APPLE
PASCAL ™

A Hands-On Approach

APPLE
PASCAL™

A Hands-On Approach

ARTHUR LUEHRMANN

University of California, Berkeley

HERBERT PECKHAM

Gavilan College

McGraw-Hill Book Company

*New York   St. Louis   San Francisco   Auckland   Bogotá   Hamburg
Johannesburg   London   Madrid   Mexico   Montreal   New Delhi   Panama
Paris   São Paulo   Singapore   Syndey   Tokyo   Toronto*

Library of Congress Cataloging in Publication Data
Luehrmann, Arthur.
  Apple PASCAL: a hands-on approach.

  (Programming language series)
  Includes index.
  1. PASCAL (Computer program language) 2. Apple
computer — Programming. I. Peckham, Herbert D., joint
author. II. Title. III. Series.
QA76.73.P2L83   001.64'24   80-27665
ISBN 0-07-049171-2 (pbk)

APPLE PASCAL™: A Hands-On Approach

  2 3 4 5 6 7 8 9 0 KPKP 8 9 8 7 6 5 4 3 2 1

This book was set in Megaron by Instant Type and
Graphics, Monterey, California. The editor was Charles E.
Stewart; the production supervisor was Joe Campanella.
The cover was designed by Oona Johnson.
Kingsport Press, Inc., was printer and binder.

ACKNOWLEDGMENTS

The Apple Pascal™ system incorporates UCSD Pascal™ and Apple® extensions for graphics, sound, paddles, and other functions. UCSD Pascal was developed largely by the Institute for Information Science at the University of California, San Diego, under the direction of Kenneth L. Bowles.

"Apple" and "Apple Pascal" are trademarks of Apple Computer Inc. "Apple" is a registered trademark of that company. "UCSD Pascal" is a trademark of the Regents of the University of California. Unauthorized use of these trademarks is contrary to the laws of the State of California or of the Federal Government.

This book is a tutorial guide to Apple Pascal, not a formal specification of the software as delivered to the buyer now or in future software revisions. Apple Computer Inc. makes no warranties with respect to this book or to its accuracy in describing any version of the Apple Pascal software product.

CONTENTS

PREFACE

Our constant goal in writing this book has been to find a sequence of compelling activities for you, the reader, to carry out on your own computer in such a way that you will come to "know" Pascal in much the same way that you came to "know" your native language without being schooled in it. We have assumed that you begin by knowing little of computers or computer languages; but we intend that, after you complete the 14 Sessions and 30 to 40 hours of hands-on activities, you will have a solid working knowledge of nearly all the vocabulary, grammar rules, and meanings that make up Pascal.

If you are studying Pascal in a school or college setting, the computer activities in this book will give you the concrete experiences so essential for understanding the rules and abstractions being presented in your classes. If you are out of school and cannot or prefer not to enroll in a formal course in Pascal, these hands-on sessions with a computer will allow you, at your own pace and under your own control, to develop a substantial knowledge of the language.

We recognized from the outset that this kind of book had to be far freer of defects than the average textbook. Since most of the learning takes place when you are sitting before the computer carrying out the tasks suggested, possibly alone or at some distance from any expert help, it was essential for us to be sure that the words were clear, the programs letter perfect, and the basic strategy an effective one.

Throughout the writing, we have been most fortunate in finding over a dozen individuals who were so frustrated in their previous attempts to learn Pascal that they could be coaxed into using (and criticizing) the early drafts of the book. They brought to the task a collection of highly developed skills in teaching, writing textbooks, programming, thinking clearly, and bringing order to unruly sentences. Alan Portis was a constant source of enthusiastic encouragement and good ideas. Tim Aaronson, who has taught programming to young people for many years, was especially sensitive to subtle misconceptions and misleading oversights. Victor Jackson had a very sharp eye for inconsistencies and flawed programs. Martha Luehrmann was absolutely tenacious in her complaints, usually justified, about statements and explanations that were off the mark. And Elizabeth Weal, who by day works in the Publications Department of Apple Computer, volunteered her critical eye and corrective skills to the rough edges of our prose. We owe her a special debt. Others who worked through the early drafts were Arthur Kessner, Harold Peters, Robert Fuller, Dean Zollman, and Marvin Marcus.

Thanks to the use of a word processing system from the beginning, we were able to absorb criticism and suggested changes and shoot back revisions in rapid succession. Some sessions went through as many as six major rewrites before all of us were content. The program segments reproduced in this book were all printed under computer control from disk files that had previously been executed. Finally, the text was automatically composed on a Compugraphic photocomposition unit from the final draft of the word-processor text files. We hope that these measures have eliminated all but a few typographic errors, and that you will forgive those.

Arthur Luehrmann

Herbert Peckham

APPLE
PASCAL™

A Hands-On Approach

If you already own this book and have access to an Apple II computer, then you are probably eager to start learning to use Apple Pascal. In that case you should skip most of this introduction except for the final section, "HOW TO USE THIS BOOK".

On the other hand, if you're in a shopper's frame of mind—trying to decide whether or not this book is for you, or whether or not Pascal is for you, or whether or not learning to use the computer is for you—then spending some time on the introduction will be worthwhile. Our goal here is to explain a bit about the design and intent of the book, to answer the question, "Why Pascal?", and to say briefly why learning to use computers is worth the effort of anyone who can read and write.

WHY THIS BOOK?

A fair question. There are a dozen or so books on programming in Pascal, including an excellent treatise by the author of the language. Does the world really need another one?

It won't come as a surprise that we think so. Here are our reasons:

- None of the books we know of deal with the details of the learner's computer, such as keytop labels, the system's editor, and file system. A beginner needs more help at first with these things than with anything else. Our goal in this book is to teach you everything that you need to know in order to write, enter, and run Pascal programs on your Apple computer system.

- Most books are written by computer scientists who teach university courses. These books feature college-level math, science, and business applications. The same programming concepts can be illustrated in other application areas accessible to more people: drawing pictures, working with text, or making music. We do that.

- Most authors seem to be concerned with coverage of every minute detail and subtle nuance of the language, as though theirs was the last book ever to be read on the subject. We care more that beginners get safely off to a good start and less about having the last word.

- Most existing Pascal books have the flavor of lectures. We think there is a need for a book written for beginners who will learn by doing rather than by listening and reading, and who will want to work at their own pace.

1

Our goal in this book is to guide you through a sequence of revealing experiences in using Pascal for the purpose of communicating with your computer. During the process of communication (and failure to communicate) you will learn the underlying grammar of the language, just the way you learned most of English grammar before going to school.

Don't try to sit back in a comfortable chair and just read this book through. It won't work that way. Go instead to the desk or table where your Apple computer is located, sit with the book open in your lap or next to the computer, and carry out all the activities in each session.

WHY PASCAL?

If you are already sold on Pascal, then the question will not be a burning one for you and you should probably skip this section. On the other hand, if your response is "Pascal who?", then better read on.

Communicating with a computer means formulating your problem and writing your instructions in a computer language. Over the years people have invented more than a hundred different computer languages, and Pascal is the name of one of them. It is a relative newcomer, defined in 1970 by the Swiss computer scientist Niklaus Wirth. Other popular languages go by the names Basic, Fortran, Cobol, Algol, PL/1, and APL.

At present more people know how to program in Basic than in any other language (thanks to the sale of nearly a million Basic-speaking computers in the past two years). Nevertheless, more lines of program statements have been written in Cobol, a standard language for business applications, than in any other language. The great majority of scientific and engineering programs are written in Fortran, one of the oldest computer languages. Applied mathematicians are especially fond of APL. Computer scientists use Algol as a standard for publishing programs in some journals. When IBM Inc. announced PL/1, they advertised it as a language that would quickly replace Fortran and Cobol by doing everything they do and more.

So, why Pascal? A frivolous, but not totally inappropriate answer would be "Why not?" Despite often vehement arguments by defenders of one language and attackers of another, no one of the common computer languages is deeply different from the others. Each one has a vocabulary of about a hundred or so words and symbols. Each one has a strict grammar, well defined and with no exceptions. Most "sentences" in any one language translate easily and directly into similar "sentences" in another language. All computer languages have about the same "expressive" range. All can be learned in a week, and experienced computerists usually know two or three languages well. So why not Pascal, or any other popular language? As the Chinese proverb goes, "Let a hundred flowers bloom..."

We are not entirely unsympathetic towards that attitude. In our view, learning to communicate with the computer is the important thing, whatever language is used. Nor are we much impressed by people who claim that this "good" language will drive out that "bad" language. All languages are human inventions, but they take on a life and cultural identity of their own. English is demonstrably inferior to Esperanto, but Shakespeare and Byron managed to say some powerful things in English, while hardly anybody says anything in Esperanto.

Actually, we think these arguments should be turned around. Since differences between computer languages are fairly small, why not start out with one that is reasonably easy to pick up and good to grow with? It happens that two of the common languages, Basic and Pascal, were designed originally for teaching computing. They are both good choices for beginners, though in different ways. Basic is much easier to get started with, partly due to language design and partly due to the very interactive way it is usually implemented. If you "boot up" your Apple II with the BASICS disk, you can type the following one-line program

```
PRINT 238 + 429
```

press the RETURN key and immediately see the program run, with the result "667" printed on your screen.

Pascal, on the other hand is a bit slower to get into and requires more knowledge of both the language and the computer's facilities for entering, editing, and running programs. The Pascal program to add 238 + 429 and print the answer is four lines long:

```
PROGRAM ADDITION;
BEGIN
  WRITELN (238 + 429)
END.
```

To type it, you have to "enter the editor". Then you have to "quit the editor". Then you have to "run the program". If you make a typing error when typing a statement in a Basic program, you are told so and may simply retype the line. In Pascal you don't discover the error until you run the program. To fix it, you must return to the editor, make the change, quit the editor, and run the program again.

So Basic wins, hands down, on ease of getting started and of quick trial-and-error programming. Trouble comes, however, when Basic programs get long and require modifications, perhaps by someone other than the original author. Here lies one of Pascal's greatest strengths: legibility by human readers. Reproduced here are Basic and Pascal versions of a program that simulates the roll of dice in a craps game. Without worrying too much about the details, decide for yourself which version looks more like it might actually represent a craps game.

Applesoft Basic Program

```
100 DEF FNR (X) = INT (1 + 6 * RND (X)) + INT (1 + 6 * RND (X))
110 LET R1 = FNR (1)
120 PRINT "YOU ROLLED A "; R1
130 IF R1 = 7 THEN 150
140 IF R1 <> 11 THEN 170
150 PRINT "YOU WIN"
160 GOTO 110
170 IF R1 = 2 THEN 200
180 IF R1 = 3 THEN 200
190 IF R1 <> 12 THEN 220
200 PRINT "YOU LOSE"
210 GOTO 110
220 LET R2 = FNR (1)
230 PRINT "NEXT ROLL IS "; R2
240 IF R2 = R1 THEN 150
250 IF R2 = 7 THEN 200
260 GOTO 220
270 END
```

Apple Pascal Program

```
PROGRAM DICEGAME;

  USES
    APPLESTUFF;

  CONST
    HELLFREEZESOVER = FALSE;

  VAR
    DICE, POINT : INTEGER;

  PROCEDURE ROLLEM (VAR TOSS : INTEGER);

    BEGIN
      TOSS := RANDOM MOD 6 + 1;
      TOSS := TOSS + RANDOM MOD 6 + 1;
      WRITELN ('YOU ROLLED A ', TOSS)
    END;

BEGIN
  REPEAT
    ROLLEM (DICE);
    CASE DICE OF
      7, 11:
        WRITELN ('YOU WIN');
      2, 3, 12:
        WRITELN ('YOU LOSE');
      4, 5, 6, 8, 9, 10:
        BEGIN
          POINT := DICE;
          REPEAT
            ROLLEM (DICE)
          UNTIL (DICE = POINT) OR (DICE = 7);
          IF DICE = POINT THEN
            WRITELN ('YOU WIN')
          ELSE
            WRITELN ('YOU LOSE')
        END
    END
  UNTIL HELLFREEZESOVER
END.
```

Unless you're already a Basic expert, you probably had a hard time seeing any plan or design in what looks like line after line of similar text in the first version. By contrast, the text of the Pascal version divides into horizontal blocks of various kinds, with names such as CONST, VAR, and PROCEDURE. Furthermore, Pascal allows the author to use indentation to clarify further the plan of the program. Most versions of Basic today treat indentation as a mistake and proceed to remove it from the program.

Basic's problem of illegibility and incomprehensibility increases drastically as a program grows in size and complexity, and Pascal's edge widens quickly. Experiments have shown that Pascal programmers are several times faster at making changes and corrections to larger programs than are people using unstructured languages such as Basic and Fortran.

There is another reason why Pascal is a good first language to learn. As a relative newcomer to the family of computer languages, it benefits from a lot of deep thinking that went on among computer scientists as to why programs written in the languages available in the early 1960's were so hard to prove to be correct. The result of their studies was a set of language requirements that make it possible merely by a careful reading of a program, block by block, to know if it will work. Pascal was among the first attempts to produce a practical language that also embodies many of these research results.

In a very real sense Pascal is a working model of modern thinking about certain goals of computer languages. Like all good models, it is being widely imitated. The new American National Standards Institute (ANSI) Fortran standard includes some of the same organizational structures found in Pascal. Work is nearing completion on ANSI Basic, which also includes all these structures, as well as long variable names, and named procedures. Among languages emerging today, it is fairly accurate to describe Ada, the language soon to be required of all contracters who want to do business with the U.S. Department of Defense, as an enhancement of Pascal.

Learning to program in Pascal, therefore, is a good way to become familiar with language ideas that appear not just in Pascal but in some older and most new and newly revised languages. Your next language will be easier if you already know Pascal.

Even so, it always pays to use the right tool for the job; and for many jobs Basic on a computer such as the Apple II is the right tool. It is easy to get into, gives you quick error diagnoses, and is a cinch to edit and try again—just the things Pascal is weakest at. Simple problems usually yield to a quick-and-dirty, trial-and-error approach and don't justify much planning. The trick, of course, is to know when that approach is likely to fail, so as to avoid it. Our rule of thumb is simple. If your program is small enough to fit on your TV screen, stick with Basic. If it's bigger or if it's probably going to grow bigger, switch to Pascal.

WHY COMPUTERS?

If the question is irrelevant to you because you already know about computers and believe that they are important, then skip this section. Unless, of course, you enjoy sermons to the faithful. If you have your doubts, however, read on.

Most everyone knows about the speed and accuracy of the modern electronic computer, its ability to carry out long and tedious calculations exactly as instructed, and its growing visibility in the workplace, stores, schools, and even homes. Today most people probably recognize that computers play a significant, even critical, role in their routine affairs: commuting to work, buying groceries, receiving bills, paying bills with checks or credit cards, making airline or motel reservations, telling time on a digital watch, tuning a TV set, receiving "personalized" junk mail, using an automatic telephone dialer, listening to a digital recording of music, watching a videodisk TV recording, setting the time and temperature of a microwave oven or of a modern home thermostat, and many other things. Not everyone is happy with what some see as a blind dependency on the new technology; especially when it or, more frequently, its human operators and programmers make errors. But even critics admit that the computer is a fixed part of life today.

Despite a general popular awareness of computers, remarkably few people today are literate users of computers. It won't come as a surprise, then, that most people have missed something fundamental about computing: namely, that it is a creative activity carried on by human beings. A computer does what it does because some person told it not only what to do but how to do it. A person who knows how to express thoughts in a computer language has a new way of talking, writing, and thinking about the ideas that he or she wants to embody in the instructions to the computer. And any time that you discover a new way to think about something, or a new language for describing your thoughts and setting them down for a closer look, then you have a new tool for solving problems. This is the main, usually overlooked point about computing.

Actually, it isn't terribly surprising that this point is missed by so many people. The time we live in is in many ways like the first decades after the printing press was invented, when nearly everyone except a small priesthood was illiterate. People recognized that printing technology would make business and government transactions and record keeping a lot easier, which in turn would have an impact on daily life. Yet few people, even several centuries later, recognized that the main effect would come when the entire public became literate and could use reading and writing for personal satisfaction and gain.

The appearance of the inexpensive personal computer is like the appearance of the printing press. In the public mind computer literacy still belongs to that small priesthood who painfully acquired their skills in the service of large, cloistered machines, unapproachable by ordinary laymen. Most otherwise educated people today believe that whatever computer needs they have must be handled by speaking in English to a member of the computer priesthood, who will translate their wishes and prayers into computer language and then communicate them to the inscrutable machine.

Of course, that is not the case; and millions of people today are discovering the ease, rewards, and personal satisfaction of direct communication with and control of a computer. In fact, recent research shows that the main reason most people buy a personal computer is not to put it to practical use but to learn to communicate with it and to become computer literate. As their skills and understanding develop, they discover uses that they could not have imagined in advance.

To conclude this sermon, you should learn computing for the same reason that you learned to read, write, and to do math: because it is good for your mind.

HOW TO USE THIS BOOK

As we said before, this book is a carefully sequenced set of activities for you to carry out at the keyboard of your computer. It will make very poor and probably confusing reading if you treat it as a conventional textbook. You will find that rules, explanations and summaries are present, but they all follow directly out of your actual experiences at the keyboard.

It is a good policy in the first five or six sessions not to stray very far from the path we have laid out for you, or to try to jump ahead in the book; if you do, don't be surprised if you occasionally get into situations that you may not be ready to handle. None of this will damage you or the computer, of course, and if worse comes to worse, you can always turn off the power switch and start over.

While our main goal here is to have an inexperienced person succeed in learning Pascal, we have not taken the easy way out and given you only a trivial subset of the language. There is little point in learning Pascal if all you get out of it are the features that are literal translations of other languages. Instead we introduce you quickly to procedure and function blocks, a variety of data types, and the main Pascal control structures. Toward the latter half of the book you will find activities on programmer-defined data types, arrays, sets, and records. While some of these are heavy-duty topics, each one builds on your previous understanding and on specific, new, concrete experiences. If your learning comes out of steady progress through these activities, we believe you will be ready for each new concept or rule. Yet, even if you decide after Session 8 or 9 or 10 that you know enough about Pascal for a while, you will have acquired a substantial understanding and will be able to write quite complex programs.

As to the specifics of your particular computer system, we assume that you have an Apple II or Apple II Plus computer, a Language System, a single disk drive, and Apple Pascal Version 1.1 diskettes. If you have two disk drives, don't conclude that this book is not for you. You will need only a single drive for all activites here, but everything that you learn will carry over to a two-drive system. If you have Version 1.0 diskettes (also called UCSD Pascal Version II.1) you may still use this book effectively. You should turn to Appendix H before doing each session, however, and acquaint yourself with any differences that will show up when using the Version 1.0 diskettes.

ONE

GETTING STARTED

First, a procedural note: this book is divided into sessions. Each session will give you about two hours activities to do with your computer. You should plan to work through a complete session at one time, without interruption, if possible. At the end of each session you will find questions and problems. It is a good idea to test your understanding by working on a few of them.

Second, don't expect each topic to be covered fully in the session where you first encounter it. Our goal at each point is to give you enough experience to be able to communicate certain instructions to your computer successfully. As your knowledge grows, we will cycle around to each topic several times, adding details and qualifications to what you already know.

Finally, if your book is more than three feet from your computer, you are in trouble. We will be continually asking you to do things with your computer. (When we do that, we'll put the instructions in **bold faced type.**) There is little point in trying to read the book without carrying out these activities. Learning is a lot easier when you can relate words and ideas to concrete experience.

> Remember this fact: like the physical world around us, a computer is what it does and not necessarily what we say about it. Test your understanding by experimentation, and believe what you see.

In order to use Pascal on your Apple computer, you need the following items:

- **An Apple II or Apple II Plus computer with 48 K bytes of memory.**

- **A Language System properly installed in your computer.**

- **A TV monitor or a TV receiver plus RF modulator, properly installed.**

- **At least one disk drive. (Two are useful for making disk copies, but you will be using only one drive while learning Pascal.)**

- **A pair of game paddles, properly installed in your computer.**

- Apple Pascal Version 1.1 diskettes marked APPLE0: and APPLE3:. (You can also use Apple Pascal Version 1.0 diskettes, but you will encounter a few differences that are explained in Appendix H.)

- At least one duplicate copy each of APPLE0: and APPLE3:.

If you have all seven of these items, then you are ready to go to work on this session. If you don't have all of the first six items, then you won't be able to do anything further until you have all of them.

If you are a new owner of the Apple Language System, then you probably have all the items except the last—the duplicates of the APPLE0: and APPLE3: diskettes. This brings up an ugly fact. On the one hand, you are *truly* asking for trouble if you go ahead and use your only copy of these precious diskettes, and risk destroying the information on them. On the other hand, making the two back-up copies is a 26-step process on a two-drive system and more than twice that on a single drive. If you are just beginning to learn your way around the Pascal System, that may be a longer journey than you are ready to take. Here is our advice:

- See whether the dealer who sold you your Language System will sell you duplicates of APPLE0: and APPLE3:.

- Failing that, borrow duplicates from a friend until you get familiar enough with the Pascal system to make your own copies.

- If these strategies fail, you'll have to go it alone. If you have two disk drives, turn now to Appendix B for a step-by-step guide through the mysteries of copying.

- If you have a single disk drive, try to borrow another drive from a friend; then turn to Appendix B.

- Failing that, your only recourse is single-drive copying. Turn now to Appendix A for a guide that leads you step by step through the process.

> In no case should you give in to the temptation to go ahead without back-up diskettes.

After you have obtained your duplicates of APPLE0: and APPLE3:, by whatever means, go on to the following section.

1-1 BOOTING UP PASCAL

Every session of this book begins with what is called the "boot-up" step. One of the things that you will learn about computers is that by means of *programming* they can be made to perform a multitude of distinct tasks. Without a program, they can do nothing. You will be using your Apple computer to write, edit, and run Pascal programs. To do that task, your computer has to be taught—that is, *programmed*—to understand Pascal. That is what is going on during the Pascal boot up. If you had wanted to write Basic programs instead, you would use the Basic boot-up procedure to teach your computer to understand Basic.

The phrase "booting up" comes from the idea of "pulling oneself up by one's own bootstraps." If the computer needs a program to do *anything*, then you might wonder how it knows enough even to move a copy of a program from diskette into its memory. How does it get started? The answer is that it pulls itself up by the bootstraps. There is a very tiny program permanently stored in one of the integrated circuits inside your computer, and it goes into effect whenever you turn on the power switch. All that it does is to turn on the disk drive, read in another short program from the diskette in the drive, and start that program running. That program, called the *bootstrap loader*, has the job of bringing from diskette all the other programs needed to enable your Apple II to "speak Pascal". The bootstrap loader program is contained on the APPLE3: diskette, while the other programs are on APPLE0:.

If this description seems overly technical, don't worry. You don't really need to know how your computer "learns" Pascal during boot up. Just follow each step below and the process will happen.

1. **Turn on the TV power switch.** Turn the volume down. If you have a game connector, switch it to GAME, TV SCOREBOARD, or the like. Turn the TV receiver to the proper channel.

2. **If the power to your Apple is on, turn it off.** The power switch is on the back and is easily reached by the left hand. When it is off, the POWER light at the lower left corner of the keyboard is also off.

3. **Insert the APPLE3: diskette into the disk drive.** Lift the drive door fully open. Hold the diskette in your right hand, palm up, with your thumb on the printed label. Insert the diskette carefully into the drive and lower the door until it snaps shut.

4. **Turn on the computer power switch.** The POWER light will come on, the red IN USE light on the disk drive will come on, and you will hear the drive spinning and clicking. On your TV screen you will immediately see the phrase "APPLE]]". In a few seconds the screen lights up with at-signs. A second later, the disk drive stops whirring, its red light goes out, and the screen clears except for a white rectangle at the upper left. Immediately after that, the following text appears:

```
INSERT BOOT DISK WITH SYSTEM.PASCAL
ON IT, THEN PRESS RESET
```

(Note: if no such text appears, it means that you are using Apple Pascal Version 1.0 diskettes. See Appendix H for further information.)

5. **Remove the APPLE3: diskette and insert the APPLE0: diskette into the disk drive.** Handle the diskettes carefully, palm up with the thumb on the label. Close the door.

6. **Press the keyboard key marked "RESET".** If nothing happens, hold the CTRL key down and press the RESET key. The RESET key is in the upper-right corner of the Apple keyboard; the CTRL key is at the extreme left. After about 15 seconds of more red lights, at-signs, and whirring disk sounds, the following message appears on your TV:

```
WELCOME APPLE0, TO APPLE II PASCAL 1.1

BASED ON UCSD PASCAL II.1

CURRENT DATE IS 30-JAN-81




(C) APPLE COMPUTER INC. 1979, 1980
(C) U.C. REGENTS 1979
```

About a second later, all activity stops and the following line appears at the very top of your screen:

```
COMMAND: E(DIT, R(UN, F(ILE, C(OMP, L(IN
```

The appearance of this line tells you that you have successfully booted up Pascal and that your computer is ready for your command. (The current date may be different.)

1-2 THE COMMAND PROMPT LINE

Actually you're looking at only a part of the COMMAND prompt line. **Do the following: hold down the key marked "CTRL" (at the left end of the keyboard) and at the same time press the A key, near it.** (We'll call this process "CTRL-A" in the future.) **Now type CTRL-A again. Do it once more.**

What you are seeing is the entire COMMAND prompt line, one half at a time. When you boot up Pascal you see the left half. When you type a CTRL-A you see the right half:

K, X(ECUTE, A(SSEM, D(EBUG,? [1.1]

When you type another CTRL-A, the left half flips back, along with any other characters that were on the left half of the screen originally.

This behavior is a general property of the Apple II Language System. The Apple screen can display lines of text that are only 40 characters long, or less. But the Pascal system is designed to work correctly with lines that are 80 characters long. You should think of the Apple screen as giving you a 40-character window for inspecting the full 80-character Pascal page. When you first boot-up Pascal the window looks out on the left half of the page. When you type CTRL-A the window quickly moves over to the right half of the full Pascal page. Another CTRL-A switches you back.

CTRL-A, therefore, is your window switch, and it is always in effect whenever you want to check the other half of the Pascal page for information or instructions. Watch out for the following **user trap**: by accident you forget to switch back to the left half, and then you type some command that produces text that appears only on the left side of the Pascal page. What happens? You don't see it, because your window is looking at the right half, which may have nothing at all on it. Very mysterious. When this happens, remember to type CTRL-A and make sure that you see the whole Pascal page before looking for more serious problems.

If you are now looking at the right half of the page, use the CTRL-A switch to get back to the left half, so that you see the beginning of the COMMAND prompt line.

The COMMAND prompt line is the most important "place" in the Pascal system. You enter the system through the COMMAND line and will often pass through the COMMAND line on your way between one part of the system and another one, as you will see in the next section.

1-3 TRAVELING AROUND THE SYSTEM

Notice that one of the "words" in the COMMAND prompt line is "F(ILE". **Type the F key and see what happens.**

The Pascal page goes blank and, after some disk activity, a new prompt line now appears at the top line. (If by chance APPLE0: is not in your drive now, just put it in. If you don't, your computer will keep looking for it forever! When the COMMAND prompt reappears, start over.) Since your window is looking at the left half of the Pascal page, you see this:

FILER: G, S, N, L, R, C, T, D, Q, [1.1]

(If, by accident, your window is looking at the right half of the page it will see nothing. Type CTRL-A to fix it.)

This new prompt line tells you that you have left the "COMMAND level" of the Pascal system and have "entered the FILER". The FILER prompt line tells you how to travel to still other places in the system. For example, you can go to the part of the system that establishes the current date.

Do that now, by typing a D on your keyboard. You should note that the FILER prompt line goes away and a new message appears. This means that you are no longer "at the level of the FILER", but have moved to the level where changing the date is possible. The new message is

```
DATE SET: <1..31>-<JAN..DEC>-<00..99>
TODAY IS 31-JAN-81
NEW DATE ?
```

Notice that at this level there is no prompt line that gives you any clues as to how to move to another level in the Pascal system. Instead you are asked to *do something*: namely, change the date from 31–JAN–81 (or whatever actual date appeared on your screen) to today's correct date.

The top line on your screen tells you the format: a number from 1 to 31, a hyphen, a 3-letter abbreviation for the month, another hyphen, and a 2-digit abbreviation for the year. **Now type today's date on your keyboard.** You're allowed to make typographical errors, by the way. If you catch them while typing on the line the errors occur in, you can correct them right away. Just press the left-arrow key (at the right end of your keyboard) enough times to move the cursor (the solid rectangle of light on the screen) to the beginning of the error. Then retype the entire part of the line you backspaced over. **Make a few mistakes right now and fix them by this method.**

When you are satisfied with your answer to the "NEW DATE?" question, **enter it into the computer by pressing the RETURN key**, at the right end of your keyboard.

Now, at what level of the system are you? *As usual, the top line of the Pascal page tells you where you are.* You have now left the date-changing level and returned to the FILER.

Let's see whether or not you succeeded in changing the date. **Type D again.** Does the screen text give the correct date? If you made a typing error before and failed to fix it, now is your chance to change the date again. **If the date is okay now, just answer the question by pressing the RETURN key.**

Again you pop back up to the level of the FILER. That is the only place you can go from the date-changing level.

Next, let's explore some other places you can get to from the FILER. Actually there are more possibilities than are shown on the prompt line. To see the rest, **type a question mark (?) (Hold down one of the two SHIFT keys while typing the key with the slash (/) and question mark on it.)** This new prompt line appears:

```
FILER: W, B, E, K, M, P, V, X, Z [1.1]
```

See what happens when you type a V. V stands for "volume" and takes you briefly to a new level. It is like the D(ATE because you can't go anywhere from it except back up to the FILER, where you came from. But it is different from D, because it simply does its task, without asking any more questions, and then pops you back to the level of the FILER. (How can you tell that you are now in the FILER, by the way?) Notice that the FILER prompt line is the way it used to be before you typed the question mark.

The task done at the V level is to display a list of various input and output devices ("volumes") connected ("on-line") to Pascal. "CONSOLE:" refers to the display screen, "SYSTERM:" to the keyboard, and "APPLE0:" to the name of the diskette in your disk drive, which the Pascal system refers to as "VOLUME #4". These details are not important for now, since you are mainly exploring the system.

Now leave the FILER again and go to the L level by typing an L on your keyboard. L stands for "list the directory of a diskette". Once more the FILER prompt line disappears and the following question appears:

```
DIR LISTING OF ?
```

Respond by typing APPLE0: (Be sure to use the zero key, not the letter O, and don't leave out the colon!). Correct any typing errors by using the left-arrow key and retyping. **Then press RETURN,** and watch as the red "IN USE" light on the disk drive comes on, the drive whirrs, and a table is printed on your TV screen. The table lists the names of all the *files* saved on your APPLE0: diskette, their lengths, and the dates they were put on the diskette. The bottom line tells how much space is left on the diskette.

As soon as the listing of the diskette directory is finished, the Pascal system pops back up to the FILER level and displays its prompt line.

You have seen three of the many ways to go "down" from the FILER to "lower levels". But how does one climb back up to the COMMAND level? **Well, type a Q and see.**

1-4 MORE THAN MEETS THE EYE

You have already seen that the COMMAND prompt line is too long to fit on the Apple screen. You had to use the CTRL-A toggle switch to move the Apple window back and forth from the left half to the right half of the Pascal page in order to see the whole prompt line. In fact, the COMMAND prompt line contains *even more* command names than can fit on the Pascal page. Try the following experiment:

With the COMMAND prompt at the top of your screen, type a question mark. At this point you should see the transformed prompt line:

```
COMMAND: U(SER RESTART, I(NITIALIZE, H(A
```

Notice that you are still looking at the left half of the Pascal page. It simply has something different written on it than it did before you typed the question mark. (You saw the same thing happen at the level of the FILER when you typed a question mark there.) **Type CTRL-A and check out the right half of the Pascal page.** It should now look like this:

```
LT, S(WAP, M(AKE EXEC
```

Now type another question mark. As before, the question mark changed the *text* following the word "COMMAND:", but it *did not* move the Apple window. That is why you are still looking at the *right half* of the original COMMAND prompt line:

```
K, X(ECUTE, A(SSEM, D(EBUG,? [1.1]
```

Type CTRL-A to see the left half of the Pascal page.

You should keep clearly in mind the following differences between CTRL-A and the question mark:

1. A question mark is legal *only* at COMMAND level and FILER level.

2. CTRL-A is legal to use in *any* part of the Pascal system at any time.

3. A question mark causes *new text* to be written on the top line of the Pascal page, but does not move the Apple window.

4. CTRL-A causes the Apple window to *move* from one half of the Pascal page to the other, without changing any text on the page.

SUMMARY

You have now returned to the top level of the Pascal system, and this is a good time to stop and summarize your journey. Table 1.1 is a sort of map of the territories you have explored and their relationships to one another.

Table 1.1 Partial table of the command levels of the Apple Pascal system. Each indented level is reached from the one above by typing the initial letter of its name.

		Exit to escape from accidental entry.
F(iler		
Q(uit the filer		F
V(olumes on line		
L(ist the directory		RETURN
D(ate setter		RETURN
? Show additional commands		RETURN

Commands Available at Any Level

CTRL-A Toggle to other half of Pascal page.		CTRL-A

During this introductory session you have found out the following things about Apple Pascal:

- **You had to use a special boot-up procedure to get Pascal started on your computer.**

- **You entered Pascal at the command level, with the COMMAND prompt line at the top of your TV screen.**

- **You typed a CTRL–A to flip your "window" from the left to the right half of the 80-character Pascal page and back again.**

- **You left the COMMAND level and went to lower levels by typing one of the initial letters listed in the COMMAND prompt line.**

- **A new prompt line often appeared when you entered a new level. It either gave you a list of still further places to go, or it asked you what to do at the current level.**

- **There was no way to get from a place at one level to another place at the same level without first going up to a higher level and then coming back down to the desired place.**

■ **You saw how to change the current date, to get a list of the input/output "volumes" available to Pascal, and to list the directory of a diskette.**

■ **You quit the FILER level, by typing a Q, and returned to the top COMMAND level of the Pascal system.**

QUESTIONS AND PROBLEMS

1. People sometimes refer to the Apple UCSD Pascal system of levels as being "tree structured". Which level is like the main trunk? Which level that you have seen is like a branch? Which levels are like leaves?

2. How many branches (or perhaps leaves) are connected to the main trunk? (Get to the COMMAND level and count the initial letters in the prompt line. Don't forget to look at both halves of the Pascal page! Now type a question mark (?) and count some more. Another question mark will get you back to the original prompt line.)

3. What happens when you type letters not included in the COMMAND prompt: for example Q, W, and Z. Type one of them. What does your Apple do?

4. What diskette needs to be in your disk drive when you first boot-up Pascal? What diskette normally remains in the drive when you are using Pascal?

5. You are now at COMMAND level. You want to see the name of the diskette that is currently in your drive. What two letters do you type? At what level do you end up after that? How do you get back to COMMAND level?

6. You have just entered the date-changing level and the computer has asked what new date to use. You decide to quit without changing the date and instead to get a listing of the directory of APPLE0:. What keys do you press to do this?

7. You are at COMMAND level and by accident your finger happens to hit the F key. How do you correct the error?

8. You are currently at COMMAND level and looking at the right half of the prompt line. You type an F. What do you see? Why? What should you do to correct the situation?

9. When you are at COMMAND level and type an F, the disk drive light comes on and the disk whirrs and clicks before the FILER prompt line appears. What do you think is going on? What would happen if the APPLE0 diskette was not in the drive when you typed F? (Try and find out. Then replace APPLE0:)

TYPING IN PROGRAMS—THE EDITOR

In Session 1 you learned how to boot up Pascal on your Apple computer and how to move from the COMMAND level down to the FILER and from there to lower levels. You also learned how to go back up from level to level. In this session you will explore a new branch of the "command tree:" the EDITOR. Like the FILER, it is connected to the main trunk, which is the COMMAND level. Your purpose, this time, is a more productive one than before. To write computer programs you need to type them into the computer, and for that purpose you will need to use the EDITOR commands.

SESSION GOALS

The primary goal of this session is to teach you how to enter the text of a program (or any other text) into the memory of your computer. In particular, you will enter the EDIT level of the Pascal system, and from there enter lower levels which will allow you to type lines of text, make deletions, and make changes. You will leave the EDIT level, write your text on a diskette, and see how the information is cataloged on the diskette. You will recover the information on the diskette and move it to the memory of the computer.

2-1 A WARM-UP EXERCISE

If you are starting this session from a "cold start"—that is, with your computer turned off, then go to Section 1-1, and read how to boot up Pascal properly.

The COMMAND prompt line should now be visible on the top line of your TV screen. (If you're trapped in some other part of the Pascal system and cannot seem to find your way out, just turn off the power and reboot, using the procedure in Section 1-1.)

Now, leave the COMMAND level and go to the FILER. You do that, you recall, by typing an F. **Next, type a D and check the current date.** (This is always good to do when you first boot up Pascal.) **Change the date if necessary, and, in any case, press the RETURN key.** You're now back at the FILER level.

You've done all that before; now for something new. **With the FILER prompt line on the top of your screen, type an N.** N stands for "New" and means you are ready to enter a new program or some other new text into your computer.

One of two things will happen as soon as you press the N key. Either you will see

```
WORKFILE CLEARED
```

followed immediately by a return back to the level of the FILER, or else you will see

```
THROW AWAY CURRENT WORKFILE ?
```

followed by a halt while the computer waits for your reply. If you get the question, it means that your particular APPLE0: diskette already has some text on it in the place where new text will go. This place on the diskette is called the *workfile*. As a precaution the computer asks you if you really want to erase the old text. The answer in the present case is yes, since you are just starting out and you want to enter new text; **so type a Y now.**

At this point, no matter which message you got, the computer has carried out some bookkeeping tasks associated with opening up a clear area in the computer for you to write new text into. This area in your computer is called your *workspace*, and you will be learning more about it during this session.

Your Pascal system is now at the FILER level. Partly for review, take a look at the directory of your APPLE0: diskette now. You probably remember from Session 1 how to do this: **type an L (for "List the directory") and then answer the question by typing the name "APPLE0:" and press the RETURN key.** (Be careful to use the zero key, not the letter O, and to include the colon.)

Note on your screen the presence of several file names that begin "SYSTEM." followed by other names. Each of these is the name of one *file*, or collection of information, that is presently stored on your APPLE0: diskette. **Right now, write down a list of all these names on a piece of paper.** You will be referring to it again in this session.

As soon as the directory listing is complete, the computer returns to the FILER level. (How do you know that?) It is now time to go to the EDIT level. The natural thing to do would be for you to type an E, right? **Well, do it and see what happens.**

You didn't get to the EDIT level, did you? In fact, when you are in the FILER, the command E takes you not over to the EDITOR but *down* a level to the "Extended list directory" level, which starts off by asking you a question about the diskette. Since you didn't mean to enter that level, just **press the RETURN key and you will be back at the FILER.**

2-2 ENTERING THE EDITOR

Evidently you can't go directly from FILER to EDITOR. They are different branches on the same tree, and you have to go back to the main trunk first. So, **quit the FILER by typing Q.**

Now you are back at the COMMAND level, and you see as the first item in the prompt line the term E(DIT. So, **type the E key.**

The new prompt line assures you that the you are, indeed, "in the EDITOR". Just below the EDIT prompt line you will see the following line:

```
NO WORKFILE IS PRESENT. FILE? ( <RET> FO
```

Actually, you are seeing only the left half of the line. **Type a CTRL-A and you get the other half,**

```
R NO FILE <ESC-RET> TO EXIT )
```

and then another CTRL-A to get back.

What this extremely mysterious message is trying to tell or ask you is this: first, there is no workfile on your diskette. (You knew this, of course, since you just cleared it out.) Second, the question "FILE?" is asking you whether you would like at this time to move some other disk file into the workspace area in your computer. (You don't want to do this now, but if you did, you would answer the question by typing the name of the file.) Finally, it tells you what other things you can type in response to the "FILE?" question. <RET> means "press the RETURN key" and <ESC-RET> means, "first press the ESC key (at the left end of the third row of keys) and then press the RETURN key."

See what happens when you carry out the ESC-RETURN sequence. What level of the system do you go to?

The reason for the ESC-RETURN option should be clear to you. If you accidentally press the E key when at COMMAND level, you can recover from the error by pressing ESC and then RETURN.

Let's get back to the editor now (by typing E) and again deal with the "FILE?" question. The right answer for you now is the simple RETURN key, since you don't want to move another file into the workspace, but you do want to use the EDITOR to type new text into the workspace. **Press the RETURN key and note a new prompt line at the top of your TV screen.**

```
>EDIT: A(DJST C(PY D(LETE F(IND I(NSRT J
```

Use your CTRL-A window switch to see the right half:

```
(MP R(PLACE Q(UIT X(CHNG Z(AP  [1.1]
```

2-3 TYPING IN NEW TEXT

Now you are "in the EDITOR", with the EDIT prompt line at the top of your screen. (If you're looking at the right half of the prompt line, press CTRL-A to get back.) Altogether there are 10 places you can go to from the EDIT level: nine lower down and one back up to COMMAND level. You will be exploring only two of these in this session.

To get started, press the I key. I stands for "Insert", and means that you are going to insert new text into your workspace starting at the position of the cursor (the solid rectangle of light), which right now is at the left end of the first line after the prompt line.

Notice that you are no longer at the EDIT level, since the new prompt line says

```
>INSERT: TEXT [<BS> A CHAR,<DEL> A LINE]
```

and on the right half of the Pascal page,

```
[<ETX> ACCEPTS, <ESC> ESCAPES]
```

Use the CTRL-A key to get back to the left half of the Pascal page.

This prompt line tells you that you are now at INSERT level and tells you the special meaning that certain keys have there.

For a start, try pressing the ESC key. Notice that you just popped back up to the EDIT level. You would use the ESC key if by accident you had pressed the I key while in the EDITOR and so had stumbled into the INSERT level. (You will find that the ESC key is very often used elsewhere in the Apple Pascal system to escape from accidental key presses.)

Now, press the I key again to reenter INSERT level. Use the alphabetic keys on your keyboard to type the following phrase:

```
HOW NOW BLUE COW
```

Now you will see what the term "<BS>" means in the prompt line: **press the left-arrow key once** and notice that the cursor has just *backspaced* over the W in "COW". **Press it repeatedly until it is just over the B in "BLUE". Now retype the following from there:**

```
BROWN COW
```

The left-arrow key allows you to delete one character at a time from what you have typed, so that you can fix errors by retyping.

2-4 MOVING INSERTED TEXT INTO THE WORKSPACE

You already know how to leave INSERT level by using the ESC key. **Press it now and see what happens.** So far, so good; it appears that you have successfully left INSERT and returned to EDIT. On the other hand, what happened to "HOW NOW BROWN COW", which is no longer visible?

Well, perhaps it is still there, but only at INSERT level. To check that idea out, **type I and see what is there.**

It looks bad. In fact, the information you typed ("HOW NOW BROWN COW") never got moved into your workspace. That is so because you took the *escape* route out of INSERT. But there is another way out. Look again at the right half of the prompt line:

```
[<ETX> ACCEPTS, <ESC> ESCAPES]
```

Since ESC throws away what you just typed, it looks as though ETX might just hang on to it. Unfortunately, your computer doesn't seem to have an ETX key. Actually it does, and you get it by typing a CTRL-C. **First use CTRL-A to get back to the left half of the page. Now, while still in INSERT, type once again:**

```
HOW NOW BROWN COW
```

Now, instead of ESC-ing from INSERT, type a CTRL-C. (Hold the CTRL key down while typing C.) Note this time that you returned to the EDITOR but that your text is still on the TV screen. This fact tells you that the text you typed while at INSERT level has now been moved into your workspace in the memory of the computer. *Whenever you are at the EDIT level your TV screen displays the top 23 lines of whatever is currently located in the workspace area of your computer's main memory.*

2-5 THE RESET KEY

There is a prominent key at the upper right corner of your keyboard, labeled RESET. It is *very* close to the RETURN key and so is easy to hit by accident. Now is a good time to stage such an accident. **Press the RESET key.** (If nothing happens, try holding down the CTRL key while pressing RESET.)

At this point you see "APPLE][" appear at the top of the screen. After a little disk activity the message "NO FILE SYSTEM.APPLE" appears in the middle of the screen. *There is only one way out of the present situation. You must turn off the power and reboot.*

Reboot Pascal using the procedure in Section 1-1. Do you think the information you typed before pressing RESET is still available? **Type E to enter the editor.** The signs are not good. You are being asked the same FILE? question you were asked the first time you entered the EDITOR. **Press RETURN to continue entering the EDITOR.**

The empty screen below the prompt line means an empty workspace. Your text is lost.

> Beware of the RESET key! We have deliber-
> ately led you into this **user trap** in a situation in
> which you had little text to lose. After entering
> 30 or 40 lines of new text into your workspace, it
> can be enormously annoying to hit the RESET
> key while reaching for the RETURN key, and
> then have to watch helplessly as your system
> comes to a halt.

In order to eliminate this user trap, recent models of Apple II and Apple II Plus computers have been shipped with a slide switch that, in one position, requires you to hold down the CTRL key while pressing RESET if you want the RESET function.

If your computer required you just now to hold the CTRL key down to activate the RESET, then you have a recent model, and should leave the slide switch as is. If not, then you may or may not have such a switch on your computer. You can check by removing the top of the Apple and looking directly under the keyboard towards the left side of the top row of keys. If you find a slide switch there, put it in the opposite position, and replace the top. Now you will need to hold down the CTRL key while pressing RESET during the boot-up process. A simple RESET will have no effect. Finally, if you have an older model that has no slide switch, you must be very careful not to press RESET by accident.

2-6 MOVING THE WORKSPACE TO DISKETTE

At EDIT level, type I to enter INSERT once more. Then type this sentence:

```
ONE MORE TIME, COW.
```

Then leave INSERT by means of CTRL-C. You have entered new text and moved it successfully into the workspace, which is now visible on your screen under the EDIT prompt line.

At this point, quit the EDITOR by typing a Q. You will note a brief bit of disk activity, suggesting perhaps that the text in your workspace has now been put on diskette for safe keeping. On the other hand, your TV screen shows the following:

```
>QUIT:
     U(PDATE THE WORKFILE AND LEAVE
     E(XIT WITHOUT UPDATING
     R(ETURN TO THE EDITOR WITHOUT UPDAT
     W(RITE TO A FILE NAME AND RETURN
     S(AVE WITH SAME NAME AND RETURN
```

When you are in the EDITOR and type a Q, you go to the QUIT level, which allows you five options. **Since the third one is easiest to deal with, type an R now and see what happens.**

Notice that after another bit of disk activity, you're back in the EDITOR, with your workspace still intact. *So the R key is used to correct the easy mistake of unintentionally hitting the Q key while in the EDITOR. It lets you get back to where you were without losing anything.*

Next, let's see what happens with the second option. **Once again type a Q, to quit the EDITOR, and then an E, to exit without updating.**

The prompt at the top of the screen now is:

```
>QUIT:
THROW AWAY CHANGES SINCE LAST UPDATE?
```

Let's answer the question with Y (for YES) and see what happens. **Type a Y.**

Now you are back at COMMAND level. **Okay, go back to EDIT level again by typing E.**

Well, now you know, to your sorrow, what "exit without updating" means. *If you leave EDIT by the Q E Y sequence of key presses, any changes you made to your workspace are lost.* Your change in the present case was the insertion of a new text into an empty workspace. The text was stored in the computer until the Q E Y sequence; after that it was lost. *There is no way to recover it.*

Now you see that you should have answered N (for NO) to the question that was asked you when you typed Q E.

One more try. **Continue entering the EDITOR by answering the "FILE?" question with a simple RETURN. Now type an I. At the INSERT level, type the following sentence**

```
THIS IS IT, BROWN COW.
```

Then leave INSERT by means of a CTRL-C, indicating that you want what you have typed to be put into your workspace area. (You can confirm your success, so far, by noting that you are at EDIT level with your new text still on the screen.)

Now quit the EDITOR by typing Q. This time, use the first QUIT option—"U(PDATE THE WORKFILE AND LEAVE"—by typing a U.

This time you see the word "WRITING" on the second line of your TV screen. A second later you hear the disk drive clicking a great deal and see a couple of dots appear on the screen after the word "WRITING". After that, you see on the next line the report that "YOUR FILE IS 24 BYTES LONG." (Each byte holds one character. If you typed in extra spaces or a RETURN, there may be more than 24 bytes in the file. An *empty* workfile contains two bytes, by the way.)

Finally you see the COMMAND prompt appear. (If you get an error message while writing, it is probably because you are not using your copy of APPLE0:, but instead have a *write-protected original*. Put in a *copy* of APPLE0: and then return to this point.)

Things definitely look more promising this time. But as a check, have a look at the directory of your APPLE0: diskette. **First enter the FILER (type an F), and then enter the "List directory" level (type an L), and finally answer the question by typing APPLE0: and pressing RETURN.**

Note that at the bottom of the directory listing on your screen is the entry:

```
SYSTEM.WRK.TEXT          4          1-FEB-81
```

(The date will actually be whatever date you entered at the beginning of this session. The number 4 tells you how many "blocks" of storage space are used on the diskette.)

This directory entry certainly looks like it might correspond to a disk file that contains the text that was in the workspace area inside the main memory of your computer. Well, there is an acid test for finding out, and you've probably guessed what it is.

Yes, turn off the computer. That will clear out whatever used to be in its memory. **Now boot up Pascal again** with APPLE3: and APPLE0: as described in Section 1-1. Now, with the COMMAND prompt line visible at the top of your screen, **enter the EDITOR again, by typing an E.**

This time you get more disk activity than before, you get a new screen message saying "READING..", and finally you see the following text on an otherwise empty screen:

```
>EDIT: A(DJST C(PY D(LETE F(IND I(NSRT J
THIS IS IT, BROWN COW.
```

You did not get the earlier "NO WORKFILE PRESENT. FILE?" question this time, because the EDITOR found a file saved on your diskette under the name SYSTEM.WRK.TEXT and proceeded to read it into the workspace of the memory of the computer. Then, when you entered the EDITOR the contents of the workspace was displayed on your screen just below the EDIT prompt line, as it always is.

This result confirms the fact that you must always leave the EDITOR with a Q U sequence of key presses if you want changes you have made to the computer's workspace to be written out of the computer and on to a diskette.

The Q E Y sequence leaves the diskette version of the workfile (if any) the way it was the previous time it was created or updated.

2-7 AN OVERVIEW OF EDITING

For work with all computers, *editing* means entering text and changing it. In the Apple UCSD editing system, you must go to the EDIT level and then to INSERT level in order to be able to type any text into your computer. Each character that you type goes into a part of the computer's memory that is usually called the *insert/delete buffer*, or simply the *buffer*. (A buffer is just computer jargon for a temporary storage location in memory.)

All of the text you type in goes into the buffer. When you leave INSERT by CTRL–C, a *copy* of the buffer contents moves into the *workspace*. But when you leave by the ESC route, *no copy* goes into the workspace.

Once a copy of the text has been moved into the workspace, you again have choices about what to do with it. If you leave the editor by the Q U route, then a *copy* of the contents of the workspace is written on your APPLE0: diskette and saved there as a file named SYSTEM.WRK.TEXT, destroying whatever was there before, if anything. But if you leave by the Q E Y route, then *no diskette copy* is made and SYSTEM.WRK.TEXT remains as it was before. (In either case, the workspace copy of the text is *destroyed* when you quit the EDITOR and go to the COMMAND level.)

Whenever you go from COMMAND level down to EDIT, a *copy* of the diskette workfile (in SYSTEM.WRK.TEXT) goes into the workspace. The *original version* remains on the diskette.

It is very helpful in working with data in computers to develop a "mental map", telling where the *data* is, and an understanding of the *processes* that affect the data and move it from place to place. Time and attention spent on this task will pay off handsomely. Figure 2.1 at the end of this session is a graphic representation of the *textual data* and the *editing processes* that lie at the heart of what you have been doing in this session. You should study it closely and see whether your ideas about how things work coincide with the picture presented there.

There is more to learn about the use of the EDITOR than you have seen here. Later sessions will add to your present knowledge. But everything that follows will be based upon the mental picture you are beginning to develop now.

SUMMARY

Figure 2.1 shows how the text that you type into the computer moves from the keyboard into the buffer, into the workspace, out to the diskette workfile, and back into the workspace. It also shows how the text in each place can be lost. Note that text on the diskette is most permanent, and least likely to be erased by accident, and is in the only form that survives when the computer is turned off.

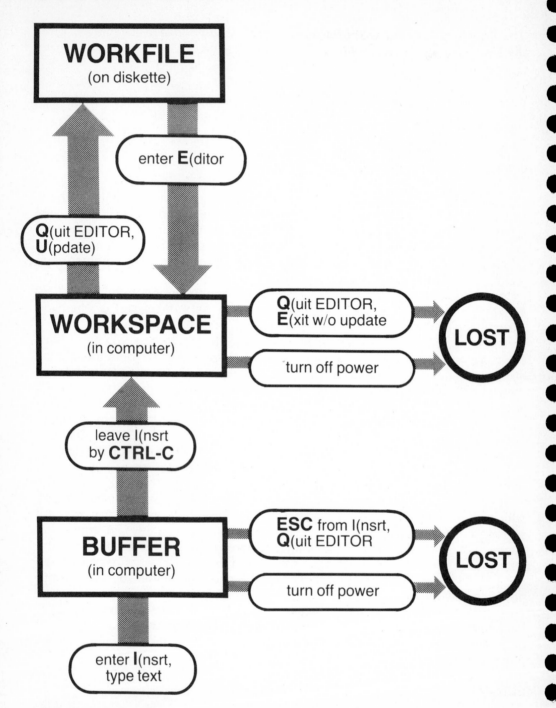

Figure 2.1 Main flow of text information in the Apple Pascal system. Rectangular boxes are places where text goes. Curved boxes are processes for moving text from place to place. New text moves from bottom to top, beginning on the keyboard and ending in a disk file. Processes that flow to the right destroy information.

It is a good idea to look over Figure 2.1 carefully as a review of this session. Try to identify each path in the diagram with processes that you have carried out during the session. You have, in fact, done every process shown in the figure.

Table 2.1 is an extension of the level structure diagram of Table 1.1. In each of the sessions, new levels and details will be added. The purpose is to remind you constantly of the underlying control structure of Apple Pascal.

Table 2.1   Amplified table of the command levels of Apple Pascal. Those features studied in this session are shown in bold face type.

	Exit to escape from accidental entry.
E(ditor	**ESC RETURN or Q E**
Q(uit editor and	**R**
U(pdate workfile	
E(xit with no update	
R(eturn to editor	**Q**
Text Changing Commands	
I(nsert text	**ESC**
CTRL-C (Normal exit.)	
F(iler	
Q(uit the filer	F
N(ew workfile	**RETURN**
V(olumes on line	
L(ist the directory	RETURN
D(ate setter	RETURN
? Show additional commands	RETURN
Commands Available at Any Level	
CTRL-A Toggle to other half of Pascal page.	CTRL-A
RESET Attempts reboot of Pascal	

During this session you have done and seen the following things.

■   **You used the FILER's N(EW instruction to clear out the workspace in your computer.**

■   **You found that you couldn't go directly from the FILER to the EDITOR, but had to go up to the COMMAND level first.**

- You entered the EDITOR and answered the "FILE?" question with a RETURN, indicating that you intended to type new text into the workspace.

- You entered the INSERT level under the EDITOR, typed in a line of text, used the back-arrow key to modify it, and CTRL–C to move it into your workspace and return to the EDITOR.

- You used the Q U sequence to quit the EDITOR and to update the diskette copy of the workfile.

- You entered the FILER, listed the directory of APPLE0: and saw there a new file named "SYSTEM.WRK.TEXT".

- You turned off the power to your computer, turned it back on, rebooted Pascal, entered the EDITOR, and discovered that your workfile had been read back into the computer workspace from APPLE0:.

- You discovered ways to get out of any level that you might have gotten into by accident.

- You experienced the RESET key user trap.

QUESTIONS AND PROBLEMS

1. List every key-press needed, starting at COMMAND level, to create a disk copy of a workfile containing only the word PASCAL. (Assume that APPLE0: does not have a SYSTEM.WRK.TEXT file on it at the start.) Hint: it will take exactly 12 key-presses, counting CTRL–C as one keypress.

2. Suppose you start at the FILER level and that APPLE0: contains a SYSTEM.WRK.TEXT file. Explain what happens as each of the following keys is pressed in sequence:

   L A P P L E 0 : RETURN N Y L A P P L E 0 : RETURN

3. When you enter the EDITOR from the COMMAND level, under what conditions do you get the "FILE?" question? When do you not get it? In the latter case what text do you see on the screen under the EDIT prompt line?

4. You are at COMMAND level and want to go to the FILER. By accident you press the E key. What happens? How do you recover if you get the "FILE?" question? If you don't?

5. You are at EDIT level and accidentally press the I key. Can you recover? If so, how?

6. You are at EDIT level and accidentally press the Q key. Can you recover? If so, how?

7. You are at EDIT level and mean to quit and update the diskette copy of your workfile area. By accident you type Q E. Can you recover? If so, how?

8. You are at EDIT level and mean to quit without affecting the contents of SYSTEM.WRK.TEXT on APPLE0:. But by accident you type Q U. Can you recover? If so, how?

THREE

WRITING, RUNNING, AND CHANGING PROGRAMS

You probably feel a bit misled at this point. We said at the beginning of the last session that you would learn how to type *programs* into your computer. In fact, all you succeeded in doing was entering some *text* about a certain brown cow! Don't feel cheated, however; the method you have just learned applies equally well to the text of a program as it does to the text of a letter to your mother. In fact, when you are in the EDITOR and entering text or changing it, your computer has no way of telling whether the information you have entered is a program or some other kind of text, or whether the text makes sense or not. The EDITOR is like a tape recorder; it takes dictation but it asks no questions about meanings or correctness.

While using the EDITOR in the last session, you found that the text you typed on the keyboard existed in the computer system in three distinct locations:

- **In the buffer. It goes directly there from the keyboard when you are at INSERT level within the EDITOR.**

- **In the workspace in the computer's main memory. A copy goes there when you leave INSERT level by means of a CTRL-C.**

- **On the APPLE0: diskette in the workfile named SYSTEM.WRK.TEXT. It goes there when you leave the EDITOR by means of the Q U (quit and update) option.**

You also saw that if you turned off the electrical power, rebooted Pascal and entered the EDITOR, then a copy of the contents of SYSTEM.WRK.TEXT was automatically moved into your workspace, ready for additional editing.

SESSION GOALS

In this session you will use what you now know about the EDITOR to enter the text of a Pascal program into the workspace. After that, you will leave the EDITOR, run the program, and see what it does. Then you will reenter the EDITOR, make changes to the program text, leave the EDITOR, and run the changed version. You will learn how typing errors are reported to you, and how to use INSERT and DELETE commands in the EDITOR to fix them. You will learn about the WRITE and WRITELN procedures, about the division of programs into lines of text, and about other divisions caused by semicolons and words such as BEGIN and END.

3-1 CLEARING THE WORKFILE

If the **COMMAND** prompt line is not visible at the top line of your TV screen, turn off the power and reboot Pascal according to the procedure in Section 1-1. Change the date to today's date whenever you reboot, using the procedure of Section 1-3.

Type an E and enter the EDITOR. After a little disk activity, the EDIT prompt line appears at the top of your screen. What you see under it will depend upon the current state of the workfile on APPLE0: . If you did the problems at the end of Session 2, then SYSTEM.WRK.TEXT will contain the last workfile that you wrote there. If you didn't do them, then it will contain the text

```
THIS IS IT, BROWN COW.
```

(If for some reason, you are starting this session with a copy of APPLE0: that doesn't have a workfile on it, then you will see the FILE? question under the EDIT prompt. If so, just press the RETURN key.)

When you entered the EDITOR, the contents of your APPLE0: workfile, whatever it is, was copied into the computer's workspace, and is now visible on your screen. Since you will be entering a Pascal program into the workfile soon, you must clear it out before doing anything else. There are several ways to do this, but the following is the one that you should always remember, since it is usually cleaner and more error-free than others.

Leave the EDITOR by the Q E option. (Quit and exit without changing the contents of SYSTEM.WRK.TEXT.)

From COMMAND level, type F and enter the FILER. Then type N, for a new, empty workfile. The computer responds by asking

```
THROW AWAY CURRENT WORKFILE ?
```

Type Y. (This means: yes, throw away disk file SYSTEM.WRK.TEXT. Incidentally, if your APPLE0: diskette does not contain a workfile, you won't be asked the above question.)

Type Q and E. (Quit the FILER, go momentarily to COMMAND level, and then enter the EDITOR.)

With the final step you see the EDIT prompt line reappear at the top of your screen, telling you that you have returned to the EDITOR.

As you become more familiar with the various parts of the Apple Pascal system, you will stop thinking of each key-press as a separate command and will start grouping them into functional *phrases*. For example, the seven key-presses you used just now might be grouped into these three phrases:

Q E	leave the EDITOR
F N Y	clear the disk workfile
Q E	go back to the EDITOR

After you have done that sequence of phrases a dozen or so times, don't be surprised if you start to remember the entire set of key-presses as a single phrase:

Q E F N Y Q E	leave the EDITOR, clear the
	disk workfile and return to the EDITOR.

This way of thinking about the command system comes naturally from use and experience. It is probably *not* a good idea to try to memorize particular key-press phrases before you have experience using them. They are hard to remember until they take on meaning from repeated use.

3-2 ENTERING PROGRAM TINY

You are now back in the EDITOR, which is asking you the question it always asks whenever you first enter it and it *fails* to find a file named SYSTEM.WRK.TEXT on your diskette. The question just below the EDIT prompt line is

```
NO WORKFILE IS PRESENT. FILE?  ( <RET FO
```

on the left half of the Pascal page, with the continuation on the right half.

Press the RETURN key, indicating that you *know* that there is no workfile on your diskette and that you intend to type one into the computer. (You did this several times in Session 2, by the way, so it should be familiar.)

To get text into the workspace, you must first enter INSERT level. **Do this by typing I.**

With the appearance of the INSERT prompt line at the top of the screen, you are at last ready to type a Pascal program into the computer. **Use your keyboard to enter the following four lines of text:**

```
PROGRAM TINY;
BEGIN
WRITELN ('HOW NOW BROWN COW')
END.
```

Read the program over carefully, making sure that it is an exact copy of the above.
There must be a space after PROGRAM, a semicolon after TINY and period after
END. The left and right parentheses are typed by holding down a SHIFT key while
typing the 8 and 9 keys, respectively. Be sure to use *single* quotes (apostrophes)
around HOW NOW BROWN COW. A single quote is a SHIFT–7. **If you find any
typing errors, use the left arrow key to backspace to the first such error. Then retype
everything from there to the end.**

Your next step is to leave INSERT so that the text of your program is copied from
the buffer into the workspace. **Recall that you do that by typing CTRL–C. Do it.**

You did it correctly if you see the EDIT prompt line appear above the four lines of
your program.

The next step is to leave EDIT so that the text of your program is moved from the
workspace area of the computer's main memory into the APPLE0: diskette workfile
SYSTEM.WRK.TEXT. **Recall that you do that by typing Q U. Do it.**

3–3 RUNNING PROGRAM TINY

Finally you are at the COMMAND level again, with the following information on
the screen:

```
COMMAND: E(DIT, R(UN, F(ILE, C(OMP, L(IN
```

At long, long last, you are ready to run your program. **Type R (for Run) and watch
your screen.**

During the next 14 seconds the following events take place:

1. The screen clears and the word

```
COMPILING...
```

appears on the top line. At the same time there is a good deal of disk activity.

2. The following two lines appear near the middle of the screen:

```
APPLE PASCAL COMPILER [1.1]
<    0>..
```

3. Quickly after the above, the following four lines are added

```
TINY      [ 1923 WORDS]
<   2>.
3 LINES
SMALLEST AVAILABLE SPACE = 1923 WORDS
```

If you don't see the above lines on your screen but instead see the report of an error on the last line, type E, and press the spacebar. This puts you back in the EDITOR with your cursor near the error. Then type Q E F N Y Q E, and start over at Section 3-2.

4. After a pause of a second or two, the screen clears and the word

```
RUNNING...
```

appears on the line just below the top.

5. Almost immediately after that, the following text appears

```
HOW NOW BROWN COW
```

6. Quickly, thereafter the COMMAND prompt line reappears and disk activity comes to a halt.

You have successfully run your first Pascal program. There were two major phases to the process: *compiling*, which was marked by the first three events above, and *running*, which included the fourth and fifth events.

You probably noticed the word TINY on the screen during the compiling phase. That is the name you gave to your program in the first line of its text. The message on the screen tells you that the computer is now working on your program in a process called *compilation*—a translation from the Pascal language into a language more nearly like the one used by the hardware in your computer.

After compiling TINY the computer begins the second phase, the *running* of the compiled program. During this phase you probably recognized the words "HOW NOW BROWN COW" as being the same as the words between single quotes in the third line of your program:

```
WRITELN ('HOW NOW BROWN COW')
```

You have probably guessed that the WRITELN statement, when the program was run, caused the text between single quotes to be *written* on your TV screen. In a moment you will be able to test whether this is true.

But first, see what happens when you run the program again. The COMMAND prompt is at the top of the screen now. **Type R again.**

Notice that the process is a lot shorter and simpler this time. It takes only four seconds from start to finish. There are none of the activities that before were associated with the appearance of the "COMPILING..." message on the screen.

Type R again. The process is repeated and again takes the same four seconds. It appears that compilation occurs only once in order to get a program ready to run, and after that, is not part of the process. Indeed, that is true.

You may be wondering where the compiled version of your program is located. **Enter the FILER, type L (for List directory), and answer the question**

```
DIR LISTING OF ?
```

with **APPLE0:.** (**Use the zero key, and don't forget to include the colon.**) **Press RETURN to enter the diskette name.**

Notice near the bottom of the directory listing on your screen a new entry with the name SYSTEM.WRK.CODE. This file was not on your diskette when you examined it in the last session. The new file was put on your diskette by the Pascal compiler (itself *also* a file on APPLE0:) and it contains the translated version of program TINY. It is this *code file* that is run by the computer after compilation ends. Once the code file has been created, there is no need to compile the *text file* again until you make a change in it. **Type Q to quit the FILER.**

3-4 CHANGING THE PROGRAM

Now that you see how to enter and run a Pascal program, you can begin to explore the language itself. For a start, let's confirm our hunch about the WRITELN statement by changing the text between single quotes, and seeing what happens when you run the changed version. **Type E to enter the EDITOR.**

As usual, the workfile SYSTEM.WRK.TEXT is copied from diskette into your workspace, which is displayed on your screen beneath the EDIT prompt line. Note carefully where the *cursor* (the solid white rectangle) is located now.

Type the right-arrow key a dozen or so times; then try the left-arrow a few times. Those keys give you character-by-character control of the position of the cursor. If they were the only ones, it would take a lot of keystrokes to move the cursor through a long program. **See what happens when you type CTRL-L and CTRL-O several times.** You have line-by-line control as well as character-by-character control. **Experiment also with the spacebar and the RETURN key.** Notice in particular how RETURN *differs* from CTRL-L. CTRL-O and CTRL-L move the cursor up and down respectively while the RETURN key moves the cursor to the beginning of the next line. (You might want to label the O key with an up-arrow and the L key with a down-arrow.)

Later on you will discover other ways to move the cursor about in a program, but right now nearly all of your use will be by means of the six *cursor control keys* you have just been experimenting with. Now let's see why one would want to move the cursor anyway.

Use cursor control keys to place the cursor on top of the H in HOW in the third line of the program text. Our goal here is to change the words between single quotes in the WRITELN statement so that we can see what happens when the program is run again.

Next, type D. This is a new EDITOR command, and it causes this prompt line to appear on the left half of the Pascal page:

```
>DELETE: < > <MOVING COMMANDS> [<ETX> TO
```

and the rest on the right half

```
DELETE, <ESC> TO ABORT]
```

Press the right-arrow key 17 times. This is the basic deletion operation, and you will use it a great deal when making program changes. You have now deleted "HOW NOW BROWN COW".

What if you delete too many chacters by accident? All is not lost. **Press the right-arrow key a few more times. Now press the left arrow the same number of times.** Deleted characters are remembered by Apple Pascal's screen editing system, just in case you need them again. This is true even when you delete past the end of line. **Try it.**

Other cursor-positioning keys can also be used when in DELETE. **Try typing CTRL-L. Then back up with CTRL-O. Next, try RETURN and follow by CTRL-O.** These keys permit rapid deletion of many lines of text, and also provide recovery from typing errors when you delete more than you intended.

Sometimes while editing text it is easiest to recover from a succession of typing errors by starting over. You can do that while in DELETE in the same way that you did when you wanted to escape from INSERT in Session 2: **Press the ESC key.** Now you are exactly where you were when you first entered DELETE, with the cursor over the H in "HOW".

Now that you know how to delete text, let's get back to the job of replacing "HOW NOW BROWN COW" by something else in the WRITELN statement. **Type D to enter DELETE. Press the right-arrow 17 times until the cursor is over the second single quote. Type CRTL-C.** CTRL-C means that you *really do* want the change to happen, just as it meant with INSERT.

At this point "HOW NOW BROWN COW" has disappeared from your workspace, you're back at EDIT level, and your cursor is positioned over the second of the two single quotes. Now it is time to insert the change.

Type I to enter INSERT. Suddenly it looks as if the right end of the line, "')", has disappeared. Actually it's just been moved over to the extreme right end of the Pascal page. **Type CTRL-A and have a look. Type CTRL-A again to get back.**

Now in INSERT, type M O O and then CTRL-C. You have, by this two-step delete/insert process, replaced "HOW NOW BROWN COW" by "MOO". The display on your screen at this moment should look like this:

```
>EDIT: A(DJST C(PY D(LETE F(IND I(NSRT J
PROGRAM TINY;
BEGIN
WRITELN ('MOO')
END.
```

(If it doesn't look like this, use D and/or I to change it until it does look like this.)

> The procedure you have used for changing text has three steps:
> 1. At EDIT level, move the cursor to the first character of the text to be changed.
> 2. Delete it. (D right-arrow(s) CTRL-C)
> 3. Insert new text. (I text CTRL-C)

You will become very familiar with this process because you will be using this procedure again and again to correct errors and make other changes in your programs.

3-5 RUNNING THE CHANGED PROGRAM

To run this changed version of TINY, type Q U R. This phrase means "Quit the EDITOR, update SYSTEM.WRK.TEXT, and run it." It is one of those key "phrases" you will become very familiar with through use.

Notice this time that the computer goes through a longer set of activities, signaled by the appearance of the COMPILING... line on your screen. After a while the word RUNNING... appears across the top of your screen, quickly followed by MOO. Immediately after that the COMMAND prompt appears.

You have changed your first program and succeeded in running it. The new version was similar to the old one except that it caused MOO instead of HOW NOW BROWN COW to appear on the screen when it was run. *It seems reasonably clear that the effect of WRITELN in Pascal is, at a minimum, to cause the text enclosed in single quotes to appear on the TV screen when the program is run.*

Another observation that you may have made is that *whenever you type a new program or change an old one and then run it, Pascal goes through the compilation step before running the program. When there have been no changes, it skips compilation and starts running immediately.*

3-6 DEALING WITH TYPING ERRORS

Let's introduce a typing error into the program and see what happens. Suppose, for example, that you had typed a space, after PRO in the first line. What would have happened? Let's find out.

Leave COMMAND level and enter the EDITOR by typing E. Move the cursor over to the G in PROGRAM. Insert a space before it by the sequence: I spacebar CTRL-C. Your screen should now look like this:

```
>EDIT: A(DJST C(PY D(LETE F(IND I(NSRT J
PRO GRAM TINY;
BEGIN
WRITELN ('MOO')
END.
```

Now use the Q U R phrase to run the changed program. Watch carefully to see what happens and when. Here's what you should see on the screen when all activity comes to a halt.:

```
COMPILING...




APPLE PASCAL COMPILER [1.1]
<   0>
PRO <<<<
LINE 0, ERROR 18: <SP>(CONTINUE), <ESC>(
```

On the right half of the Pascal page you will find the rest of the bottom line:

```
TERMINATE, E(DIT
```

This situation is an example of a *compile-time error* detected in your program. The next to the last line on your screen shows you the precise point in the text of your program where the compiler discovered that there was a problem. The last line on the screen tells you which text line it occurred in, (line 0 is the first line), what its *error number* is, and what your options are at this moment. The three options are

■ <SP>: **Press the spacebar to continue trying to compile the program.**

■ <ESC>: **Press the ESC key to quit and go back to COMMAND level.**

■ E(DIT : **Type E to go to the EDITOR and fix the error.**

The first option is always risky, since one real error usually misleads the compiler into thinking that there are several others when in fact there may not be. The second option is there so that you can get out of the RUN command if you accidentally touched the R key while at COMMAND level. You want the third option.

Type E now and notice that, after some disk activity, your workfile is back in the workspace and is visible on the screen. Instead of the EDIT prompt line, the following *error message* appears:

```
ERROR IN DECLARATION PART.   TYPE <SP>
```

Sometimes these messages are right to the point and quite helpful. At other times, they may seem obscure and even misleading. Of one thing you may be certain, however: *an error of some kind exists at or before the point in the text where the cursor now is positioned.* Your job is to find it.

In the present case, you know what the error is, because you introduced it yourself. **Press the spacebar to continue entering the EDITOR.** The cursor is properly located for you to delete the erroneous space. **Type D right-arrow CTRL-C.**

Check the program to make sure it works again: type Q U R and watch. (If you get additional error messages, go back to the EDITOR, make changes as above so that the program matches exactly the program text at the end of Section 3–4, and run again.)

The last page or two of this book contain a list of all Compiler Error Messages. Later, when you get more experienced, you can use them during the compiling process to decide whether to continue compiling or to return to the editor.

3-7 TEXT LINES IN PASCAL PROGRAMS

You have seen two slightly different versions of a Pascal program. The text of the program was four lines long. You may have concluded (especially if you know other computer languages) that this particular arrangement of text into lines is important. Let's find out.

Enter the EDITOR. Put the cursor just to the right of the last character in the first line. Type the sequence: D right-arrow CTRL-C. You have just succeeded in deleting the RETURN character that you typed when you originally entered that line of the program. **Now, type this sequence: I space CTRL-C.** This sequence has inserted a blank space between the end of the original first line and the beginning of the second line. In effect, you have substituted a space character for the RETURN character.

The program is now only three lines long. **Repeat the above process, moving the cursor just beyond the new end of the first line, deleting the RETURN and inserting a space. Do it a third time.** At this point your program is one line long. It looks like this:

```
PROGRAM TINY; BEGIN WRITELN ('MOO') END.
```

(If it doesn't look exactly like this, keep using INSERT and DELETE to edit it until it does.)

Next try to run this new version by typing Q U R. Now what do you think about the importance of lines in the text of a Pascal program? **Enter the EDITOR again.**

To reinforce this fact, let's change the program so that it looks like this:

```
PROGRAM
TINY;
BEGIN
WRITELN
('MOO')
END.
```

To make each change, first move the cursor to the character that will begin a new line, and then type I RETURN CTRL-C. In this way you insert a RETURN character just before the T in TINY, the B in BEGIN, etc.

Check it out when you have finished and make sure that it looks exactly like the above. **Now type Q U R and see whether this version will run.**

As a final experiment on line divisions, **go back to the EDITOR, move the cursor to the G in the first line, and insert a RETURN there by means of the I RETURN CTRL-C sequence.** The program should look like this:

```
PRO
GRAM
TINY;
BEGIN
WRITELN
('MOO')
END.
```

Now type Q U R and see the result.

Your last experiment ended with a compile-time error. In fact, the error number here is the same one you got when you inserted a space into the word PROGRAM. **Type E and then press the spacebar to return to the EDITOR.**

On the basis of all these experiments, can you formulate a theory as to when it is legal and when it is illegal to use RETURN in the text of a Pascal program?

3-8 WRITE AND WRITELN

For the following experiments you will need a clear workfile. **Make sure the EDIT prompt is at the top of your screen. Then type the sequence Q E F N Y Q E.** You did this at the start of this session for the same purpose. Think through the meaning of each command in this seven-letter sequence.

Continue entering the EDITOR now by answering the "FILE?" question with a RETURN, indicating that you will type in the workfile. At this point you are in the EDITOR with an empty workfile, ready to enter new text. **Study the following program:**

```
PROGRAM WRITEIT;
BEGIN
  WRITE ('HOW ');
  WRITE ('NOW ');
  WRITE ('BROWN ');
  WRITELN ('COW')
END.
```

As you type it into the computer's buffer, make certain of the following points:

1. The *program name,* WRITEIT, contains no spaces.

2. There is a semicolon after the program name.

3. The third line is indented two spaces. You use the spacebar to create the indentation. After that, the next three lines automatically start at the same indentation.

4. Three semicolons separate the four *program statements* between the words BEGIN and END.

5. The seventh line is "undented" two spaces, back to the left margin. You do this by typing the left-arrow key two times before typing END.

6. The program ends with a period.

Type I, and then enter the program above. Move the text into your workspace by typing CTRL-C. (If you discover an error in the text at this point, move the cursor to the error and fix it with INSERT and/or DELETE operations, just as before.)

Type Q U R to run WRITEIT. As usual with new or changed programs, the process starts with the "COMPILING..." message. If you typed the program correctly there are no compile-time error mesages. (If you do get an error message, then type E followed by spacebar to get back to the EDITOR and fix the error.) After the run is complete, your screen should look like this;

```
COMMAND: E(DIT, R(UN, F(ILE, C(OMP, L(IN
RUNNING...
HOW NOW BROWN COW
```

It looks as though WRITE and WRITELN have very similar meanings in Pascal. They both display text on the screen. Perhaps you are wondering what caused these four words to appear, strung together on a single line on your screen. Two ideas may have crossed your mind:

1. One possibility is that WRITE and WRITELN may be different. WRITELN may start a new line after writing its text on the screen, but WRITE may not.

2. Another possibility is that the semicolon after WRITE may prevent a new line from being started. Absence of a semicolon may cause a new line to begin.

The first idea can be tested easily by changing WRITE to WRITELN in the program. **Type E to enter the EDITOR. Use the cursor control keys to place the cursor immediately after the E in "WRITE ('NOW ');". Enter INSERT by typing I. Type L N and CTRL-C.**

The result should be that you have changed WRITE to WRITELN in that line of your program text and are back in the EDITOR. The screen now looks like this:

```
>EDIT: A(DJST C(PY D(LETE F(IND I(NSRT J
PROGRAM WRITEIT;
BEGIN
   WRITE ('HOW ');
   WRITELN ('NOW ');
   WRITE ('BROWN ');
   WRITELN ('COW')
END.
```

Run the program by typing Q U R. As before, you see on the screen a report of progress during the *compiling* phase and, if there are no errors a quick transition to the *running* phase. At the end, your screen looks like this:

```
COMMAND: E(DIT, R(UN, F(ILE, C(OMP, L(IN
RUNNING...
HOW NOW
BROWN COW
```

As you now can see, the first explanation is correct. The big difference between WRITE and WRITELN is that WRITELN ends its writing activities on the screen by issuing a RETURN, so that the next characters sent to the screen will start on a new line at the left margin. WRITE does not issue a RETURN.

3-9 ABOUT THOSE SEMICOLONS

Just because the first explanation is correct doesn't necessarily mean that the second is totally wrong. Even if WRITELN *does* start a new line, it could also be necessary to use a semicolon after WRITE to keep it from doing the same thing.

More investigation is in order, and the obvious experiment is to see what happens when you delete a semicolon after WRITE.

Enter the EDITOR. Move the cursor to the semicolon after the first WRITE in the BEGIN/END block. Delete it. Be sure to exit from DELETE by CTRL-C, so as to move the change into your workspace when you return to the EDITOR. The program should look like this:

```
PROGRAM WRITEIT;
BEGIN
   WRITE ('HOW ')
   WRITELN ('NOW ');
   WRITE ('BROWN ');
   WRITELN ('COW')
END.
```

From the EDITOR, type Q U R to run the program. What happened? What is ERROR 6? **Type E to return to the EDITOR** with the text of the error message at the top of your screen. It says

```
ILLEGAL SYMBOL (POSSIBLY MISSING ';' ON
```

on the left half of the Pascal page, and

```
LINE ABOVE) . TYPE <SP>
```

on the right.

The hint in this case is correct. The semicolon you deleted is the missing semicolon referred to in the error message. Evidently the second explanation is wrong. In fact, the semicolon is required.

> In Pascal, semicolons are required between any two statements. They signify the end of one statement and the beginning of another. Semicolons have no effect on the way WRITE and WRITELN work.

The contrast between the role of the semicolon and the RETURN in the text of a Pascal program is very sharp. You may, without breaking any of Pascal's grammatical rules, type a RETURN quite literally *anywhere* you would have typed a space. But you have little freedom regarding semicolons. *Whenever two consecutive statements occur, a semicolon must occur after the first statement and before the second.* (The semicolon itself may be preceeded or followed by spaces, or for that matter, RETURNs.

If you have read the last paragraphs very carefully, then you are probably thinking that we must be mistaken. The original version of WRITEIT worked fine even though it seemed to be lacking a couple of semicolons. There was no semicolon between BEGIN and the first WRITE, and there was none between the WRITELN and END. The rule about *always* needing semicolons between statements must be wrong, you might think.

We agree that a semicolon is not needed after BEGIN nor before END. We insist, however, that a semicolon *must* separate consecutive statements. You've probably already guessed the way out of this apparent contradiction: *BEGIN is not a "statement" in Pascal, nor is END.* In fact, you should think of BEGIN and END as nothing more nor less than punctuation marks. BEGIN is like an opening bracket and END is like a closing bracket. Statements *within* brackets need to be separated by semicolons, but no semicolons are needed to separate the statements from the brackets themselves.

The above paragraph is so important that you probably should reread it now and make certain that you understand it. You will see many BEGINs and ENDs in this book and it is essential that you stop thinking of them as a kind of statement. It is natural to think of them as statements if you are familiar with other languages, since programmers almost always put BEGIN or END on a line by itself. Recall, however, the other main fact about the text of a Pascal program: arrangement into separate lines is left up to the author. BEGIN and END, therefore, really aren't either *lines* or *statements*. They are only *words* that stand as major punctuation marks of the language.

> If this concept seems strange to you, keep reminding yourself that a RETURN in the text of a program has exactly the same significance—no more and no less—that a space character has. Either one may be used whenever it is necessary to separate the words of the language from one another.

As you have already seen, the same program can be typed as one long line, with no RETURNs, or as a vertical column of single words and symbols, with no spaces. Since the structure of the program is *not* based on text lines, Pascal has to have other means of grouping and separating statements: hence BEGIN, END, semicolons and other formatting devices that you will learn later.

The structure of Pascal programs is not based on text lines.

If you're like us, you will at first find it a nuisance to have to keep remembering to put a semicolon between Pascal statements. You will forget to do it once in a while and will get a sometimes obscure error message at a later point in the program. On the other hand, you will also come to recognize that the meaninglessness of text lines in Pascal allows you more *stylistic freedom* when you write than other programming languages offer.

We have used that stylistic freedom here to adopt an *indentation scheme* in program WRITEIT. The four statements between BEGIN and END were each indented two spaces. These additional spaces were not required by Pascal. *It is a general rule that whenever a space (or RETURN) is required, two or more spaces (or RETURNs) may be used.* If you went back to the original version of WRITEIT in Section 3-7 and deleted all the indentation spaces, the program would still be grammatically correct and would produce the same results. We have used indentation here specifically to call attention to the fact that the four indented statements form a group that is bracketed between the opening BEGIN and the closing END. As programs become longer they become more complex and harder to read. A consistent indentation style will help you to read and understand what you (and others) have written.

By way of example, and to conclude this session, turn now to the Introduction of this book and remind yourself of the way program DICEGAME looked in its neatly indented form. Well, folks, here is another version of the *same* program, and it is as grammatically correct as the one in the Introduction. Let's hear it for style!

```
PROGRAM DICEGAME;USES APPLESTUFF;CONST
HELLFREEZESOVER=FALSE;VAR DICE,POINT:
INTEGER;PROCEDURE ROLLEM(VAR TOSS:
INTEGER);BEGIN TOSS:=RANDOM MOD 6+1;
TOSS:=TOSS+RANDOM MOD 6+1;WRITELN(
'YOU ROLLED A ',TOSS)END;BEGIN REPEAT
ROLLEM(DICE);CASE DICE OF 7,11:WRITELN
('YOU WIN');2,3,12:WRITELN('YOU LOSE');
4,5,6,8,9,10:BEGIN POINT:=DICE;REPEAT
ROLLEM(DICE)UNTIL(DICE=POINT)OR(DICE=7);
IF DICE=POINT THEN WRITELN('YOU WIN')
ELSE WRITELN('YOU LOSE')END END UNTIL
HELLFREEZESOVER END.
```

Anybody who claims that Pascal is good because it *forces* clear writing is obviously overstating the case. The truth is that Pascal is defined in such a way as to *allow* clear writing, where some other languages would treat as errors any attempts at indentation or using blank lines.

At the present time your computer is still halted, waiting for you to attend to the missing semicolon error it found in your program. **Press the spacebar to get fully into the EDITOR. Then quit the EDITOR and return to the COMMAND level.**

SUMMARY

During this session you have done and seen the following things:

- **You used EDIT/INSERT to enter the text of a short Pascal program.**

- **You used the Q U R sequence to run the program.**

- **Running was a two-phase process: compiling, or translating Pascal into a language closer to the one used by the hardware, and running the translated program.**

- **You found that the compiler translates the diskette text file of the program into a code file on the same diskette.**

- **You used EDIT/DELETE followed by EDIT/INSERT to make changes in the program.**

- **You used the arrow keys, CTRL-L, CTRL-O, space and RETURN to position the cursor in the workfile prior to insertion or deletion.**

- **You introduced typographic errors into a program and saw how compile-time errors are reported and repaired.**

- **You discovered that it is illegal to put a space in the middle of the word PROGRAM.**

- **You discovered that division of Pascal program text into lines is permitted anywhere a space is allowed.**

- **You also saw that consecutive Pascal statements must be separated by semicolons, and that the words BEGIN and END serve to bracket statements into functional blocks.**

- **You used WRITE and WRITELN in programs to generate textual output on your screen.**

Now let's also update the tables that mark your progress into the level structure of the Apple Pascal system.

Table 3.1A Amplified table of the EDITOR levels of Apple Pascal. Those features studied in this session are shown in bold face type.

	Exit to escape from accidental entry.
E(ditor	ESC RETURN or Q E
Q(uit editor and	R
U(pdate workfile	
E(xit with no update	
R(eturn to editor	Q

Cursor Moving Commands

Right-arrow (Move cursor right)
Left-arrow (Move cursor left)
CTRL-L (Move cursor down
CTRL-O (Move cursor up)
RETURN (Move cursor to beginning
             of next line)
Spacebar (Move cursor to next
             character)

Text Changing Commands

I(nsert text	ESC
CTRL-C (Normal exit)	
D(elete text	**ESC**
CTRL-C (Normal exit.)	

Table 3.1B Amplified table of other command levels of Apple Pascal. Those features studied in this session are shown in bold face type.

	Exit to escape from accidental entry.
F(iler	
Q(uit the filer	F
N(ew workfile	RETURN
V(olumes on line	
L(ist the directory	RETURN
D(ate setter	RETURN
? Show additional commands	RETURN
R(un the program in workfile	
Commands Available at Any Level	
CTRL-A Toggle to other half of Pascal page.	CTRL-A
RESET Attempt reboot of Pascal	

Table 3.2 These are the five Pascal words that you used in Session 3. A similar table will appear at the end of all future sessions.

BEGIN	END	PROGRAM
WRITE	WRITELN	

QUESTIONS AND PROBLEMS

1. If you are at the COMMAND level, what keystrokes are necessary to clear out the workfile?

2. You have just finished entering a Pascal program, have pressed CTRL-C to move the program from the input buffer to the workspace in Apple's memory. What key presses are required to run the program?

3. If you are at the EDIT level, give the keypresses necessary to display a list of the files on APPLE0: if you *don't* wish to update the workfile.

4. As far as Pascal is concerned, how are spaces and RETURNs treated?

5. If you are in the EDIT/INSERT mode and press the ESC key, what will happen?

6. A program line reads

```
WRITELN ('FAT CAT')
```

If you have just entered EDIT level, explain how you would change the line to read

```
WRITELN ('BAD CAT')
```

7. Suppose your workspace contains the lines

```
HI DIDDLE DIDDLE,
THE CAT AND THE FIDDLE.
THE COW JUMPED OVER THE
MOON.
```

Explain how you would delete the lines

```
THE CAT AND THE FIDDLE
THE COW JUMPED OVER THE
```

from the workspace.

8. What is wrong with the following program?

```
PROGRAM ZIP;

BEGIN
   WRITELN ('ZIPPITY')
   WRITELN ('DOO')
   WRITELN ('DAH')
END
```

9. What will happen if the following program is run?

```
PROGRAM QUOTE;

BEGIN
   WRITE ('IT WAS THE ');
   WRITELN ('BEST OF TIMES,');
   WRITE ('IT WAS THE ');
   WRITELN ('WORST OF TIMES.')
END.
```

10. Write a program to print out the following letter patterns on the screen of your computer.

```
A
AB
ABC
ABCD
ABCDE
```

FOUR

GENERATING SOUND

You have now reached an important plateau in your understanding of Apple Pascal. The dozen or so single-letter *system commands* that you have learned are the ones that you will use 90% of the time in the future. You used them in the previous session to write, compile, run, change, recompile, and rerun your first Pascal program. You will be doing this sequence of activities again and again throughout the rest of this book. Your programs will get longer. They will contain new types of statements. They will exercise new features of the language and the computer. But the sequence, write — compile — run — change — recompile — rerun, will be with you forever.

One of the problems you have probably already encountered is that the screen is often filled with information that comes from different sources. Did a particular line of text show up there because you typed it in? Or, perhaps the Pascal operating system generated the line: or perhaps the line came from the compiler or from the program when it was run. Perhaps lines from all these sources are on the screen at the same time. Not to worry, however, since after a few hours of practice at your computer you will automatically sort out where information on the screen is coming from.

The reason for bringing this issue up is that it gets in the way of learning about Pascal. It is enough for you to concentrate on the details of Pascal without having to worry about what process generated a display on the screen. Consequently, we will avoid the problem as much as possible in this session by using the sound and game paddle features of the Apple. The main advantage of this strategy is that it will always be perfectly clear where information is coming from.

Be certain that the two game paddles are properly installed in your Apple computer before starting this session.

SESSION GOALS

You will mainly review the elements of Pascal programs learned in Session 3 and extend this knowledge to programs that use loops. The and sound paddle controls will be used to demonstrate output, input, and the loop process. As part of an on-going process you will review the manner in which Pascal programs are entered, modified, and run.

4-1 A SHORT REVIEW

If your computer is on, turn it off. Boot up Pascal using the procedure described in Section 1-1. You should now see the COMMAND line at the top of the screen. Remember that it's always a good practice to set the current date after booting up Pascal. **Press F to move into the FILER. With the FILER prompt at the top of the screen, press D to call the date-setting facility.** The date previously recorded on APPLE0: will be displayed. It may not be the current date. **Follow the instructions, set the current date, and press RETURN.** When you do so, you are returned automatically to the FILER. **Type Q to return to COMMAND level.**

In the next section you will enter a new program into the workfile. There may or may not be a program currently in SYSTEM.WRK.TEXT on APPLE0:, but to be sure, let's see what's there before destroying it in preparation for a new program. (This is *always* a good practice.)

From COMMAND level, type E to enter the EDITOR. As you probably recall, one of two things always happens when you do this. If there is no SYSTEM.WRK.TEXT file on the diskette, you will see the "NO WORKFILE PRESENT. FILE?" message. But if SYSTEM.WRK.TEXT *does* exist, then the system copies it into the workspace of your computer and displays the top 23 text lines on your screen. If you are using the same APPLE0: diskette that you were using in Session 3, then the second situation will occur, and you will see the last program that you wrote. Because you won't be using it any more, you may get rid of it as shown below. (If, on the other hand, you picked up a different APPLE0: that has text on it that should *not* be destroyed, now is your chance to start over with the right diskette.)

Recall that from the EDITOR the seven-letter sequence for clearing out SYSTEM.WRK.TEXT is Q E F N Y Q E. If the file needs to be cleared, type the letters now. As we suggested in Session 3, it will help you to group the letters into three short phrases:

    Q E   Quit the EDITOR
    F N Y   From FILER, get new workfile
    Q E   Quit FILER, enter EDITOR

Whichever state your APPLE0: diskette was in originally, it is now cleared of file SYSTEM.WRK.TEXT, and the "FILE?" question is now on your screen and waiting for a reply from you. **Press RETURN.**

4-2 GENERATING SOUND

After a few moments the EDIT prompt line will appear at the top of the screen. Since you want to type in a program **press I** to switch into the insert mode. You should see the INSERT prompt line at the top of the screen.

Examine the short program below. Note the vertical spacing between parts of the program and how the indentation emphasizes the structure of the program. As you type in this program, check each line carefully before going on. If mistakes are noted, remember that you can use the left-arrow at the right side of the keyboard to move the cursor back to the location of the error. Then just retype the remainder of the line correctly. **Okay, now type in the program.**

```
PROGRAM SOUND;

   USES
       APPLESTUFF;

   BEGIN
      NOTE (20, 100)
   END.
```

You should see the program on the screen exactly as shown above. The INSERT prompt line should still be at the top of the screen. **Press CTRL-C to move the program into the workspace of the computer memory.** After this is done, you should see the EDIT prompt line at the top of the screen.

The program isn't much more complicated than the ones you worked with in Session 3, and seems reasonably transparent. The *program name* is SOUND which reflects the purpose of the program. This is the first program you have seen which has the "USES block". APPLESTUFF is a collection of special *procedures*. It is stored in in APPLE0:SYSTEM.LIBRARY. The APPLESTUFF procedure used in this program is named NOTE. When the program is compiled, the computer brings APPLESTUFF into the program. If a program does not use any of the special procedures, there is no need for the APPLESTUFF declaration.

Now you can try out the program. Remember that at the EDIT level, Q causes the computer to leave the EDITOR and prompt you about the workfile. U causes the workfile to be updated on the diskette APPLE0:. Finally R starts the compilation and execution ("running") process. You can type the three letters all together and the computer will pick them up as needed. **Press the keys Q U R.**

After a few seconds of disk whirring and various messages flashing on the screen during compilation, the program will run. If there were no errors in the program, you should have heard a single tone (approximately middle C) that lasted a little more than a second. Really not too exciting, right? Have patience: more impressive results are close by.

(If you didn't get the results described above but instead got an error message during the compilation process then there must be a typing error in the program. **If so, press E to call the EDITOR and then press the spacebar.** Find the error and correct it with the delete and insert operations you learned about in Session 3.)

It should be clear to you that the source of the tone was the command NOTE *inside* the program. No action on your part was required after you signaled the computer to run the program. **Type R and listen again.** There were no compiler messages this time, since you had made no changes between runs. **Now rapidly type**

three Rs in a row. Notice that the computer shores up the extra commands and carries them out in sequence.

Now let's see what happens when you change the numbers in parentheses after NOTE and then rerun. **Type E to enter the EDITOR. Move the cursor to the "2" in "20". Change it to "3" by the usual delete/insert sequence: D right-arrow CTRL-C I 3 CTRL-C.**

At this point you should be back at EDIT level. **Type Q U R, and listen.**

Return to the EDITOR and repeat the editing steps in the previous two paragraphs, changing "100" to "200". Run (Q U R) the new version. What is the effect? What do you think the two numbers in the NOTE statement control?

4-3 ANOTHER WAY TO MAKE THE SAME SOUND

Go to the EDITOR again and use delete/insert steps to change the program text so that it looks like this:

```
PROGRAM SOUND;

    USES
       APPLESTUFF;

    VAR
       PITCH, DURATION : INTEGER;

BEGIN
    PITCH := 30;
    DURATION := 200;
    NOTE (PITCH, DURATION)
END.
```

Perhaps the easiest way to insert the two lines that begin with VAR is to use the following procedure:

1. Place the cursor just to the right of the semicolon after APPLESTUFF.

2. Type I to enter INSERT mode.

3. Press RETURN once to start a new line.

4. Press RETURN again to enter a blank line.

5. Press the left arrow twice to adjust the indentation.

6. Type VAR and press RETURN.

7. Press the spacebar twice (not the right arrow) for indentation.

8. Type

```
PITCH, DURATION : INTEGER;
```

and do not press RETURN.

9. Type CTRL–C to exit INSERT mode.

Notice that in this method, you start out on the line above the place you want to insert one or more new lines. The first thing you insert is a RETURN. Then you enter the new line or lines but do not put a RETURN at the end of the last line.

You can use the same strategy to insert the two new lines after BEGIN, starting with the cursor just to the right of BEGIN. (Only a single RETURN is needed at the start this time, since you are not inserting any blank lines here.) Finally, you can use delete/insert to change the numbers "30, 200" into "PITCH, DURATION".

Type Q U R to run the new version. (If there is a compile-time error, type E, press the spacebar, and make the necessary changes.) What do you hear? **Type R and listen again.**

If all went well, then you heard exactly the same sound in the new version that you did with the immediately previous one. This may not seem like progress to you, since we made the program larger and didn't get anything new out of it. Yet it is progress, for we have separated the program into two distinct phases. The first phase assigns numerical values to the words PITCH and DURATION. The second phase uses these values, whatever they are, to make a sound. In just a few minutes you will see how to make use of this separation to produce many different sounds by changing the values of PITCH and DURATION.

In Pascal, PITCH and DURATION are called *variables*. The first thing you probably noticed about them is that each variable name occurs in two different sections in the program: in the text line after the word VAR, and again in the BEGIN/END block.

Let's see what happens if you delete DURATION from the line after VAR. **Return to the EDITOR, move the cursor to the comma before the "D" in DURATION, and delete ", DURATION". Leave DELETE mode (CTRL-C) and run (Q U R) the changed program.** What happened?

Toward the middle of your screen you should see the compile-time message "LINE 20, ERROR 104". **Type E to return to the EDITOR.** The error message at the top of the screen says

```
UNDECLARED IDENTIFIER. TYPE <SP>
```

The cursor is just to the right of the word DURATION in the BEGIN/END block of the program. Note that the compiler did not make a similar complaint about the word PITCH.

> You have just discovered a basic grammar rule of Pascal: except for a few words already known to the Pascal compiler, you have to define all words before you use them.

Words such as BEGIN, END, WRITELN, and NOTE are known to the compiler. But variable names, such as PITCH and DURATION, are not. Pascal requires that you declare them in the VAR section of your program. (VAR is an abbreviation for VARIABLE.) If you forget to do so, the compiler reminds you of any undeclared identifiers. "Identifier" is just a fancy word for "name", by the way.

Fix the error as follows. Press the spacebar. Use CTRL-O and arrow keys to move the cursor just after PITCH in the VAR section. Reinsert ", DURATION". Exit with CTRL-C. Make certain that your program is now exactly the same as it was at the beginning of this section. (If you're in doubt, run it. Then return to the EDITOR.)

There is nothing magical about the names we have used here for our variables. You have immense freedom of choice, and it is a good idea to use that freedom to create meaningful names. It may seem cute to use variable names like FOO or SALLY, but you'll have a tough time understanding your program a week later.

Although your freedom here is great, it isn't total. Try the following experiment. **With the cursor to the right of DURATION, type I and insert ", BEGIN". Leave the INSERT mode via CTRL-C.** The VAR block now looks like this

```
VAR
   PITCH, DURATION, BEGIN : INTEGER;
```

RUN (Q U R) the program. Again you get a compile-time message that says "LINE 16, ERROR 2". **Type E and read the error message on your screen.** Notice that the cursor is located just after BEGIN in the VAR block. The slightly obscure message

```
IDENTIFIER EXPECTED
```

means that the compiler did not want you to use BEGIN as a variable name. Why not? Because BEGIN is a word that has a special meaning in Pascal. We say that it is a *reserved word*.

> Altogether, Apple Pascal has 41 reserved words, and you may not use any of them as a variable name. If you do, then you will get the "IDENTIFIER EXPECTED" message in the VAR block where you first try to define it.

Appendix C has a complete list of Apple Pascal reserved words. It also gives more detailed rules governing legal names for variables. If you start your names with letters and follow with letters and numbers, omitting spaces and punctuation marks, you'll be okay, except for a rare time when you accidentally pick a name that is the same as a reserved word.

In order to call your attention to the reserved words, we will adopt a printing convention in all future programs shown in this book. The convention is that all reserved words will be printed in bold face type. As you see them again and again, you will be reminded to stay away from them as variable names.

There is another class of words that sometimes can lead to problems. **If you are still looking at the error message, press the spacebar. From the EDIT level, delete BEGIN from the VAR block. Now change PITCH to WRITELN in the VAR block and in both places in the BEGIN/END block.** When finished, the program should look like this

```
PROGRAM SOUND;

    USES
        APPLESTUFF;

    VAR
        WRITELN, DURATION : INTEGER;

BEGIN
    WRITELN := 30;
    DURATION := 200;
    NOTE (WRITELN, DURATION)
END.
```

You have used WRITELN several times before, but certainly not in this context. WRITELN is a procedure normally used to send information to the screen. Will the computer accept WRITELN as a variable? Well, let's find out. **Leave the EDITOR and run the program.** Were you surprised at the the results?

Okay, now **return to the EDITOR and insert the shaded line below so that the BEGIN/END block looks like this**

```
BEGIN
    WRITELN := 30;
    WRITELN (WRITELN);
    DURATION := 200;
    NOTE (WRITELN, DURATION)
END.
```

Well, you saw that before this last change, the program ran and the computer didn't complain about the use of WRITELN as a variable name. Will the computer complain now that WRITELN is being used both in its usual function (to send information to the screen) and also as a variable name?

Leave the EDITOR and run the program. This time things didn't work out as well, right? ERROR 59 means error in variable. The problem arose because you declared WRITELN as a variable and then attempted to use WRITELN as a procedure to send information to the screen.

In addition to the reserved words in Pascal (which you cannot use as variable names) there is another class of words which may be used for variable names under some circumstances. This new class is called *built-in* words, and WRITELN is in this class.

The computer understands these built-in words so they do not have to be declared in a VAR block. You may declare and use a built-in word for another purpose provided you don't subsequently try to use the word in its usual meaning in the same program. WRITELN is acceptable as a variable name provided you don't then try to use it to send information to the screen in the same program.

We will not print the built-in words in Pascal programs in bold face type as we will for reserved words. Instead, beginning with this session, a listing of the built-in words encountered to date (as well as the reserved words) will be given in each session summary.

As already pointed out, you do have great freedom in the choice of variable names, but you do not have license. Even though it is possible to use built-in words for variable names, the prudent programmer will not do so.

Press E and the spacebar to get to the EDITOR. At the EDIT level, use the insert/delete modes to put the program back in it's original form. When finished, your program should once more look like this

```
PROGRAM SOUND;

  USES
    APPLESTUFF;

  VAR
    PITCH, DURATION : INTEGER;

BEGIN
  PITCH := 30;
  DURATION := 200;
  NOTE (PITCH, DURATION)
END.
```

4-4 THE THREE PROPERTIES OF VARIABLES

Let's see what this program has told us so far about variables. First, they have unique names, such as PITCH and DURATION. Second, they can be given values by statements such as these:

```
PITCH := 30;
DURATION := 200
```

Statements like these are called assignment statements because they assign values (like 30 or 200) to variables (like PITCH or DURATION). About half the statements in most programs are assignment statements, by the way. The symbol ":=" is called the assignment operator. You may not put a space between the colon and the equal sign, but you may put spaces on either side of the assignment operator. The only thing that you may put on the left side of the ":=" is the name of a variable. The single exception to this rule is discussed in Session 6.

Variables have a third and final property, and the following experiment will show you what it is:

Variables have a third and final property, and the following experiment will show you what it is: **Return to the EDITOR if you're not already there. Change the PITCH assigment line to read**

```
PITCH := 30.5;
```

and then run the program.

This tiny change resulted in compile-time error number 129. **Type E and check the error message.** It says

```
TYPE CONFLICT OF OPERANDS. TYPE <SP>
```

The cursor is at the right side of the semicolon after the PITCH assignment statement.

What you have discovered by this experiment is that variables have something called *type*, and furthermore, that in most situations type conflict is an error. Notice the word INTEGER in your VAR block. It means that you have declared your PITCH and DURATION variables to be of type integer. (An integer is just a whole number, such as 5, 239, or –8723.) But once you get into the BEGIN/END block of the program, your first assignment statement tries to give PITCH a value that is not an integer but is a decimal fraction. A decimal fraction in Pascal is said to be of type real. So you are trying to assign a thing of one type to a variable of another, and Pascal calls this a type conflict.

> The important things to remember about variables are their three properties: name, type and value. Name and type must always be declared in a VAR block, and value is assigned somewhere in the BEGIN/END block.

4-5 INPUTTING VALUES FROM OUTSIDE THE PROGRAM

In this section you will begin to see the real power of being able to refer to values by their names without knowing what the values actually are. In the programs you have written so far, the variables PITCH and DURATION were assigned numeric values within the program itself. In this section you will write new programs in which PITCH and DURATION have no known values at the time you write the program. Instead, they take on values when you run the program, by a process called input.

Here is a preliminary example of the sort of thing we're talking about. **If you're still looking at the error message, press the spacebar and enter the EDITOR. Then use INSERT and DELETE to change your program so that it looks like this:**

```
PROGRAM SOUND;

  USES
     APPLESTUFF;

  VAR
     PITCH, DURATION : INTEGER;

BEGIN
  PITCH := PADDLE (0);
  DURATION := PADDLE (1);
  NOTE (PITCH, DURATION)
END.
```

You have made two editorial changes. In the first line of the BEGIN/END block you deleted the numerical value 30.5 and inserted the expression "PADDLE (0)". Be sure to use zero in the parentheses following PADDLE and not O. In line two, you changed the value 200 to the expression "PADDLE (1)".

At EDIT level, type Q U R and run the program. Listen to the sound. Now turn the knobs on the two paddles connected to your computer to new settings. Type R and run the program again. Do this five or six more times varying one paddle control knob at a time.

What is going on? How is the sound being controlled? Why did it change?

To get more information about what is happening, let's add one new statement to the program. **Go back to the EDITOR and put the cursor just to the right of the semicolon in the DURATION assignment statement. Type I. Insert a RETURN and this new line:**

```
WRITELN (PITCH, '    ', DURATION);
```

Since you put a RETURN at the beginning of the line you don't need another one at the end. **Exit via CTRL-C.** The new BEGIN/END block should look like this:

```
BEGIN
  PITCH := PADDLE (0)#
  DURATION := PADDLE (1)#
  WRITELN (PITCH, '   ', DURATION)#
  NOTE (PITCH, DURATION)
END.
```

Most of the spaces in the program are cosmetic and are used to make the block easier to read. The spaces inside the quotes in the WRITELN statement *do* have meaning however, as you will see.

Now run the program via Q U R. Watch and listen. Change the paddle knob settings and type R a few more times.

Each time you ran the program you heard a sound and you also saw a pair of numbers appear on your screen near the top. The numbers were separated by three blank spaces. The numbers changed when you changed paddle settings. What is going on?

Well, you already know from Session 3 that WRITELN causes text to appear on your screen, but this is a new situation. In Session 3 you used a statement such as

```
WRITELN ('HOW NOW BROWN COW')
```

and found that the text *between quotes* appeared on the screen. Now you are using a different version of WRITELN:

```
WRITELN (PITCH, '   ', DURATION)
```

There are no quotes around the words PITCH or DURATION. Furthermore, these words are the *names of variables.*

What you have discovered is that when you used an unquoted variable name in a WRITELN statement, the current *value* of that variable was written on the screen. (The three spaces between quotes in WRITELN are also written *literally* on the screen and act as a separator between the two numbers.

So now you know how those numerical values got on your screen. But how did they change from run to run? Well, you did change the paddle settings; and your program does have the new words PADDLE (0) and PADDLE (1). Evidently, the answer is tied up in these facts, and here it is. In Apple Pascal, PADDLE is an example of a *function*. A function is very much like a variable in that it has a *name*, a *type* and a *value*. The difference is that a variable can only get its value by having the value assigned to it explicitly, as in

```
PITCH := 20
```

whereas a function gets its value by some process of its own which depends upon the way the function is defined. The value of the PADDLE function depends on two things: first, whether the number appearing in parentheses after the word PADDLE is a zero or a one; second, the physical setting of the corresponding paddle control knob. Whenever during the run of a program, a statement containing the PADDLE function is reached, the computer *inputs* one of the two paddle controls attached to your Apple and the function *returns a value,* as we say, corresponding to the setting of the knob.

In your program, therefore, the statement

```
          PITCH := PADDLE (0)
```

first causes the computer to input a number corresponding to the setting of the knob on paddle zero. Then the function takes on a value equal to that number. Finally, that value is assigned to the variable PITCH.

You may have wondered where PADDLE was defined since its name does not appear in the *declaration section* (the part of your program that precedes the BEGIN/END block). PADDLE, like NOTE, is defined in APPLESTUFF. Both are brought into your program by the compiler as a result of the USES block at the beginning of your declaration section.

Here is a good way to think about the difference between a variable and a function. Think of a variable as a *place* in the memory of the computer where an item of data is stored. Whenever you put a variable name on the left side of an assignment statement, it means that you want to put some new data in the place in memory corresponding to that variable name. Whenever you put a variable name on the right side of an assignment statement or in a WRITELN statement or almost anywhere else, it means that you want the variable name to be replaced by the data currently located in that variable's place in the memory of the computer.

In contrast, think of a function as a *process* that produces an item of data whenever the function name appears in a program statement. With this idea in mind, you will see that it would be wrong to use the statement

```
          PADDLE (1) := PITCH
```

in a program, since PADDLE is not a *place* in the computer memory, and so cannot have a value assigned to it by an assignment statement. Another way of saying the same thing is that PADDLE can *give* a value to something else, but PADDLE cannot *be given* the value of something else. Instead, the value of PADDLE or any other function is determined strictly by the rules that define it. In Session 6 you will learn how to define functions of your own and see how they work in more detail.

> A variable is a place in memory where an item of data is stored. A function is a process that produces an item of data.

What is the *type* of function PADDLE? Well, you didn't get any "type conflict" error when you ran the program, so PADDLE must be of the same type as PITCH, which is of type integer. You may have also noticed that the values it returns are not negative. In fact, PADDLE returns only integers from zero through 255.

4-6 THE FOR STATEMENT

Let's explore this program a bit more. You probably got tired of typing R again and again while experimenting with different paddle settings. Well, Pascal has a statement that will save you that bother. **Go back to the EDITOR. Compare the present version of your program with the following one:**

```
PROGRAM SOUND;

  USES
    APPLESTUFF;

  VAR
    PITCH, DURATION, COUNT : INTEGER;

BEGIN
  FOR COUNT := 1 TO 500 DO
    BEGIN
      PITCH := PADDLE (0);
      DURATION := PADDLE (1);
      WRITELN (COUNT, '    ', PITCH, '    ', DURATION);
      NOTE (PITCH, DURATION)
    END
END.
```

You will be changing your program to look like this new version. There are several steps to this editing job, but you'll soon see the advantage. **First, insert ", COUNT" in the VAR block. Second, with the cursor to the right of BEGIN, insert a RETURN, two spaces of indentation, and the two new lines**

```
FOR COUNT := 1 TO 500 DO
  BEGIN
```

without pressing RETURN after the last line. Then CTRL-C out of INSERT mode.
You will discover that the indentation of the next four lines is all wrong. Fortunately,
there's an easy fix for that. **At EDIT level, press RETURN to get the cursor to the next
line. Type A to enter ADJUST mode.** You will see a new prompt line:

```
>ADJUST: L(JUST R(JUST C(ENTER <LEFT,RIG
```

on the left half of the Pascal page and on the right half,

```
HT,UP,DOWN-ARROWS> [<ETX> TO LEAVE]
```

Now is a good time to experiment a bit with the ADJUST commands. **Press the
right-arrow and left arrow keys a few times. Use the right-arrow key enough times to
position the line so that it is indented a total of six spaces from the left margin.**

At this point, the first line is properly indented and you're still at ADJUST level.
Now comes the magic. **Type CTRL-L.** The second line is now correctly indented.
Type CTRL-L twice more. The third and fourth are also okay. **Finally, type CTRL-C
and go back to the EDIT level with the new indentations still intact.** (You can't ESC
out of ADJUST, by the way, but you can always undo anything you've done by using
the arrow, CTRL-L and CTRL-O keys before pressing CTRL-C.)

**Move your cursor to the "P" in PITCH in the WRITELN statement. Insert
"COUNT, ' ', " and type CTRL-C.** (Your WRITELN statement is now more than 40
characters long, so part of it is on the right half of the Pascal page.)

**Move the cursor just beyond the closing parenthesis of the NOTE line. Now type I
to enter INSERT. Press RETURN. Press the left-arrow twice, insert "END" and
CTRL-C back to the EDIT level once more.**

At this point you have made all the changes and your new version should look
exactly like the one printed at the start of this section. **Check it carefully. Fix any
errors.**

Now you are ready to run the new version. **Put the paddles close by and type Q U
R. After compilation, play with each paddle knob while the program runs.** What is
happening?

First, there are many text lines on the screen, and three numbers on each line.
The first number in the line starts at 1 and increases by one on each successive line.
Each of the other two numbers stays about the same from line to line if you do not
touch the paddle controls. Otherwise they change in response to the paddle
settings.

Now is a good time to find out which paddle is which and to mark them. **Turn both
knobs all the way to the left (counterclockwise). If the program has stopped running,
type R again.** Notice the zeros in columns two and three, and the silence. **Slowly turn
just one of the knobs, watch the numbers, and listen.** If the second column of
numbers starts changing and you start hearing sounds, then you are holding paddle
zero. But if silence remains and the third column of numbers starts changing, you
have paddle one. **Mark the paddles correctly now.**

Run again with both paddles all the way to the left. Turn paddle one to the right slowly until the number in column 3 is around 50. Now turn paddle zero to the right very slowly and listen.

You probably heard a sequence of steadily increasing pitches at first, while the numbers went from one to 50. After that the pitches were fairly random.

Turn paddle zero to the right until the pitch value (column two) is about 30. Turn paddle one all the way to the left and then very slowly to the right.

As soon as the duration value (column three) changed from zero you heard a sudden shortening in the length of time the note was held. Small numbers gave short notes and larger ones gave longer notes, except that zero gives the longest note. (You may also have found that the duration numbers suddenly got small again despite the fact that you continued to turn the knob slowly to the right. Don't worry about that now. It happened because your program input the value from paddle one right after paddle zero. The results can be inaccurate unless more time is allowed between the two inputs.)

4-7 GRAMMAR RULES FOR THE FOR STATEMENT

Now let's see what these new program features have done. You've probably guessed that the FOR statement is the cause of these 500 lines of output to your screen. Its effect is *exactly* the same as if you had duplicated the original four-line BEGIN/END block 500 times. Instead of having to duplicate the program block many times, all you have to do is put the block in a FOR statement, sometimes also called a FOR/DO loop, or simply a FOR loop.

The FOR statement has this general form:

FOR *variable* := *initial-value* **TO** *final-value* **DO** *statement*

where "statement" after DO, means either a single statement (called a *simple statement*) or else a block of statements preceded by BEGIN and followed by END. In Pascal, a BEGIN/END block is also called a *compound statement*. As before, you should think of BEGIN and END as giant brackets that enclose the compound statement. A compound statement can contain other compound statements within it.

Now let's see how the FOR loop works. It starts out by setting the value of the variable equal to the initial value (COUNT := 1 in your program). Next it tests to see whether the variable has already exceeded the final value (500 in your program). If so, nothing further happens and we say *the loop is exited*. Otherwise the simple or compound statement after the word DO is executed once. In your program, it is the following compound statement that is executed:

```
BEGIN
   PITCH := PADDLE (0);
   DURATION := PADDLE (1);
   WRITELN (COUNT, '    ', PITCH, '    ', DURATION);
   NOTE (PITCH, DURATION)
END
```

Then, one is added to the value of the variable. Finally we *loop back* to the top, and start over, seeing whether the variable has yet exceeded the final value, and then either exiting or continuing.

In your particular program you can see that the compound statement shown above must be executed 500 times, since the initial value of COUNT is one and the final value is 500.

4-8 REFINING THE PROGRAM

You have successfully written the prototype of *all* computer programs. It takes *input* from the outside world. It *processes* the input, and it generates *output*. Every useful program performs these three functions.

In the process of creating the program you have learned how to write a FOR loop, how to use the PADDLE function to get input values, how to assign those values to variables, and how to use the NOTE procedure to convert the variables to sound output.

The next step is to refine the program to make it more usable. You noticed, for example, that the range of pitch values between zero and fifty gave you a musical scale, plus silence. Higher values produced random pitches. It would be nice to do a little more *processing* on the input from paddle zero to force the numbers to be in the range zero through 50. Let's see how to do this.

You saw earlier that the PADDLE function always returns values between zero and 255. One way to keep the PADDLE numbers from being too big is to divide them by a number bigger than one. For example, if you divided all the PADDLE values by two, you would get numbers between zero and 127.5. On the other hand, numbers like 127.5 are not integers, so won't that lead to one of those *type conflict* errors you saw before? Not to worry. Pascal provides a special kind of *integer division operation* that first does the division and then throws away the *fractional part* if there is any. The operation is called DIV, and the following experiment will show how to use it.

Enter the EDITOR and insert " DIV 5" at the end of the first line containing the PADDLE function, as shown here:

```
PITCH := PADDLE (0) DIV 5;
```

Quit the EDITOR and run this new version.

As you see, except when you twist the the knob on paddle zero all the way to the right, PITCH stays within the limits that NOTE needs in order to produce a musical scale.

Now let's see whether we can fix up that occasional inaccuracy problem caused by inputting paddle one too soon after paddle zero. This difficulty is one of timing caused by the way the computer works, not by your program. **Get back to the EDITOR and insert this line immediately after the semicolon of the PITCH assignment statement:**

```
FOR WAIT := 1 TO 3 DO;
```

You have introduced a new variable, WAIT, so you must be sure to *declare* it. **At EDIT level, move the cursor to the space after COUNT and insert ", WAIT".** With these two changes your program should look like this:

```
PROGRAM SOUND;

   USES
      APPLESTUFF;

   VAR
      PITCH, DURATION, COUNT, WAIT : INTEGER;

BEGIN
   FOR COUNT := 1 TO 500 DO
      BEGIN
         PITCH := PADDLE (0) DIV 5;
         FOR WAIT := 1 TO 3 DO;
         DURATION := PADDLE (1);
         WRITELN (COUNT, '   ', PITCH, '    ', DURATION);
         NOTE (PITCH, DURATION)
      END
END.
```

Run it and experiment with paddle one to see whether the durations increase steadily now as you turn the knob from left to right.

The fix works. But *how* does it work? What you did was to insert a particularly simple form of the FOR statement between the two statements that input the paddle settings. This form of the FOR statement probably looks illegal to you because there is *no other statement at all* after the word DO, but only a concluding semicolon. We said earlier, when we defined the FOR statement, that there *always* had to be a statement (either simple or compound) after the word DO. Isn't there a contradiction?

No, and if you understand why, then you're in good shape for sorting out some other seeming contradictions or surprises in the way Pascal is defined. The way out of this contradiction is simply to recognize that one kind of statement is the so called *null statement*—that is, a statement whose text contains *no characters*. (The idea may sound silly at first, but then so did the idea of *zero* when folks were still using Roman numerals.)

So, in fact, the little FOR statement you just added to the program does indeed contain a *statement* after the word DO and before the semicolon. It is the null statement. You may not see it, but it's there.

Okay, given that it is legal Pascal, what does it *do*? Well, like your *outer loop*, which counts from one to 500, this *inner loop* counts from one to three. The outer loop executed its big compound statement 500 times. Likewise, the inner loop executes its null statement three times each time around the outer loop. *In effect, it does nothing, three times.* You may think that it takes no clock time to do nothing three times; but if so, you've forgotten that it takes time to do the counting itself. The WAIT variable starts out with a value of one, and each time through the loop, one gets added to it and its value gets tested to see whether it has exceeded three. This all takes time—not much, but enough to let things settle down between paddle inputs. And that is why the second paddle value is now correct.

Run the final version of your program a few more times. Check out a pitch of zero; a pitch of one with a duration of one. Compare a pitch of 12 with one of 24, 36, and 48. What scale does Apple Pascal use?

You may have wanted to stop the program while it was running to inspect the text on the screen, and then continue execution. Apple Pascal has such a facility. **While your program is running, type CTRL-S. Now touch a few other keys at random (but not the RESET key!) After a few seconds, type CTRL-S again.** The CTRL-S facility may be used at any level of the Pascal system.

> Watch out for this **user trap**: by accident you type a CTRL-S without knowing it, and suddenly it appears that your computer is broken and will not respond to any keypresses. If this happens, just type another CTRL-S and continue.

Note that CTRL-S only stops programs that generate output to the TV screen. It will also stop *system* programs that generate screen output, such as the EDITOR and nearly anything else.

4-9 STORING PROGRAMS ON A SEPARATE DISKETTE

The workfile, APPLE0:SYSTEM.WRK.TEXT, is exactly the right place to keep a program while you are in the process of writing, running, debugging, and changing it. When you enter the EDITOR, the workfile is automatically loaded into your workspace for easy editing. When you leave the EDITOR with the Q U option, the workspace is automatically written back into the APPLE0: workfile. When you type R at the COMMAND level, the computer automatically compiles the workfile on APPLE0:, stores the resulting code file on APPLE0:, and then executes the latter.

Because the workfile is such a good place to keep a program during development, it is also a very bad place to keep a finished program. There can be only one workfile on APPLE0: and if the completed program remained there it would be very difficult to work on any other programs without destroying the finished one. So, you should move a program out of APPLE0:SYSTEM.WRK.TEXT as soon as no further work is planned for it. This section will show you how to do that.

You may have noticed in your earlier work that the system files on APPLE0: occupy about 90 percent of the space on your diskette. In fact, version 1.1 of Apple Pascal leaves only 32 blocks of free storage out of the 280 block total. Although a block contains 512 characters (bytes), the shortest possible text file is four blocks long, and the shortest code file is two blocks long. This means that you will need at least 6 free blocks on APPLE0: for both forms of the workfile, even when the program is only a few dozen characters long. For this reason it is a bad idea to move a copy of a finished program from the APPLE0: workfile into a new file on that crowded diskette, even though it is legal to do so.

The following is our recommended method of moving a copy of the APPLE0: workfile into a new file on a separate diskette. (Other methods exist, but you are somewhat more likely to make errors if you use them.)

1. Move the APPLE0: workfile into the EDITOR workspace for a visual checkout.

2. Write a copy of the workspace on to a second diskette.

To do this you must already have a Pascal formatted diskette with enough free space on it to hold the new file. It need not contain any of the system files, however.

For the following steps we will assume that you already have such a formatted diskette and that its name is BLANK:, the name that the FORMATTER program gives to freshly formatted diskettes. If you do not have one, now is a good time to format a blank diskette, using the procedure specified in Appendix A–3. (If you do not have a blank, you can temporarily use any one of your system diskette copies, such as APPLE3:, to store the workfile copy. In that case, skip the next paragraph, which tells how to change the diskette name.)

First, let's change the name of BLANK: to one that suggests you will be using the diskette to store your programs. PROGRAM: is the name we'll use in this description.

1. **From COMMAND level, type F C to enter the FILER and go to the CHANGE level.** The prompt line will read "CHANGE ?"

2. **Open the disk drive door. Remove APPLE0: and insert BLANK:**

3. **Type "BLANK:" and press RETURN.** A second prompt line asks "CHANGE TO WHAT ?"

4. **Type "PROGRAM:" and press RETURN.** If all goes well, the third line of the screen will say "BLANK: — — > PROGRAM:"

5. **Remove the diskette, now named PROGRAM:, from the drive and insert APPLE0:** Use a felt tip pen to write the name on the diskette label.

6. **Type Q to quit the FILER.**

Incidentally, you can also use the FILER's C(HANGE command to change the name of a file on a particular diskette. Just add the file name after the colon at the end of the diskette name when responding to the "CHANGE ?" query. Then type the new file name in response to the "CHANGE TO WHAT ?" question.

Now that you have a diskette named PROGRAM: let's see how to move a copy of your workfile from APPLE0: to PROGRAM:.

1. **From COMMAND level, type E to enter the EDITOR.** This moves a copy of SYSTEM.WRK.TEXT from APPLE0: to the workspace where you can check it out visually before taking the next step.

2. **Type Q to quit the EDITOR.** As usual, you must choose a further option at this point. (You have used the U, E, and R options in the past.)

3. **Type W.** This means that you want to write the contents of the workspace into a diskette file. You should see the following screen prompt

```
>QUIT:
NAME OF OUTPUT FILE(<CR> TO RETURN) --
```

4. **Remove the APPLE0: diskette from the drive and insert PROGRAM:** Be sure the door is closed tightly.

5. **Type CTRL-A followed by PROGRAM:SOUND.TEXT followed by a RETURN.** (If PROGRAM: already contained a file named SOUND.TEXT, you would be asked whether or not to destroy its previous contents.)

6. **Type CTRL-A a few times to read both sides of the Pascal page.** You are still at the QUIT level. If all went well you got a message telling how many bytes long your file was, and you are being asked whether to "E(XIT FROM OR R(ETURN TO THE EDITOR?"

7. **Remove PROGRAM: from the disk drive and insert APPLE0:**

8. **Type E to return to COMMAND level.** (WARNING: If you type R and APPLE0: is not in the drive, the screen goes blank and you will have to reboot.)

You have succeeded in writing a copy of APPLE0:SYSTEM.WRK.TEXT into the file SOUND.TEXT on your PROGRAM: diskette. Unless you plan some additional work on the program, this is an excellent time to clear out your workfile.

To clear the workfile from COMMAND level, type F N Y Q, returning to COMMAND level.

If you did the last step, the old workfile is gone from APPLE0: and a copy is now on diskette PROGRAM: in the file SOUND.TEXT. *It is a good idea now to review all the above steps and remind yourself what was going on during each one.*

4-10 RECALLING PROGRAMS FROM A SEPARATE DISKETTE

Now we come to the other half of the process: getting a file back from another diskette into the APPLE0: workfile for further editing or running. In the following exercise you will move SOUND.TEXT from the PROGRAM: diskette into the APPLE0: workfile.

1. **From COMMAND level, type F T to enter the FILER and go to the TRANSFER level.** The prompt line at the top of the screen should ask the question "TRANSFER ?"

2. **Remove APPLE0: from the disk drive and insert PROGRAM:, closing the door tightly.**

3. **Type PROGRAM:SOUND.TEXT and press RETURN.** If all goes well, the next prompt asks "TO WHERE ?" (If not, you will be told so and will be bounced back to the FILER level. You probably left off ".TEXT". Type T and try the transfer again.)

4. **Without changing diskettes, respond to the new prompt by typing APPLE0:SYSTEM.WRK.TEXT and pressing RETURN.** The prompt line now asks you to insert APPLE0:.

5. **Remove PROGRAM: from the disk drive, insert APPLE0:, and then press the spacebar.** If APPLE0: already has a workfile on it, you will be asked as a safety measure whether or not to destroy the workfile. Normally you want to, so would type Y. If there is no workfile, you will not see the question. In either case you will know that the transfer was successful when you see the message

```
PROGRAM:SOUND.TEXT
  --> APPLE0:SYSTEM.WRK.TEXT
```

6. **Press Q to quit the FILER. When the COMMAND prompt appears, type I to reinitialize the system.**

7. **When the COMMAND prompt reappears, type E and verify the transfer with your own eyes.**

   Sections 4–9 and 4–10 call attention to the only serious shortcoming of working with a single-disk-drive system. On a two-drive system you always have two diskettes (APPLE1: and APPLE2:) in the drives, and each of them has a great deal of free space left over after that taken up by the system files. Consequently it is a simple matter to make a copy of the workfile or to move a copy of another file into that workfile without having to handle the diskettes.

   Bear in mind, however, the fact that while using this book you will only notice this shortcoming when you decide to move copies of programs back and forth between the workfile and your program diskette. That doesn't happen very often.

SUMMARY

During this session you have learned the following new things about Pascal on the Apple:

■ **You saw that APPLESTUFF is a collection of built-in procedures located in APPLE0:SYSTEM.LIBRARY.**

■ **You used NOTE (one of the APPLESTUFF procedures) to generate sound.**

■ You saw that NOTE needs two values. The first determines the pitch and the second the duration of the note.

■ You learned that variables in Pascal are declared in the VAR block in a program.

■ You discovered that reserved words in Pascal cannot be used for variable names.

■ You saw that built-in words in Pascal can be used for variable names but the original purpose of the name is then lost to the program.

■ You saw that variables in Pascal have three properties; name, type, and value.

■ You used the PADDLE function to provide input to a program.

■ You saw that the FOR loop causes the simple, compound, or null statement following DO to be executed a specific number of times.

■ You used the A(djust feature of the EDITOR to adjust the indentation of a program.

■ You used the DIV function to accomplish division with integers.

■ You used a FOR loop with a null statement after DO to produce a delay in a program.

■ You used CTRL-S to stop and restart program output to the TV screen.

■ You learned how to change the name of a diskette or file using the C(HANGE function in the FILER.

■ You learned how to use the Q W exit from the EDITOR to move a copy of the workfile on APPLE0: to another diskette.

■ You used the TRANSFER function in the FILER to move a program from a separate diskette to the file SYSTEM.WRK.TEXT on APPLE0:

To finish the summary, the tables marking your progress through the Pascal level structure should be updated to reflect the ideas you have learned in this session.

Table 4.1A Amplified table of the EDITOR levels of Apple Pascal. Those features studied in this session are shown in bold face type.

	Exit to escape from accidental entry.
E(ditor	ESC RETURN or Q E R
Q(uit editor and	
U(pdate workfile	
E(xit with no update	
R(eturn to editor	Q
W(rite to named file	**RETURN**
Cursor Moving Commands	
Right-arrow (move cursor right)	
Left-arrow (Move cursor left)	
CTRL-L (Move cursor down)	
CTRL-O (Move cursor up)	
RETURN (Move cursor to beginning of next line)	
Spacebar (Move cursor to next character)	
Text Changing Commands	
I(nsert text	ESC
CTRL-C (Normal exit	
D(elete text	ESC
CTRL-C (Normal exit)	
Formatting Commands	
A(djust indentation	
CTRL-C (Normal exit)	

Table 4.1B Amplified table of other command levels of Apple Pascal. Those features studied in this session are shown in bold face type.

	Exit to escape from accidental entry.
I(nitialize the system	
R(un program in workfile	
F(iler	
Q(uit the filer	F
N(ew workfile	RETURN
V(olumes on line	
L(ist the directory	RETURN
C(hange name	**RETURN**
T(ransfer a file	**RETURN**
D(ate setter	RETURN
? Show additional commands	RETURN
Commands Available at Any Level	
CTRL-A Toggle to other half of Pascal page	CTRL-A
CTRL-S Stop and restart screen output	**CTRL-S**
RESET Attempts reboot of Pascal	

Table 4.2 Cumulative Pascal vocabulary. New words introduced in this session are printed in bold face. (Code: a = declared in APPLESTUFF)

Reserved Words	Built-In Procedures	Built-In Functions	Other Built-Ins
PROGRAM	WRITE	Integer	Types
USES	WRITELN	**a PADDLE**	**INTEGER**
VAR	a **NOTE**		
BEGIN			Units
FOR			**APPLESTUFF**
TO			
DO			
END			
DIV			

QUESTIONS AND PROBLEMS

1. If you are in the EDITOR, what keystrokes are necessary to clear out the workfile and return to the editor?

2. How are the name and type of variables established in Pascal? What about the value?

3. What is meant by "type conflict" in Pascal?

4. Discuss the similarities and differences between a *function* and a *variable* in Pascal.

5. Write a Pascal program to display the numbers 1, 2, ..., 14, and 15 vertically on the screen.

6. Write a program to cause the computer to play a scale with pitches equal to 12, 13, 14, ..., 23, and 24.

7. Explain how you would change a diskette name from BLANK: to TAXES:.

8. Assume you have a program named SOUND.TEXT on diskette PROGRAM:. What steps must be taken to change the name to FURY.TEXT?

9. Suppose you have finished writing a program and it is currently in the file SYSTEM.WRK.TEXT on the APPLE0: diskette. Explain how to move the program to a diskette named ABC: where it will have the name SONIC.TEXT.

10. Assume the program SONIC.TEXT is stored on the diskette ABC:. What must you do to move this program into SYSTEM.WRK.TEXT on the APPLE0: diskette?

11. Explain how you would *insert* a line in the middle of a Pascal program. Assume you begin in the EDIT mode.

12. Explain how you would *delete* a line in the middle of a Pascal program. Assume you begin in the EDIT mode.

13. Discuss the similarities and differences between *reserved* words in Pascal (like BEGIN, FOR, END, etc.) and *built-in* words (like WRITE and NOTE).

14. Explain precisely how a FOR loop works.

15. What is a simple statement? A compound statement? A null statement?

INVENTING NEW WORDS: PROCEDURES

In the last two sessions you have been using several different kinds of statements. One kind was the *assignment* statement, such as

```
PITCH := 20
```

Another was the *FOR* statement, an example of which is

```
FOR COUNT := 1 TO 10 DO
    NOTE (50, 20)
```

We have not given a precise name to other statements that you have used, such as

```
WRITE ('HOW NOW');
WRITELN ('BROWN COW')
```

and

```
NOTE (PITCH, DURATION)
```

You may have decided that each one of these so-far unnamed statements is a different *kind* of statement (especially if you are familiar with other programming languages). In Pascal, however, they are all examples of a *single* kind of statement, called a *procedure* statement, or a *procedure reference*, or a *procedure call*.

Procedures and their close relatives, *functions*, are the main topic of this session and the next one. As you develop a clear picture of the significance of the procedure idea, you will see why it is that Pascal has only a very small number of distinct kinds of statements. In fact, there are only nine different kinds of Pascal statements, and you already have used three of them. In Sessions 7 and 8 you will use three more, so things are moving right along.

SESSION GOALS

To start with, you will review use of the FOR statement to generate musical scales that go up in pitch and, with the DOWNTO word, go down also. You will use the EDITOR's C(OPY B(UFFER command to duplicate program lines and to move text lines from one place to another. Your main activity, however, will be to define program subunits, such as the ones that play musical scales, to give these subunits names of your choosing, such as UP and DOWN, and then to use the subunits in a program by calling them by name. In other words, you will write *procedures* and *call* them. You will then see how to *parameterize* a procedure, so that instead of always doing the same thing, its behavior is controlled by the data *passed* to it. You will explore the concepts of *local* and *global* variables, and will see that a procedure can have its own VAR block.

5-1 STARTING UP

This session starts off like all the previous ones, so the instructions this time are a bit more concise. If you need more details, turn to the start of the previous session. Here are the standard start-up steps:

- **Boot up Pascal if your computer is off.**

- **Enter the FILER and set the current date.**

- **Enter the EDITOR and inspect the current workfile.**

- **Clear out the workfile, if necessary, by typing Q E F N Y Q E.**

- **Press RETURN to complete entry into the EDITOR, and then enter INSERT mode.**

At this point, the INSERT prompt is at the top of your screen and you are ready to type in a new Pascal program and move it into the EDITOR's empty workspace. **Study the following program and then type it in.**

```
PROGRAM SCALES;

  USES
    APPLESTUFF;

  VAR
    PITCH, DURATION : INTEGER;

BEGIN
  DURATION := 100;
  FOR PITCH := 8 TO 20 DO
    NOTE (PITCH, DURATION)
END.
```

CTRL-C out of INSERT. Read for typing errors, repair any, and then run the program.

As the program name implied, this program creates a fairly musical scale starting at about C below middle-C and rising in pitch one note of the chromatic scale (the white keys and the black keys) at a time until it reached middle-C.

Suppose you wanted a descending scale instead. Well, let's do the obvious thing and see what happens. **Return to the EDITOR and change the FOR statement so that it reads:**

```
FOR PITCH := 20 TO 8 DO
     NOTE (PITCH, DURATION)
```

Now run the changed program.

Well, that didn't work. The program compiled correctly and ran with no reports of errors, but no sound came out. Let's try again.

Return to the EDITOR. Change the FOR statement again so that it looks like this:

```
FOR PITCH := 20 DOWNTO 8 DO
     NOTE (PITCH, DURATION)
```

Run the result.

This version of the FOR statement works, and you have added another Pascal *reserved word*, DOWNTO, to your vocabulary. *In the FOR statement the word TO means that the variable is to be increased; DOWNTO means it is to be decreased.* Notice, however, that it is *not illegal* to use TO when the initial-value is greater than the final-value. The result in that case is that the FOR loop is *not executed* at all, since the variable begins with a value that is already greater than the final value. *If you want a FOR loop to count down instead of up, you have to say so by substituting DOWNTO for TO.*

Incidentally, you now know everything that there is to know about the FOR statement. There are no new words and no new grammar rules to be learned.

5-2 DUPLICATING BLOCKS OF TEXT

You can now make a scale that goes up or down. Let's combine the two: begin with a rising scale and follow it with a descending one. Furthermore, let's make the descending scale happen in half the time of the rising one. The main program block will look like this (but don't type the changes yet):

```
BEGIN
  DURATION := 100;
  FOR PITCH := 8 TO 20 DO
    NOTE (PITCH, DURATION);
  DURATION := 50;
  FOR PITCH := 20 DOWNTO 8 DO
    NOTE (PITCH, DURATION)
END.
```

Since the text of the first three lines is very similar to that of the second three, and both are similar to the present text of your program, it would be nice if there were some easy way to make a duplicate copy of what you now have and then patch up the differences. As you have probably guessed, we wouldn't have brought up the idea if it weren't possible. Here goes.

Return to the EDITOR. Move the cursor so that it is on top of the D in the assignment statement

```
DURATION := 100
```

Now enter DELETE mode and press RETURN three times. Then CTRL-C out.

It probably looks to you as though things are getting worse. We said that you were going to make a duplicate copy and we've left you without *any* copy. But don't lose faith; magic is around the corner.

Without moving the cursor, type C and enter COPY mode. The top line of your screen contains the COPY prompt line:

```
>COPY: B(UFFER F(ROM FILE <ESC>
```

It tells you that you can type one of three things: B, F, or ESC. **Press the ESC key.** Evidently this is the escape route out of COPY if you accidentally fall into it from the EDITOR.

Type C again to enter COPY. Now type B.

Wonder of wonders! The three lines of text you previously deleted are now back in your program, and you're back at EDIT level with the cursor on D where it started out. Now comes the best part. **Type C and B again.**

And so, as advertised, you have made an exact copy of the original three lines. Your main program block should now look like this:

```
BEGIN
   DURATION := 100;
   FOR PITCH := 20 DOWNTO 8 DO
      NOTE (PITCH, DURATION)
   DURATION := 100;
   FOR PITCH := 20 DOWNTO 8 DO
      NOTE (PITCH, DURATION)
END.
```

You're still not where you want to be, but let's stop for a moment and take note of the way copy worked. The text that you deleted from the EDITOR's workspace was *not* totally destroyed. Instead it went into the *insert/delete buffer.* This is the same buffer where your text is stored when you enter INSERT and then type the text on your keyboard. That is why it is called the *insert/delete* buffer. (We'll simply call it the *buffer* from now on.)

Whenever you enter COPY and type B, a copy of the current contents of the buffer is inserted into the text at the current position of the cursor.

From the above description, you can see that whenever you delete some text from your workspace, you can get it back by typing C B. It will be inserted where it was before (provided that you have not moved the cursor after the deletion). Thus, for an accidental deletion, "C B" is the "Oops!" button.

The other thing to note is that after you type C B the buffer still contains whatever text it had before. So if you type C B again, you get *another* copy at the current cursor location. That is exactly what happened in the present case. If you had wanted 10 copies you would have had only to type C B 10 times.

Now let's get back to the editing job on the SCALES program. Three changes have to be made:

Change the first occurrence of "20 DOWNTO 8" to "8 TO 20".
Change the second occurrence of ":= 100" to ":= 50".
Insert a semicolon after the first FOR statement.

Read that last instruction very carefully. Don't put the semicolon right after the DO, since that is *not* the end of the FOR statement. Every FOR statement begins with the word FOR and ends with the simple or compound statement that is to be repeated. The FOR statement is on two text lines in the present example, so the semicolon has to go at the end of the second line of the pair.

If by mistake you *had* put the semicolon after the DO the result would have been grammatically correct but it would not have been what you wanted: the FOR statement would have counted from 8 to 20, each time executing our old friend, the *null* statement. Then the NOTE procedure, the statement after the FOR statement, would have been executed exactly once with a PITCH value of 21.

A misplaced semicolon is the easiest Pascal **user trap** to fall into. To stay out of it, you need a very clear mental picture of the structure of each kind of Pascal statement.

If you made the three editorial changes, then your program should now look exactly like this:

```
PROGRAM SCALES;

  USES
    APPLESTUFF;

  VAR
    PITCH, DURATION : INTEGER;

  BEGIN
    DURATION := 100;
    FOR PITCH := 8 TO 20 DO
      NOTE (PITCH, DURATION);
    DURATION := 50;
    FOR PITCH := 20 DOWNTO 8 DO
      NOTE (PITCH, DURATION)
  END.
```

There is no semicolon after the final FOR statement because it is bracketed by the END. (Remember, BEGIN and END are *not* statements.) Semicolons are required *between* statements, not *after* statements.

Read the program over carefully. Then run it.

5-3 DEFINING NEW WORDS

You now have a program that does one up-scale and one somewhat shorter down-scale. In fact, if the computer knew what you were talking about by UP and DOWN, then you could write the main program block as

```
BEGIN
  UP;
  DOWN
END.
```

You could also make longer and more complicated programs very easily, such as

```
BEGIN
  UP; DOWN; UP; UP; UP; DOWN
END.
```

The problem is that Pascal has never heard of UP and DOWN. These are not words in its standard vocabulary. However, Pascal does have a way for you to define new words of your own choosing and to give them whatever meaning you want, in terms of existing words. Let's do it and then see what we've done.

You are going to be using the EDITOR to make three major changes in the text. Step 1 will be to create a new main program block that uses UP and DOWN, as if they had meaning to Pascal. Step 2 will be to create the definition of UP. Step 3, similar to step 2, will be to create the definition of DOWN. Let's do the main block.

Enter the EDITOR and put the cursor on the B in BEGIN. Enter DELETE mode. Press RETURN to delete the whole line. CTRL-C out of DELETE. At EDIT level again, move the cursor to the E in END. Type C B.

You have deleted BEGIN from its previous location and inserted it six lines down. In effect you *moved* it by this sequence: delete, position cursor, copy buffer. No other command for moving text exists. You only moved one word, but you could have moved a dozen lines in the same way. Now let's finish up Step 1.

Put the cursor on the E in END, enter INSERT mode. Indent two spaces. Type the following line:

```
UP; UP; DOWN; DOWN; UP
```

Press RETURN at the end of the line and then CTRL-C out of INSERT.

At this stage your partially edited program text should look like this:

```
PROGRAM SCALES;

  USES
    APPLESTUFF;

  VAR
    PITCH, DURATION : INTEGER;

  DURATION := 100;
  FOR PITCH := 8 TO 20 DO
    NOTE (PITCH, DURATION);
  DURATION := 50;
  FOR PITCH := 20 DOWNTO 8 DO
    NOTE (PITCH, DURATION)
BEGIN
  UP; UP; DOWN; DOWN; UP
END.
```

Now, for step 2, we need to define what UP means. Here's the way to do that:

At EDIT level, put the cursor on the D in the first assignment statement in the text. Enter INSERT and type these two lines:

```
PROCEDURE UP;
  BEGIN
```

Be sure to indent BEGIN, and to press RETURN after it. CTRL-C out of INSERT mode. Enter ADJUST mode next. Press the right-arrow key four times to move the start of the assignment statement under the G in BEGIN. Press CTRL-L twice to indent all three lines similarly. Now CTRL-C out of A(DJUST. At EDIT level, press RETURN to put the cursor at the start of the next line, the second assignment statement. Enter INSERT again. Indent two spaces and type this line:

```
END;
```

Finally press RETURN twice, and CTRL-C back to the EDIT level.

Well, that was a long trip through the EDITOR, but it was mainly a review of things you had done in earlier sessions. Step 2 is now complete and your job in progress should look like this:

```
PROGRAM SCALES;

  USES
    APPLESTUFF;

  VAR
    PITCH, DURATION : INTEGER;

  PROCEDURE UP;
    BEGIN
      DURATION := 100;
      FOR PITCH := 8 TO 20 DO
        NOTE (PITCH, DURATION)
    END;

  DURATION := 50;
  FOR PITCH := 20 DOWNTO 8 DO
    NOTE (PITCH, DURATION)
BEGIN
  UP; UP; DOWN; DOWN; UP
END.
```

Step 3 is exactly like step 2, except for a change in the *name* after PROCEDURE. **Follow the above editing steps on the second three-line block, changing UP to DOWN so that the complete program now looks like this:**

```
PROGRAM SCALES;

  USES
    APPLESTUFF;

  VAR
    PITCH, DURATION : INTEGER;

  PROCEDURE UP;
    BEGIN
      DURATION := 100;
      FOR PITCH := 8 TO 20 DO
        NOTE (PITCH, DURATION)
    END;

  PROCEDURE DOWN;
    BEGIN
      DURATION := 50;
      FOR PITCH := 20 DOWNTO 8 DO
        NOTE (PITCH, DURATION)
    END;

BEGIN
  UP; UP; DOWN; DOWN; UP
END.
```

Before you run the new version, note its general structure. You won't be able to see the whole program on your screen at once, but as you move the cursor up and down you can see the hidden parts.

Here is a way to move the cursor quickly over large distances. **From EDIT level type J, for J(UMP.** The prompt line at the Jump level says

```
>JUMP: B(EGINNING E(ND M(ARKER <ESC>
```

As with other EDIT commands, ESC is the escape route for accidental entry. **Type B. Type J E.** These commands move the cursor quickly to the first and last characters in the workspace. (We won't discuss the M command here. Later, you can learn about it in the Apple Pascal Operating System Reference Manual.)

The new version of your program has a heading, a USES block, a VAR block, two different PROCEDURE blocks, and finally, the main BEGIN/END block. Note also that each procedure block looks like a miniature program: it has a heading and a BEGIN/END block. A semicolon separates the heading from the BEGIN/END, and a semicolon after END terminates the PROCEDURE. The main program block is the shortest part of the program. (This situation is characteristic of well-written programs, by the way.)

Now, run the program, fix any compile-time errors, and listen to the results. Go back to the EDITOR, change the sequence of UP and DOWN statements in your main block, and then run the new program. Go to the EDITOR again and delete all the UP and DOWN words in the main block. Run this version.

Notice, first of all, that the sequence of scales you heard each time was the same as the sequence of UP and DOWN statements in your main block. When you removed all of them you heard nothing. This observation should convince you that it is the main program block that is in full command at all times. The FOR statements and NOTE statements in the PROCEDURE blocks only came alive when the main program block *calls* upon them to do so.

In the first new version of your program the word UP appeared in the main block several times. In each appearance, UP was a statement by itself. (Remember that semicolons separate statements.) The same was true of DOWN. When the program was run, each statement in the main block was executed, one after the other. When UP was executed, it *called upon* its definition in the PROCEDURE UP block. At that moment the statements in that block began execution. When they finished, the execution of that UP statement was complete, and the next statement in the main BEGIN/END block began execution. If it was another UP, the same thing happened. If it was DOWN, then a *call* went out to PROCEDURE DOWN and the defining statements there were carried out.

As you have seen, the power of being able to define your own procedures has two different dimensions. First, it often makes your main program much shorter and therefore easier to change and experiment with. At least as important, it allows you to organize a program into meaningful units and to name each unit according to the purpose it serves in the overall design.

> Programs that use procedures well are generally far easier to read, easier to under- stand, easier to change, and easier to get working. Often they also make more efficient use of computer resources; but that is a far less important benefit as computers get cheaper every year and human resources get more costly.

5-4 CHANGEABLE PROCEDURES

In your experiments so far, each one of your procedures did the same thing each time it was called. It would be a lot more interesting if you had some way to control certain aspects of the procedure at the time when it was called.

Your UP procedure always began an ascending scale at C below middle C. It would be a somewhat more interesting musical object if, for example, we could have it start at middle C when called the first time, and at F above middle C the next time. You could, of course, accomplish this by separate procedures for each starting note; but that would be tedious. Especially when there is another way.

Edit your PROCEDURE UP block so that it looks like this:

```
PROCEDURE UP (KEY : INTEGER);
  BEGIN
    DURATION := 100;
    FOR PITCH := KEY TO KEY + 12 DO
      NOTE (PITCH, DURATION)
  END;
```

The new word KEY appears in the first and fourth line; the remainder of the procedure is unchanged.

Make similar changes in the PROCEDURE DOWN block. In this case, "20 DOWNTO 8" should be replaced by "KEY DOWNTO KEY − 12". If part of the right side of the FOR statement disappears, you can use CTRL-A to see it.

Next, edit the main block so that it looks like this:

```
BEGIN
  UP (8); DOWN (20); UP (8);
  UP (20); UP (32); DOWN (20)
END.
```

With these three additions to program SCALES, it should look like this:

```
PROGRAM SCALES#

   USES
     APPLESTUFF#

   VAR
     PITCH, DURATION : INTEGER#

   PROCEDURE UP (KEY : INTEGER)#
     BEGIN
       DURATION := 100#
       FOR PITCH := KEY TO KEY + 12 DO
         NOTE (PITCH, DURATION)
     END#

   PROCEDURE DOWN (KEY : INTEGER)#
     BEGIN
       DURATION := 50#
       FOR PITCH := KEY DOWNTO KEY - 12 DO
         NOTE (PITCH, DURATION)
     END#

   BEGIN
     UP (8)# DOWN (20)# UP (8)#
     UP (20)# UP (32)# DOWN (20)
   END.
```

Check the text carefully. Run the program and listen. Rerun a few times and listen for each procedure call to happen.

The first UP and DOWN did nothing new, nor did the next UP. But the following UP went an octave higher, and the one after that went another octave higher. How did it work? What is KEY? Where in the program was it defined (declared)? **Get back to the EDITOR and look closely at the PROCEDURE UP block and at the main program block.**

The thing that stands out in both places is the addition of something in *parentheses* after the procedure name. In the PROCEDURE block, the item in parentheses is a *declaration* telling Pascal that KEY is a *variable of type integer.* In the main program block, we see particular integers, such as 8, 20, and 32, between parentheses.

The next thing to note is that the same variable name, KEY, appears in parentheses after procedure UP and also in the FOR statement within that same procedure. Obviously, there must be some connection, and there is. KEY is called a *parameter variable.* Like any variable, it has a *name* (KEY), a *type* (integer), and a *value.* However, this parameter variable did *not* get its value by means of an assignment statement, the way ordinary variables do. Instead, it had its value *passed to it* at the time the procedure was *called.* In your program you had the statement

```
UP (8)
```

When that statement was executed, it *called* procedure UP and it *passed* a value of 8 to *parameter variable* KEY. While procedure UP was running, it used KEY's value in the FOR statement, with the result that the initial PITCH value was 8 and the final value was 8 + 12, or 20. Later, your program executed the statement

```
UP (32)
```

which *called* UP again but this time *passed* a value of 32 to parameter variable KEY. That caused the initial and final PITCH values to be 32 and 44, respectively.

> The concept of calling a procedure and passing values to it is a very powerful one— perhaps the most powerful one in programming.

You should stop here for a moment, review what you have done, and reflect a bit on how it all works and what it means. You will be using procedures and parameters a great deal in the remainder of this book, so you'll be gathering experience as you go. Perhaps the main thing to notice now is that procedures give you a way of breaking a complicated programming job down into manageable chunks, each of which performs some fairly simple task. When you adopt this strategy (which, by the way, is a good problem-solving approach in many real-life situations; more about that later) you will find that your main program is largely a sequence of procedure calls.

5-5 PARAMETERS, LOCAL AND GLOBAL VARIABLES

You may have wondered about the fact that the parameter KEY was declared twice: once in the PROCEDURE UP heading and once in the PROCEDURE DOWN heading. Isn't it true that variables in Pascal are supposed to be declared only once? The answer to that is "yes and no". It is certainly true, for example, that a particular variable name can appear only once in a particular VAR block. We will see, however, that a procedure can have variables of its own that the main program does not know about by name. Parameter variables are in that class, as the following experiment will show.

   Go to the EDITOR and change the main BEGIN/END block to look like this:

```
BEGIN
   UP (18);
   WRITELN (KEY)
END.
```

What do you think will happen when you run this version? Will 18 be written on your screen? Or 31? Or what? **Run the program.**

You got compile-time error number 104. **Go to the EDITOR and read the message. Then press the spacebar.** The compiler gives you the familiar "undeclared identifier" complaint about variable KEY in the WRITELN statement. This tells you that the main program doesn't even know about the word KEY in UP and in DOWN. In the same way, the KEY in UP is *distinct from* KEY in DOWN and each one is unknown to the other.

The situation with the DURATION variable may or may not be different. Let's think about that. First, note that DURATION is declared in the VAR block of the main program. Then, note that its name appears inside UP and again inside DOWN. Since your program compiled and ran, it is safe to conclude that procedures UP and DOWN *do* know about the existence of DURATION. You'd probably expect the main program also to know about it, but let's make certain.

Change the main block again so that it looks like this:

```
BEGIN
   UP (20);
   WRITELN (DURATION);
   DOWN (32);
   WRITELN (DURATION)
END.
```

Run the program, listen, and watch the screen. You should see this:

```
RUNNING...
100
50
```

Do you understand why? Procedure UP assigned a value of 100 to DURATION. The first WRITELN wrote on the screen the value of DURATION after the call to UP. Then came the call to DOWN, which assigned 50 to DURATION. The second WRITELN wrote the new value on the screen. *There is only one variable named DURATION and it is known to the main program and to both procedures.* The same is also true of PITCH, of course. We say that PITCH and DURATION are *global* variables, because they are known to all parts of the program. Let's do another experiment to sharpen the concept of a global variable.

Go to the EDITOR and use DELETE to eliminate the lines

```
VAR
   PITCH, DURATION : INTEGER;
```

from the main program. Then use COPY BUFFER to place an exact copy of them at the beginning of UP and also at the beginning of DOWN.

In case you don't recall the steps for making these changes, here they are:

1. Put the cursor on the V in VAR.

2. Enter DELETE mode.

3. Press RETURN twice.

4. CTRL-C out.

5. Put the cursor on the B in BEGIN in procedure UP.

6. Type C B

7. Use ADJUST to indent both lines.

At this point the two lines should appear just before BEGIN. Finally, repeat steps 5, 6, and 7 for procedure DOWN. The program should look like this now:

```
PROGRAM SCALES;

USES
  APPLESTUFF;

PROCEDURE UP (KEY : INTEGER);
  VAR
    PITCH, DURATION : INTEGER;
  BEGIN
    DURATION := 100;
    FOR PITCH := KEY TO KEY + 12 DO
      NOTE (PITCH, DURATION)
  END;

PROCEDURE DOWN (KEY : INTEGER);
  VAR
    PITCH, DURATION : INTEGER;
  BEGIN
    DURATION := 50;
    FOR PITCH := KEY DOWNTO KEY - 12 DO
      NOTE (PITCH, DURATION)
  END;

BEGIN
  UP (20);
  WRITELN (DURATION);
  DOWN (32);
  WRITELN (DURATION)
END.
```

Check it out carefully. Run it and see what happens.

Well, there you are again with the "undeclared identifier" message on the screen. The main program didn't know about the DURATION variable.

Make one last change. **Delete both WRITELN statements and try to run again.**

There shouldn't be any error messages this time, and the program should run just as it did when the VAR block was in the main program only.

What do you conclude about the new situation, with a VAR block declaring PITCH and DURATION *inside* UP and *inside* DOWN? First off, DURATION can't be a *global* variable any longer, since the main program doesn't know about it. On the other hand, UP certainly knows about a variable named DURATION, since it assigns a value to it and uses it in the NOTE statement. DOWN also knows about a variable with the same name. Finally, there was no problem in declaring DURATION to be a variable in *two* places. (All of these facts are also true of PITCH.)

In the last version of your program, you converted PITCH and DURATION into what are called *local* variables. Local variables are known *within* the procedure block where they were declared, but not outside. You created local variables by putting the VAR block that contained the variables *inside* the procedure block. Although UP and DOWN each declare a variable named DURATION, UP's DURATION is a different variable from DOWN's DURATION.

> Any names defined within a procedure block are known locally everywhere within that block, but they are not known outside that block.

Parameter variables lie somewhere between *local* variables and *global* variables. If a variable is local to a procedure, neither its name nor its value is known outside the procedure. If it is global, both name and value are known outside. If it is a parameter, then its name is not known outside, but its value is passed to it from outside at the moment the procedure is called.

You will find that the ability to declare local variables is very useful in writing a library of procedures, since the writer doesn't have to worry that a variable in the main program might accidentally have the same name as one in a procedure. If the one in the procedure is local, then it will have no effect on the one in the main program. They can coexist peacefully.

Here's a **user trap** to watch out for. In the main program you declare X to be a variable. The program contains a procedure. You use X as a variable in the procedure, but by accident, you forget to declare it within the procedure, even though you were thinking of X there as a *local* variable. When you compile the program you get no error messages, since the compiler thinks you mean X to be *global* and intended the procedure's X to be the same as the main program's X.

This gives surprising results that are extremely hard to diagnose. The way out of the trap is to avoid using the same names for local and global variables even though it is legal to do so. If you had used Y instead of X for one of the variables in this example, the compiler would have reported an "undeclared identifier" because of the missing VAR block.

5-6 PROCEDURES AND PROBLEM-SOLVING

This section is mainly philosophical. If you are eager to get on with doing things, skip ahead.

We said earlier that breaking a complicated task into simpler subtasks, and then working with each subtask more or less independently, was a good general approach to problem solving, not just in computer programming, but also in the real world. You actually do that all the time.

Consider the task of going to work or to school in the morning. If you were asked to describe the task, you would probably say that you get out of bed, do bathroom chores, get dressed, have breakfast, and drive or take a bus to work or school. That is what is called a *top-level* description of the main task. In fact, it is nothing more than a list of *procedure calls*. What does "get out of bed" mean? Well, it means this: turn off alarm; rub eyes; throw back covers; put on slippers; stand up; make bed. But this list is nothing more than another description in terms of still lower level subsubtasks. For example, "put on slippers" means this: find slipper; if left slipper, put on left foot; if not, put on right foot; find other slipper; put on other foot.

You may think that the description of procedure put-on-slippers is already fairly detailed. In fact, it too is merely a description in terms of *calls* to still lower level procedures. At some point you will get exasperated if asked to specify all this detail and you will say, "Oh, you know what I mean by that!" In other words, you are claiming that some procedures are *predefined* or *built-in* and don't require definition. For example, you might say that find-a-slipper or put-left-slipper-on-left-foot is a built in procedure.

It is, and it isn't. It is if you are talking to another person who understands your meaning. But if you are talking to a child who is still having trouble with left and right, or a very young child who is still working on simple hand-eye coordination, these low-level procedures, to you, are still high-level descriptions to the child who is trying to master them and is working on the still lower-level tasks that compose them.

There is a related point to be made here. It often happens that a person has a good top-level description of a task, but makes mistakes lower down in defining or carrying out a subtask. The child who knows how to do the get-out-of-bed procedure but walks out of the bedroom with an unmade bed or with the left slipper on the right foot, clearly knows how to get up in the morning but still has a few *bugs* in the lower level procedures. Recent research is showing that many school children who seem to make "dumb mistakes" in addition and subtraction are, in fact, calling on buggy procedures at the lower level, while their top-level understanding is perfect.

The philosphical point to be made here is this: the concepts of main program, procedure, subprocedures, and debugging, which arise out of computer programming needs, are *powerful ideas* for thinking about knowledge itself and about how people acquire knowledge. In a sense that is probably more than just poetic, learning seems to be a matter of programming, debugging, and reprogramming the mind.

Whether you buy that conclusion or not, you will have to agree, we think, that the real world is chock full of procedure calls, and we conclude this section with an example. Flip open the pages of your favorite French *haute cuisine* cookbook and look up a recipe or two. Very soon you will come upon some simple-looking dish that has only a few ingredients. Looking more carefully, you see that it needs "a cup of your favorite white sauce." What white sauce? They don't sell that at the supermarket. So you go to the index of your cookbook and, behold!, there are 10 pages devoted to the preparation of various white sauces. You have just discovered a procedure call.

5-7 GRAMMAR RULES FOR PROCEDURES

The grammatical structure of a procedure is almost the same as that of the program itself. Both begin with a *heading*, followed by a *declaration block*, followed by a *BEGIN/END block*. The precise grammatical form of the program and procedure structures are:

prog-head prog-declaration-block **BEGIN** *statement(s)* **END**.

proc-head proc-declaration-block **BEGIN** *statement(s)* **END**;

Thus, the text of a procedure, like that of a program, begins with a heading and ends with the reserved word END and a punctuation mark.

The program heading has the form

prog-head = **PROGRAM** *name parameter-list;*

while the procedure heading format is

> proc-head = **PROCEDURE** name parameter-list;

So far, the program parameter-list has been a *null list*—i.e., a list whose text contains *no* characters, like the null statement. You have also seen null parameter-lists in the first version of procedure UP and DOWN, and also lists that were not null.

With only a few exceptions, the declaration block of a procedure has the same general form as that of a program: both declaration blocks can contain a VAR block, any number of PROCEDURE blocks, and other types of blocks you will learn about later. Note especially that this grammar rule allows you to define a *local procedure* within another procedure, and still another "local-local" procedure within that one, and so on, as deeply as you want. (It is unusual to find actual programs with more than two or three procedure levels, by the way.)

The BEGIN/END block of statements in a procedure is subject to exactly the same grammar rules that apply to statements in a program. Whatever is legal in one is legal in the other. Note, however, that a period comes after the main BEGIN/END while a semicolon comes after a procedure BEGIN/END.

In the activities you carried out in this session, you learned that there were rules about which *variable* names were known to which parts of a program. These rules are called *scoping rules,* and they also apply to the names of *procedures* and to the names of other things that you will learn to define in later sessions: *functions, constants,* and *data types.*

> In Pascal there is a single rule that tells the *scope* of any name: the name is known *only* within and *everywhere* within the text of the *program unit* where the name was defined.

The simplest application of this rule is to names of *global scope.* For a name to be known everywhere within a program it must either be a built-in name, such as WRITELN, or else it must be defined in the declaration section of the main program. A variable declared in the main program VAR block is a global variable. A procedure defined in the main program's declaration is a global procedure—that is, it may be called by the main program, or by another procedure defined in the main program's declaration section, or even by a procedure defined within the declaration section of another procedure. Global names are known everywhere.

Another application of Pascal's scoping rule tells what is meant by *local scope.* If a name is defined within the declaration section of a procedure (or a function), the name is *unknown* to the program unit in which that procedure (or function) was defined. But such a name is known *everywhere within* the procedure (or function) where it was defined.

There is an easy way to think about Pascal's scoping rule. A given program unit (i.e., a procedure or a function or the main program itself) is like an individual person. A person can have grandparents, parents, siblings, children, nieces and nephews, grandchildren, etc. A procedure defined in the main program has a *parent* which is the main program. If the main program declaration block defines other procedures or functions, these are *siblings*. If the procedure in question contains a declaration block that defines another procedure or function, that is a *child*. If a sibling has children, they are *nieces and nephews*. If a child has children, they are *grandchildren*.

With this analogy in mind, Pascal's scoping rule says that names defined in a particular program unit are known to it, its children, its grandchildren, its great-grandchildren, etc. But the names are *not* known to parents, grandparents, great-grandparents, etc. Nor are the names known to siblings, nieces and nephews, etc.

> If you are a procedure, you and all your direct lineal descendents are the only ones who know the names you define.

SUMMARY

In this session you learned how to declare procedures within a program and how to call them from statements in the program. While learning these main facts about procedures you also learned a number of new things:

- **You had to use the word DOWNTO in a FOR statement if the variable was to decrease by one each time through the loop.**

- **The familiar WRITELN and NOTE statements used in earlier sessions were identified to be examples of a single type of Pascal statement: the procedure call.**

- **You used the EDITOR's C(OPY B(UFFER commands to make duplicate copies of program text, and also to move text from one place to another.**

- **You edited two sections of your main program and converted them into procedures.**

- **You changed the main program into a list of procedure calls.**

- **You used J B and J E in the editor to move the cursor to the beginning and end of the workspace.**

- **You added a parameter list to your procedure declarations, and modified the procedure calls to pass data values to the parameter.**

■ You discovered the difference between global variables and local variables, and saw the relation between them and parameter variables.

■ You saw that conflicts do not arise when a calling program declares a variable with the same name as a local variable declared in the called procedure. The local variable is used within the called procedure, as if the other one did not exist, and vice versa.

Finally, let's update the Pascal level structure table, and the Pascal vocabulary table.

Table 5.1A Amplified table of the EDITOR levels of Apple Pascal. Those features studied in this session are shown in bold face type

	Exit to escape from accidental entry.
E(ditor	ESC RETURN or Q E
Q(uit editor and	R
U(pdate workfile	
E(xit with no update	
R(eturn to editor	Q
W(rite to named file	RETURN
Cursor Moving Commands	
Right-arrow (Move cursor right)	
Left-arrow (Move cursor left)	
CTRL-L (Move cursor down)	
CTRL-O (Move cursor up)	
RETURN (Move cursor to beginning of next line)	
Spacebar (Move cursor to next character)	
J(ump to	**ESC**
E(nd of text	
B(eginning of text	
Text Changing Commands	
I(nsert text	ESC
CTRL-C (Normal exit)	
D(elete text	ESC
CTRL-C (Normal exit)	
C(opy text from	**ESC**
B(uffer	
Formatting Commands	
A(djust indention	
CTRL-C (Normal exit)	

Table 5.1B Table of other command levels of Apple Pascal. No new features appeared in this session.

	Exit to escape from accidental entry.
R(un program in workspace	
I(nitialize the system	
F(iler	
Q(uit the filer	F
N(ew workfile	RETURN
V(olumes on line	
L(ist the directory	RETURN
C(hange name	RETURN
T(ransfer a file	RETURN
D(ate setter	RETURN
? Show additional commands	RETURN
Commands Available at Any Level	
CTRL-A Toggle to other half of Pascal page	CTRL-A
CTRL-S Stop and restart screen output	CTRL-S
RESET Attempts reboot of Pascal	

Table 5.2 Cumulative Pascal vocabulary. New words introduced in this session are printed in bold face. (Code: a = declared in APPLESTUFF)

Reserved Words	Built-In Procedures	Built-In Functions	Other Built-Ins
PROGRAM	WRITE	Integer	Types
USES	WRITELN	a PADDLE	INTEGER
VAR	a NOTE		
PROCEDURE			Units
BEGIN			APPLESTUFF
FOR			
TO			
DOWNTO			
DO			
END			
DIV			

QUESTIONS AND PROBLEMS

1. What three kinds of Pascal statements have you used so far in this book?

2. Suppose a program contains these two statements:

```
FOR I := 5 DOWNTO N DO
   WRITELN (I);
WRITELN (I)
```

What will appear on the screen if the value of N is 1? 4? 5? 6?

3. Answer question 2 for the situation in which there is a semicolon immediately after DO. (How many statements would there be in that case?)

4. From the EDITOR, explain what each of the following key press sequences will do. Assume the cursor is at the beginning of line 1 and that there are 10 lines in the workspace.

    a. D RETURN RETURN ESC

    b. D RETURN RETURN CTRL-C

    c. D RETURN RETURN CTRL-C C B

    d. D RETURN RETURN CTRL-C RETURN RETURN C B C B

    e. J E

    f. J B

    g. J ESC

5. Explain how adding a PROCEDURE block to a program can shorten it.

6. Explain how adding a PROCEDURE block can make a program easier to understand.

The next three questions refer to the following program text. For ease of identifying lines, we have put number labels on each text line.

```
 1:   PROGRAM TOP;
 2:     VAR
 3:        HENRY : INTEGER;
 4:     PROCEDURE MIDDLE;
 5:       VAR
 6:          GWEN : INTEGER;
 7:       PROCEDURE BOTTOM;
 8:         VAR
 9:            LUKE : INTEGER;
10:         BEGIN
11:           <statement 1>
12:         END;
13:       BEGIN
14:         <statement 2>
15:       END;
16:   BEGIN
17:     <statement 3>
18:   END.
```

7. Which line or group of lines of program TOP contain

   a. The heading?

   b. The declaration block?

   c. The BEGIN/END block?

   (Hint: These three parts must add up to the whole program.)

8. Answer question 7 for procedure MIDDLE. Do the same for procedure BOTTOM.

9. You are procedure MIDDLE. In terms of family relationships, what sort of relatives are TOP and BOTTOM?

10. In the family (TOP, MIDDLE, BOTTOM, HENRY, GWEN, LUKE), who knows HENRY? Who knows GWEN? Who knows LUKE?

11. Consider these three possible statements:

```
HENRY := 5;
GWEN := 10;
LUKE := 2
```

For each one, decide whether it would lead to the "undeclared identifier" error message if used as statement 1? As statement 2? As statement 3? Which variable is known globally, throughout the program?

12. Consider these two possible procedure call statements:

```
MIDDLE
BOTTOM
```

   Decide for each one whether it would lead to the "undeclared identifier" error message if used as statement 3?

13. How does a parameter variable of the kind you used in this session receive its name? Its type? Its value?

14. The diatonic scale in the key of C major, starting at middle C, consists of these eight pitches: 20, 22, 24, 25, 27, 29, 31, and 32. Write a procedure that plays such an ascending scale, and where the duration of each note is determined by paddle one. (Hint: You will need eight NOTE call statements.)

15. "Transposing", in music means adding the same pitch value to every note in the diatonic scale. Rewrite the procedure in Problem 14 so that there is a parameter called KEY which is added to the pitch value in each NOTE call statement. If KEY has the value zero, the C major scale should result.

16. Section 5–6 showed how you can describe the everyday task of going to work as a sequence of procedure calls to subtasks, which in turn were calls to subsubtasks, etc. Pick another common task and describe it in the same way. Write the name of each task on one line, and indent under it each of its subtasks, etc.

17. Based on your task analysis in Problem 16, give an example showing how a bug in executing a low-level task can give unexpected results, even though the top-level description of the task is accurate.

MORE INVENTED WORDS: FUNCTIONS

In Session 5 you saw how to enlarge on the *built-in* vocabulary of the Pascal language by inventing new words of your own and defining precisely what you mean by them. You invented the words UP and DOWN and, you used PROCEDURE blocks to define their meanings in terms of known words and statements, such as NOTE and FOR. Once defined, you were able to use these words as commands, just as though they were part of the language. The result was that your main program became both shorter and more meaningful to a reader.

In this session you will explore a very close relative of the procedure, called a *programmer-defined function*. You are familiar with the idea of a function, since you have already used the built-in PADDLE function and have seen that it carries out a process that returns an integer value. In this session you will learn how to define your own functions.

SESSION GOALS

You will experiment with the built-in RANDOM function and RANDOMIZE procedure and discover their properties. You will use the MOD operator and learn its relationship to the DIV operator you used earlier with integers. You will use MOD and RANDOM together to produce a smaller set of random integers, useful in programming chance events, such as games. You will define a new function of your own that returns a random integer lying between two given integers. You will test the function by using it to make sounds with random pitches in a given octave. You will meet the famous Off-By-One Bug. You will refine your programs to use paddle input. You will see how to place comments in the text of a program, and will review how to write the finished version on your PROGRAM: diskette. Finally you will explore new features of the EDITOR.

6-1 RANDOM NUMBERS

Although your main goal here is to learn how to define functions of your own devising, this session begins with a side trip that will introduce you to a new function that has already been defined for you in the APPLESTUFF unit. You have already used one such *built-in* (also called *intrinsic*) function: namely PADDLE. The new one is called RANDOM. Let's see how it works.

Boot up Pascal and enter the date if necessary. Enter the EDITOR to check the workfile. Clear it out if necessary and return to the EDITOR. Enter INSERT mode and type the following program.

```
PROGRAM NOISE;

USES
    APPLESTUFF;

VAR
    CHAOS, COUNT : INTEGER;

BEGIN
  FOR COUNT := 1 TO 20 DO
    BEGIN
      CHAOS := RANDOM;
      WRITELN (COUNT, '      ', CHAOS)
    END
END.
```

Check it over for errors. Then run it. If there are compile-time errors, fix them.

The program produces two columns of integers. The first column is just the steadily increasing value of the FOR-loop variable, COUNT. But what about the second column? The numbers there are mostly five-digit numbers, but not always. None of them is negative and there seems to be a ceiling at about 32,000.

Note down the first three or four numbers in the second column and run the program again.

Again, you got similar results. In fact, the numbers you noted down were *repeated exactly* the second time. Whatever process produced them before, it did the same thing again. But the sequence of numbers produced seems to be very chaotic.

It is clear how the numbers got on the screen. Your WRITELN procedure call had as the third item in its parameter list a variable named CHAOS. CHAOS got its value in the assignment statement

```
    CHAOS := RANDOM
```

RANDOM must be the source of all those strange numbers. As we said earlier, RANDOM is a *built-in function* that comes along with the rest of APPLESTUFF. A function, you recall, is a precisely defined process that produces a value. Whenever a statement containing the name of the function is executed, the process happens and the function *returns the value* that the process produced. (If you're hazy about the notion of a function and how it differs from a variable, you might review Section 4–5.)

So RANDOM is a function that returns positive integers. Successive calls of the RANDOM function produce new integers, but there appears to be no predictable pattern, except that they don't seem ever to be much over about 32,000. Although there is no obvious order, something fairly definite must be going on, since a second run of the program produced the exact same sequence of values as the first.

You might guess that somewhere in the memory of the computer there is a long table of these numbers; but that isn't the case. In fact, each one is computed by a precise formula from the number before. The initial number, called the *seed*, determines the whole sequence. Although the numbers aren't really produced by chance, the formula used to generate them is chosen carefully to make the numbers seem as random as the roll of a die, or the toss of a coin.

Go to the EDITOR and insert, just before the FOR statement, this line, including a RETURN:

```
RANDOMIZE;
```

Run the program. Then run it again.

The sequence of numbers changed each time, didn't it? It looks as though the computer now may actually have produced "real" random numbers. Not so! RANDOMIZE is a call to a *built-in procedure* in APPLESTUFF. When called, it uses some chance physical event to produce one number, which is used as the *seed* for the formula discussed above. But each number after that is computed from the one before.

The point of this discussion is to let you know that the computer doesn't actually have a true dice-rolling capability. Nevertheless, the RANDOMIZE procedure and the RANDOM function are close approximations and are very useful in introducing chance-like events into a computer program when you want that—in a game, for example.

6-2 THINK OF A NUMBER FROM 1 TO 10

You now know how to produce random numbers between 0 and some big number (32,767 to be precise). That's fine, we hear you saying, but how about random numbers over some other interval? To simulate the roll of a die, one wants numbers between 1 and 6 to occur with equal chance, for example. How can that be done?

Go to the EDITOR and change your assignment line to look like this:

```
CHAOS := RANDOM MOD 6;
```

Run the program. Run again.

You're almost there. Variable CHAOS is receiving random values between zero and five. All that you would have to do now is to change the assignment line to read

```
CHAOS := 1 + RANDOM MOD 6;
```

and you would have it.

But, how did the phrase "MOD 6" do the job? What does MOD mean? Why 6? **To answer that, go to the EDITOR and change the assignment line again:**

```
CHAOS := COUNT MOD 6;
```

Run the program.

The program now writes on each line of the screen the value of COUNT, followed by the value of COUNT MOD 6. The values are identical when COUNT is between zero and 5. But at COUNT = 6, COUNT MOD 6 goes back to zero. In the same way, 7 MOD 6 is 1, 8 MOD 6 is 2, etc., until we reach 12. At that point you see that 12 MOD 6 is zero again.

If you haven't seen the rule yet, here is it: *COUNT MOD 6 is the remainder of COUNT divided by 6.* For example, 13 divided by 6 is 2 with a remainder of 1; and, as you can see on your screen, 13 MOD 6 is indeed 1.

Actually you use MOD all the time, but in another context. If it is now 10 p.m. and you have 4 more hours of work to do, when can you go to bed? At 2 a.m., of course: (10 + 4) MOD 12 is equal to 2. This kind of counting is called *modular arithmetic* (hence the Pascal word MOD) and you do it every day.

It is a good idea to lump X MOD Y and X DIV Y together in your mind. Both are *integer operators* in the same sense that + and – are called integer operators. They go together in a complementary way: each one performs a division of X by Y, but one of them (DIV) throws away the remainder, while the other (MOD) reports the remainder and throws away the integer quotient. If you like formulas, the following statement is always true:

```
X = Y times (X DIV Y ) + (X MOD Y)
```

(If you hate formulas, forget it; it isn't especially important anyway.)
Go to the EDITOR and again change the assignment line as follows:

```
CHAOS := RANDOM MOD 2;
```

Predict what you will see, and then run the program.

This sequence of zeros and ones could be used in a program to represent a coin-toss or some other two-way situation in which you wanted equal probability on both sides.

You've probably already figured out that "MOD 1" gives zero all the time. After all, every integer is exactly divisible by one and leaves no remainder. But what about "MOD 0"? Let's find out.
Again change the assignment line to:

```
CHAOS := RANDOM MOD 0;
```

Run again.

Compiling went fine, but you got the run-time error message, "DIVIDE BY ZERO", plus some other information. Evidently a MOD of zero is illegal. So are negative MODs. **Press the spacebar to start over at COMMAND level.**

6-3 BUILDING A BETTER FUNCTION

You now have the tools to build a more usable version of the built-in RANDOM function. It is rare that a program of yours will need random numbers between zero and 32,767. Typically, you will want a set of numbers somewhere between a lowest and a highest value. Of course, the particular values of these extreme numbers will be different from application to application.

Here is an example. Suppose you want to generate random musical notes in the octave between pitch numbers 24 and 36. It would be very nice to be able to do that by using a new random number function—call it RND—such that the main program would look as follows:

```
BEGIN
  RANDOMIZE;
  FOR COUNT := 0 TO 200 DO
    BEGIN
      CHAOS := RND (24, 36);
      WRITELN (COUNT, '    ', CHAOS);
      NOTE (CHAOS, 20)
    END
END.
```

If RND existed, it would make your programming job easier; but more important, it would make the *intent* of the program clearer to a reader of its text. RND (24, 36) practically says, "return a random integer in the range 24 to 36."

Your job now is to build yourself such a function, and you can do it in almost exactly the same way you did when building procedures in the last session. You *declare* each function in a separate FUNCTION block. FUNCTION blocks must follow the VAR block in the *program unit* in which the function is defined. (A program unit can be the main program, a procedure, or another function.) FUNCTION blocks can go before, after, or among PROCEDURE blocks in the same program unit. Of course, like any named object in Pascal, they have to be declared in the text of the program *before first use* by anything else. For example, if you have a PROCEDURE block and if a statement in the procedure contains the name of the function, then the FUNCTION block has to precede that PROCEDURE block.

6-4 THE FORM OF THE FUNCTION BLOCK

Your RND block will look like this:

```
FUNCTION RND (LOW, HIGH : INTEGER) : INTEGER;
  BEGIN
    RND := ???
  END;
```

Before going ahead with completion of the assignment statement that ends with question marks, notice the general form of this block. It is very much like a PROCEDURE block. It begins with a *heading* followed always by a semicolon, and concludes with a BEGIN/END block. (It could also have, between the two, a *declaration section* containing a local VAR block and perhaps its own local PROCEDURE and FUNCTION blocks. This simple example, however, has no declarations.) The heading begins with the reserved word FUNCTION, followed by a *name* of your choice, followed by a *parameter list*, followed by a *type declaration*. Except for the last item and the keyword FUNCTION, the grammatical form of the heading is exactly like that of the PROCEDURE heading and also of the PROGRAM heading.

Let's examine that last, distinguishing item. Why is there a type declaration both inside the parameter list (within the parentheses) and after the parameter list (beyond the parentheses)? The phrase ": INTEGER" inside the parentheses should be familiar to you from your work with procedures. It tells that the parameter variables, LOW and HIGH, are of type integer. When the main program *calls* RND, it must supply the function with data values that are integers.

But, what about the second ": INTEGER" type declaration? The answer is that it refers to the type of the function itself. Remember, from your work in Session 3 with the built-in PADDLE function, that every function must have a *name*, a *value*, and a *type*. The final declaration says that your function RND is of type integer. That means that it will *return* integer data values to the calling program. The writer of the program that calls RND has to know that fact and has to use the word RND only in a place where *integer constants* would also be legal to use. (If not, then the compiler would report our friend, the "type conflict error.")

To summarize a bit, a function is very much like a procedure, both in form and in purpose. Each one is a defined *process*. Each process is set in action by a *call*, or *reference*, made when some statement containing its name is executed. The only difference is that a procedure call is performed by a statement that consists of nothing more than the name of the procedure. In contrast, a function call is made by using the name of a function in *any Pascal statement* where a constant of the same type could also have been used.

A function always returns an item of data of that same type. In effect, the data item it returns "takes the place of the name of the function" wherever it appeared in the calling program.

Now let's see how it is that you can specify the number that your RND function is going to return. First of all, there is a *grammar rule* and it is very simple: somewhere in the BEGIN/END block of the FUNCTION block, there has to appear some statement that will assign a value to the name RND. We have written that statement somewhat sketchily before as

```
RND := ???
```

In this example, then, RND gets a value by appearing on the left side of an assignment statement *within the function definition*. Thus, the function will return as a value, whatever is computed on the right side of the assignment operator.

The only place in a Pascal program where it is legal to have a function name appear on the left side of an assignment statement is within the BEGIN/END block of the definition of that function. It would be illegal, and make no grammatical sense, for the main program to say this:

```
RND (3, 9) := 87
```

6-5 DEFINING FUNCTION RND

Let's get back now to the completion of your definition of RND. We have to replace all those question marks with some computation that will produce random integers in the range between LOW and HIGH. How do you compute the numbers? Well, you know that RANDOM gives random numbers from zero to 32,767. You know that RANDOM MOD N gives random numbers starting at zero and extending up to N-1. So, it *looks* like you should subtract LOW from HIGH to get the range of numbers, right? And then add LOW to the result, so that the numbers will start not at zero but at LOW, right? Well, do it.

Go to the EDITOR and change the program NOISE to the following text. You will have to use CTRL-A here to see the right half of the Pascal page when you type the FUNCTION line.

```
PROGRAM NOISE;

  USES APPLESTUFF;

  VAR
    CHAOS, COUNT : INTEGER;

  FUNCTION RND (LOW, HIGH : INTEGER) : INTEGER;
    BEGIN
      RND := LOW + RANDOM MOD (HIGH - LOW)
    END;

BEGIN
  RANDOMIZE;
  FOR COUNT := 0 TO 200 DO
  BEGIN
    CHAOS := RND (24, 36);
    WRITELN (COUNT, '    ', CHAOS);
    NOTE (CHAOS, 20)
  END
END.
```

Check it carefully. Run the program.

It *seems* okay, doesn't it? The notes are all in the same octave and seem randomly distributed. In fact, there's a subtle *bug* in your program. If you are unusually sharp-eyed, you may have caught it. Look at the numbers on the screen while the program is running.

If the program has stopped, run it again. While it is running type CTRL-S from time to time and inspect the numbers. Type CTRL-S again to start the program going again.

The problem is that you aren't getting all the pitch numbers out of RND that you asked for. You are okay at the low end, where a value of 24 shows up once in a while. But you asked for a top pitch of 36. Look closely—no 36.

This is an example of the most famous and most common bug in computing: the Off-By-One Bug. You wanted a top pitch of 36, but you got only as far as 35. You will get to know this creature very well.

Let's see what happened. Quickly, without thinking at all, answer this question: "How many numbers are there in the range 7 to 12?" The answer is 5, right? Twelve minus 7 is 5, so the answer must be 5, okay? No, not okay. There are 6 numbers in the range 7 to 12: 7, 8, 9, 10, 11, and 12. *You always have to add one after taking the difference between the numbers that define the two ends of the range.*

Return to the EDITOR and change the assignment statement in the FUNCTION block to read:

```
RND := LOW + RANDOM MOD (1 + HIGH - LOW)
```

Run the program. Now it is working as you asked it to, reaching a high pitch of 36.

> There is only one sure defense against the Off-By-One Bug: substitute simple numbers into your expressions and see whether they work out.

In your case, the actual numbers you used will do. With LOW = 24 and HIGH = 36, HIGH – LOW = 12. Well, RANDOM MOD 12 gives numbers in the range zero to *eleven*. Adding LOW (24) to that gives numbers in the range 24 to *35*, not 36. Clearly, we needed to add one to HIGH – LOW to fix the error. *This trick, substituting simple numbers for variables and then checking the results by hand, will save you many hours of grief.*

6-6 PROGRAM REFINEMENTS

You can make a few additions to program NOISE that will let you control the sounds by means of the paddle control knobs. Most of what follows in this section will be review, by the way.

Go to the EDITOR and change the second parameter in your NOTE procedure call so that it looks like this:

```
NOTE (CHAOS, PADDLE (1))
```

Run the program and use paddle one to speed up and slow down the sequence of sounds.

You can use the other paddle to control the bottom note of the octave out of which the notes are picked at random, rather than have them always come out of the octave between 24 and 36. Let KEY be the name of the bottom note. We want random pitches in the range between KEY and KEY + 12.

Go to the EDITOR and change the RND parameters as follows:

```
CHAOS := RND (KEY, KEY + 12);
```

Two tasks remain. You have to declare KEY to be a variable, and you have to assign a value to it before it is used. The goal is to have paddle zero control KEY. As you remember, the PADDLE function will return numbers between zero and 255; but the range of good musical notes is only zero to 50. That means KEY must be zero or larger, but KEY + 12 shouldn't be greater than 50. That limits KEY to between zero and 38. We come close to that range if we use PADDLE (0) DIV 7 as the value for KEY. (What exact range does this correspond to?)

From the EDITOR, add KEY to the VAR block, and add an assignment statement for KEY. The revised program should look like this:

```
PROGRAM NOISE;

  USES APPLESTUFF;

VAR
  CHAOS, COUNT, KEY : INTEGER;

FUNCTION RND (LOW, HIGH : INTEGER) : INTEGER;
  BEGIN
    RND := LOW + RANDOM MOD (1 + HIGH - LOW)
  END;

BEGIN
  RANDOMIZE;
  FOR COUNT := 0 TO 200 DO
    BEGIN
      KEY := PADDLE (0) DIV 7;
      CHAOS := RND (KEY, KEY + 12);
      WRITELN (COUNT, '    ', CHAOS);
      NOTE (CHAOS, PADDLE (1))
    END
END.
```

Now run program NOISE a few times, controlling it with the two paddle knobs.

6-7 ADDING COMMENTS TO YOUR PROGRAM

If you use a clear, consistent indentation style when you write Pascal programs, and if you choose meaningful names for things, the text of your programs will usually be self-explanatory. Once in a while, however, there may be a need to add a word or phrase to help clarify a meaning or distinguish similar-looking words from one another. For example, the last two lines of program NOISE contain the word END. The first END closes the FOR statement, while the second one closes the entire program. (In longer programs it is not uncommon to see three or four ENDs in a row.) Adding a word or two of comment would help clarify the situation. This section shows how to do that.

Change the NOTE statement as follows:

```
(* NOTE (CHAOS, PADDLE (1)) *)
```

Run the changed program. If you succeeded in surrounding the NOTE statement by the symbols (* and *), then you saw that it was effectively deactivated when you ran the program. Everything else worked as before, but there was no sound.

Go to the EDITOR again and change the last two lines of the FOR statement as follows:

```
(* WRITELN (COUNT, '    ', CHAOS);
NOTE (CHAOS, PADDLE (1)) *)
```

Run again. This time the program ran, but there was *no* output. It appears that *all* of the text enclosed by the symbols (* and *) simply vanished from the compiled program. In fact, that is exactly what happened. The symbols are called *comment brackets*. If a space occurs between the parenthesis and the asterisk, the result is *not* a comment bracket. When the Pascal compiler comes upon the *opening* bracket, (*, it simply ignores all characters until it finds a *closing* bracket, *).

In the example above, you have used this feature of the Pascal compiler to *comment out* a part of your program without actually deleting the text. This practice is often useful while *debugging* a long program. You can, for example, add four or five extra WRITELN statements to output intermediate results useful in figuring out what is going on. Then you can selectively comment out the ones that are not useful at the moment.

That, however, is not the main use of comment brackets. Instead, they give you a way to add to the text of your program those helpful phrases we talked about at the beginning of this section. The following listing shows an example of the use of comments to clarify the intent of program NOISE. **Delete the comment brackets now in your program. Then add the following changes:**

```
PROGRAM NOISE;

    (* PLAYS RANDOM NOTES IN ONE OCTAVE.
       PADDLE (0) CONTROLS LOWEST NOTE.
       PADDLE (1) CONTROLS DURATION. *)

    USES APPLESTUFF;

    VAR
      CHAOS, COUNT, KEY : INTEGER;

    FUNCTION RND (LOW, HIGH : INTEGER) : INTEGER;

      (* RANDOM INTEGER IN RANGE LOW..HIGH *)

      BEGIN
        RND := LOW + RANDOM MOD (1 + HIGH - LOW)
    END; (* RND *)

BEGIN
  RANDOMIZE;
  FOR COUNT := 0 TO 200 DO
    BEGIN
      KEY := PADDLE (0) DIV 7;
      CHAOS := RND (KEY, KEY + 12);
      WRITELN (COUNT, '   ', CHAOS);
      NOTE (CHAOS, PADDLE (1))
    END (* FOR *)
END.
```

Check these changes carefully. Run the program to check for errors. The result should be exactly the same as for the version you ran at the end of Section 6–6.

There is one horrible **user trap** that comes along with comments, and now is a safe time to fall into it. **Go to the EDITOR and delete the asterisk in the closing comment bracket of the first comment in the program text.** What do you think will happen when you try to compile this program? Where does the first comment end? **Run the program and find out. Then return to the EDITOR.**

Understanding what went on was fairly easy in the present case, because you were conscious of the cause of the problem. But if the missing asterisk had been an unnoticed typing error, you would have been very hard pressed to figure out why the compiler complained that RND was an "undeclared identifier". It was obviously declared in the FUNCTION heading. The problem is that the FUNCTION heading is (by accident) *inside the initial comment*, which doesn't get closed until the symbol *) is reached *after* the FUNCTION heading. The USES block and the VAR block are also part of the comment.

Beware of unclosed and improperly closed comments.

Restore the asterisk that you removed from the initial closing comment bracket. Run once more to make sure all is in order.

6-8 FILING YOUR PROGRAM AWAY

Program NOISE is now in shape for writing out on your PROGRAM: diskette and saving for future reference. You learned how to do that in Section 4–9, and this is a good opportunity to review the steps.

At EDITOR level, type Q W. The screen prompt is this:

```
>QUIT:
NAME OF OUTPUT FILE (<CR> TO RETURN, --
```

Remove APPLE0: from the drive and insert your diskette PROGRAM:. Type CTRL-A. Then type the diskette name and the file name as follows:

```
PROGRAM:NOISE
```

Press RETURN. Type CTRL-A again. The new screen prompt is this:

```
>QUIT
WRITING..
YOUR FILE IS 607 BYTES LONG.
DO YOU WANT TO E(XIT FROM OR R(ETURN TO
```

Remove PROGRAM: from the drive. Re-insert APPLE0:. Type R.

At this point you have added a new file named NOISE.TEXT to your PROGRAM: diskette. A copy of the same program is also in your EDITOR workspace, and another copy is on APPLE0: in the workfile.

It is essential in this process to have the right diskette in the drive at the right time. If APPLE0: is in the drive when you press RETURN after typing PROGRAM:NOISE, the writing-out operation fails, but no great harm is done. You just start over with a Q W. But if PROGRAM: is in the drive when you type R (or E) in the final step, you are in trouble, since PROGRAM: lacks the necessary system files, such as SYSTEM.EDITOR. The computer gives up in despair and tries to do a cold-start reboot, putting the message APPLE][at the top of the screen. If that happens, remove whatever diskette is in the drive, replace it with APPLE3:, and follow the regular boot-up procedure. The EDITOR workspace will have been lost, but the APPLE0: workfile will still be intact.

6-9 MORE ABOUT THE EDITOR

You should now be back in the EDITOR and on your screen you should see a copy of program NOISE exactly as it was at the end of Section 6-7. Now that you have safely tucked away a copy of NOISE on your PROGRAM: diskette, this is a good time to exercise a few new features of the EDITOR without worrying about losing information. Furthermore, the text is now long enough to use commands that would have been useless before.

We begin with tools for moving the cursor around in the workspace, starting with a revew of the J(UMP command. **Type J E. Type J B.** These commands put the cursor at the end and beginning of the text. They give the biggest moves possible.

Now let's do a slightly smaller big move. **Type P.** This command moved the cursor about one page (23 text lines) down the screen. **Type P again.** As before, it tried to move forward a full page, but this time there were not enough lines. The cursor moved to the end of the text.

Next, let's take even smaller steps. **Type J B to get back to the beginning. Then type 5 and press RETURN. Type 10 and press RETURN. Type / and press RETURN.** These experiments show that a numeric prefix, followed by RETURN, has the same effect as an equal number of RETURNs. That is, 3 RETURN is equivalent to RETURN RETURN RETURN. You also saw that / RETURN meant to issue as many RETURNs as possible. The effect was the same as J E.

Type 4 CTRL-O. Type 20 CTRL-0. Type 10 CTRL-L. These experiments show that the numeric-prefix idea also works with CTRL-O and CTRL-L. **Type 22 and press the right-arrow key. Type 22 and press the left-arrow key. Type 22 and press the spacebar. Type / and press the left arrow.** As you probably guessed, the number or slash prefix works in the same general fashion with all of the cursor-move commands in the EDITOR.

Now for another new wrinkle. **Press the RETURN key about ten times. Notice the greater-than sign (>) just before the word EDIT in the prompt line. Type the key that has the comma and the less-than sign (<) on it. Notice that a less-than sign now appears before EDIT. Now press the RETURN key a few times.** The symbol in front of the word EDIT establishes what is called the *set direction*. The effect of the RETURN key *at EDIT level* is determined by the set direction. The normal direction is *forward,* indicated by a greater-than sign (>), and causes a RETURN to move the cursor forward to the start of the next line. The *reverse* direction, indicated by a less-than sign (<), causes a RETURN to move the cursor backward to the start of the preceding line.

Now let's see what else is affected by the set direction. **With the reverse direction set, type the right-arrow key a few times. Type the left-arrow key. Type CTRL-L. Type CTRL-O.** These keys move the cursor in fixed directions, irrespective of the set direction. **Press the spacebar a few times.** The effect is a backspace because the set direction is backwards.

Type J B. Type J E. Type P. Type the key that has the period and greater-than sign (>) on it. Notice that a greater-than sign again appears in front of the EDIT prompt. **Type another P.** This experiment shows that the P(AGE command moves the cursor one page *in the set direction,* but that the J(UMP command is not affected by the set direction.

To summarize a bit, you have found that the RETURN, spacebar, and P keys move the cursor in the set direction. The other cursor-move keys are unaffected by the set direction. The direction may be set *forward* by the period, greater-than, and plus keys; it may be set *backward* by the comma, less-than, and minus keys.

There is another nice way to move the cursor to a location defined not by the number of steps to get there but by the text that is to be found there. For example, if you wanted to find the first occurrence of the NOTE call, here is all you would have to do. **Type J B. With the direction set to forward, type F.** You see this prompt line:

```
>FIND[1]: L(IT <TARGET> =>
```

Type the following response:

```
/NOTE/
```

As you saw, the cursor was moved just beyond the first occurrence of the word NOTE as soon as you typed the second slash. If your response had been

```
.NOTE.
```

the result would have been identical. The slash or period is called a *delimiter*. You can choose any delimiter that is not a letter or a number. The word you type between delimiters must be a complete word in the text of your program and not just a fragment, such as OTE, if the search is to be successful. F(IND is affected by the set direction. A numeric prefix to F tells *which* occurrence to search for. A slash prefix to F means to find the *last* occurrence.

So much for moving the cursor about while at EDIT level. Next, let's see how to make it easier to enter long lines and to read them. So far, you have been using CTRL–A to toggle the viewing window back and forth to each half of the Pascal page. The problem with that is that you lose the context of the line you are trying to read or type. The Apple Pascal EDITOR gives you another option, called *horizontal scrolling*. **Move the cursor to the beginning of the FUNCTION RND heading. Type CTRL–Z. Press the right-arrow key repeatedly and notice what happens as the cursor approaches the right side of the screen. Keep pressing the right-arrow key until the cursor moves to the next line.**

This mode is especially nice when you are typing long lines into the computer, since the window moves right along with the new letters you type. **Type CTRL–A to leave the horizontal-scroll mode.** When you do so you will sometimes end up looking at the right half-page and sometimes at the left. Another CTRL–A will get to the other half, as usual.

The last EDITOR command to be introduced in this session is the X(CHANGE, which is nothing more than a shortcut for combining a D(ELETE with an I(NSERT. Suppose you wanted to change the first FOR statement so that it counted from zero to 832 instead of zero to 200. Here is the shortcut. **Move the cursor to the 2 in 200. Type X. Type 832. Type CTRL–C.** That's all there is to it. Note that this approach works only when the *number* of characters is the same before and after the exchange. Also, you cannot make an exchange beyond the end of a text line. ESC get's you out of the X(CHANGE mode without changing the workspace.

SUMMARY

The most important things you learned in this session were the grammar rules for *declaring* functions and for *calling* them into execution. You saw how to declare the *type* of the function in the heading of the FUNCTION block, and how to use an assignment statement within the FUNCTION block to specify the *value* to be returned by the function. You learned that a FUNCTION block goes after the VAR block in the program and comes before, among, or after any PROCEDURE blocks or other FUNCTION blocks. You also were told that a procedure or another function could have a locally defined FUNCTION block within it.

In addition to these fundamental facts about functions, you also experienced a few other things.

- You used the RANDOM function (defined in APPLESTUFF) and found that it produced a chaotic-looking stream of numbers between zero and 32,767.

- You used the RANDOMIZE procedure (defined in APPLESTUFF) to generate a random seed for the sequence of numbers produced by RANDOM.

- You found that the integer expression X MOD N gave a value equal to the remainder of X divided by N; and that X DIV N gave the integer quotient.

- You used RANDOM MOD N to generate chaotic-looking integers in the range zero to N–1.

- You met OBOB, the famous Off-By-One Bug and found a strategy for fixing it.

- You refined a random tone program to use paddle input for more user control.

- You used comment brackets (* and *) both to comment-out program segments and to add explanatory text.

- You used the Q W exit option from the EDITOR and saved the workspace copy of your program in a named file on the PROGRAM: diskette.

- You used the P(AGE command to move the cursor a page at a time.

- You saw that a number or a slash preceding a cursor move command in the EDITOR caused a repetition of the command.

- You saw how to change the set direction, and found that the RETURN, spacebar, P, and F commands each moved the cursor in the set direction.

- You used the F(IND command to move the cursor to a selected word in the text.

- You used CTRL–Z to set horizontal scroll mode.

- You used the X(CHANGE command as an delete/insert shortcut.

Tables 6.1A and 6.1B show the expanded command level structure of the Apple Pascal system. Since there will be no major additions to these tables in the remainder of the book, only the cumulative Pascal vocabulary tables will be given in future sessions. The complete command level structure is given in Appendix D.

Table 6.1A Amplified table of the EDITOR levels of Apple Pascal. Those features studied in this session are shown in bold face type.

	Exit to escape from accidental entry
E(ditor	ESC RETURN or Q E
Q(uit editor and	R
U(pdate workfile	
E(xit with no update	
R(eturn to editor	Q
W(rite to named file	RETURN
Cursor Moving Commands	
Right-arrow (Move cursor right)	
Left-arrow (Move cursor left)	
CTRL-L (Move cursor down)	
CTRL-O (Move cursor up)	
RETURN (Move cursor to beginning of next line)	
Spacebar (Move cursor to next character)	
J(ump to	ESC
E(nd of text	
B(eginning of text	
P(age move	
F(ind text pattern	**ESC**
Text Changing Commands	
I(nsert text	ESC
CTRL-C (Normal exit)	
D(elete text	ESC
CTRL-C (Normal exit)	
C(opy text from	ESC
B(uffer	
X(change characters	**ESC**
CTRL-C (Normal exit)	
Formatting Commands	
A(djust indentation	
CTRL-C (Normal exit)	

Table 6.1B Amplified table of other command levels of Apple Pascal. Those features studied in this session are shown in bold face type.

Exit to escape
from accidental
entry.

F(iler
    Q(uit the filer   F
    N(ew workfile   RETURN
    V(olumes on line
    L(ist the directory   RETURN
    C(hange name   RETURN
    T(ransfer a file   RETURN
    D(ate setter   RETURN
    ? Show additional commands   RETURN

R(un program in workspace

I(nitialize the system

Commands Available at Any Level

    CTRL-A Toggle to other half of   CTRL-A
            Pascal page
    CTRL-S Stop and restart screen   CTRL-S
            output
    CTRL-Z Set horizontal scroll   **CTRL-A**
    RESET Attempts reboot of Pascal

Table 6.2   Cumulative Pascal Vocabulary. New words introduced in this session
are printed in bold face. (Code: a = defined in APPLESTUFF)

Reserved Words	Built-In Procedures	Built-In Functions	Other Built-Ins
PROGRAM	WRITE	Integer	Types
USES	WRITELN	a PADDLE	INTEGER
VAR	a NOTE	**a RANDOM**	
PROCEDURE	**a RANDOMIZE**		
FUNCTION			Units
BEGIN			APPLESTUFF
FOR			
TO			
DOWNTO			
DO			
END			
DIV			
MOD			

QUESTIONS AND PROBLEMS

1. What are the results of these integer expressions?

   a. 13 DIV 5

   b. 13 MOD 5

   c. 5 DIV 13

   d. 5 MOD 13

   e. 5 MOD 5

   f. 5 MOD 1

   g. 5 MOD 0

   h. 5 MOD –5

2. Given a number N, how can you use MOD to tell whether it is exactly divisible by 17? How can you use DIV for the same purpose?

3. Suppose the 37th day of the year is a Monday. How can you compute whether the 237th day will be a Monday? If it isn't a Monday, how can you tell what day it is?

4. How can you tell whether a given number is even or odd?

5. One common way for a computer to produce random-looking sequences of numbers is the following:

   a. Pick a 2-digit *seed* and a 2-digit *factor*.

   b. Set the *next-number* equal to the *seed*.

   c. Multiply the *next-number* by the *factor*.

   d. Remove the units digit and thousands-digit (if there is one).

   e. Let the *next-number* equal the two inner digits. (This is the beginning of the random sequence of numbers.)

   f. Repeat steps c through f.

   Experiment with this procedure. Start with a factor of 37 and a seed of 1. Find the first dozen or so numbers produced. (A pocket calculator will help.)

6. Change the seed in Question 5 and repeat. Are there "bad seeds"?

7. Change the factor in Question 6 and repeat. Are there "bad factors"?

8. If function HENRY is declared within procedure GEORGE, does the main program know about the existance of HENRY?

9. In Question 8, is a variable declared by HENRY known to GEORGE? Is a variable declared by GEORGE known to HENRY? Is HENRY known to GEORGE?

10. Why does the type of a function have to be declared?

11. What kind of statement is used to give a function its value?

12. Write the complete FUNCTION block for a function that returns the square of an integer. (N*N equals the square of N.)

13. Change the assignment statement of the function in Question 12 to make it return the fifth power of N.

14. Referring to the FUNCTION RND as defined at the end of Section 6–5, decide in each case below whether the *call* to RND is legal or not. If not, explain why.

   a. X := RND (2, 2)

   b. Z := RND (2, 1)

   c. Q := RND (–10, 10)

   d. R := RND (0, 32768)

   e. M := RND (0, 98.6)

15. Which cursor move commands in the EDITOR are affected by the set direction?

16. List all of the keys that can change the set direction when used at the EDIT level.

17. Explain what a numeric prefix and a slash do when used with cursor moving commands.

18. Suppose the workspace is 35 lines long, and each line has at least 20 characters. Where will the cursor be after each of the following sets of key presses:

   a. J B

   b. J B . 9 RETURN

   c. J E , 9 RETURN

d. J B / CTRL-L

e. J B + 6 spacebar

f. J B > P < P

19. What key presses would you use to find:

a. the first occurrence of the word BEGIN in the workspace.

b. the second occurrence of the word BEGIN.

c. the last occurrence of the word BEGIN.

DRAWING PICTURES

The functions and procedures that you learned to define in the last two sessions are the basic building blocks out of which all but the simplest Pascal programs are composed. The existence of these types of program units is your invitation to break any larger programming problem into smaller "chunks" which can be attacked one at a time. The functions and procedures that you define will determine the overall "shape" that your program takes.

With this topic behind you, you have already reached an important plateau in your understanding of the *organization* of Pascal programs into program units. You have also learned nearly all of the Apple Pascal system commands that will be needed in this book. (For that reason, we now stop reproducing the table of system commands at the end of each session.) At this point, you have learned your way around the EDITOR and the FILER, and you can write a fairly long, multipart program.

There is more to learn, but it will all proceed on the solid base established so far. There are more statement types; one new one appears in this session and two more in the next. There are additional *data types* beyond the integers you have been using. And there are new elementary capabilities, such as graphic output. That is the main topic of this session.

SESSION GOALS

In this session your main task will be to learn how to generate line drawings on the screen. You will learn about a new data type called *boolean*. You will be introduced to the REPEAT statement, which is used to control looping in a way different from the FOR statement. You will learn the difference between *constants* and *variables*. You will write a graphic procedure.

7-1 PADDLE SKETCH

Carry out the standard startup steps: boot up Pascal, set the date, inspect the workfile, clear it out if necessary, and, finally, enter INSERT mode in the EDITOR.

These items, which are probably old hat to you by now, make your computer ready for you to type in a new Pascal program and then move it into the now empty workfile. You should see the INSERT prompt at the top of the screen, the cursor at the left of the line below it, and an otherwise blank screen.

Type in the following program.

```
PROGRAM SKETCH;

USES
    TURTLEGRAPHICS, APPLESTUFF;

VAR
    I, X, Y, WAIT : INTEGER;

BEGIN
    INITTURTLE;
    PENCOLOR (WHITE);
    FOR I := 1 TO 2000 DO
      BEGIN
        X := PADDLE (0);
        FOR WAIT := 1 TO 3 DO;
        Y := PADDLE (1);
        MOVETO (X, Y)
      END (* FOR *)
END.
```

Check each line carefully as you enter it, using the left-arrow key to delete errors. Leave INSERT via CTRL-C. Check the semicolons especially carefully. If you find errors, use DELETE/INSERT to repair them.

There are a few new things and several old things in this program. Starting at the top, the *name* of the program is SKETCH. It has a USES block, which you saw in the last two sessions, but this time there are two words following USES: TURTLEGRA-PHICS as well as APPLESTUFF. The first and second statements in the main BEGIN/END block, INITTURTLE and PENCOLOR (WHITE), are both new. The third statement is the familiar FOR statement.

Within the FOR statement there is a *compound statement*, bracketed by BEGIN and END. It contains four simple statements. The first is an assignment. The second is the simplest form of the FOR statement, since the word DO is followed by a *null* statement and a semicolon. The third statement is another assignment. The fourth statement, MOVETO (X, Y), is a new procedure call. Note that *three* semicolons separate the *four* statements making up this compound statement. No semicolon is needed after the fourth one because the word END brackets it. Note similarly that *two* semicolons separate the *three* statements that make up the main BEGIN/END block of the program. The third statement (the outer FOR statement) is *not* followed by a semicolon, since it is bracketed by the final END.

First of all, you should recognize that there are no new statement *varieties* here. INITTURTLE, PENCOLOR, and MOVETO are examples of the familiar *procedure call* statement. Other examples are WRITELN and NOTE. You *will* be seeing a new statement variety in this session, so keep your eyes peeled.

Your immediate goal is to understand these new elements in your program and to see how they work together. **From the EDITOR, type Q U R to run the program.** (If there are compile-time errors, go back to the EDITOR, fix them, and run again.)

Turn the knobs on your paddles back and forth, first using one paddle at a time and then using them together. If time runs out, type R and run again. What position does paddle zero control? What about paddle one? Recall that the PADDLE function returns the number zero when the knob is all the way to the left (counterclockwise) and 255 when all the way to the right. What position on the screen corresponds to zero for paddle zero? Zero for paddle one? 255 for paddle one? Try to draw a square as large as possible; is its top visible on your screen?

Return to the EDITOR after you've finished these experiments.

You've probably guessed that all the action is going on in the compound statement of the outer FOR loop. Let's examine these statements. The first one is a familiar *assignment* statement, like the one you used in Session 4. It *inputs* the current setting of paddle zero, returns a number between zero and 255, and assigns that value to the variable named X. The next statement is a make-work loop, which you also used in Session 4 to allow the required amount of time between paddle inputs. The third statement assigns to variable Y the value corresponding to the setting of paddle one. The last statement, MOVETO (X, Y), is the only new one here; and it is the one that causes *graphic output* to your screen, just as WRITE and WRITELN cause *text output* and NOTE causes *sound output*.

Perhaps the easiest way to understand how the MOVETO procedure works is by imagining that you are giving commands to a little creature who can crawl about your screen and who posesses a set of pens. For historical reasons, we'll call this little fellow a *turtle*, though you've already seen that this particular turtle can crawl pretty fast.

The effect of MOVETO (X, Y) is to move the turtle to a point that is a distance of X from the left edge of the screen and a distance Y from the bottom edge. The turtle moves to the new point along a straight line path from wherever it was when MOVETO was called. While moving, the turtle draws a line with whichever pen color it currently holds.

The turtle is left in its new position until told to do something different. Because the paddle inputs and the MOVETO statement occur inside a FOR loop which goes from one to 2000, the turtle is getting a sequence of 2000 commands to move to positions with X and Y values determined by your paddle settings. If you don't change either paddle control, the turtle moves to where it already is, so you don't see any action. If you change only paddle zero, only the X value (the distance from the left edge of the screen) changes. The turtle moves on a horizontal line. If you change only paddle one, then only the Y value (the distance from the bottom edge) changes. The turtle moves up and down. If you change both paddles at once, you change both X and Y and the turtle moves diagonally.

> MOVETO is very powerful. With it, a program can draw any figure that can be represented by a sequence of straight line segments.

7-2 DRAWING IN COLORS

Let's investigate the notion of *pencolors* referred to in the above section, where we said that as the turtle moves it "draws a line with whichever pen color it currently holds." You have probably guessed where in the program SKETCH the turtle is told what pen color to use: it's the PENCOLOR (WHITE) statement just before the outer FOR loop. Let's change it to another color.

From the EDITOR, use DELETE and INSERT to change WHITE to ORANGE. Back at the EDIT level, type Q U R and run the program. Go back to the EDITOR, change ORANGE to BLUE or GREEN, or VIOLET, and run again.

If you have a color TV display, then you saw that the turtle can draw lines in several colors.

7-3 A NEW PASCAL STATEMENT: THE REPEAT LOOP

You probably have begun to feel that these experiments would be a lot easier to do if the program loop wasn't always set to exactly 2000 steps. Sometimes it ran out before you were ready to quit, and sometimes you had to wait for it to run out. What you'd like is some way to have the steps *repeat* again and again *until* you signal that you're ready to quit.

Well, folks, you're in luck: the Pascal language has the words REPEAT and UNTIL in its vocabulary, and they mean just what you'd expect. To use them in program SKETCH you're going to make two changes. The text beginning with "FOR I := " and ending on the next line with "BEGIN" will be deleted and replaced by the word "REPEAT". The word "END" on the line after MOVETO (X, Y) will be deleted and replaced by the text "UNTIL BUTTON (0)". (That's a zero between parentheses, not an O.) **Use INSERT, DELETE, and ADJUST to change the main BEGIN/END block of your program to look like this:**

```
BEGIN
   INITTURTLE;
   PENCOLOR (WHITE);
   REPEAT
      X := PADDLE (0);
      FOR WAIT := 1 TO 3 DO;
      Y := PADDLE (1);
      MOVETO (X, Y)
   UNTIL BUTTON (0)
END.
```

(If you want to be very tidy, you can also delete "I," from the VAR block, since I is not used anywhere in the new version.)

From the EDITOR, type Q U R and run the new version.

Don't be alarmed when the program runs on and on. How do you stop it? **Try pressing the little button on paddle zero.** What happened? **Type R to run again, and again press button zero. Return to the EDITOR and inspect the program.**

You have changed your main program from a *FOR loop* to a *REPEAT loop*. The FOR loop always results in a predetermined number of repetitions, but the REPEAT loop continues again and again until some stated *condition* comes *true*.

Here's an important item of nomenclature: we refer to *all six lines* of text in your REPEAT loop as forming a *single REPEAT statement*. Remember that in Pascal the division of text into lines is fairly arbitrary. As far as the definition of the language is concerned, a single statement can appear on one line or on many lines. A statement can start in the middle of one text line and continue until the middle of the next. We will *not* commit such stylistic blunders in this book, and you shouldn't either; but the point here is that you will have a much clearer idea of the way Pascal *statements* are defined if you stop thinking about lines of text and start thinking of larger structures.

Note, for example, that the single REPEAT statement in program SKETCH contains four statements *within* it. This concept will come as a surprise to people familiar with languages like Basic or Fortran, where each statement is a thing unto itself. In Pascal, the majority of statements contain other statements. You have now seen two examples: the REPEAT and FOR statements.

Now let's see what the formal definition of the REPEAT statement is. Every grammatically correct REPEAT statement must fit the following format rule:

REPEAT *statement(s)* **UNTIL** *condition*

That is, it begins with the reserved word REPEAT, followed by one or more statements, followed by the reserved word UNTIL, followed by an expression that can be either true or false. If there are several statements in the *body* of a REPEAT statement, they must be separated by semicolons, as usual in Pascal. It is also legal to have no text (except a space of course) between REPEAT and UNTIL; our friend the *null statement* takes care of the legalities in that case. Note here that BEGIN and END are not required around the body of the REPEAT loop, since REPEAT and UNTIL serve the same purpose of bracketing the set of statements in the body.

The following example shows that you can use a REPEAT loop to get the same effect as the FOR loop that you have been using.

```
I := 1;
REPEAT

   (* BODY OF LOOP *)

   I := I + 1
UNTIL I > 2000
```

In this case the *condition*, "I > 2000" is *false* while I is less than 2000 or equal to 2000, but becomes *true* when I reaches 2001. But, by means of the statement before UNTIL, each time through the loop, one is added to the old value of I and the result is assigned back to I. Hence, the body of the loop will be done 2000 times.

Now let's look again at the REPEAT loop in your program SKETCH. The only element that still needs explanation is the phrase BUTTON (0) after UNTIL. According to the grammar rules of the REPEAT statement, the thing that follows UNTIL has a *true* or *false* value. In fact, BUTTON satisfies that requirement.

You've probably guessed that BUTTON, like PADDLE is a *function* that gets *input* and *returns a value*. PADDLE gets input from the rotating knob and returns as a value some *integer* between 0 and 255. BUTTON gets input from the little button switch on the paddle housing, and it returns a value that is either *true* (if the button is being pressed) or *false* (if not pressed).

Since *true* and *false* are not integers, you're probably wondering about the *type* of function BUTTON. It is certainly not *of type integer* is it? In fact, it is a Pascal data type called *boolean* (after George Boole, the great logician). Other languages often call this type *logical*. Don't worry about the name: the important thing to remember about functions and variables of type boolean is that they can only take on values equal to *true* or *false*. The BUTTON function is of type boolean and so is the expression "I > 2000", which you saw earlier in this section. Both can take on only these two values.

So far in your study of Pascal you have found only one kind of statement that uses boolean expressions: the REPEAT statement. In the next session you will meet the IF statement, the Pascal statement that most often uses boolean expressions. Since you will get much more experience there, we'll drop the subject now and return to graphics.

7-4 INVISIBLE LINES AND BACKGROUND COLORS

You may have realized that we are missing an essential graphic tool for drawing pictures. We've seen how to make the turtle draw lines in white, orange, blue, green, and violet. But, how do you move the turtle to a new starting location *without* *drawing a line*? If that capability were lacking, you'd be pretty limited in the kind of drawings you could make. Well, try this experiment.

Edit your program so that the PENCOLOR line looks like this:

```
PENCOLOR (NONE);
```

Run the changed program. Press button zero when you get bored.
You may feel that seeing *nothing* happen is pretty unexciting. (If so, you probably weren't too turned on by the *null statement* either.) But getting nothing to happen is sometimes of critical importance. By using the color value NONE in the PENCOLOR statement you have succeeded in moving the turtle all over the screen without leaving a trace. By alternating between NONE and WHITE, say, you could draw any set of *disconnected* lines. We won't pursue that right now, because it would change the program quite a bit to do so.

Instead, let's see what we can do about the background color. So far it's always been black. **Edit your program so that the main body looks like this:**

```
BEGIN
   INITTURTLE;
   PENCOLOR (BLACK);
   FILLSCREEN (WHITE);
   REPEAT
      X := PADDLE (0);
      FOR WAIT := 1 TO 3 DO;
      Y := PADDLE (1);
      MOVETO (X, Y)
   UNTIL BUTTON (0)
END.
```

There are only two changes. First, you have used a new color, BLACK, for the turtle's pen. Second, you have introduced a new graphic command, FILLSCREEN, with the color WHITE.

Run the new version, exercise the two paddles, and finally quit by pressing button zero. Return to the EDITOR. Change BLACK and WHITE to ORANGE and BLUE, or VIOLET and GREEN, and run again.

Procedure FILLSCREEN obviously does just what its name suggests: it fills the screen between certain boundaries, using whatever color was passed as a parameter to the procedure.

7-5 RANDOM SKETCHING

The combination of *random numbers* with graphics is often quite wonderful to see. In this section you will change two lines of your program and get a significant change of output.

Enter the EDITOR and change the REPEAT loop so that it looks like this:

```
REPEAT
   X := RANDOM MOD 280;
   Y := RANDOM MOD 192;
   MOVETO (X, Y)
UNTIL BUTTON (0)
```

You recall from the last session that the expression "RANDOM MOD N" gives an approximately random integer lying in the range zero to N-1. Thus these changes will result in X getting a random value between zero and 279 and Y getting a random value between zero and 191. Why these particular ranges?

> The numbers 0, 279, 0, and 191 define the extreme left, right, bottom, and top of the visible points on your Apple II screen.

In effect, therefore, this program now picks *random visible points* and draws lines from one to the next. **Run the new version and watch. Press button zero as usual to quit.**

7-6 LOOPS INSIDE OF LOOPS

After running your program for a while, the screen gets pretty well covered with lines. It would be nice to erase and start over without stopping the program. Here's one way to do that:

Return to the EDITOR and change the body of your program to look like this:

```
BEGIN
   INITTURTLE;
   PENCOLOR (WHITE);
   REPEAT
      FILLSCREEN (BLACK);
      REPEAT
         X := RANDOM MOD 280;
         Y := RANDOM MOD 192;
         MOVETO (X, Y)
      UNTIL BUTTON (0)
   UNTIL BUTTON (1)
END.
```

Except for new indentation, the important thing that you have done here is to insert a new REPEAT after PENCOLOR, and a new UNTIL BUTTON (1) before END. In effect, you have now *nested* one REPEAT loop (the old one) inside another REPEAT loop (the new one). The body of the *inner* loop will be repeated until BUTTON (0) has the value *true*, as in the past. The body of the *outer* loop will be repeated until BUTTON (1) is *true*. But the inner loop is part of the body of the outer loop, so the situation is a little subtle.

Think it over a while. Then run this new version. What happens when you press button zero alone? What happens when you press button one alone? What happens when you press both together? Why? **Return to the EDITOR and study the program.**

It's a good strategy in understanding any program to go at it line by line, starting at the top. In this case, the first statement is a call to INITTURTLE. (Don't worry now about what it does.) Next, PENCOLOR sets the pen to WHITE. Next we enter the outer REPEAT loop. Next FILLSCREEN (BLACK) does what its name implies: turns every point on the screen black. Continuing to read down the program text, we enter the inner REPEAT loop. Within that loop, X and Y get random values and the turtle moves to the corresponding point, drawing a line.

The next line of text is UNTIL BUTTON (0), which closes the inner loop. If button zero is not being pressed, then the BUTTON (0) function is *false*, and the inner loop is repeated, adding a new line to the screen. (Note that while the program is in this inner loop, it is not even examining the state of button one, so it won't matter whether or not you press it *at this time*.)

If button zero is pressed, then BUTTON (0) becomes *true* and the inner loop stops looping. We go to the next line of the program and find UNTIL BUTTON (1), which closes the outer loop. If at this particular instant, button one is *not* being pressed, then the *entire outer loop* gets repeated. The first statement in the outer loop is FILLSCREEN (BLACK); so the screen is restored to black, erasing all the lines that were drawn on it previously. The next statement in the outer loop is the *inner* REPEAT statement. So, almost immediately, the program is back in the inner loop, drawing random lines and waiting for button zero to be pressed.

Now you can see why both buttons have to be pressed at the same time to stop the program: button zero has to be pressed to get out of the inner loop. At that instant, button one is examined. If it is being pressed then, the outer loop stops looping and the program ends.

Run the program again and make sure that it behaves the way we said. Then return to the EDITOR.

7-7 A LESSON IN USER-ENGINEERING

From the point of view of the *user* of this program, who may have no idea how it was written, it would have made much better sense if each button had its own unique function, instead of requiring the user to press both buttons at the same time to end the program. A small change will do that.

Go to the EDITOR and insert " OR BUTTON (1)" after "UNTIL BUTTON (0)". The two UNTILs should now look like this

```
UNTIL BUTTON (0) OR BUTTON (1)
UNTIL BUTTON (1)
```

This change requires a little explanation, since it introduces the new word OR. However, its meaning is the same as the common meaning of the English word "or". In the present case the entire expression

```
BUTTON (0) OR BUTTON (1)
```

is *true* if either BUTTON (0) or BUTTON (1) is *true* or if both are *true*. The expression is *false* only if BUTTON (0) and BUTTON (1) are both *false*.

In the present situation, that means that the *inner* loop will quit if either button zero or button one is held down. But the outer loop will quit only if button one is held down. From the point of view of the *user*, therefore, button zero means "erase and start over", while button one means "stop the program". The two buttons *seem* to function independently.

> This kind of careful attention to the way the user sees a program—the so-called "user interface"—is the single most important thing for programmers to learn. It makes the difference between programs that are friendly, forgiving, conversational, and humane and others that are hostile, rigid, obscure, and machine-like.

Run the changed program and confirm the fact that button zero and button one now appear to function independently.

7-8 COUNTING PASCAL STATEMENTS

The present short program gives a good opportunity to deal with a source of confusion about the text of a Pascal program. How many statements do you think there are in the main BEGIN/END block of program SKETCH? Count them now and find out.

That sounds easy, but it really isn't. What does counting mean in the case of a statement such as FILLSCREEN (BLACK) that is part of another statement? In some sense it is fair to say that the program contains only *three* statements: INITTURTLE, PENCOLOR (WHITE), and the outer REPEAT statement. Yet it obviously also contains assignment statements, other procedure calls, and another REPEAT statement. One could count as many as *eight* different statements.

The way out of this confusion is to talk about *levels of detail*. At the outermost level of detail there are only the three statements described above. But one of them, the REPEAT statement, contains two statements within it. Furthermore, the second one of those is another REPEAT statement containing three simple statements within it. In the following listing of the main BEGIN/END block we show a way of talking about the "statement number" of each statement in the program.

```
Line   Statement   Program

A                  BEGIN
B      1               INITTURTLE;
C      2               PENCOLOR (WHITE);
D      3               REPEAT
E      3.1                 FILLSCREEN (BLACK);
F      3.2                 REPEAT
G      3.2.1                   X := RANDOM MOD 280;
H      3.2.2                   Y := RANDOM MOD 192;
I      3.2.3                   MOVETO (X, Y)
J                            UNTIL BUTTON (0)
K                        UNTIL BUTTON (1)
L                  END.
```

At the coarsest level of detail, program SKETCH has three statements, the third of which extends from lines D through K. Looking at it more finely, we see that statement 3 contains two statements, 3.1 and 3.2. Looking at 3.2 more carefully, we find that it contains three statements; 3.2.1, 3.2.2, and 3.2.3. Using this approach you can see, indeed, that SKETCH contains only three statements, but it also contains eight statements.

You should notice that we have always used *indentation* of the text of our programs to call attention to the way that Pascal statements are *nested* within one another. As you become more familiar with statement nesting, you will also discover that you understand when semicolons are required and when they are not needed. For example, line H needs a semicolon to separate statement 3.2.2 from 3.2.3. But line I does *not* need a semicolon since there is no statement 3.2.4. Likewise, line J, which ends statement 3.2, needs no semicolon because there is no statement 3.3; and line K, which ends statement 3, needs no semicolon because there is no statement 4. If you now inserted a statement after line K, it would become statement 4, and you would have to go back to the UNTIL in line K and add a semicolon.

7-9 CONSTANTS

The following statements have appeared in the last several versions of your program:

```
X := RANDOM MOD 280;
Y := RANDOM MOD 192
```

You know what the numbers 280 and 192 mean, because you have just been working with them: 280 is the width of the screen and 192 is the height. But how would these statements look to someone else who was reading your program and who might not be aware that the Apple graphic screen had these dimensions? Or, how would they look to you a few months from now when you may have forgotten the significance of these particular numbers? And, even if you remember them, will you also recognize 140 and 96 as being the middle of the screen? What about 210 and 144? What do they represent? The recognition problem gets much harder in longer programs, which might easily be sprinkled with a mixture of numbers, each with its own meaning in the proper context, but hard to recognize by its literal appearence as a number in a program statement.

There is another important consideration that bears on this issue. Suppose that your program is scattered with literal numbers like 280, 140, 70, 210, etc., all of which derive from the actual width of the screen. Now, suppose you want your existing program to run on a different Pascal computer system which has a screen that can plot 320 or 512 points horizontally. To change your program you would have to read it carefully, locate all of the subtle ways that 280 and its relatives had been included in the text, and then laboriously edit each one to conform to the correct numbers for the new screen width.

What to do? Well, for a start, you could certainly clarify the intent of your program by writing the statements like this:

```
X := RANDOM MOD WIDTH;
Y := RANDOM MOD HEIGHT
```

Substituting the words, WIDTH and HEIGHT, for 280 and 192 makes your meaning vastly clearer than it was. In a longer program that had to make use of the point at the middle of the screen, WIDTH DIV 2 and HEIGHT DIV 2 are much more obvious than the mere numbers, 140 and 96.

Part of the solution to the problem is clear: *it is always better to use meaningful names for things than to use literal numbers.* But how can one do that in Pascal? Well, you already know one way to do that. You could declare WIDTH and HEIGHT in the VAR block as new variables of type integer. That would get the *names* into existence, all right, but it would *not* give any *values* to those names. You would have to take care of that toward the beginning of your BEGIN/END block, probably by means of assignment statements such as these:

```
WIDTH := 280;
HEIGHT := 192
```

prior to the first use of those names elsewhere in the text of the program. Furthermore, you would have to take care that no later statements assigned new values to these variables.

That course of action would be the recommended one indeed, if Pascal did not offer an even better solution. What you really need is something which has two properties: a *meaningful name* and an *unchangeable value*, once it is specified. Such objects are called *constants* in Pascal, and are different in concept from *variables*, which may change in value throughout the program.

Let's include the constants WIDTH and HEIGHT in your present program. **Go to the EDITOR and change your program so that it has the CONST block and changed assignment statements shown below:**

```
PROGRAM SKETCH#

   USES
      TURTLEGRAPHICS, APPLESTUFF#

   CONST
      WIDTH = 280#
      HEIGHT = 192#

   VAR
      X, Y : INTEGER#

BEGIN
   INITTURTLE#
   PENCOLOR (WHITE)#
   REPEAT
      FILLSCREEN (BLACK)#
      REPEAT
         X := RANDOM MOD WIDTH#
         Y := RANDOM MOD HEIGHT#
      MOVETO (X, Y)
      UNTIL BUTTON (0) OR BUTTON (1)
   UNTIL BUTTON (1)
END.
```

Note carefully the grammar and punctuation rules for the CONST block. After the *reserved word* CONST there appears a sequence of phrases of the general form

name = literal-constant semicolon

The *name* is up to you, subject to the usual rules that apply to any Pascal names—i.e., it must start with a letter and be followed by zero or more letters or numeric digits or both. After the name there comes an equal-sign, *not a colon-equal-sign*. This is *not* an assignment operation, but rather a definition of the very meaning of the word. After the equal-sign there must be a *literal constant*. In the case of integer numbers, for example, a literal constant is just the set of characters that you ordinarily use to write the number down on paper. It is *not* grammatically correct to write

```
WIDTH = 140 + 140#
```

since "140 + 140" is *not* a literal constant. Note also, that the *type* of a constant is never declared explicitly. That isn't necessary, after all, since the type is evident by looking at the literal constant: 280 is obviously an integer. Last of all, note that each constant definition always concludes with a semicolon.

So much for the CONST block in the *declaration section* of your program. What about the use of such defined constants? Well, for openers, the name of a constant, once defined, can by used in most places just like the name of a variable. Your program, for example uses WIDTH in the expression

```
RANDOM MOD WIDTH
```

and there is no way to tell, just by inspecting that expression, whether WIDTH is a constant or a variable (or a function, for that matter). The usage rule for named constants is actually a little different than for variables. *The name of a constant can be used anywhere in a program, including the declaration section itself, where the literal constant it stands for would also be allowed.* You will see examples of this in Session 11.

Check the program text carefully, and then run it. There should be no change in its behavior.

To drive home the point about the unchangeability of Pascal constants, let's make one more change. **Go to the EDITOR and insert the following line just before the X assignment statement:**

```
WIDTH := 140;
```

Run the changed version, and note the error message. Then delete the above line.
The reason you got the error message is *exactly* the reason you would get one if you had included the statement

```
280 := 140;
```

That just doesn't make sense and Pascal says so, whether you use a literal constant or a named constant in a nonsensical way. The truth of the matter is that naming a constant is just specifying another way to "spell" the literal constant. In your program, the five characters "W-I-D-T-H" here have *exactly* the same meaning as the three characters "2-8-0". Once given in the CONST block, there was no way to take that meaning back, or to change it in the remainder of the program. That is what a constant is.

The addition of the CONST block brings to five the number of distinct types of blocks that can appear in the declaration section of a Pascal program. They are the USES, CONST, VAR, PROCEDURE, and FUNCTION blocks. All except the USES block may also appear in the declaration section of procedure and function definitions. The first three blocks are similar in that there can be no more than one of each in a program, and the blocks have to appear in that order: USES, then CONST, then VAR. PROCEDURE and FUNCTION blocks, if any, must occur after the other blocks; there may be several of each and they may be intermixed with one another. Later you will learn about a few additional blocks allowed in the declaration section, but the ones you have used thus far are the main ones that you are likely to see in most Pascal programs.

The *scoping rules* for names, which you learned in Session 5, apply also to named constants. If declared in the main program they are known *globally*. Constants declared in a procedure or function are local to it and to all its direct lineal descendents.

7-10 VIEWPORTS

So far, you have been drawing pictures on the whole screen of your TV display. There will be times when you want to limit the picture to a smaller part of the screen. **Return to the EDITOR and add the following line immediately after INITTURTLE:**

```
VIEWPORT (70, 210, 0, 100);
```

Run the changed program.

This experiment shows you how to define limits for your picture. *The numbers (of type integer) in your call to the VIEWPORT procedure define the left, right, bottom, and top of a rectangle on the screen. No graphic output will occur outside that rectangle, called the "viewport", until it is changed. Line segments that cross a viewport boundary are "clipped" so that only the interior part is drawn. FILLSCREEN fills the viewport only. The full dimensions of the screen are achieved by VIEWPORT (0, 279, 0, 191), which is exactly what you get if the program contains no VIEWPORT statement. A program can contain more than one VIEWPORT statement; each one (potentially) redefines the viewport; and there is only a single viewport in effect at one time.*

7-11 TURTLEGRAPHICS AND INITTURTLE

You've undoubtedly been wondering about these words and their meanings. They have been in each of the programs you have written in this session. In order to discover their meanings, let's delete them, one at a time, and see what happens.

Return to the EDITOR. Delete TURTLEGRAPHICS and the comma after it. Run the program.

You got compile-time error 104. **Type E and read the error message at the top of the screen.** Since the cursor is now just to the right of INITTURTLE, that is the word that is being complained about as being an "undeclared identifier".

Remember that in Pascal, all names (identifiers) have to be defined (declared) prior to their first use. Without the word TURTLEGRAPHICS in the USES block, you get the error message; with it, you don't. You saw a similar situation with APPLESTUFF in Session 4. TURTLEGRAPHICS is a special package of graphic routines, stored on APPLE0: in file SYSTEM.LIBRARY. It is there that the names INITTURTLE, FILLSCREEN, VIEWPORT, PENCOLOR, and MOVETO are defined, along with the colors BLACK, WHITE, BLUE, ORANGE, GREEN, VIOLET and NONE. If you leave TURTLEGRAPHICS out of the USES block, then all these names are undefined.

Press the spacebar. Reinsert TURTLEGRAPHICS and the comma. Delete INITTURTLE. Run the program.

You do not get an error this time, but you don't get a picture either. The "RUNNING..." message suggests that all is in order. Is your program running? **Press button one and see whether it stops as it should.**

The INITTURTLE statement is necessary before any other graphic statements are executed. It takes care of *initializing* several things so that future graphic activity will take place properly. Most notably, it sets your TV display into *graphic mode*. When any Pascal program first starts running, the TV display is in *text mode*. When WRITE or WRITELN statements are executed, they output characters which are visible on the screen when in *textmode*. This is because WRITE and WRITELN send their output to what we have been calling the *Pascal page*, the left half of which is normally visible on your screen.

> In fact, there are really two Pascal pages: the *text page* and the *graphic page*. The Apple window looks out at only one or the other, but both exist at the same time. A program can be invisibly outputting text to the text page while the graphic page is visible on the screen, and *vice versa*.

The main thing that INITTURTLE does is to erase the graphic page and to set the Apple window so that it is looking at the graphic page. (In addition, it sets PENCOLOR to NONE, puts the turtle in the center of the graphic page, and sets the viewport to be the full screen.) If INITTURTLE is left out, the program may run correctly, but you will not *see* any graphic output because you are still looking at the text page.

The TURTLEGRAPHICS unit contains two additional procedures that enable you simply to switch the Apple window back and forth between the graphic page and the text page. Neither one changes what is on the pages. The statement

```
TEXTMODE
```

is a procedure call that sets the Apple window to the text page. Likewise, the statement

```
GRAFMODE
```

is a procedure call that sets the window to the graphic page. No parameters are passed to either procedure. We will not explore TEXTMODE or GRAFMODE now, but they will be useful in cases where you need to use both text and graphic output.

Return to the EDITOR and restore INITTURTLE and a semicolon to your program.

7-12 MAKING YOUR OWN GRAPHIC PROCEDURES

The TURTLEGRAPHICS unit defines all the graphic procedures that you have used in this session. The ones you have seen, plus one or two more, are the basic tools you have available for all your graphic tasks. As you have used them you must have gotten the impression that they are quite primitive tools. In fact, people in the computer world would refer to this set of procedures as *the graphic primitives*, meaning that everything else has to be built out of these procedures. Search as you may, you won't find in TURTLEGRAPHICS any procedures for drawing squares, or circles, or graphs, or pie charts. It is up to you to create those procedures yourself.

Your work in Session 5 and 6 showed you a general method for defining and naming your own procedures and functions. In this section you will use that method to create a procedure to draw a rectangle of any size on the screen at any location. Such a procedure might be used, for example as a building block in another graphic program or to box in some text in a program that mixes text with graphics on the graphic page.

Before defining the details of this procedure, let's first agree on a *name* for it and on the data to be *passed* to it that will specify the precise rectangle to be drawn. We'll call the procedure BOX, as a reminder that it will draw a rectangular box. The data to be passed to BOX when it is *called* will have to tell (a) how big the box is and (b) where it is to be drawn. There are many ways to do that. For example, we could pass to BOX the width, height, and location of the lower-left corner (two more numbers). Or else we could pass the location of the lower left and the upper-right corners. Or, we could pass the width, height, and location of the center. Once we decide on the *meaning* of the data to be passed, we must next decide on the *order* in which the four items of data are to appear in the parentheses after BOX in the call statement.

In one sense, it doesn't matter how you decide these questions. Any one of the above specifications will work and is sensible. Despite that fact, *this is not the time to toss a coin or make a thoughtless decision.* Whenever you define a procedure or a function, you are making an *extension to the language*. It is always a good idea to think about the language and to look around for existing linguistic models for what you want to do. If you find one, then make your extension "sound like" or "have the flavor of" words and patterns already present. If you do that, the result will have a natural quality that makes it easy to learn, easy to use, and easy to remember.

It so happens that TURTLEGRAPHICS does indeed have a nice model for your BOX procedure. It is the VIEWPORT procedure, which also specifies a rectangular area on the screen, as you have seen. The four items of data for VIEWPORT are the locations at the left, right, bottom, and top of that rectangle, as measured from the left edge or the bottom edge of the screen in each case. Obviously, you will find it easier to learn, use, and remember the BOX procedure if it uses these same pieces of data in the same order.

Now we turn to the task of *declaring* procedure BOX and specifying the detailed drawing instructions the turtle will need to draw the box. A reasonable set of instructions would be these:

1. Move to the lower-left corner, without drawing a line.

2. Draw a horizontal line to the lower-right corner.

3. Draw a vertical line to the upper right.

4. Draw a horizontal line to the upper left.

5. Draw a vertical line to the lower left.

Here is a direct, line-for-line translation of those instructions from English into TURTLEGRAPHICS primitives:

```
PROCEDURE BOX (L, R, B, T : INTEGER);
   BEGIN
      PENCOLOR (NONE); MOVETO (L, B);
      PENCOLOR (WHITE); MOVETO (R, B);
      MOVETO (R, T);
      MOVETO (L, T);
      MOVETO (L, B);
   END; (* BOX *)
```

Note that once the pen color is set to white, it stays that way; therefore, the last three lines of the BEGIN/END block don't need a PENCOLOR call.

This procedure, like ones you wrote in Session 5, has a *parameter list* with several variables (L, R, B, and T) *declared* as integers. The names are chosen to remind a reader that the order of the parameters must be *left, right, bottom, and top*. In the main body of BOX, these parameter variables are used in the five calls to MOVETO. Look at the first one:

```
MOVETO (L, B);
```

It says, in effect, "Move to the left-hand, bottom point of the rectangle." That is the lower-left corner. The other moves can be understood in the same way.

Go to the EDITOR and insert the PROCEDURE BOX declaration into your program text. Remember to put it after the VAR block.

Now let's use our new word by *calling* BOX in the main program. It would be easy enough to modify the main BEGIN/END block to make your program draw *random rectangles* on the screen. All that is necessary is to select *two* random horizontal positions (one for the left edge and the other for the right) and *two* random vertical positions (for bottom and top). Then, call BOX with these four values.

Below is the complete program. The name has been changed. The VIEWPORT call has been deleted. Variables have been added or changed. The main BEGIN/END block has been changed. **Edit your program to look like this:**

```
PROGRAM BOXES;

  USES
    TURTLEGRAPHICS, APPLESTUFF;

  CONST
    WIDTH = 280;
    HEIGHT = 192;

  VAR
    X1, X2, Y1, Y2 : INTEGER;

  PROCEDURE BOX (L, R, B, T : INTEGER);

    BEGIN
      PENCOLOR (NONE); MOVETO (L, B);
      PENCOLOR (WHITE); MOVETO (R, B);
      MOVETO (R, T);
      MOVETO (L, T);
      MOVETO (L, B)
    END; (* BOX *)

BEGIN
  INITTURTLE;
  PENCOLOR (WHITE);
  REPEAT
    FILLSCREEN (BLACK);
    REPEAT
      X1 := RANDOM MOD WIDTH;
      X2 := RANDOM MOD WIDTH;
      Y1 := RANDOM MOD HEIGHT;
      Y2 := RANDOM MOD HEIGHT;
      BOX (X1, X2, Y1, Y2)
    UNTIL BUTTON (0) OR BUTTON (1)
  UNTIL BUTTON (1)
END.
```

Check the changes carefully. Then run the new program. As before, button zero erases the screen and button one stops the program.

After running the program a few times, you might like to keep a copy of it, under its own name, on your PROGRAM: diskette. You can do that from the EDITOR by using the Q W option. See Section 4–9 for details.

SUMMARY

During this session, you learned the following new things about Pascal:

- **You found that TURTLEGRAPHICS must be declared in the USES block if graphic commands are in a program.**

- **You learned that INITTURTLE must be used in a program before graphic commands to initialize the graphics package.**

- You saw that PENCOLOR is used to set the color of drawings on the screen.

- You used the MOVETO (X, Y) to cause the turtle to draw a line from its present position to the new screen position X and Y.

- You used the REPEAT/UNTIL statement to loop until the condition following UNTIL was true.

- You met a new type of data called boolean which can take on only the two values: true or false.

- You saw that OR can connect two boolean expressions with the same meaning as the English "or".

- You learned that the turtle can be moved from one position on the screen to another without drawing a line by employing PENCOLOR (NONE).

- You found out the difference between a variable and a constant.

- You learned to declare constants in a CONST block, ahead of the VAR block.

- You used the VIEWPORT command to restrict graphic output to a specified part of the graphic page.

- You wrote a graphic procedure.

    The last part of the summary is to update the Pascal vocabulary table.

Table 7.1 Cumulative Pascal vocabulary. New words introduced in this session are printed in boldface. (Code: a = declared in APPLESTUFF; g = declared in TURTLEGRAPHICS)

Reserved Words	Built-In Procedures	Built-In Functions	Other Built-Ins
PROGRAM	WRITE	Boolean	Constants
USES	WRITELN	**a BUTTON**	**g NONE**
CONST	a NOTE		**g WHITE**
VAR	a RANDOMIZE	Integer	**g BLACK**
PROCEDURE	**g FILLSCREEN**	a PADDLE	**g GREEN**
FUNCTION	**g GRAFMODE**	a RANDOM	**g VIOLET**
BEGIN	**g INITTURTLE**		**g ORANGE**
FOR	**g MOVETO**		**g BLUE**
TO	**g PENCOLOR**		
DOWNTO	**g TEXTMODE**		Types
DO	**g VIEWPORT**		**BOOLEAN**
REPEAT			INTEGER
UNTIL			
END			Units
			APPLESTUFF
DIV			**TURTLEGRAPHICS**
MOD			
OR			

QUESTIONS AND PROBLEMS

1. What is meant by a boolean variable? How is it different from an integer variable?

2. What will happen if you attempt to use screen graphics without the INITTURTLE command in your program?

3. Suppose you use the line

        REPEAT UNTIL BUTTON (0);

   in a program. What would its effect be?

4. How is the Apple window switched from the graphic page to the text page? How is it switched back to the graphic page?

5. Can you write on the text screen while looking at the graphic screen?

6. How do you set the background color of the graphic screen?

7. Write a program to generate and display on the screen random integers between 0 and 100. Use button zero to stop the program.

8. Explain why procedure BOX (Section 7–12) works even if R < L or T < B. In these cases, what is the order of the lines drawn by BOX?

9. The problem is to generate rectangles of varying size on the screen. Write a program to draw black rectangles on a white screen. Each time you press button zero, a new rectangle whose size and location is chosen randomly is to be drawn on the screen. Make sure that all such rectangles fit on the screen. Use button one to stop the program.

10. Write a program to draw a tic-tac-toe diagram (black lines on a white screen) in a viewport that occupies the upper right quarter of the screen.

11. Modify program SKETCH (the version in Section 7–9) to draw random black lines on a white screen in a viewport occupying the lower left quarter of the screen. Choose all the random points inside the viewport so that there is no clipping of lines. Use button zero to stop the program.

12. Write a program to draw horizontal white lines on a black screen. The lines are to be started at some random point on the screen and extend to the right a random part of the remaining length to the right edge of the screen. Stop the program with button zero.

13. Write a program to cover a white screen with black grid lines (both horizontal and vertical) spaced 20 screen units apart starting at the lower left corner of the screen.

EIGHT

BRANCHING STATEMENTS: IF AND CASE

You have already met two of Pascal's five *control statements*. In Session 4 you learned to use a FOR statement to control the repeated execution of a simple or compound statement some predetermined number of times. In Session 7 you used a REPEAT statement for a similar purpose, except that the repetition continued until some logical condition became true. The FOR and REPEAT statements provide *loop control* over other statements that make up the *body* of the loop. In Session 9 you will meet the WHILE statement, Pascal's third and final kind of loop control statement.

In this session you will learn about two new statements, IF and CASE, that allow *branching control* over other statements. By using IF and CASE statements you will be able to write a program that does different things under conditions established by the *branching logic* of the program. Without these two new statements, all of your programs would have no choice but to march through all statements in succession, possibly looping back over some or all of them. Very few practical computer programs could be written without using branching control statements.

SESSION GOALS

Your main goal is to understand how to use IF and CASE statements to control execution of various alternative sets of statements in a program. Along the way you will use variables of a new type called CHAR, and will gain further experience with variables and expressions of type BOOLEAN. You will use the built-in READ and READLN procedures to get user input into a running program. You will write a BOOLEAN function. You will learn to use three new graphic procedures.

151

8–1 A SIMPLE TWO-WAY BRANCH

Boot up Pascal. Set the date. Clear out the workfile. Go to the EDITOR/INSERT level and enter the following program:

```
PROGRAM QUESTION#

   VAR
      ANSWER : CHAR#

BEGIN
   WRITE ('IS EVERYBODY HAPPY? ')#
   READLN (ANSWER)#
   WRITELN ('THE ANSWER IS ', ANSWER)
END.
```

CTRL–C out of INSERT mode. Check for typing errors and fix any you find.
This initial program has two new features: a variable of type CHAR, and a call to procedure READLN. The best way to learn their meanings is by experimentation. **Run the program.** You should see

```
RUNNING...
IS EVERYBODY HAPPY?
```

on the screen; then everything halts. What is happening? **Look at the first line in the BEGIN/END block.** You have seen the WRITE statement many times before. It produced the question "IS EVERYBODY HAPPY?" on the screen. The fact that nothing is happening now probably has something to do with the next line—the READLN statement. The name of the procedure implies its function. READ is the opposite of WRITE. If WRITE and WRITELN output information on the screen, then READ and READLN should input information from somewhere. Any ideas where? The most likely candidate at this point *has* to be the keyboard. The variable in the READ parameter is of type CHAR, a new data type which you haven't seen before.
   Let's try a keystroke on the keyboard to see if that will get the program running again. **Press the Y key and then the RETURN key.**
   What happened? You should have seen "THE ANSWER IS Y" written on the screen. At the top of the screen you should see the COMMAND line which indicates that the program has finished running. Our hunch that READLN asks for information from the keyboard seems to be correct since the program finished as soon as you pressed Y and then the RETURN key. **Run the program a few more times, each time typing a response and pressing RETURN.** These experiments show that a call to READLN causes a program halt until the user types something, ending with a RETURN. Then an attempt is made to assign to the variable in the READLN parameter list a value equal to what was typed by the user. In the present case the

variable, ANSWER, was of type CHAR, which is the Pascal abbreviation for *character*. So the *initial* character of the string of characters that the user types is assigned as the value of ANSWER. Finally, the third statement in your program writes the value of ANSWER on the screen. Note that WRITELN accepts parameters of type CHAR as well as INTEGER.

Now that you know how to get user input from the keyboard into a running program, let's see how to use that input to *control* the operation of the program. **Replace the WRITELN line with the five new lines shown below.**

```
BEGIN
   WRITE ('IS EVERYBODY HAPPY? ');
   READLN (ANSWER);
   IF ANSWER = 'Y' THEN
      WRITE ('GOOD ')
   ELSE
      WRITE ('BAD ');
   WRITELN ('NEWS')
END.
```

Note that there is only a single semicolon in the five new lines you added. That means you have added only two Pascal statements. The interesting one begins with the reserved word IF, is four lines long, and contains two other unfamiliar reserved words, THEN and ELSE. Familiar calls to the WRITE procedure follow these two new reserved words. Thus you can see just from the general grammar rules of Pascal that the IF statement contains other statements within it.

We'll come back to this point in a moment. **Now run the program. Type a Y in answer to the question on the screen. Press RETURN.** What happened? Why did it happen?

Well, does the message "GOOD NEWS" make sense in light of the fact that the character "Y" was typed in? Look at the line following READLN (ANSWER). There is a *condition* stated there, and it is "IF ANSWER = 'Y'". The letter you typed in at the keyboard was *assigned* to the variable ANSWER so ANSWER *is* equal to Y. But the statement says that if ANSWER does equal Y THEN what? The next line is the statement WRITE ('GOOD'), which is the source of part of the message you saw on the screen.

So far, so good. If the condition is true, evidence points to the fact that the statement following THEN will be executed. What do you suppose will happen if you type in a character other than Y? Let's find out.

Press R again to run the program. This time, enter N and press the RETURN key. This time you got "BAD NEWS" displayed on the screen and you probably saw this coming. If the condition following IF is true, the statement following THEN is executed. If the condition following IF is false, the statement following ELSE will be executed. The IF/THEN/ELSE structure works exactly the way you would expect it to when you read it.

Note that *either* the statement following THEN was executed *or else* the statement following ELSE was executed, depending upon the condition following IF. But in either situation the statement following the entire IF statement

```
WRITELN ('NEWS')
```

was executed. The IF statement in your program contains two *branches*, only one of which was taken when you ran it. After that branch was completed, the statement after the entire IF statement was executed. That is how the complete message "GOOD NEWS" or "BAD NEWS" was constructed on your screen.

Let's vary the program. **Return to the EDITOR and change the BEGIN/END block to the following:**

```
BEGIN
  WRITE ('IS EVERYBODY HAPPY? ');
  READLN (ANSWER);
  IF ANSWER = 'Y' THEN
    WRITELN ('HOORAY')
END.
```

Note that this time the IF statement contains a THEN branch but lacks an ELSE branch. What will happen when you run it? **Run and see. Type a Y and press RETURN. Run again, this time typing something other than Y. Press RETURN.**

This experiment shows that the IF statement does not need to have an ELSE branch. If the condition "ANSWER = 'Y'" is true, the THEN branch is taken. But if the condition is false, the abbreviated form of the IF statement has no effect at all.

8-2 BOOLEAN VARIABLES AND FUNCTIONS

A very small change in your program will introduce a useful new topic. **Go to the EDITOR and change your program so that it looks like this:**

```
PROGRAM QUESTION;

  VAR
    ANSWER : CHAR;
    YES : BOOLEAN;

BEGIN
  WRITE ('IS EVERYBODY HAPPY? ');
  READLN (ANSWER);
  YES := ANSWER = 'Y';
  IF YES THEN
    WRITELN ('HOORAY')
END.
```

You have added a new variable whose name is YES and whose type is BOOLEAN. In the BEGIN/END block, YES is assigned the value ANSWER = 'Y'. What value is that? **Run the program and find out.**

Did it surprise you that this version of QUESTION behaved exactly as before? What you have found out here is that "ANSWER = 'Y'" is a legal expression, that it has a value of some kind, and that you can assign it to the variable YES. Since you didn't get a "type conflict" error, that must mean that the expression also is of type

BOOLEAN. As you recall from your experience with the BUTTON function, there are only two BOOLEAN values: *true* and *false*. Thus YES is assigned the value *true* if ANSWER = 'Y' and the value *false* otherwise. The name of your program points up one big difference between the := symbol and the = symbol. The := symbol always means to *assign a value* to a variable. The = symbol is used here to *compare* two values. It is the result of that comparison that gets assigned to YES.

From there on everything should be fairly clear. The behavior of the IF statement depends only upon the value of YES. If *true*, the THEN branch is taken and HOORAY appears on the screen. If *false*, nothing happens.

The example you have seen here is slightly artificial, but you should recognize that the ability to assign a BOOLEAN value to a named variable means that you can write procedures that operate on these variables without knowing what their values are. You can also pass BOOLEAN values as parameters to a function or procedure. Perhaps the most common occurrence of named BOOLEAN objects, however, is BOOLEAN-valued functions, such as BUTTON. The following change in your program shows how you might define your own BOOLEAN function.

```
PROGRAM QUESTION;

  FUNCTION YES : BOOLEAN;
    VAR
      ANSWER : CHAR;
    BEGIN
      READLN (ANSWER);
      IF ANSWER = 'Y' THEN
        YES := TRUE
      ELSE
        YES := FALSE
    END; (* YES *)

BEGIN
  WRITE ('IS EVERYBODY HAPPY? ');
  IF YES THEN
    WRITELN ('HOORAY')
END.
```

The main change here has been to convert YES from a variable into a function. When YES is referred to in the main BEGIN/END block, the result is a *call* to the function. The first thing the function does is to call READLN and receive keyboard input. Note that the variable ANSWER is now local to function YES, since the main program no longer has need to know about it. Next the function compares ANSWER to 'Y'. If equal, then YES returns the value TRUE; if not, YES returns the value FALSE. Note that TRUE and FALSE are the "standard spellings" of the two values that BOOLEAN data can have. Thus, TRUE and FALSE are *constants* of type BOOLEAN, just as 'Y' is a constant of type CHAR, and 24 is a constant of type INTEGER.

Go to the EDITOR and make the above changes to your program. Run it a few

times. The fact that it works the same as before shows that your BOOLEAN function is doing exactly what we said above.

This example of BOOLEAN functions is fairly typical of their use in other situations. Notice that the function does more than just return a true or false value. It also performs the input from the keyboard. A more complete version of function YES would also verify that ANSWER was equal to either 'Y' or 'N' and, if not, prompt the user to type one or the other. Then it would repeat the verification. Thus, when the main program calls YES it is both enacting an input procedure and also determining which of two possible situations occurred. That is a characteristic use of BOOLEAN functions.

8-3 READ AND READLN

Run the program for each of the keyboard inputs listed below. In each case, watch what happens in response to your input.

```
YES
YOOHOO
NO
NUBILE
spacebar
WHOOPEE!
```

Now let's review what happened. You saw that Y, YES, and YOOHOO caused HOORAY to be written out. Only the first character of the input is assigned to the variable ANSWER. *Anything* beginning with Y results in Y being assigned to ANSWER, which in turn causes HOORAY to be printed out. Anything *other* than input beginning with a Y will cause nothing to be displayed.

Go back to the EDITOR and delete the LN in the READLN statement. Leave the EDITOR and run the program. After the message IS EVERYBODY HAPPY?, press the Y key but not the RETURN. What happened? The point of interest here is whether or not the RETURN key is required after a character is typed in.

Run the program again, but this time type the letters R F D in quick succession, but again don't press the RETURN key.

Well how did you wind up in the date-setting facility? It's simple. If you were watching the screen you saw that as soon as you pressed R, the program decided that ANSWER was *not* equal to Y, and it ended. The computer went back to the COMMAND mode and looked for further instructions. Recall that the computer stores up commands when more than one letter is pressed in succession. Of course the next letter you typed in was F, which called the FILER. Then the D moved you into the date-setting facility. This another of the **user traps** that you can stumble into occasionally.

Press RETURN and Q to get back to the COMMAND level.

Changing READLN to READ had two effects. First, the program started running again as soon as you typed a single character. Second, since you did not type a

RETURN, the text on your screen at the end of the run looked like this

       IS EVERYBODY HAPPY? YHOORAY

when you typed a Y in response to the question. If you want "HOORAY" to appear on the next line, you will have to make the program itself output a RETURN immediately after the input. **Change the READ line in function YES as follows:**

      `READ (ANSWER)# WRITELN#`

Run again and type a Y. This time "HOORAY" should have appeared on the next line.

8-4 THE SEMICOLON BUG

Change the main BEGIN/END block as follows:


```
BEGIN
   WRITE ('IS EVERYBODY HAPPY? ')#
   IF YES THEN#
     WRITELN ('HOORAY')
END.
```


Run it. Type Y. Run again. Type N. Why did the insertion of the semicolon after THEN cause "HOORAY" to be written on the screen no matter what you typed in response to the question?

    The explanation here is quite simple. Adding the semicolon after THEN had the effects of signaling the end of the IF statement and of removing the final WRITELN call from the body of the IF. Since it is now outside the IF statement, it is carried out *every* time, regardless of what the user typed in answer to the question.

    What, then, is the IF statement doing now? The complete statement looks like this

      `IF YES THEN#`

This may not seem to agree with the form of the abbreviated IF statement:

IF *condition* **THEN** *statement*

since there doesn't seem to be a statement after THEN. But there is, of course, and it is our friend the *null statement*, which you met in Session 4. The upshot of this experiment is that the accidental insertion of a semicolon after THEN does *not* always lead to a compile time error, but it *does* change the logic of the program.

Watch carefully for extra semicolons within your IF statements.

In the present example, the null statement is executed if YES is *true* and not executed otherwise. (There is no practical difference, of course, since the null statement doesn't do anything.) But in either case, program execution continues with the final WRITELN ('HOORAY') call, now no longer a part of the IF statement.

It will help you to avoid dropping needless semicolons into IF statements if you recognize that the *reserved words* THEN and ELSE, like BEGIN, END, REPEAT, and UNTIL, act just like punctuation marks themselves. Extra punctuation is never needed immediately before or immediately after THEN or ELSE. If you find a semicolon so situated, remove it.

8-5 NESTED IF STATEMENTS

You have seen how an IF statement creates a two-way branch in a program, each branch of which is a Pascal statement. So far the branch statements have always been WRITE or WRITELN procedure calls, but they might have been any Pascal statement, simple or compound. One particularly interesting branch statement would be another IF statement. The following version of program QUESTION shows such an example of one IF statement nested within another.

```
PROGRAM QUESTION;

VAR
   WEEKDAY, RAINY : BOOLEAN;

FUNCTION YES : BOOLEAN;
   VAR
     ANSWER : CHAR;
   BEGIN
     READ (ANSWER); WRITELN;
     IF ANSWER = 'Y' THEN
       YES := TRUE
     ELSE
       YES := FALSE
   END; (* YES *)

BEGIN
   WRITE ('IS TODAY A WEEKDAY? ');
   WEEKDAY := YES;
   WRITE ('IS IT RAINING? ');
   RAINY := YES;
   IF WEEKDAY THEN
     IF RAINY THEN
       WRITELN ('DRIVE TO WORK')
     ELSE
       WRITELN ('WALK TO WORK')
   ELSE
     IF RAINY THEN
       WRITELN ('GO TO MUSEUM')
     ELSE
       WRITELN ('PLAY TENNIS')
END.
```

Notice that the outer IF statement contains a THEN branch and an ELSE branch. The THEN branch is a simple IF statement, also containing THEN and ELSE branches. Likewise, the outer ELSE branch is another simple IF statement with THEN and ELSE branches. The net result is a *four-way branch* that depends upon the combined BOOLEAN values of WEEKDAY and RAINY.

Make the above changes in your program. Run it several times, typing in all four combinations of Y/N responses to the two questions.

If you have any doubts about how each pair of inputs generates its own output, you should study the main IF statement and run the program again. Note that the indentation scheme used in the program text helps to clarify the nesting of the IF statements. Each ELSE is indented the same amount as the IF that it goes with. To get the meaning of any particular ELSE, all that you have to do is look directly above it to the IF that has the same indentation. For example, the first ELSE in the main BEGIN/END block goes with IF RAINY; so it means IF NOT RAINY. The second ELSE goes with IF WEEKDAY and means IF NOT WEEKDAY.

Another thing to notice here is the lack of semicolons in the ten lines containing the main IF statement. None is needed or permitted because the THEN branch and the ELSE branch each consist of a single simple statement; namely, an IF statement. Likewise, the branches of each of the inner IF statements are simple WRITELN statements. Since there are only simple statements, no semicolon separators are needed.

8-6 THE ABBREVIATED-IF BUG

You saw at the end of Section 8–1 that it is legal to have an IF statement with only a THEN branch. While such abbreviated IF statements are very useful and are common in practical programs, they are also a frequent source of a nasty bug that can be hard to decipher. We'll lead you into this trap slowly so that you can see how it happens.

Go to the EDITOR and comment out the outer ELSE branch of the IF statement in your main program. It should look like this:

```
IF WEEKDAY THEN
  IF RAINY THEN
    WRITELN ('DRIVE TO WORK')
  ELSE
    WRITELN ('WALK TO WORK')
(* ELSE
  IF RAINY THEN
    WRITELN ('GO TO MUSEUM')
  ELSE
    WRITELN ('PLAY TENNIS') *)
```

Run the program four times, testing all combinations of Y and N responses to the two questions. Were there any surprises?

Next, remove the opening comment bracket from the outer ELSE line and place it in front of the inner ELSE in the next to last line of the main IF statement. Your outer ELSE branch should now look like this:

```
ELSE
  IF RAINY THEN
    WRITELN ('GO TO MUSEUM')
  (* ELSE
    WRITELN ('PLAY TENNIS') *)
```

Run it four times, testing all Y/N combinations. As before, there should be no surprises with this abbreviated IF statement. Three of the combinations (YY, YN, NY) give appropriate messages, while the fourth (NN) gives no message, since the corresponding ELSE branch has been commented out.

Delete both comment brackets. Now actually delete the ELSE branch that is inside the outer THEN branch. Your IF statement should look like this:

```
IF WEEKDAY THEN
   IF RAINY THEN
      WRITELN ('DRIVE TO WORK')
ELSE
   IF RAINY THEN
      WRITELN ('GO TO MUSEUM')
   ELSE
      WRITELN ('PLAY TENNIS')
```

Run it and test all four Y/N response combinations. Any surprises this time? The YY response should have been okay: you should have seen the rainy weekday message "DRIVE TO WORK". But the YN response probably surprised you. You deleted the branch for a weekday with no rain, so you probably expected to get *no* message at all. Instead you got the sunny weekend message, "PLAY TENNIS", which makes no sense for a weekday. The other two response pairs, NY and NN, were probably just as puzzling, since they *caused no* message to appear. *Why was the main ELSE branch missed?* Surely it is right there in your program text. What is going on?

The phenomenon you have discovered here is the famous Pascal abbreviated-IF bug, and it is a real puzzler the first time you encounter it. The problem comes from a built-in *ambiguity* of the language. You interpreted the five-line ELSE branch as belonging to the *outer* IF WEEKDAY statement. But you *could have* interpreted that same ELSE branch as belonging to the *inner* IF RAINY statement. Your indentation suggests that you wanted the first interpretation to be true; but recall that Pascal pays no attention to your indentation scheme. In fact, by changing *only* the indentation, you could arrive at a program text that suggests the second interpretation:

```
IF WEEKDAY THEN
   IF RAINY THEN
      WRITELN ('DRIVE TO WORK')
   ELSE
      IF RAINY THEN
         WRITELN ('GO TO MUSEUM')
      ELSE
         WRITELN ('PLAY TENNIS')
```

In fact, your experiment proved that the Pascal compiler chose this second interpretation over the first one. It associated the five-line ELSE branch with the *immediately preceding* IF statement.

> The Pascal compiler *always* associates an ELSE branch with the immediately preceding *open* IF statement. If you do not want that association, then you must *close* the immediately preceding IF statement.

Let's see how to *close* the IF RAINY statement so that the ambiguous ELSE branch will be associated with the outer IF WEEKDAY statement. You already know one way to close a statement: end it with a semicolon. Let's try that. **Insert a semicolon after the inner IF RAINY statement.** The first three lines of the IF WEEKDAY statement should look like this:

```
IF WEEKDAY THEN
  IF RAINY THEN
    WRITELN ('DRIVE TO WORK');
```

Run this version. Bad news. It looks as though the semicolon is a case of overkill. It not only closed out the inner IF RAINY statement, it also closed out the outer IF WEEKDAY statement. Then the compiler got into trouble when it tried to interpret ELSE as the *beginning* of the next statement, which is illegal. That is why you got the compile-time error message at that point. Note that the error message is not at all helpful.

Return to the EDITOR and delete the semicolon. That stategy did not work. We need a more limited way to close the inner IF without closing the outer one at the same time. If we could simply *bracket* the inner IF, that might do the trick. Since Pascal has the bracketing words BEGIN and END, let's try the following strategy.

Bracket the entire IF RAINY statement between the words BEGIN and END. Your text should look like this now:

```
IF WEEKDAY THEN
  BEGIN
    IF RAINY THEN
      WRITELN ('DRIVE TO WORK')
  END
ELSE
  IF RAINY THEN
    WRITELN ('GO TO MUSEUM')
  ELSE
    WRITELN ('PLAY TENNIS')
```

Run the new version and test out all four Y/N combinations. Your results should prove that the bracketing strategy was successful. The five-line ELSE branch was associated with the outer IF WEEKDAY statement because the BEGIN/END brackets closed off the inner IF RAINY statement.

For completeness you should know about one other way to close an abbreviated IF statement in ambiguous situations like this. **Go to the EDITOR. Delete the BEGIN and change END to ELSE.** Your IF WEEKDAY statement should now look like this:

```
IF WEEKDAY THEN
   IF RAINY THEN
      WRITELN ('DRIVE TO WORK')
   ELSE
ELSE
   IF RAINY THEN
      WRITELN ('GO TO MUSEUM')
   ELSE
      WRITELN ('PLAY TENNIS')
```

Run this version and confirm that it behaves exactly like the previous one.
Here is how the extra ELSE worked. When the compiler reached it, it closed out the immediately preceding open IF statement, which was the IF RAINY, by encoding a null ELSE branch for it. When the compiler reached the second ELSE, it correctly associated the following branch with the immediately preceding *open* IF statement, which at that point was the IF WEEKDAY statement.

Which of these two methods is best? It is largely a matter of taste and you will find both in common use. We prefer the BEGIN/END brackets because the intent of the programmer seems clearer. Using null branches strikes us as being tricky and obscure.

Finally, you should note that this particular logic bug arises only when you use a single abbreviated IF statement as the THEN branch of an outer IF statement. If the THEN branch contains an abbreviated IF and even one additional statement, then you will need BEGIN/END brackets around them anyway and the problem goes away. You also saw that there was no problem using an abbreviated IF statement as the ELSE branch of an outer IF. So the bug does not happen very often, which is probably why the results are so surprising when it does happen.

8-7 ANOTHER APPROACH TO MULTIWAY BRANCHES

You have seen that under certain unusual circumstances nested IF statements can get you into trouble. In fact, most people seem to have a hard time interpreting the meaning of nested IF statements, especially as the nesting gets deeper. Sometimes you can clarify the branching logic of a program by using the IF statement in a different way.

Go to the EDITOR and change your BEGIN/END block to look like this:

```
BEGIN
  WRITE ('IS TODAY A WEEKDAY? ');
  WEEKDAY := YES;
  WRITE ('IS IT RAINING? ');
  RAINY := YES;
  IF WEEKDAY AND RAINY THEN
    WRITELN ('DRIVE TO WORK')
  ELSE
    IF WEEKDAY AND NOT RAINY THEN
      WRITELN ('WALK TO WORK')
    ELSE
      IF NOT WEEKDAY AND RAINY THEN
        WRITELN ('GO TO MUSEUM')
      ELSE
        WRITELN ('PLAY TENNIS')
END.
```

Note that we have introduced two new reserved words: AND and NOT. "WEEKDAY AND RAINY" is a BOOLEAN expression. Its value is TRUE if both WEEKDAY *and* RAINY are TRUE; its value is FALSE if either or both are FALSE. The point you should note here is that the logic of the first THEN branch is now easier to follow than before: WEEKDAY and RAINY both have to be TRUE in order to get the message "DRIVE TO WORK". If either or both are FALSE, then the ELSE branch is taken.

The ELSE branch is another IF statement. The condition this time is "WEEKDAY AND NOT RAINY". The phrase "NOT RAINY" is a BOOLEAN expression that is TRUE when RAINY is FALSE and FALSE when RAINY is TRUE. It follows from this that "WEEKDAY AND NOT RAINY" is TRUE *only if* WEEKDAY is TRUE and RAINY is FALSE. In that case the THEN branch is taken and we get the message "WALK TO WORK". Otherwise the next ELSE branch is taken.

There we find another IF statement with condition "NOT WEEKDAY AND RAINY". Note here that NOT goes with WEEKDAY and not with the whole expression "WEEKDAY AND RAINY". That is, the condition "NOT WEEKDAY AND RAINY" is TRUE *only if* WEEKDAY is FALSE and RAINY is true. In that case the THEN branch is taken and we get the message "GO TO MUSEUM". Otherwise we get to the final ELSE branch.

A look at the previous steps will show that the only way the program could have reached the final ELSE branch is for the expression "NOT WEEKDAY AND NOT RAINY" to be TRUE. So no additional IF statement is needed this time. Instead, the ELSE branch simply writes the message "PLAY TENNIS".

Run the program and confirm that it works as advertised.

You may have noticed that the logic of this version of your program really breaks down into four successive cases. This fact would be somewhat clearer if we adopted a special *formatting convention* for situations in which each ELSE branch is a simple IF statement. **Change your IF statement as follows:**

```
IF WEEKDAY AND RAINY THEN
    WRITELN ('DRIVE TO WORK')
ELSE IF WEEKDAY AND NOT RAINY THEN
    WRITELN ('WALK TO WORK')
ELSE IF NOT WEEKDAY AND RAINY THEN
    WRITELN ('GO TO MUSEUM')
ELSE
    WRITELN ('PLAY TENNIS')
END.
```

In a situation like this each ELSE has the meaning "take this branch if *none* of the preceding conditions is true."

8-8 GRAMMAR RULES FOR THE IF STATEMENT

Now is a good time to summarize what you have learned about the IF statement. The general form of the IF statement is the following:

IF *condition* **THEN** *statement1* **ELSE** *statement2*

The words IF, THEN, and ELSE are reserved words. The *condition* is any word or expression that has a value equal to TRUE or FALSE. In other words, it is any expression of type BOOLEAN. *Statement1* and *statement2* may be any legal Pascal statement of any kind, including assignment statements, procedure calls, the FOR, REPEAT, and WHILE statements and even an IF or CASE statement. *Statement1* or *statement2* can be either a simple statement or a compound statement, bracketed as usual by BEGIN and END, or a null statement.

Note especially that THEN and ELSE act like punctuation marks in the structure of the IF statement, separating the *condition*, *statement1*, and *statement2* from one another.

For that reason it is always incorrect to place a semicolon immediately before or after THEN or ELSE.

The only place a semicolon may be required within an IF statement is inside a compound statement, if a compound statement is present in the IF statement. Any other semicolon will signal the end of the IF statement, and the compiler will try to interpret the word following the semicolon as the start of a new statement outside the IF statement.

The meaning of the IF statement is fairly direct. If the *condition* is true then *statement1* is executed. If it is false, *statement2* is executed.

The IF statement has an abbreviated form:

IF *condition* **THEN** *statement*

It means that if the *condition* is true then the *statement* is performed. If it is false nothing happens.

As you have seen, the abbreviated form of the IF statement contains a potential **user trap** that is very hard to detect. If you use an abbreviated IF statement as the THEN branch of another IF statement that also has an ELSE branch, then you have an ambiguous situation. Does the ELSE branch belong to the inner IF statement or to the outer IF statement? The compiler resolves the ambiguity by always associating an ELSE branch with the innermost open IF statement when one IF is nested within another. If that interpretation is not the one you intended, then you are in trouble. Furthermore, you get no warning. The following rule will keep you out of trouble.

> If you nest an abbreviated IF statement inside the THEN branch of another IF statement, bracket the entire inner IF statement between BEGIN and END.

This is how such a nested IF statement should look:

```
IF condition1 THEN
   BEGIN
      IF condition2 THEN
         statement1
   END
ELSE
   statement2
```

By this arrangement you will connect the ELSE branch unambiguously with the outer IF statement.

8-9 THE READ AND READLN PROBLEM

We will turn soon to the CASE statement, the other *branching control* statement available in Pascal; but we do so in stages. **Clear out your workfile and enter the following new program.**

```
PROGRAM CALCULATOR;

  VAR
    A, B : INTEGER;
    OPERATION : CHAR;

BEGIN
  REPEAT
    READLN (A, OPERATION, B);
    IF OPERATION = '+' THEN
      WRITELN (A + B)
    ELSE IF OPERATION = '-' THEN
      WRITELN (A - B)
    ELSE IF OPERATION = '*' THEN
      WRITELN (A * B)
    ELSE IF OPERATION = '/' THEN
      WRITELN (A / B)
  UNTIL FALSE
END.
```

Note that the program runs in an *infinite loop*. Since FALSE is a constant and can *never* be equal to TRUE, the REPEAT loop will go on forever. How can the program be stopped? In just a while you will see.

Within the REPEAT loop, the first statement is a call to READLN with parameter variables A, OPERATION, and B. A and B are integers and OPERATION is a character. The rest of the loop is one long IF statement containing a THEN branch and three ELSE IF/THEN branches. As you saw in Section 8-7, this type of structure defines a set of separate cases. Which case is executed depends upon the character value of OPERATION.

Run the program. When it halts, type 2+3. Do not include spaces. Press RETURN. Then type 8–5 and press RETURN. Try 8X9 and RETURN. Try 8*9 and RETURN, and 15/2 and RETURN.

Your program behaves like a simple four-function calculator, and you should be able to see fairly clearly how it works. The READLN procedure reads characters as the user types them on the keyboard. It interprets the first character(s) as the digit(s) of an integer. When it finds a character that is not a digit, it stops processing the integer and assigns it to the variable A. Next it assigns the nondigit character to OPERATION. Then it interprets the next character(s) as digit(s) of another integer. That process stops when a nondigit is typed or when RETURN is pressed, and the resulting integer value is assigned to B. After the RETURN is pressed the program halt (caused by READLN) ends.

The IF statement making up the rest of the REPEAT loop then decides which of the four cases to carry out, depending upon the value of OPERATION. The actual arithmetic takes place inside the WRITELN parameter list. The symbols +, −, *, and / are used by Pascal to stand for addition, subtraction, multiplication, and division. Nothing happened when you typed 8X9 because there was no case corresponding to OPERATION = 'X'.

If you followed the directions above, then your program is still running, waiting for more input. How can you stop it? There are several ways, but this is the most direct, dependable one: **Hold down the CTRL key and the SHIFT key at the same time while pressing the P key.** We will call this operation CTRL-SHIFT-P or CTRL-@, since @ is the same as SHIFT-P.) You should see the following message on your screen:

```
PROGRAM INTERRUPTED BY USER
S# 0, P# 7, I# 310
TYPE <SPACE> TO CONTINUE
```

Don't worry about the numbers on the second line. They indicate where in your program the interruption occurred. **Now press the spacebar.** You should see the screen clear, hear disk activity, and see the message

```
SYSTEM REINITIALIZED
```

quickly followed by the appearance of the COMMAND prompt line.

CTRL-@ is one of those system commands, like CTRL-A, CTRL-S, and CTRL-Z, that can be typed at any level of the system, at any time. CTRL-@ always causes a fatal halt of any process, including system processes. When you then press the spacebar the system does a "warm reboot", equivalent to what it does when you insert APPLE0: and press RESET during the regular boot-up procedure. CTRL-@ is also equivalent to the I(NITIALIZE command, which can only be used at COMMAND level.

Run your program again. This time type 3 * 4, including a space after the 3. Notice that as soon as you typed the asterisk the program halted with this message:

```
IO ERROR: BAD INPUT FORMAT
S# 1, P#1, I# 30
TYPE <SPACE> TO CONTINUE
```

Press the spacebar. Again the system does a warm reboot. The inclusion of an innocuous space character in the user input caused a fatal error. Why? Here is the story. The arrival of the space character signaled the end of the first integer. So A received the value 3. Then OPERATION received the value ' '. Finally, the READLN procedure was ready to receive numeric digits for B. Instead, the next character typed was an asterisk, which is not legal as part of an integer: hence the BAD INPUT FORMAT complaint.

As a programmer you need to be aware of the fact that READ and READLN can cause fatal errors when used with numeric variables. In fact, the only completely safe way to get input from a user is by using READ with a variable of type CHAR. Practical Pascal programs intended for general use will contain quite long and complex procedures to get user input one character at a time and to attempt to convert it to numbers or strings. Such procedures must take care of input format errors without bringing the program to a halt. We will not go into detail here, but will leave the subject with the following warning:

> Never use READ or READLN with numeric parameters in any program intended for use by other people.

Since your current program is just for your own use, leave the READLN statement as is; but type input responses carefully and do not include spaces.

8-10 THE CASE STATEMENT

In the previous section you got no response when you typed 8X9 because the program didn't recognize X as a legal operation. You can change the program to allow X as a synonym for *. **Go to the EDITOR and change the second ELSE IF line as follows:**

```
ELSE IF (OPERATION = 'X') OR (OPERATION = 'X') THEN
```

Note that parentheses are needed when OR or AND are used between expressions involving *relational operations* (=, >, <, >=, <=, <>). **Run the program and press RETURN. Type 9×8 and press RETURN.** Having taken care of that problem, let's turn now to the general structure of the program. As you have seen, it amounts to a set of four separate *cases*. Each case is discrete and no case overlaps with any other. Whenever you have such a situation, you should see whether a CASE statement can be used to better effect than an IF statement. You can do so in program CALCULATOR. **Halt the program via CTRL-SHIFT-P. Go to the EDITOR. Make the following change to the REPEAT statement:**

```
REPEAT
  READLN (A, OPERATION, B);
  CASE OPERATION OF
    '+': WRITELN (A + B);
    '-': WRITELN (A - B);
    '*', 'X': WRITELN (A * B);
    '/': WRITELN (A / B)
  END (* CASE *)
UNTIL FALSE
```

Note that each WRITELN statement is preceded by one or more constants of type CHAR and a colon. Each WRITELN statement is followed by a semicolon, except the last, which is followed by END. This whole object, beginning with CASE and ending with END, is a single CASE statement. **Run the new version and confirm that it works as before. Try typing 8,9 and RETURN.**

The CASE statement is usually preferable to the IF statement when you have simple, discrete cases. The CASE statement is more compact, clearer, and usually more efficient.

8–11 GRAMMAR RULES FOR THE CASE STATEMENT

The CASE statement always has the following general form:

CASE *expression* **OF** *case-list* **END**

Expression stands for anything that has an INTEGER, CHAR, or BOOLEAN value. (In Session 11 we will extend this set of types.) *Expression* can be the name of a variable, a function, a constant, or an arithmetic expression, among other things. *Case-list* stands for a list of items, separated from one another by semicolons, with each item having the following form:

label-list : *statement*

Label-list stands for one or more constants of the same type as the *expression* above. If there are several constants, they must be separated by commas. *Statement* stands for any Pascal statement, whether simple, compound, or null. As usual, a compound statement needs to be bracketed by BEGIN and END.

The first thing that happens when a CASE statement is executed is that the *expression* is evaluated. Next, a match is looked for between the resulting value and one of the constants in one of the *label-lists*. If no match is found nothing happens. If a match is found, the corresponding *statement* is executed.

It is illegal for the same constant to appear in two *label-lists*. The compiler detects this situation and reports an error. Note that only *constants* may be used in *label-lists*. Variables, functions, and expressions are illegal. This fact limits the use of the CASE statement to situations in which exact matches occur.

Use CTRL–SHIFT–P to stop your program.

8–12 A GRAPHIC APPLICATION

Now let's apply the CASE statement to a graphic application. **Clear out the workfile. Enter the following program.**

```
PROGRAM DRIVER;

USES
    TURTLEGRAPHICS, APPLESTUFF;

VAR
    CH : CHAR;

BEGIN
    INITTURTLE;
    PENCOLOR (WHITE);
    REPEAT
        REPEAT
            MOVE (1)
        UNTIL KEYPRESS;
        READ (CH);
        CASE CH OF
            'L': TURN (90);
            'R': TURN (-90)
        END (* CASE *)
    UNTIL CH = 'Q'
END.
```

This program has several familiar features as well as some new ones. At the coarsest level of detail the BEGIN/END block contains three statements. INITTURTLE does graphic initializations, putting the turtle in the center of the screen headed to the right. PENCOLOR (WHITE) enables drawing with a white pen. The third statement is a REPEAT loop that exits if CH equals 'Q'.

Within the REPEAT loop is another REPEAT loop that exits if something called KEYPRESS becomes TRUE. Since you didn't declare KEYPRESS, you've probably guessed correctly that it is a BOOLEAN function defined in an external unit—APPLESTUFF in this case. KEYPRESS is normally false. It becomes true whenever a key on the Apple keyboard is pressed. It goes to false again if you READ the keyboard.

As soon as the inner REPEAT loop is exited, the program executes a READ (CH) call, which inputs the character that was typed when KEYPRESS became true. Finally, the value of CH is used to decide which of the cases to execute in the CASE statement. If CH = 'L' then TURN (90) is executed. If CH = 'R' then TURN (-90) is executed. (Any other value of CH causes nothing to happen.) The statement TURN (90) makes the turtle do a 90 degree left turn away from its current heading. TURN (-90) is a 90 degree right turn. So typing L causes a left turn, and typing R causes a right turn. At that point the outer REPEAT loop occurs (unless the user has typed a Q) and the program is quickly back in the inner REPEAT loop.

Run the program. While it is compiling, get your fingers positioned over the L and R keys. As soon as you see a line being drawn on the screen press the L key a few times. Now press the R key a few times. If the turtle gets off the screen, type Q and run again.

As you have seen, the MOVE (1) graphic procedure call has the effect of moving the turtle *forward* one screen unit in whatever direction the turtle is headed. The screen, you recall, is 280 units wide and 192 units high. The MOVETO (X, Y) procedure also causes the turtle to move, but not necessarily in the direction it is headed. MOVETO (X, Y) does an "absolute move" from the turtle's current position to a new one X screen units from the left edge and Y screen units from the bottom. MOVE (N) does a "relative move" of N screen units in the direction the turtle is currently headed. Neither MOVETO nor MOVE affects the heading of the turtle. The TURN procedure does that, as you have seen. TURN (D) turns the turtle D degrees to the left (counterclockwise) from its current heading.

There is also a TURNTO procedure, and it is an "absolute turn" to a specific heading. The following modifications to your CASE statement incorporate calls to TURNTO.

```
CASE CH OF
    'R': TURNTO (135);
    'T': TURNTO (90);
    'Y': TURNTO (45);
    'F': TURNTO (180);
    'H': TURNTO (0);
    'V': TURNTO (-135);
    'B': TURNTO (-90);
    'N': TURNTO (-45)
END (* CASE *)
```

Note that the eight letters chosen here as *case labels* form a sort of square around the G key. The key to the right of it is H, and the corresponding case in the CASE statement says TURNTO (0). In fact a TURNTO of zero degrees corresponds to a heading to the right. TURNTO (90) means an upwards heading, and you see indeed that the T key is above the center G key. In general, the direction of each key away from the center key tells the direction you want the turtle to be headed.

Enter this new version of the CASE statement and run the program. Use the eight new keys to control the absolute heading of the turtle.

If you're having trouble controlling things, you can slow the process down a bit by putting a wait loop inside the inner REPEAT loop. **Change the REPEAT loop as follows:**

```
REPEAT
   MOVE (1);
   FOR WAIT := 1 TO 100 DO
UNTIL KEYPRESS;
```

Be sure to add WAIT to your VAR block.

The final form of program DRIVER is shown below:

```
PROGRAM DRIVER;

   USES
      TURTLEGRAPHICS, APPLESTUFF;

   VAR
      CH : CHAR;
      WAIT : INTEGER;

BEGIN
   INITTURTLE;
   PENCOLOR (WHITE);
   REPEAT
      REPEAT
         MOVE (1);
         FOR WAIT := 1 TO 100 DO
      UNTIL KEYPRESS;
      READ (CH);
      CASE CH OF
         'R': TURNTO (135);
         'T': TURNTO (90);
         'Y': TURNTO (45);
         'F': TURNTO (180);
         'H': TURNTO (0);
         'V': TURNTO (-135);
         'B': TURNTO (-90);
         'N': TURNTO (-45);
      END (* CASE *)
   UNTIL CH = 'Q'
END.
```

Run this final version.

SUMMARY

In this session you saw and did the following things:

- You used READ and READLN to get user input into a running program.

- You used variables of types CHAR and BOOLEAN.

- You defined a BOOLEAN valued function.

- You used IF and CASE statements to control logically alternative branches of a program.

- You found that the ELSE branch of an IF statement can be omitted.

- You experienced a common bug associated with nesting an abbreviated IF statement within the THEN branch of a regular IF statement.

- You found that extra semicolons within an IF statement can introduce bugs.

- You used AND, OR, and NOT in BOOLEAN expressions.

- You used a succession of ELSE IF constructions to define logical cases.

- You found that CTRL-@ can be used at any time to interrupt a running program and start a "warm reboot" of Pascal.

- You found that it is dangerous to use READ or READLN with numeric variables.

- You used the CASE statement in a graphic application to associate different key presses with different turtle headings.

- You used the BOOLEAN KEYPRESS function to detect any Apple keyboard activity.

- You used the MOVE, TURN, and TURNTO graphic procedures.

Here is the updated Pascal vocabulary table.

Table 8.1 Cumulative Pascal vocabulary. New words introduced in this session are printed in boldface. (Code: a = declared in APPLESTUFF; g = declared in TURTLEGRAPHICS)

Reserved Words	Built-In Procedures	Built-In Functions	Other Built-Ins
PROGRAM	**READ**	Boolean	Constants
USES	**READLN**	a BUTTON	**FALSE**
CONST	WRITE	**a KEYPRESS**	**TRUE**
VAR	WRITELN		g NONE
PROCEDURE	a NOTE	Integer	g WHITE
FUNCTION	a RANDOMIZE	a PADDLE	g BLACK
BEGIN	g FILLSCREEN	a RANDOM	g GREEN
FOR	g GRAFMODE		g VIOLET
TO	g INITTURTLE		g ORANGE
DOWNTO	**g MOVE**		g BLUE
DO	g MOVETO		
REPEAT	g PENCOLOR		Types
UNTIL	g TEXTMODE		BOOLEAN
IF	**g TURN**		**CHAR**
THEN	**g TURNTO**		INTEGER
ELSE			
CASE			Units
OF			APPLESTUFF
END			TURTLEGRAPHICS
DIV			
MOD			
AND			
OR			
NOT			

QUESTIONS AND PROBLEMS

1. What problems can arise if a program uses READLN with numeric variables?

2. When is it legal and when is it illegal to have a semicolon appear within the text of an IF statement?

3. What causes function KEYPRESS to return a value of TRUE? What causes it to return a value of FALSE?

4. Explain the difference between the effects of the MOVE and MOVETO procedures.

5. Explain the difference between the effects of the TURN and TURNTO procedures.

6. What is an abbreviated IF statement, and what problems can it cause?

7. Consider the following CASE statement:

```
CASE X > 5 OF
   TRUE: WRITELN ('GREATER');
   FALSE: WRITELN ('LESS THAN OR EQUAL')
END (* CASE *)
```

Is it legal? Justify your answer.

8. Consider the following CASE statement:

```
CASE X OF
   X > 5: WRITELN ('GREATER');
   X <= 5: WRITELN ('LESS THAN OR EQUAL')
END (* CASE *)
```

Is it legal? Justify your answer.

9. One of the two CASE statements in questions 7 and 8 is legal. Rewrite it as an IF statement.

10. Consider the following IF statement:

```
IF A > 0 THEN IF B > 0 THEN WRITE ('X') ELSE WRITE ('Y')
```

a. Indent it to clarify the meaning.

b. What output would the statement generate for the following values of A and B?

i)	A = 1,	B = 1
ii)	A = 1,	B = -1
iii)	A = -1,	B = 1
iv)	A = -1,	B = -1

11. In question 10, change the IF statement so that "ELSE" is replaced by "ELSE ELSE". Repeat parts 10(a) and 10(b) for this new version of the statement.

12. In question 10, change the IF statement so that "IF A > 0 THEN" is replaced by "IF A < 0 THEN;". Repeat parts 10(a) and 10(b) for this new version of the above statement.

13. The toll charged at a bridge is based on the type of vehicle, the number of passengers, and the time of day. All trucks are charged $1.00 regardless of the number of passengers or the time of day. During rush hours, cars with three or more passengers are free; otherwise the toll is 50 cents. During non-rush hours, the toll for all cars is 25 cents regardless of the number of passengers. Set up a program that gets answers to the following three questions:

    a. "Is it a car?"

    b. "Is it rush hour?"

    c. "Are there three or more passengers?"

    The program should then write the appropriate toll on the screen.

14. Organize the program in question 7 so that it asks no unnecessary questions.

15. Write a program that inputs an arbitrary integer and then generates an output that depends on the number input as follows:

Input	Output
< 1	Nothing
1	1ST
2	2ND
3	3RD
4 . . 20	4TH . . 20TH
> 20	Nothing

16. Change the program in question 15 so that it works correctly for integers greater than 20. For example, if you input 33, the output should be 33RD; or if you input 101, the output should be 101ST, etc. (Hint: use the MOD operator.)

17. Consider the following program:

```
PROGRAM TEST;

VAR
    N1, N2, N3 : INTEGER;

BEGIN
WRITELN ('TYPE IN THREE INTEGERS');
WRITELN ('SEPARATED BY SPACES.');
WRITELN ('THEN PRESS RETURN');
READLN (N1, N2, N3);
IF N1 > N2 THEN
IF N2 > N3 THEN
WRITELN (N3, ' ', N2, ' ',  N1)
ELSE IF N1 > N3 THEN
WRITELN (N2, ' ', N3, ' ', N1)
ELSE WRITELN (N2, ' ', N1, ' ', N3)
ELSE
IF N3 > N2 THEN
WRITELN (N1, ' ', N2, ' ', N3)
ELSE IF N1 > N3 THEN
WRITELN (N3, ' ', N1, ' ', N2)
ELSE WRITELN (N1, ' ', N3, ' ', N2)
END.
```

Change the indentation to clarify the meaning.

18. If the program in question 17 is run using the following inputs, what will the output be in each case?

a. 10 20 30

b. 20 10 30

c. 20 30 10

d. 30 10 20

e. 30 20 10

f. 10 30 20

19. In an earlier session you learned that in the NOTE function, PITCH values of 20, 21, 22, ..., 31, and 32 generate a very nearly chromatic scale beginning at middle C. Consider the following pattern:

Piano key	PITCH	Apple keyboard key
C1	20	A
C#	21	W
D	22	S
Eb	23	E
E	24	D
F	25	F
F#	26	T
G	27	G
G#	28	Y
A	29	H
Bb	30	U
B	31	J
C2	32	K

Look at the Apple keyboard and you will discover that the Apple keys listed above approximate the layout of a piano keyboard. Write a program to "play" notes until button zero is pressed. If you press key A, for example, you should hear middle C; J should produce the note B, and so on. Use the READ function to call for input at the keyboard. Disable the keys Q, R, I, O, P, Z, X, C, V, B, N, M, the comma, and the period, so that if you press these keys, nothing is heard. This can be done by setting PITCH equal to zero if these keys are pressed.

NINE

STRING VARIABLES AND WHILE LOOPS

This session will deal with collections of characters called *strings*. The concept of a string of characters is a powerful one and finds a wide range of applications. Word processing, for example, is solely concerned with inputting, manipulating, and outputting strings of characters.

Actually, you have already made use of string *constants* in WRITE and WRITELN calls. When you wrote WRITELN ('MOO') in Session 3, you were passing the string constant 'MOO' as a parameter to procedure WRITELN.

The ideas about procedures and functions introduced in Sessions 5 and 6 will be generalized here to apply to strings as well as numbers. You have already used the READ and READLN procedures to input single characters. In this session you will learn how to extend READ and READLN to input strings of characters.

SESSION GOALS

You will primarily learn how to work with *strings* of characters, a new type of data, and will learn how to use the *built-in* string functions LENGTH, CONCAT, POS, and COPY, and the *built-in* string procedure DELETE. Finally, you will learn to use the WHILE statement to create a program loop different from either the FOR or REPEAT loop.

9-1 GETTING STARTED WITH STRINGS

Boot up Pascal and get a clear workfile. Of course, be sure not to throw away anything valuable when you clear the workfile.

The first program that we will work with in this session should be quite familiar to you. It's program TINY from Session 3, but with a different name. Here it is:

```
PROGRAM WORDS;

BEGIN
  WRITELN ('HOW NOW BROWN COW')
END.
```

181

Type in the program. Run it and verify that our old friend HOW NOW BROWN COW is displayed on the screen.

Let's look carefully at this simple program. First, the message HOW NOW BROWN COW is the *parameter* of the WRITELN procedure. By parameter, we mean that it is what the procedure needs to carry out the task involved. The single quotes on either end of the message set off a *string constant*, whose value is passed to the WRITELN procedure.

As the program stands, it couldn't be simpler, or more useless, for that matter. There simply isn't much call for messages about brown cows.

Modify the program so that it appears as follows:

```
PROGRAM WORDS;

VAR
    PHRASE : STRING;

BEGIN
    PHRASE := 'HOW NOW BROWN COW';
    WRITELN (PHRASE)
END.
```

The modifications include adding a VAR block, inserting an assignment statement in the BEGIN/END block, and modifying the WRITELN statement.

Notice the declaration of a new *STRING* data type in the VAR block. You have now seen four different data types: INTEGER, BOOLEAN, CHAR, and STRING.

The variable PHRASE is of type STRING and receives its *value* in the assignment statement in the BEGIN/END block. The *variable* PHRASE is assigned the *value* HOW NOW BROWN COW in the assignment statement. Finally, the *value* of PHRASE is passed to the WRITELN procedure. The parameter of the WRITELN procedure is a variable that has a *string value* rather than the numeric and character values studied previously.

Leave the EDITOR and run the program. You should have seen exactly the same output as that of the first program. The output is the same but the method of obtaining it is fundamentally different than in the first version of WORDS. In this version, the value of the STRING *variable* PHRASE is passed to the WRITELN procedure. Earlier, the value of the string *constant* 'HOW NOW BROWN COW' was passed to WRITELN.

You should note that Pascal has a simple "spelling rule" for writing string constants in the text of a program. *The first and last character must be a single-quote mark (also called an apostrophe). The sequence of characters typed between single quotes is the value of the string. The quote marks are not part of the value.*

You've probably noticed a problem with this rule, namely that you'd have a hard time making string constants out of sentences *containing* apostrophes. If you wrote

```
PHRASE := 'YOU'VE PROBABLY';
```

the Pascal compiler would interpret the apostrophe as the *closing quote mark* for the string value YOU. Then the compiler would expect a semicolon or END or other delimiter. So it would get in trouble and complain about the word VE.

Here's the way out. **Change the line containing your assignment statement as follows:**

```
PHRASE := 'IT''S JOHN''S BOOK.';
```

Run the new version.

So you see that the spelling rule for string constants contains a special feature. *A consecutive pair of single-quotes within the text of a string constant is interpreted as a single quote character within the string and not as a delimiter of the string.*

Change the line containing your assignment statement to read,

```
PHRASE := '';
```

Leave no space between the quote marks. Run the program.

As you saw, that was grammatically acceptable; but *nothing* appeared on the screen when you ran it. Pascal allows you to deal with strings that contain *zero* characters. Such a string is called a *null* string, and you have now seen how to type a null string as a constant.

9-2 THE LENGTH FUNCTION

Now, let's look at the first of the *built-in string functions*. **Insert the following line just before END.**

```
WRITELN (LENGTH (PHRASE))
```

Don't forget to insert a semicolon at the end of the preceding line.

Okay, leave the EDITOR and run the program. This time the first line of the output was blank, as before and the second line contained a zero. Why a zero?

Go back and change your assignment statement back the way it was originally:

```
PHRASE := 'HOW NOW BROWN COW';
```

Leave the EDITOR and run the program. The output is the same except the number 17 is typed out below the BROWN COW message. What is the significance of the number 17? **Count the number of characters in the phrase HOW NOW BROWN COW (Don't forget to count the spaces too.)**

You probably have already figured out what the LENGTH function does but it won't hurt to go over the details. LENGTH is an example of a built-in function that has a name, a type, and a value, just like the functions you have already met. Of course, its name is LENGTH. Its type is declared somewhere in the Pascal system, so we don't have to declare it. It's easy enough to see what its type is, however. The *value* of the string variable PHRASE is *passed* to the LENGTH function. The function produces, or *returns*, an integer equal to the number of characters in the string passed to it. This means that LENGTH is of type INTEGER. When the function is evaluated, the integer result of the function takes its place in the Pascal expression.

In turn, the *value* of LENGTH (PHRASE) is *passed* to the procedure WRITELN which displays the numeric value 17 on the screen.

It probably seems as though we have been using unnecessarily stilted words to describe a simple idea. However, we feel that it is difficult to overemphasize the importance of the concepts of passing parameter values to functions or procedures and having a result returned or a process carried out. Once you have these ideas sorted out in your mind, you will have mastered one of the most important ideas of programming in Pascal, or in any other language.

Just to firm up the notion of passing parameter values of functions, let's try an experiment. **Go to the EDITOR and modify program WORDS as follows:**

```
PROGRAM WORDS;

   VAR
      PHRASE : STRING;
      SENTENCE : INTEGER;

   BEGIN
      SENTENCE := 12345;
      PHRASE := 'HOW NOW BROWN COW';
      WRITELN (LENGTH (PHRASE));
      WRITELN (LENGTH (SENTENCE))
   END.
```

A new integer variable has been added to the VAR block; its value is assigned in the BEGIN/END block. Finally, a new WRITELN statement has been added just before END. **Run the program.**

We hope you saw Error 125 (error in type of standard procedure) coming. If you think about the last changes made to the program, it isn't hard to see why the error message surfaced. SENTENCE has an INTEGER value but LENGTH requires a STRING value to be passed to it. The variable SENTENCE may *look* like it should have a string value but it was declared to be of type INTEGER. *It's the value of a variable, not its name, that gets passed.*

One more change. **Change the WRITELN statement containing the variable SENTENCE to read**

```
WRITELN (SENTENCE)
```

and then run the program.

This time everything works fine. *You can pass either the value of a string expression or an integer expression to the WRITELN procedure.* (You can also pass character values to WRITELN.)

Let's sum up what you've learned about the LENGTH function. LENGTH *requires* the value of a string to be passed to it, and returns an integer equal to the number of characters in the string.

9-3 MAKING LONG STRINGS OUT OF SHORT ONES

The LENGTH function seems simple enough. Now let's experiment with another built-in string function. **Go to the EDITOR and modify program WORDS to look as follows:**

```
PROGRAM WORDS;

VAR
    PHRASE, WORD1, WORD2, WORD3, WORD4 : STRING;

BEGIN
    WORD1 := 'HOW ';
    WORD2 := 'NOW ';
    WORD3 := 'BROWN ';
    WORD4 := 'COW ';
    WRITELN (WORD1, WORD2, WORD3, WORD4)
END.
```

You've added four more *string variables* in the VAR block. The values of these new variables are assigned in the first four lines of the BEGIN/END block. The list of parameters passed to WRITELN has been changed.

What's happening in the WRITELN statement? Now there is a *parameter list* consisting of the variables WORD1, WORD2, WORD3, and WORD4. The *values* of the words in the parameter list are passed to the WRITELN procedure. Incidentally, be sure that there is a blank space at the end of each of the strings being assigned to WORD1 through WORD4. The reason for the spaces is cosmetic, as you will see shortly.

Run the program. You get the same old sentence about the BROWN COW but it is being produced in a different way than in the first two versions of the program that you ran in this session. The phrase is built up from the individual string variables in the parameter list passed to the WRITELN procedure. Of course, if you change the order of the words in the parameter list, the order of the displayed words will also be changed.

All right, it's clear that you can build up long strings by putting the parts of the string in a parameter list and passing the values to the WRITELN procedure. There is a slicker way to accomplish this that depends on another built-in function.
Change the program as follows:

```
PROGRAM WORDS;

    VAR
        PHRASE, WORD1, WORD2, WORD3, WORD4 : STRING;

BEGIN
    WORD1 := 'HOW ';
    WORD2 := 'NOW ';
    WORD3 := 'BROWN ';
    WORD4 := 'COW ';
    PHRASE := CONCAT (WORD1, WORD2, WORD3, WORD4);
    WRITELN (PHRASE)
END.
```

The values of the parameter list (WORD1 through WORD4) are passed to the function CONCAT. The result of CONCAT (that is, its value) is then assigned to the string variable PHRASE. The value of PHRASE is passed to the WRITELN procedure. But what does CONCAT do? **Run the program and observe the results.**

Once more we are reassured about the BROWN COW, but this result was produced in still a different way than in the first three versions of program WORDS. One thing is clear: the result of the CONCAT function must be of type *string* since it is assigned to PHRASE, which has already been declared to be a string variable. CONCAT "puts together" the string values of the variables in the parameter list to form the phrase HOW NOW BROWN COW. You may have two or more strings, or string variables, as parameters of CONCAT. (CONCAT stands for *concatenation*, by the way.) The function then glues them together into a single string. It is the value of this new string that gets assigned to PHRASE and then passed to WRITELN in your program.

Recall that we advised you to insert a blank space at the end of each of the assignments of WORD1, WORD2, WORD3, and WORD4 for cosmetic reasons. If the spaces are missing, the program will display HOWNOWBROWNCOW. If you include a space at the end of each of the words in the parameter list passed to CONCAT, there will be normal spaces between the words.

Now let's do an experiment which will reveal an unfortunate characteristic of this version of Pascal. **Go to the EDITOR and make a few changes to program WORDS. The new version is shown below:**

```
PROGRAM WORDS#

  VAR
    PHRASE, WORD1, WORD2, WORD3, WORD4 : STRING#
    LETTER : CHAR#

BEGIN
  WORD1 := 'HOW '#
  WORD2 := 'NOW '#
  WORD3 := 'BROWN '#
  WORD4 := 'COW'#
  LETTER := 'S'#
  PHRASE := CONCAT (WORD1, WORD2, WORD3, WORD4, LETTER)#
  WRITELN (PHRASE)
END.
```

You've added a new variable (LETTER) of type CHAR, deleted the space at the end of COW, assigned the character S to the variable LETTER, and added LETTER to the parameter list being passed to PHRASE. You're probably way ahead and see that if we concatenate (or glue on) S to our familiar message, we can consider the BROWN COW in the plural. This certainly seems like a neat way to put things together.

Run the program. Surprise, surprise! The problem involves a mismatch of variable types. WORD1 through WORD4 are all of type STRING, so there's no problem there. However, LETTER is of type CHAR. You certainly ought to be able to append a character to a string, but Pascal doesn't permit it. Sad but true! So here is another **user trap** to avoid. Even if it makes logical sense to glue on or concatenate a character to a string, Apple Pascal won't allow it.

One final experiment, and we'll be finished with the CONCAT function. **Go to the EDITOR and delete LETTER from the parameter list in CONCAT.** Now we want to rearrange the order of WORD2 and WORD3. **Use the X(chng feature of the EDITOR to change the CONCAT parameter list to the following:**

```
PHRASE := CONCAT (WORD1, WORD3, WORD2, WORD4)#
```

Leave the EDITOR and run the program. As you see, changing the order of the variables in the parameter list changes the order in which the words are glued together.

Remember that the parameter list passed to CONCAT must consist of either strings or string variables. We could have added an S to the BROWN COW phrase by doing this:

```
PHRASE := CONCAT (WORD1, WORD2, WORD3, WORD4, 'S')#
```

This time it isn't a *variable* of type CHAR that is being glued on, it is the *constant string* 'S'. You can mix constant strings with string variables in the parameter list any way you desire. You can't, however, use anything other than values of type string in the list.

Actually, Apple Pascal is quite forgiving about *single-character constants* such as 'S'. It will treat them as being either of type STRING or of type CHAR, as appropriate. You don't have to worry about the ambiguity.

9-4 LOCATING ONE STRING IN ANOTHER

You've learned all there is to know about the LENGTH and CONCAT functions. LENGTH required a string to be passed to it and returned an integer. CONCAT required a parameter list of strings or string expressions to be passed to it and returned a longer string consisting of the parts glued together. The next string function to experiment with is like LENGTH in that it returns an integer, but is quite different in that it requires exactly two strings as parameters.

Modify program WORDS until it looks as follows:

```
PROGRAM WORDS;

    VAR
       PHRASE, WORD1, WORD2, WORD3, WORD4 : STRING;
       FIRSTLETTER : INTEGER;

    BEGIN
       WORD1 := 'HOW ';
       WORD2 := 'NOW ';
       WORD3 := 'BROWN ';
       WORD4 := 'COW';
       PHRASE := CONCAT (WORD1, WORD2, WORD3, WORD4);
       WRITELN (PHRASE);
       FIRSTLETTER := POS ('BROWN', PHRASE);
       WRITELN (FIRSTLETTER)
    END.
```

Here are the changes. An INTEGER variable FIRSTLETTER has been added to the VAR block. A new function POS has appeared. Its parameters are the constant 'BROWN' and the variable PHRASE. The value of the function is assigned to the INTEGER variable FIRSTLETTER. Okay, great! So what does POS do? As always, the best way to find out is to run the program and see.

Run the program. You certainly were expecting HOW NOW BROWN COW. But what does the 9 indicate? Well, the string 'BROWN' is involved, as is the string PHRASE which has the value HOW NOW BROWN COW. Note that the B in BROWN is the 9th character in PHRASE (don't forget to count the spaces as characters).

The first string in the parameter list of POS is called the *target* string. It is the string you are shooting for. The second string in the parameter list, the *source* string, is the one that may contain the target string. The value returned by POS is an integer and is equal to the *character position* of the *first* occurrence of the target in the source string.

What would happen if you turned the arguments around in the POS function? **Modify the statement containing the POS function to**

```
FIRSTLETTER := POS (PHRASE, 'BROWN');
```

and run the program. How can you interpret the result of 0? It's easy. The value of PHRASE (the string HOW NOW BROWN COW) does *not* occur in the string BROWN. *If the target string cannot be found in the source string, a value of 0 is returned by POS.*

Here's a different wrinkle. **Change the FIRSTLETTER assignment statement to read**

```
FIRSTLETTER := POS (WORD4, PHRASE);
```

When you first used the POS function, the target string was the string constant 'BROWN'. Now it is the *string variable* WORD4. In CONCAT, it didn't make any difference whether you used a string constant or a string variable, so it should be okay here. If so, then the POS function will look for the target WORD4, which has the value COW, in the source string PHRASE, which has the value HOW NOW BROWN COW. Do a little counting, and if everything works as advertised, FIRSTLETTER should have the integer value 15. **Run the program and see what is printed out.** Were you right?

How about this variation?

```
FIRSTLETTER := POS ('OW', PHRASE)
```

There are four occurrences of 'OW' in HOW NOW BROWN COW. Which one will be located by POS?

Make the necessary changes in the program and run it. That settles the issue of multiple occurrences of the target in the source string. POS locates the *first* occurrence, starting from the left.

Change the assignment statement for FIRSTLETTER to read

```
FIRSTLETTER := POS (' ', PHRASE);
```

and then run the program. The question here is "Does it make any sense to use a space for a target string?" The result of 4 shows that the answer is yes. The space character is a perfectly good target string and is routinely used to locate word boundaries in strings.

The last thing to check about the POS function is whether or not the *null* string can be used as a target string. **Change the FIRSTLETTER statement to**

```
FIRSTLETTER := POS ('', PHRASE);
```

There are no characters inside the single quotes that define the target string; hence the target is the null string. **Run the program and see what happens?**

You could probably have predicted what happened. By definition, PHRASE consists of characters. A character certainly can't be a null string. Thus, there is no match of the null string in the source string PHRASE and POS returns a value of 0.

So, chalk up another function. POS requires a target string and a source string as parameters, and returns an integer value equal to the position of the first character of the target at the first occurrence of the target in the source string. If the target can't be found in the source string, POS returns a value of zero. Any string, can be used for the target or the source. You may not use values of type CHAR as parameters of POS.

9-5 EXTRACTING PIECES OF STRINGS

Let's plunge right ahead to the next string function. **Modify program WORDS to appear as follows:**

```
PROGRAM WORDS;

    VAR
        PHRASE, WORD1, WORD2, WORD3, WORD4 : STRING;
        PIECE : STRING;

    BEGIN
        WORD1 := 'HOW ';
        WORD2 := 'NOW ';
        WORD3 := 'BROWN ';
        WORD4 := 'COW';
        PHRASE := CONCAT (WORD1, WORD2, WORD3, WORD4);
        WRITELN (PHRASE);
        PIECE := COPY (PHRASE, 5, 9);
        WRITELN (PIECE)
    END.
```

There are a couple of interesting things about this version of program WORDS. First, note that there are two separate declarations of string variables. This is the first time this has been done in the book. As a matter of fact, you may have as many declarations of any of the variable types as you want, and in any order. Sometimes it makes more sense to use two declarations of variables of type string (the case above) than to have a long list of variables extending over into the right half of the Pascal page. It is a matter of taste.

There are no other changes in the program down through the WRITELN (PHRASE) statement. COPY is a new function. As you can see, it has a string and two integers as parameters. COPY must return a value of type STRING since the result is assigned to PIECE, which was declared to be a variable of type STRING.

Run the new version of the program. Did you anticipate what happened? As you can see, COPY extracts a *substring* from the source string which, in this case, is the string variable PHRASE. The substring begins at character number 5 and extends for 9 characters. The first item in COPY's parameter list is the source string. The second item is an integer giving the starting position of the substring to be extracted. The third item in the list is an integer giving the length of the substring in characters. So, if you count over 5 characters in HOW NOW BROWN COW and take the next 9 characters, you get the substring NOW BROWN, which is exactly what the computer did in the above example.

Of course, there are several questions that arise immediately. What happens if the starting point is outside the length of the source string? What if the length of the substring is a negative number? What happens if the length of the substring extends past the end of the source string? What happens if the length of the substring is set to zero?

You are capable of answering these questions without any further specific directions. **Modify the COPY function in program WORDS to obtain the answers to the questions in the paragraph above.**

9-6 ELIMINATING PIECES OF STRINGS

There is another string operation that is closely related to COPY. This is the DELETE procedure. It works exactly the same as COPY except that DELETE returns what is left of the source string after the substring is deleted.

To see how this works, modify program WORDS as follows:

```
PROGRAM WORDS;

VAR
    PHRASE, WORD1, WORD2, WORD3, WORD4 : STRING;

BEGIN
    WORD1 := 'HOW ';
    WORD2 := 'NOW ';
    WORD3 := 'BROWN ';
    WORD4 := 'COW';
    PHRASE := CONCAT (WORD1, WORD2, WORD3, WORD4);
    WRITELN (PHRASE);
    DELETE (PHRASE, 9, 6);
    WRITELN (PHRASE)
END.
```

DELETE is fundamentally different than the other string operations studied thus far because it is a *procedure* rather than a function. Note that the result of DELETE is not assigned to anything. DELETE clearly does something to the source string

PHRASE. Based on what we have said and your experience with COPY, you can probably figure out what it does.

Run the program. Did you anticipate what happened? If you begin at character number 9 in string variable PHRASE (which has the *value* HOW NOW BROWN COW), and delete 6 characters, the result is HOW NOW COW.

You should note an important Pascal capability here: the string variable PHRASE in the call to DELETE is used both to pass a parameter value *to* that procedure and also to *return the result* back to the caller. That is why the value of PHRASE is *different* before and after the call to DELETE. *This is one of the few times that you have seen a variable name (PHRASE) used to pass a value back to the caller after the call to a procedure or a function.*

Let's look at this more closely. **Change your call to DELETE as follows;**

```
DELETE ('HOW NOW BROWN COW', 9, 6);
```

Run the program. Did that result surprise you?

The reason the change got you into trouble is that you cut off the two-way communication channel between the main program and procedure DELETE. The main program *sent* the value HOW NOW BROWN COW to DELETE, but there was *no way for it to receive* the shortened string with BROWN deleted. *The rule is that you must always use a variable name as the parameter of a procedure (or function) that will change that parameter.*

Obviously, one of the things you must know about any built-in procedure or function is whether any of its parameters are of this kind. Such parameters are called *reference parameters*, while the other kind of parameters that only pass values into procedures or functions are called *value parameters*. The DELETE procedure has one reference parameter and two value parameters.

When you write procedures of your own you must distinguish reference parameters from value parameters. We haven't shown you how to do that, but you will see an example soon.

As with the COPY function, there are a number of additional questions that should be answered. Can the length of the substring to be deleted be negative? What happens if the length of the substring to be deleted extends past the end of the source string? What happens if the starting point of the substring is either negative or extends past the end of the source string? **Use the computer to answer these questions.**

9-7 COMBINING STRING OPERATIONS

We've gone about as far as we can with program WORDS. Now it's time to see several of the string operations combined together in a program.

Clear out program WORDS from your workfile and enter the program below.

```
PROGRAM SENTENCE;

VAR
    PHRASE : STRING;

BEGIN
    READLN (PHRASE);
    WRITELN;
    WRITELN (PHRASE)
END.
```

As you can see, this program is a simple one. PHRASE is declared a string, as in program WORDS. The difference in this program is that PHRASE gets its *value* from the READLN *procedure*. Recall from your experience with the READLN procedure that information typed in at the keyboard is assigned to the variable that is named in the READLN parameter list. (Note that READ and READLN have *reference parameters* while WRITE and WRITELN have *value parameters*. This means that you may use only variables as parameters for READ and READLN.)

You should be able to predict correctly what will happen if you run the program. Think about it a minute and then **run the program.** What happened?

The problem seems to be that nothing is happening. The usual "RUNNING..." line appears at the top of the screen indicating that the computer is running the program, but then everything halts. There is nothing wrong; the computer is executing the READLN (PHRASE) statement and is waiting for you to type in a string.

Type in THE QUICK BROWN FOX and press RETURN. What produced the blank line between your input and the same line typed back by the program? If you said the *empty* WRITELN statement, then you're right. There is no parameter for WRITELN so nothing is printed. However, after printing nothing, it output a RETURN so a new line can be started. Simply stated, an empty WRITELN statement produces a blank line. The value of PHRASE is the string you typed in (THE QUICK BROWN FOX) and this value is passed to the second WRITELN procedure.

It would make more sense from the user's point of view if a prompt appeared on the screen before the READLN statement, giving some clue about what was expected. This would avoid the possible confusion that results when the program runs and nothing seems to be happening.

Go to the EDITOR and insert the line

```
WRITELN ('TYPE IN A SENTENCE AND PRESS RETURN');
```

just after BEGIN; then run the program.

All right, it is clearer now. If you type in the same sentence, the screen display should be

```
RUNNING...
TYPE A SENTENCE AND PRESS RETURN
THE QUICK BROWN FOX

THE QUICK BROWN FOX
```

By now, you should be getting quite adept at sorting out the source of the information on the screen. The *computer* generated the top line. The *program* was the source of the second line. *You* were the source of the third line. The *program* was the source of the blank line and line five.

Let's introduce a few familiar string functions into this program. **Modify the program so it looks as follows:**

```
PROGRAM SENTENCE;

   VAR
      PHRASE : STRING;
      COUNT : INTEGER;

   BEGIN
      WRITELN ('TYPE IN A SENTENCE AND PRESS RETURN');
      READLN (PHRASE);
      WRITELN;
      FOR COUNT := 1 TO LENGTH (PHRASE) DO
         WRITELN (COPY (PHRASE, 1, COUNT))
   END.
```

A new variable COUNT, of type INTEGER has been added. Instead of the last WRITELN statement, a FOR statement involving both COUNT and LENGTH (PHRASE) has been added. Notice particularly that there is a single statement following the FOR statement. That is why there is no need to bracket it in a BEGIN/END block.

Well, what does the program do? Before running it, why don't you see if you can figure out what will happen? Give the program a few moments thought.

Now run the program, and at the input prompt, type in the string ABCDEFGH-IJKLMNOPQRST. As you can see, a COPY function embedded inside a FOR statement can produce interesting results. Were you correct about the output?

Now let's try to make the program type out fragments of the input string beginning with the complete string. **Change the last WRITELN statement to read:**

```
WRITELN (COPY (PHRASE, 1, LENGTH (PHRASE) - COUNT))
```

Run the program, and at the input prompt type in ABCDEFGHIJKLMNOPQRST.
Check the output carefully. The last letter in your input was T, but the last letter in the first line of the output is S. What's wrong? Well folks, it's our old friend OBOB the *Off-By-One-Bug*. Once identified, the problem is easy to correct. **Change the WRITELN statement to read:**

```
WRITELN (COPY (PHRASE, 1, LENGTH (PHRASE) - COUNT + 1))
```

Run the modified program and type in any sentence or phrase you want. Now everything works as advertised.
This program is a good one to demonstrate the use of several string operations and how they can be combined.

9–8 MISCELLANEOUS FACTS ABOUT STRINGS

In most practical computer applications, strings play the main role of communicating textual information to the user and receiving textual input from the user. Despite a few shortcomings, the Apple version of strings in Pascal is one of its most attractive features. The built-in functions and procedures you have been using will allow you to produce clear tabular output and to analyze responses typed by a user. This section summarizes additional facts about Apple Pascal strings.
As you have seen, a given string variable, such as PHRASE in your current program, can be assigned strings of different lengths. You may have wondered whether there is an upper limit to the size of strings. There is. If you had typed in a sentence longer than 80 characters, for example, your current program would have come to a halt and reported a "value range error".
You can change the 80 character limit. **Go to the EDITOR and change the VAR block as follows:**

```
VAR
   PHRASE : STRING [10];
   COUNT : INTEGER;
```

Your Apple keyboard seems to lack the square bracket keys, but they are there. Type CTRL–K for the left bracket and SHIFT–M for the right bracket. **Run the program. When prompted, type a single short word. Then run again, and this time, type a sentence with more than 10 characters. Note that PHRASE starts with only 10 characters.**
This shows how to shorten the maximum length of a string variable. You can use the same method to increase the maximum length up to a ceiling of 255 characters. That is the upper limit in Apple Pascal. As you have seen, if you do not specify a maximum length for a string variable, then a length of 80 characters is assumed to be the maximum. **Go to the EDITOR and delete the string length specification from your VAR block.**

So far you have seen how to use COPY and DELETE to get at *substrings* within a string value. There is also a very different way to get at the individual characters that make up a string. **Change the FOR statement of your program as follows:**

```
FOR COUNT := 1 TO LENGTH (PHRASE) DO
    WRITELN (PHRASE [COUNT])
```

Run the new version. If all went well, you should see each character of the sentence you typed, one under the other at the left margin of the screen. PHRASE [COUNT] refers to a single character of the string PHRASE. When COUNT = 1, it is the first character; when COUNT = 2, it is the second, etc.

You can also use this method to assign values to the individual characters in a string. The following changes in your program will change all space characters in PHRASE into plus signs:

```
FOR COUNT := 1 TO LENGTH (PHRASE) DO
    IF PHRASE [COUNT] = ' ' THEN
        PHRASE [COUNT] := '+';
WRITELN (PHRASE)
```

Make these changes and run the program. In general, you can use PHRASE [COUNT] in the text of a program whenever it is legal to use a variable of type CHAR.

> Note that the whole string is of type STRING, but each character is of type CHAR. You will get a type-conflict error if you use a character component of a string in a place where a string is expected.

To drive that point home, think about the fact that a string with length equal to one is *different* from data of type CHAR, even if they equal the same letter of the alphabet. If CH is a variable of type CHAR and ST is a variable of type STRING, the following statements are legal:

```
ST := 'A';
CH := 'B';
ST [1] := CH
```

But all these are *illegal*:

```
ST := CH#
CH := ST#
ST := CONCAT (ST, ST [1])#
IF ST = ST [1] THEN#
```

The final facts to consider here are restrictions on the use of strings. First, you may not define a function of your own that returns a string value. (This is a pity, since, as you have seen in your work with built-in functions such as COPY and CONCAT, user-defined string functions would be very useful.) Second, you may not use strings as case labels in a CASE statement. (This is another pity; the application need is quite common.) In contrast, character-valued functions are legal, and character constants may be used as case labels in a CASE statement. Perhaps some future version of Pascal will finish the job of building the string data type into the language in a more complete and natural way. In the meantime, you should be aware of present limitations; but you should also be thankful that you have strings at all. Many versions of Pascal have no string data type.

9-9 A WORD PROCESSING PROGRAM

With a few changes, program SENTENCE can be converted into a program that is the heart of most word processing systems. Let's look at the new program and then review the changes.

```
PROGRAM SCANNER#

  CONST
    SPACE = ' '#

  VAR
    PHRASE : STRING#
    FIRST : INTEGER#
BEGIN
    WRITELN ('TYPE IN A SENTENCE AND PRESS RETURN')#
    READLN (PHRASE)#
    WRITELN#
    REPEAT
      FIRST := POS (SPACE, PHRASE)#
      WRITELN (COPY (PHRASE, 1, FIRST - 1))#
      DELETE (PHRASE, 1, FIRST)
    UNTIL FIRST = 0
END.
```

You may want to clear out the workfile and enter the program from scratch. If you want to modify program SENTENCE, here are the changes: the program name has been changed to SCANNER, a new constant called SPACE has been declared, the integer COUNT has been changed to FIRST, and a REPEAT block has been inserted after WRITELN.

Either way, make sure that you have the program exactly as listed above. Now let's discuss what is going on. The constant SPACE has been set equal to the space character in the CONST block. (Pascal will treat SPACE as being of type CHAR or STRING as needed.) The significant changes are in the REPEAT block. In the first line of this block, FIRST is assigned the *value* of the POS function which locates the first occurrence of a space in the string PHRASE. This value is an integer and is one greater than the length of the first word in the string PHRASE. In line two of the REPEAT block the first *word* of PHRASE is written out. You can see it is a word because it is the *value* of COPY working on PHRASE, starting at character 1, and continuing for one less than FIRST characters. This writes everything up to the first space, but not including the space. In the next line, DELETE deletes the first word from PHRASE *and the space following the word*. This process repeats until FIRST has a value of zero, which will occur when there are no spaces left in PHRASE.

It should be reasonably clear to you that the program is intended to break apart into separate words any phrase you enter, and then write out these words in a vertical column. **Run the program and type in EVERY GOOD BOY DOES FINELY at the input prompt.** Did you get the five words typed back in a vertical column?

It's OBOB again, but this time in different clothing. You got four words instead of the expected five. We are *Off-By-One* but this time it's a *word* that is involved. What's wrong?

Try the program again, and enter EVERY GOOD BOY DOES FINELY, but this time type a space after FINELY. Okay, this time it works, but you would have to remember to include a space at the end of your input string whenever you type it in. This is artificial and flies in the face of good user engineering. How can the problem be fixed?

Notice that the test (UNTIL FIRST = 0) in the REPEAT loop is done *after the loop is executed*. Here is where the problem lies. After the next to last word is typed out, there are no spaces left; so the program exits from the REPEAT loop, losing the last word. Having the user add the extra space solved this problem, but there surely must be a better way to straighten things out.

One way to repair the error is to use an IF statement *inside* the REPEAT block. **Go to the EDITOR and change the REPEAT block as follows:**

```
REPEAT
   FIRST := POS (SPACE, PHRASE);
   IF FIRST > 0 THEN
      BEGIN
         WRITELN (COPY (PHRASE, 1, FIRST - 1));
         DELETE (PHRASE, 1, FIRST)
      END
   ELSE
      WRITELN (PHRASE)
UNTIL FIRST = 0
```

Study this segment carefully and be sure that you can explain the presence or absence of a semicolon at the end of each line.

Now, as long as FIRST > 0, the program works as it did in its original form. When FIRST = 0, the ELSE clause is invoked, which causes PHRASE to be written out. But at this point, PHRASE is simply the last word in the sentence that was entered. This is precisely the condition we were seeking; we have cleared up the problem without the user having to include a space at the end of the input phrase.

Run the program and type in a sentence. Verify that you get all the words back, typed in a vertical column.

As with most problems in programming, there is usually more than one solution; and our problem with SCANNER is no exception. **Delete most of the IF statement from the program and add one line. The program should look like this:**

```
PROGRAM SCANNER;

  CONST
    SPACE = ' ';

  VAR
    PHRASE : STRING;
    FIRST : INTEGER;

  BEGIN
    WRITELN ('TYPE IN A SENTENCE AND PRESS RETURN');
    READLN (PHRASE);
    WRITELN;
    PHRASE := CONCAT (PHRASE, SPACE);
    REPEAT
      FIRST := POS (SPACE, PHRASE);
      WRITELN (COPY (PHRASE, 1, FIRST - 1));
      DELETE (PHRASE, 1, FIRST)
    UNTIL FIRST = 0
  END.
```

You are back to the original form of the program but there is a new statement just before REPEAT. By using the CONCAT function to glue on a space at the end of the input sentence, the user doesn't have to remember to put one there.

Try this new program. The only problem remaining is a subtle one. There is a blank line at the bottom of the display that wasn't planned. Let's see yet another way to cure the initial problem, and while we're at it, avoid the extra line that showed up in the last version.

Go to the editor and modify the program to appear as follows:

```
PROGRAM SCANNER;

  CONST
    SPACE = ' ';

  VAR
    PHRASE : STRING;
    FIRST : INTEGER;

BEGIN
  WRITELN ('TYPE IN A SENTENCE AND PRESS RETURN');
  READLN (PHRASE);
  WRITELN;
  PHRASE := CONCAT (PHRASE, SPACE);
  WHILE LENGTH (PHRASE) > 1 DO
    BEGIN
      FIRST := POS (SPACE, PHRASE);
      WRITELN (COPY (PHRASE, 1, FIRST - 1));
      DELETE (PHRASE, 1, FIRST)
    END (* WHILE *)
END.
```

The new feature in this version of SCANNER is the WHILE control statement. Its structure is very similar to that of the FOR statement. As long as the condition stated in the WHILE statement is true, the statement following the word DO will be executed. The essential difference between the WHILE and REPEAT statements is that the test is made *before executing the loop* in the WHILE statement, whereas it is made *after executing the loop* in the REPEAT statement.

> The body of a WHILE statement may or may not be carried out. The body of a REPEAT statement is always carried out at least once.

Try out this new version. It accomplishes precisely what was desired. There are no extra lines at the bottom of the screen, and the user needn't remember to include an extra space at the end of the input string.

This program, or one like it, is the heart of any word-processing system. It breaks a string apart into words, which can then be handled by other parts of the word processing program.

It is worth noting that you have now been introduced to *all* the major Pascal statements that you will meet in this book. There are a few more capabilities that you will learn but the major work is done.

You will need this program in Session 11. **Save it on your PROGRAM: diskette under the name SCANNER using the method described in Section 4-9.**

9-10 GRAMMAR RULES FOR THE WHILE STATEMENT

Since Pascal contains only a small number of distinct statement types, it is a good idea to learn the "sentence structure" of each kind. The WHILE statement form is particularly easy to remember, since it is very close to that of the FOR statement. As you know, the FOR statement's structure is this:

FOR *variable* := *initial-value* **TO** *final-value* **DO** *statement*

(An alternative form uses the reserved word DOWNTO in place of TO.) Similarly, the WHILE statement has the form

WHILE *boolean-expression* **DO** *statement*

Note that in *both* cases the term *statement* can represent either a *simple* statement or else a *compound* statement. In other words, if more than one simple statement forms the body of a FOR loop or of a WHILE loop, then the statements must be separated by semicolons and bracketed by a BEGIN/END pair.

The other type of loop, the REPEAT loop, has a slightly different grammatical structure, in which the reserved words REPEAT and UNTIL play the same bracketing role as BEGIN and END. For that reason there is no need for a BEGIN/END pair to enclose the set of statements that make up the body of the REPEAT loop.

The term *boolean-expression* in the definition of the WHILE statement stands for anything you can write that has a value that is either *true* or *false*. For example, expressions such as $N < 20$ or $X = 0$ are legal, as are boolean-valued functions, such as BUTTON, or variables declared to be of type BOOLEAN.

As you have seen, the first thing that happens when a WHILE statement is executed is that the boolean value is computed. If it is *false* nothing else happens, and the body of the loop is *not* executed. If the value is *true*, however, then the body of the statement (simple or compound) is executed once. Then the boolean value is computed again. If false, the loop terminates. If true, the loop continues.

We can use this understanding of the WHILE loop to state more clearly how a FOR loop works. Consider the following FOR statement:

```
FOR I := initial-value TO final-value DO
   loop-statement
```

The following WHILE statement has *exactly* the same effect:

```
I := initial-value;
WHILE I <= final-value DO
   BEGIN
     loop-statement;
     I := I + 1
   END
```

If in the FOR statement the word TO was changed to DOWNTO, then the equivalent WHILE statement would be

```
I := initial-value;
WHILE I >= final-value DO
  BEGIN
    loop-statement;
    I := I - 1
  END
```

A simple example of the use of the WHILE statement arises when one needs to get from the user of a program a yes or no answer to a question. Here is an example of a first cut at such a program segment:

```
WRITELN ('DO YOU WANT INSTRUCTIONS?');
READLN (ANSWER);
IF ANSWER = 'YES' THEN
  yes-procedure
ELSE
  no-procedure
```

The problem with this approach is that if the answer was YEP or OK or SURE, then the program would do the *no-procedure*. The easy way to deal with this difficulty is to insert a WHILE statement as follows:

```
WRITELN ('DO YOU WANT INSTRUCTIONS?');
READLN (ANSWER);
WHILE (ANSWER <> 'YES') AND (ANSWER <> 'NO') DO
  BEGIN
    WRITE ('PLEASE TYPE YES OR NO -- ');
    READLN (ANSWER)
  END; (* WHILE *)
IF ANSWER = 'YES' THEN
  yes-procedure
ELSE
  no-procedure
```

In the above example, the WHILE loop is not executed at all if the answer is YES or NO. Other answers result in the prompt PLEASE TYPE YES OR NO — and a new READLN, repeated until the answer is YES or NO. After the WHILE loop is exited, the IF statement works correctly.

SUMMARY

Let's summarize the key points that you have learned in this session.

- **You learned that LENGTH is a string function that has an integer value equal to the number of characters in its string parameter.**

- **You used the string function CONCAT to glue together the strings in its parameter list.**

- **You used POS to find the position of the first appearance of a target string in a source string.**

- **You used COPY to extract a copy of a substring from a source string.**

- **You saw that DELETE is a procedure to remove a substring from a source string.**

- **You learned how to specify the maximum length of a string variable.**

- **You found that the longest allowed string was 255 characters long.**

- **You used square-bracket notation to refer to individual characters in a string.**

- **You found that individual characters were of type CHAR and that errors occur if you use them where STRING variables are expected.**

- **You used the built-in string functions and procedures to write a program to scan an entire phrase and pick off each word separately.**

- **You used the WHILE statement to cause a loop to be executed as long as the condition expressed in it was true.**

- **You saw that the WHILE statement could be used to give a precise definition of the way the FOR statement works.**

Here is the updated Pascal vocabulary table.

Table 9.1 Cumulative Pascal vocabulary. New words introduced in this session are printed in boldface. (Code: a = declared in APPLESTUFF; g = declared in TURTLEGRAPHICS)

Reserved Words	Built-In Procedures	Built-In Functions	Other Built-Ins
PROGRAM	**DELETE**	Boolean	Constants
USES	READ	a BUTTON	FALSE
CONST	READLN	a KEYPRESS	TRUE
VAR	WRITE		g NONE
PROCEDURE	WRITELN	Integer	g WHITE
FUNCTION	a NOTE	**LENGTH**	g BLACK
BEGIN	a RANDOMIZE	**POS**	g GREEN
FOR	g FILLSCREEN	a PADDLE	g VIOLET
TO	g GRAFMODE	a RANDOM	g ORANGE
DOWNTO	g INITTURTLE		g BLUE
DO	g MOVE	String	
REPEAT	g MOVETO	**CONCAT**	Types
UNTIL	g PENCOLOR	**COPY**	BOOLEAN
WHILE	g TEXTMODE		CHAR
IF	g TURNTO		INTEGER
THEN	g VIEWPORT		**STRING**
ELSE			
CASE			Units
OF			APPLESTUFF
END			TURTLEGRAPHICS
DIV			
MOD			
AND			
OR			
NOT			

QUESTIONS AND PROBLEMS

1. What is the type of function CONCAT?

2. What values are required as parameters for DELETE?

3. What is the type of function COPY?

4. What values are required as parameters for POS?

The following three problems are based on strings that have these values:

```
S1 := 'A BIRD IN THE HAND '
S2 := 'IS WORTH TWO IN THE BUSH '
S3 := 'BUSH'
```

5. What is the value of:

   a. LENGTH (S1)

   b. CONCAT (S2, S1)

   c. POS ('THE', S1)

   d. POS ('BUSH', CONCAT (S1, S2, S3))

   e. POS (S3, S1)

   f. POS (S3, S2)

   g. POS (S3, S3)

6. What is the value of:

   a. COPY (S1, 1, 1)

   b. COPY (S2, 4, 9)

   c. COPY (S3, 3, 5)

   d. COPY (S1, 1, 0)

   e. COPY (CONCAT (S1, S2), 23, 5)

   f. COPY (S1, POS ('TWO', S2), 5)

7. What are the values of S1 or S2 after the following procedure calls:

   a. DELETE (S1, 1, 2)

   b. DELETE (S2, 3, POS ('H', S3))

   c. DELETE (S1, 5, LENGTH (S3))

8. Which of the following WRITELN calls are legal? For the legal ones, what will be written on the screen?

a. WRITELN (')

b. WRITELN (")

c. WRITELN (''')

d. WRITELN ('''')

e. WRITELN (''', ''')

9. Modify program SCANNER so that if multiple spaces occur in the input string, the program will not print out "null" words.

10. Write a program to count and print out the number of times each vowel occurs in an input string to be typed in at run time.

11. Write a program to find the number of times STRING 1 occurs in STRING 2, if both strings are to be typed in at run time.

12. Write a program to call for input of a string. Search through the string and replace each occurrence of 'A' with 'Z'; then print the modified string on the screen.

13. If ST is a string with value equal to 'ABCDEF', A is a variable of type CHAR, and B is a variable of type STRING, which of the following assignment statements are legal?

a. A := ST [4];

b. A := COPY [ST, 4, 1];

c. A := 'D';

d. B := ST [4];

e. B := COPY [ST, 4, 1];

f. B := 'D';

14. Write a program to call for the input of a string; then print the string back on the screen in reverse order.

15. If you run the following program and at the input prompt type in any string of characters and press RETURN, what will be displayed on the screen?

```
PROGRAM GUESS;

  VAR
    ST, BLANK : STRING;
    COUNT : INTEGER;

BEGIN
  WRITELN (' TYPE IN A STRING');
  WRITELN;
  READLN (ST);
  WRITELN;
  BLANK := '';
  FOR COUNT := 1 TO LENGTH (ST) DO
    BEGIN
      BLANK := CONCAT (' ', BLANK, COPY (ST, COUNT, 1));
      WRITELN (BLANK);
      DELETE (BLANK, COUNT + 1, 1)
    END (* FOR *)
END.
```

TEN

NUMBER TYPES AND ARITHMETIC

Now that you have completed nine sessions and used nearly all the Pascal statement types, it has probably occurred to you that you have learned a great deal about Pascal without getting involved in detailed manipulation of numbers. The fact is that that you needn't do "number crunching" simply because you are programming a computer. Even in scientific and engineering programs there are many more statements that deal with loops, conditions, procedure definitions, and the like than there are statements that carry out numerical computations. Nevertheless, sooner or later, you will want to make use of the numeric and arithmetic facilities of Pascal. If your mathematical skills are rusty, relax. We are *not* going to embark upon a dissertation on esoteric mathematics. We *are* going to show you the various number types in Pascal, and how they can be used.

SESSION GOALS

You will learn about *long integer* and *real* numbers in addition to the type *integer* that you have already used. You will discover the largest values that integer and long integer variables can have, and the largest and smallest non-zero values the real variables can have. You will use the *arithmetic operators* and discover the order in which these operations are performed. You will explore an important user trap in computer arithmetic, in which one plus one isn't always two. You will use an assortment of numeric functions. Finally you will study the connections between the different number types.

10-1 HOW BIG AND HOW SMALL?

The Apple, like *any* computing device has both a largest and smallest number that it can handle. Moreover, the situation is a bit more complicated in Pascal since there are three *kinds* of numbers available. It is important that you be *aware* that these largest and smallest values exist. Otherwise, you may stumble into very surprising user problems.

Let's work first with numbers of type *integer* since you have already used them in programs. **Boot up Pascal, clear out the workfile, set the date, and enter the following program:**

```
PROGRAM SIZE;

   VAR
      X : INTEGER;
      INKEY : CHAR;

BEGIN
   X := 1;
   REPEAT
      X := X * 2;
      WRITELN (X);
      READ (INKEY)
   UNTIL INKEY = 'Q'
END.
```

The asterisk in the first line of the REPEAT statement means *multiplication.* The interesting part of the program takes place in this REPEAT loop. Each time the computer goes through the loop, the value of X gets multiplied by 2, and the result is assigned back to X. The new value is displayed on the screen. The main purpose of the READ statement is to halt the display so you can watch what is taking place. As the program stands, it will loop through this block until you type a Q.

Leave the EDITOR and run the program. Press the spacebar three times. Now you should see the numbers 2, 4, 8, and 16 displayed in a vertical column on the screen. Each time you press the spacebar, you will see two times the value of X that appeared previously on the screen. **Keep pressing the spacebar until you see something interesting happen.**

When X reached 16384, something interesting certainly happened. Instead of the 32768 which *should* have been the next number, you got –32768, and after that only zeros. What happened between 16384 and 32768? The answer is that there is a largest integer that the Apple can handle in Pascal, and it lies between these two numbers.

It turns out that Pascal has a name for this *largest integer.* It is called MAXINT and is a predefined *constant.* On the Apple, MAXINT has the *value* 32767. You don't have to remember the value 32767 when writing Apple Pascal programs. You can simply use the MAXINT and the Apple will put in the correct value. A big caution flag should go up here. On other computers MAXINT may have different values. This is one of the details you should check when writing Pascal programs for other systems.

If you lose sight of the fact that integer values in Apple Pascal should not exceed 32767, you can fall into a user trap that would be almost impossible to troubleshoot. Notice what happened when program SIZE pushed the value of X past MAXINT. The WRITELN procedure generated a surprising value of –32768, and then nothing but zeros. When this happened, you could continue to run the program by pressing the spacebar, *and there was no error message.* There is nothing to prevent you from writing a program that will routinely generate integer values greater than MAXINT. If this happens, the integer will take on unexpected values. Needless to say, you would have a very confusing time trying to explain what happened.

This is a very malignant type of program bug. The program runs and produces correct results *some* of the time, and nonsense *some* of the time. It is far easier to find a bug in a program that doesn't work at all, than in one that works *part of the time.*

At any rate, to be forewarned is to be forearmed. If you declare a variable as type integer, the largest value it can accurately take on is MAXINT, which on the Apple II has the value 32767. If the program tries to push the value past this point, it will be incorrect.

You are probably wondering why MAXINT is 32767 rather than, for example 99999. The reason is that variables of type INTEGER are represented internally as *binary numbers* with digits zero and one, and not as *decimal numbers*. The biggest positive binary number allowed is 111111111111111 which is the decimal number 32767.

Let's make a small change in your program and check out negative numbers. **Press the Q key to end the program run. Go to the EDITOR and change the first assignment line to**

```
X := -1;
```

Run the program as before and look for the largest negative integer.

There is some asymmetry here. The first troublesome *positive* integer is 32768, but –32768 is a perfectly acceptable *negative* integer. More experimentation would prove that –32769 cannot be represented correctly as an integer, however.

> The valid range of integers on the Apple II implementation of Pascal is –32768 through 32767.

Press the Q key to end the program. Go to the EDITOR and change the declaration of variable X to

```
VAR
   X : INTEGER [24];
```

Also change the assignment line back to

```
X := 1;
```

You need square brackets to modify the INTEGER declaration for X. As you may recall from Session 9, you can produce a [character by typing CTRL-K, and the] with SHIFT-M. You might consider marking this fact on pieces of paper and gluing them to the keytops if you haven't already done so.

Once the difficulty of the missing characters is solved, it doesn't seem as though anything drastic has happened to your program. What is the purpose of the square brackets, and what does the 24 signify?

Leave the EDITOR and run the program. Press the spacebar 14 times. The last two numbers on the screen are 16384 and 32768. Wasn't MAXINT supposed to be 32767? This time, the computer went right on past MAXINT with no difficulty.

Keep pressing the spacebar until pressing it further causes no change on the screen. When this happens you will see the number

$$604462909807314587353088$$

on the screen. Apart from being a very large number, what is its significance? The significance lies not in this number, but the *next* number that should come up on the screen. Multiply the number above by 2 (remember, that is what is happening in the program) and the result is

$$1208925819614629174706176$$

Count the number of digits in the two numbers. The first has 24, and the second 25. Remember the [24] that you added to the declaration of the integer X in the VAR block? Now it should be clear what this did. It created a *new* type of integer called a *long integer* that can be larger than MAXINT. In the present example, the maximum length of the long integer as set out in the VAR block is 24 *decimal* digits.

Now it's clear why the computer refused to display the second number above. It was too long. Notice something else. **Try to press any of the keys except RESET.** Well folks, your system has just died a horrible death! The ball game is over as far as this program is concerned. You have only one way out. **Turn the power off, insert the APPLE3: diskette and reboot the system.**

When the system tried to exceed the maximum length of the long integer X, strange things happened and the system died. The only safe thing to do at this point is to turn the power off and boot up Pascal from scratch as you did above. Not even CTRL-SHIFT-P will work here.

Now let's tidy up some loose ends about the long integers. You declared X to be a long integer of maximum length 24 decimal digits. In the present case, the range of X is

$$-999999999999999999999999$$

through

$$999999999999999999999999$$

(The negative sign does *not* count as a digit.) As all these 9's may have suggested, long integers are represented internally as decimal rather than binary digits.

In Apple Pascal, you can extend the range of long integers to a maximum of 36 digits. If you leave off the square brackets containing the maximum number of digits, the type changes to *ordinary integers* with a range from −32768 to 32767. These two types of integers are different from one another.

When using long integers you must be very careful not to exceed the maximum length. If you do, your system will die the horrible death witnessed above. You probably are wondering why anyone would ever need long integers having a length of 36 digits anyway; we'll return to that question later in this session.

Incidentally, you should make note of the fact that the WRITELN procedure (and also WRITE, READLN, and READ) accept parameters of type long integer.

Let's investigate a third type of number. **Go to the EDITOR and change the declaration of X in program SIZE so that the VAR block reads**

```
VAR
    X : REAL;
```

Again, this seems like a small change, but it introduces a new type of number. Now X is of type REAL. Do you have any ideas about what a real number is? Aren't *all* numbers real? Mathematicians make a sharp distinction between real and integer numbers. We can see some of the characteristics of this distinction by trying out the program.

Run the program but don't press the spacebar quite yet. The first number on the screen is a two, but it looks different from the twos you have seen so far. This is the first major difference between integer and real numbers. The WRITE and WRITELN procedures will accept values of type REAL, but they always output a decimal point in them, even when the value is a whole number.

Press the spacebar 3 times. Here is the second surprise with real numbers. What does 1.60000E1 mean? You probably were expecting the number sixteen, and that's really what you got; however it is *displayed* in a new way. The E1 means that the decimal point belongs one place to the right of its present position, so, the number displayed is really 16.0000. The E notation is called *power of ten* or *scientific notation.* The number following E is the *exponent* of ten.)

All right, go on pressing the spacebar until the program halts. You may find it comfortable to hold down the REPT (which stands for REPEAT) key and spacebar at the same time. You will have to press the spacebar many times, so be patient.

When the computer stopped, the last part of the display was

```
8.50706E37
1.70141E38

FLOATING POINT ERROR
S# 1, P# 1, I# 16
PRESS RESET
```

Clearly, you have asked the computer to go beyond its upper limit for *real* numbers. Based on the information above, you know that the maximum value for a real number must be greater than 1.70141 with the decimal point moved 38 places to the right. In fact, the maximum real value is about twice that number: 3.402823E38, or

$$340,283,200,000,000,000,000,000,000,000,000,000,000.$$

which, by any standards, is an awfully large number. (If you are impressed by this sort of thing, it's 340.2832 billion billion billion billion.)

The last thing to note about real numbers is that the computer displays only 6 significant digits. In that big number above, only approximately the first 7 digits have significance. The rest of the zeros serve only to indicate where the decimal point belongs. This is in sharp contrast to long integers where the computer keeps track of *all* the digits involved.

Do not follow the instructions on the screen. Instead, remove APPLE0: from the drive. Replace it with APPLE3: and then press RESET to start a "cold" bootup. As you can see, the system was re-initialized. The problem is this: the next number would have been greater than the maximum value of real numbers in Apple Pascal. What value should the program assign to X? The Apple decides to give up. (Some computer languages will warn you that a potential problem exists, assign the maximum real value, and continue.)

In the case of real numbers, you can also find out what the *smallest* positive real number is. **Modify the REPEAT statement to appear as follows:**

```
REPEAT
   X := X / 2;
   WRITELN (X);
   READ (INKEY)
UNTIL INKEY = 'Q'
```

X / 2 means to *divide* 2 into the value of X. Now instead of X growing as you press the RETURN key, it will decrease in size. **Run the program.**

The first number out is 5.00000E-1. Well, 1 divided by 2 is 0.5 and if you move the decimal point one place to the *left*, you do have 0.500000. **Keep pressing the spacebar until the computer stops.**

The last number displayed is 1.17549E-38 which means 1.17549 with the decimal point moved 38 places *to the left*. The smallest legal positive number in Apple Pascal is

$$0.0000000000000000000000000000000000000001175495$$

and is, as you can plainly see, a *very* small number. The same error message surfaced again because the next number that should be assigned to X is outside the bounds of real numbers on the Apple. (Again, some languages will simply set the result equal to zero and go on.) **As before, insert APPLE3: and do a cold reboot of Pascal.**

Real numbers may be negative as well as positive. The absolute values of negative real numbers must lie in the same range as positive real numbers.

There are two important things to remember about real numbers. First, unless you get involved in scientific calculations, you will usually have little need to use them. Second, even if you do, the odds of generating numbers outside the range of reals is small.

Of course, the main use of real numbers is to represent numbers that have a fractional part. They are the natural choice in some situations. One quite typical exception is financial calculations involving dollars and cents. The problem with using real numbers here is that they give you only about 6 or 7 significant figures; that will introduce *rounding errors* for numbers such as 112000.81. A better approach is to make your basic financial unit the *penny* and then use *long integers* with enough digits to handle your biggest number.

10-2 THE UNINITIALIZED-VARIABLE BUG

One of the commonest and subtlest bugs in programming is forgetting to assign a value to a variable and then using that variable in some expression in your program. Let's see what happens when you deliberately introduce this bug into the current version of program SIZE. **Delete the first assignment statement, X := 1, and replace it with WRITELN (X). Run the altered version.**

Note first of all that the compiler does *not* report an error, even though your program never assigned a starting value of X. The very first statement attempts to write the value of X on the screen. Then the first statement inside the REPEAT loop takes the initial value of X (whatever that is), divides it by 2, and assigns the result back to X. The next statement writes the new value of X on the screen.

When you ran the program you saw that the computer was undaunted by the fact that you never *initialized* the value of X. The computer somehow generated its own strange starting value for X, wrote the value on the screen, and then proceeded to divide it by 2 (correctly) and write the new value on the screen. Your program made an error, but the computer failed to detect it and instead went ahead computing incorrect results. This category of unreported bug is especially pernicious.

You should not get the idea that uninitialized variables will always start out with the same predictable value, such as zero for numeric variables. Remember that a variable is just a *place* in the computer's memory. When you declare a variable in a VAR block, the Pascal compiler decides what physical memory location to use for that variable. *But it does not do anything to the data already there.* Whatever "garbage" happens to be there becomes the initial value of that variable on that particular run of the program. A different run might find different "garbage" in the same memory cells.

> The only way to avoid this bug is by a careful reading of your program. For every variable that you declare there must be a statement somewhere that defines its value *before* executing any other statement that makes use of the value.

Type Q and exit your program.

10-3 ARITHMETIC WITH INTEGERS

In this section, the main topic will be the arithmetic operations of type integer that are available in Pascal, and the rules for the *order* in which various operations are done. First, let's be certain about what is meant by an integer. Stated in the simplest terms, an integer is just a whole number. This includes the positive counting numbers 1, 2, 3, 4, ..., the negative of the counting numbers –1, –2, –3, –4, ..., and a very special whole number, 0. Notice that if you add two whole numbers together you always get a whole number. The same is true for subtraction and multiplication. Consequently, you can perform addition, subtraction, and multiplication with integers and get integers; you do not get another number type as a result of the computation. Division is another matter. If you divide the integer 3 by the integer 2, the result is the *real* number 1.5. Therefore, if you are working with numbers of type integer and want to do division, you have to have special operators.

Remember that A DIV B is the *whole number* part of the *quotient* of A divided by B. On the other hand, A MOD B is the *remainder* of A divided by B. You have used these rules in previous programs, but it's a good idea to review them here.

Clear out the workfile and enter the following program:

```
PROGRAM ORDER;

BEGIN
   WRITELN (20 DIV 6)
END.
```

This is a very simple program whose sole purpose is to experiment with the order of operations and the functions that are available in Pascal. You will make a number of modifications to the *numeric expression* whose value is passed to the WRITELN procedure.

The first experiment won't be much of an experiment since you already know what the answer should be. What is 20 DIV 6? **Run the program.** Of course, you got the expected result of 3.

Change the WRITELN statement to read

```
WRITELN (17 MOD 5)
```

What answer will be produced now? **Run the program.** You should have anticipated the answer of 2, since 2 is the remainder of 17 divided by 5.
Next, change the line to

```
WRITELN (2 + 3 * 5)
```

There is some ambiguity here unless there are well defined rules for the *order* in which the calculations are to be done. If addition is done first, the answer is 25. If multiplication is done first, the answer is 17.

Well, you can easily find out which way it is. **Run the program.** The result gives you a valuable piece of information to file away for reference. (We'll summarize all the rules at the end of this section, so you don't have to write anything down at this point.)

Just to test the idea that multiplication is always done *before* addition and to see whether the *order* of the terms makes a difference, **change the WRITELN statement again as follows:**

```
WRITELN (2 + 3 * 5, 3 * 5 + 2)
```

This gives you the answer, but the *output format* is rather cramped. The result on your screen looks like this:

```
1717
```

You have to read this as "seventeen, seventeen," and it confirms the idea that multiplication is done ahead of addition, no matter what the order of the terms. We say that multiplication has a "higher priority" than addition.

Now let's try to improve the output format. **Change the WRITELN call again as follows:**

```
WRITELN (2 + 3 * 5 : 6, 3 * 5 + 2 : 6)
```

Now run the program. Note here that the two seventeens are each located in a *field* that is six characters wide, and that they appear on the right side of that field. That is the effect of ": 6" after any parameter in a WRITE or WRITELN call. (Other numbers could be used in place of 6.)

Now let's see what happens in an expression that contains multiplication and *subtraction*. **Change the WRITELN call as follows and rerun.**

```
WRITELN (-2 + 3 * 5 : 6, 3 * 5 - 2 : 6)
```

This result confirms that multiplication has a higher priority than subtraction as well as addition.

What about expressions that contain both addition and subtraction? What is the order of carrying out these two operations? **Change WRITELN again as follows:**

```
WRITELN (2 + 3 - 5 : 6, 3 - 5 + 2 : 6)
```

Notice that if addition is done first, the result will be

   0   -4

But if subtraction is done first, the result will be

   0   0

Run the program and see.

This test is inconclusive about the first expression (2 + 3 - 5), since your zero result would occur regardless of whether the addition or the subtraction was done first. But the second result shows that subtraction *in the second expression* was done before the addition. Let's clear this ambiguity up.

Change the WRITELN again as follows:

```
WRITELN (9 - 3 - 2 : 6)
```

If the subtraction on the left is done first, the result will be 4; but if the one on the right is done first, the result will be 8. **Run the program and find out.**

The easiest way to summarize all this is to say that multiplication takes place before addition or subtraction, and that additions and subtractions are done from left to right. **Read over the previous results and make sure that you can explain everything you have seen according to this rule.**

Now let's find out where DIV and MOD fit into this scheme. **Change the WRITELN parameter again to this:**

```
WRITELN (2 + 3 DIV 5 : 6, 3 DIV 5 + 2 : 6)
```

Using the fact that 3 DIV 5 = 0, 5 DIV 5 = 1, and 3 DIV 7 = 0, you should be able to verify the following possible results before running:

1	0	if + is first
2	2	if DIV is first
1	2	if the order is left-right

Run the test program and find out.

This result suggests that DIV is like * : both operations are carried out before + or –. Indeed, that is the case in Pascal. You probably guessed that MOD is like DIV and * also, and that is also true, though we will not investigate it experimentally now. Instead, let's see what can be done to *break the rules of order*.

Consider the following version:

```
WRITELN (5 DIV 2 + 3 * 4)
```

Again, it makes a difference in what order the calculations are done. From what you saw in the previous example, you can safely conclude that the result will be 2 + 12, or 14.

Don't bother to run that. Instead, change the WRITELN call to read

```
WRITELN (5 DIV 2 + 3 * 4 : 6, (5 DIV 2 + 3) * 4 : 6)
```

Run it. Notice that the arithmetic *inside* the parentheses is done *before* the result (5) is multiplied by 4.

Let's try a harder one. **Change the WRITELN call as follows:**

```
WRITELN (((2 * 3 MOD 2) * (2 + 3 * 2)) * 2)
```

In the leftmost inner parentheses you can see that it makes a great difference whether the multiplication or MOD is done first. If the multiplication is done first, the result of the expression in parentheses is 6 MOD 2 or 0. If the MOD operation is done first, the result is 2 * 1 or 2. You should have gathered from the last few experiments that division and multiplication are done at the same level of priority. In this expression we have two operations of the same priority. Now it becomes important to know in which direction the computer scans the expression. **Run the program. Inspect the answer and work backwards to discover whether the computer scanned the first nested set of parentheses from left to right, or right to left.** Well, what did you find out?

In a few moments we'll return to the question of order and scanning direction of arithmetic expressions, but now let's look at some of the *built-in numeric functions* that are available in Pascal.

Change the WRITELN statement in program ORDER to read

```
WRITELN (ABS (38))
```

and run the program. Nothing much seemed to happen to the 38, right? **Change the parameter of the ABS function to –251 and run the program again.** What happened this time? ABS evidently takes the *size* of the number and ignores the sign. ABS(–5) is 5, ABS(14) is 14, and so on.

We'll make an important point here and will return to it later. Your parameters for ABS were of type integer, and ABS returned an integer value. (How could you tell?) In the section after next, you will try to use a real argument for ABS. What do you suppose will be returned in that case?

The last function to experiment with in this section is SQR. **Modify the WRITELN statement to read as follows:**

```
WRITELN (SQR (5))
```

Run the program. What is the relationship of the answer to 5? Do you know yet what SQR does?

Change the argument of SQR to –6 and run again. Okay, now you should have the purpose of SQR nailed down. If not, experiment some more until you are sure.

Let's sum up what you should have learned. There are three familiar arithmetic operations on integers in Pascal. They are addition (+), subtraction (–), and multiplication (*). There are two types of division; MOD and DIV. The computer scans arithmetic expressions from left to right until the innermost set of parentheses is located. Then, the operations inside are done according to priority rules, again scanning from left to right. The operations with the highest priority are division and multiplication. Then addition and subtraction are done.

There is a good rule of thumb to keep in mind. *If there can possibly be any confusion about the order in which operations are to be done, use extra parentheses to make it clear. Too many parentheses rarely cause trouble, but too few certainly can.*

10-4 ARITHMETIC WITH LONG INTEGERS

Why long integers anyway? As we said earlier, they are usually needed for financial calculations. As you will discover in this session, calculations with *real* numbers usually produce approximations of the correct answer. The approximations may be very good, but nevertheless, they are still only approximations. This sort of thing makes bankers and auditors very nervous. However, calculations with integers are *exact*.

The best way to approach financial calculations is to let integers represent the number of pennies in the transaction. It's clear that data of type INTEGER won't be of much value unless you have a very small company. Remember that MAXINT has the value 32767. If this is the number of pennies, then none of the calculations could amount to more than $327.67.

On the other hand, *long integers* can be specified to have lengths up to 36 digits. The maximum financial amount that could be handled with long integers is therefore

$$\$9,999,999,999,999,999,999,999,999,999,999.99$$

This is big enough even for government calculations. The long integers can be *sized* to any type of financial calculation you wish.

Let's return to the question of arithmetic, this time with long integers. **Modify program ORDER so it appears as follows:**

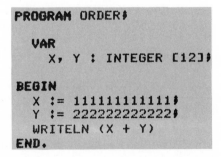

```
PROGRAM ORDER;

  VAR
    X, Y : INTEGER [12];

BEGIN
  X := 111111111111;
  Y := 222222222222;
  WRITELN (X + Y)
END.
```

Can you *add* long integers together? **Run the program and find out.** The answer should convince you that you can. It is also true that subtraction can be done with long integers.

Change the last two lines of the BEGIN/END block to read

```
Y := 5;
WRITELN (X * Y)
```

Well, what about multiplication? **Run the program.** No problem yet. Addition, subtraction, and multiplication are all permitted with long integers.

There is only one basic arithmetic operation left. **Change the last two lines as follows:**

```
Y := 100;
WRITELN (X DIV Y)
```

If the DIV operation is permitted, you should get 1111111111 as an answer. (There are ten 1s in this number) **Run the program.** What's the answer; is DIV permitted?

The next obvious operation to try is the MOD type of division. **Modify the WRITELN statement to read**

```
WRITELN (X MOD Y)
```

If MOD is permitted, then the answer ought to be 11. (Do you see why?) If not, then an error message should probably show up.

Run the program. Error 134 seems ominous. **Press E to see what the error is.** The illegal operand message confirms our fears. Unfortunately, MOD is *not* permitted with long integers. **Press the spacebar to get back to the EDITOR.**

Addition, subtraction, multiplication, and the DIV form of division can be done with long integers. The MOD form of division is *not* permitted. The same priority rules you discovered for these operators when using integers also apply when using long integers. Remember that you can pick any length of long integers up to 36. Be careful that your calculations don't wind up with a number longer than the maximum size of the long integers. If you do, your system will die the horrible death you saw earlier. *Note also that ABS and SQR do not work with long integers.*

10-5 ARITHMETIC WITH REAL NUMBERS

Now let's turn our attention to arithmetic involving *real* numbers. **Change program ORDER until it appears as follows:**

```
PROGRAM ORDER;

VAR
    X, Y : REAL;

BEGIN
    X := 4.256;
    Y := .172;
    WRITELN (X + Y)
END.
```

The two variables X, and Y have been declared to be of type *real,* and are assigned real values in the assignment statement. The arithmetic seems perfectly clear. **Run the program.** What happened?

Judging by the position of the cursor, the problem seems to lie in the definition of Y. **Press E to move into the EDITOR where you can read the error message.** The message ERROR IN < FACTOR > seems rather cryptic. Well, the problem is in the *way you "spelled"* the constant in the text of that assignment statement. First, *all* real numbers must be written with a decimal point in them. If you were considering the number four as a real number it would have to be written as 4.0 with a decimal point and a zero appended. If there is no digit before the decimal point or after it, you *must* insert a 0 there.

Change .172 to 0.172 in the assignment statement for Y and run the program again.

This time the program ran with no difficulties. You probably expected to get an answer of 4.428, but you got 4.42800 instead. This is one of the characteristics of arithmetic with real numbers. They are represented internally with an accuracy of about 7 decimal digits. The 7th digit is rounded off and six digits are displayed in any real result output by the WRITE or WRITELN procedure. If necessary, zeros are added to the end of the number, as happened in this example, to fill out the result to six digits.

Change the WRITELN statement to read

```
WRITELN (X - Y)
```

and run the program. There were no surprises this time, and you got the expected answer of 4.08400.

Change the - to * in the WRITELN statement and check out multiplication. Did everything work out out as expected? The only difference was in the way the answer was displayed. Of course, 7.32032E–1 is the way the computer represents 0.732032.

There is one last arithmetic operator to check out. **Change the WRITELN call statement to**

```
WRITELN (X / Y)
```

and run the program. You saw earlier that / is the operator for division of real numbers. The answer is 2.47442E1 which is the computer representation of 24.7442.

There are few surprises in arithmetic with real numbers. You haven't looked at the *order* of operations with real numbers, but you don't have to; the order is precisely the same as for integer and long integer arithmetic. Division and multiplication have priority over addition and subtraction. The computer scans expressions from left to right, and works from the deepest set of parentheses out.

You have already learned that the ABS function returns a value equal to the parameter, but always with a positive sign. You saw that ABS (–3) = 3. If the parameter of the ABS function is an integer, so is the value of the function.

Let's check this out with real numbers. **Modify the BEGIN/END block of program ORDER to read:**

```
BEGIN
  X := -4.256;
  WRITELN (ABS (X))
END.
```

The answer of 4.25600 indicates a *real* result. ABS is a curious function because it can be passed either a real or an integer parameter. The type of the value of the function is determined by the type of the parameter. If the parameter is real, the value of ABS is real; if the parameter is integer, the value of ABS is integer. (Incidentally, Pascal doesn't give you a way to define a function of your own with this adaptive property.)

Change ABS to SQR and run the program. What happened? It seems clear that SQR has the same adaptive characteristic as ABS. *The type of the value of either ABS or SQR is the same as that of the parameter of the function.*

The next two functions to experiment with are TRUNC and ROUND. **Modify program ORDER so that it appears as follows:**

```
PROGRAM ORDER;

VAR
  X : REAL;

BEGIN
  X := 4.256;
  WRITELN (TRUNC (X) : 10, ROUND (X) : 10)
END.
```

Run the program. What do TRUNC and ROUND do? The result of 4 (without the decimal point and trailing zeros) indicates that these functions return an *integer*. Both of them seem to throw away the fractional part of the real number. In the present case, with X = 4.256, both functions returned a value of 4.

Change the assignment line to the following

```
X := 4.856;
```

and run again. For this value of X, TRUNC and ROUND returned *different* integers. **Experiment with other positive numbers in the assignment statement.**

Now let's check out the negative cases. **Change the assignment line to the following**

```
X := -4.256;
```

and run the program. Next, try

```
X := -4.856;
```

and run again. These experiments should give you a clear idea of how TRUNC and ROUND work.

> For any real parameter X, ROUND returns the integer *nearest* to X. If X is positive, TRUNC returns the nearest integer that is less than or equal to X. If X is negative, TRUNC returns the nearest integer that is greater than (i.e. more positive than) or equal to X.

Thus, ROUND "rounds off" real numbers to the nearest integer, while TRUNC "truncates" (chops off) the fractional part of real numbers and returns just the integer part. The following facts may be useful in helping you to understand the connection between these functions:

If X > = 0 then ROUND (X) = TRUNC (X + 0.5)

If X < 0 then ROUND (X) = TRUNC (X – 0.5)

An important use of the TRUNC function is to *convert* a value of either type real or type long-integer to a value of type integer. Of course, the real or long-integer value has to be within the standard range (–32768 through 32767) of integer values. We will return to this use of TRUNC later in this session.

Let's turn to a different function. **Modify your program to appear as follows:**

```
PROGRAM ORDER;

  VAR
    X : INTEGER;

BEGIN
  X := 4;
  WRITELN (PWROFTEN (X))
END.
```

X, which is of type integer is assigned the value 4. The new function is PWROFTEN. PWROFTEN rather sounds like "power of ten", doesn't it? **Run the program.** What was printed out? PWROFTEN does indeed compute a power of ten and returns the result as a real number. The parameter of PWROFTEN *must* be an integer value, and the value of the function is a real number. Negative parameter values are illegal and will cause the system to die.

10-6 SOME MATHEMATICAL FUNCTIONS

If you are familiar with functions such as the square root, sine, cosine, and logarithms, you'll probably be interested in this section, and should read on. If not, skip to the next section.

Apple Pascal includes a package of mathematical functions in a special unit called TRANSCEND. If you wish to use any of the functions, you must include TRANSCEND in a USES declaration block, just as you did with TURTLEGRAPHICS and APPLESTUFF. TRANSCEND is the third and last of these special units supplied with Apple Pascal and saved in the file SYSTEM.LIBRARY on APPLE0:.

The functions are these: SQRT, SIN, COS, EXP, ATAN, LN, and LOG. Let's look briefly at each of these.

SQRT (X) returns the square root of X. Both X and SQRT (X) are real. The only restriction is that you can't take the square root of a negative number.

SIN (X) takes the sine of the real parameter X. X is assumed to be in radians. The value of SIN (X) is also real. COS (X) has the same characteristics except that the cosine of X is returned. There is no tangent function defined in TRANSCEND. You can compute it easily, though, by evaluating SIN (X) divided by COS (X).

ATAN (X) returns the arctangent of X. X is a real number, and ATAN (X) is also real and is expressed in radians.

EXP (X) returns a real value equal to e (the base of the natural logarithms) raised to the power X. Both X and the value returned by EXP (X) are real.

LN (X) takes the natural logarithm of X. Both X and LN (X) are real, and X must be a positive number. LN is the inverse of EXP.

There is no exponential operator in Pascal. You can't, for example, raise X to the Yth power where X and Y are real numbers, or even when Y is a simple integer. At least, you can't do it directly. You can, however, compute it using the EXP and LN operators. To compute X to the Yth power, use the following recipe:

```
EXP (Y * LN (X))
```

LOG (X) returns the logarithm of X to the base ten. Both X and LOG (X) are real. Note that PWROFTEN can have only integer values, so it is not a proper inverse of the LOG function.

The discussion of these mathematical functions has deliberately been kept brief. If you understand what we've been talking about, then the description should suffice. If not, then far too many pages would be needed to lay out the details.

10-7 AN APPLICATION OF REAL NUMBERS

If you exclude scientific calculations, most routine problems can be handled quite well with integers. On the other hand, the following problem is one that does require real numbers: the problem of computing the average of a set of numbers. We start by generating a set of random *integers* from 0 to 10 inclusive, using the RANDOM function. Then we compute their average, which will be *real*.

Clear out the workfile and enter the following program:

```
PROGRAM FINDAVERAGE;

  USES
    APPLESTUFF;

  VAR
    COUNT, HOWMANY : INTEGER;
    SUM, AVERAGE : REAL;

BEGIN
  RANDOMIZE;
  WRITE ('HOW MANY NUMBERS? ');
  READLN (HOWMANY);
  SUM := 0;
  FOR COUNT := 1 TO HOWMANY DO
    SUM := SUM + RANDOM MOD 11;
  AVERAGE := SUM / HOWMANY;
  WRITELN ('AVERAGE IS ', AVERAGE)
END.
```

There are some details about the program that are worth discussing. First, SUM (which will be used to accumulate the sum of the random numbers) is declared to be real. If SUM had been declared an integer, and HOWMANY (the number of random numbers to be generated) was large enough, it is possible that SUM would have been greater than MAXINT which would then set SUM equal to incorrect values. With SUM declared to be real, the difficulty is avoided.

Another item you may have spotted is that AVERAGE (a real value) is assigned the quotient of SUM (a real) and HOWMANY (an integer). This looks like a type conflict, but isn't. This whole issue will be discussed thoroughly later in this session.

The random numbers are generated by RANDOM MOD 11. You have used the RANDOM function many times before. This expression will generate integers at random from the set 0, 1, 2, ..., 9, and 10. If you average a large number of these random numbers, what should you get? If you said 5, then you are right. However, it won't usually be *exactly* 5 will it? Also, as the number of random numbers generated increases, shouldn't the average get closer to 5?

Run the program and answer the prompt with a 10. Run the program several more times keeping HOWMANY at 10. Did you get the same average each time?

Run the program several more times, this time using an input value of 100. Are the results grouped closer about 5?

Finally, try it again, but this time run the program several times with a value of 1000. How do the results check out this time?

It should be clear that as the number of random numbers in the average increases, the average gets closer to 5. This program in addition to revealing some facts about statistics, also illustrates a case where real numbers are required.

10-8 ONE PLUS ONE ISN'T ALWAYS TWO

The introduction of the *real* data type brings with it a lot of advantages, but also one or two **user traps.** If you fall into one of these traps with your eyes open, perhaps you won't have as much trouble recognizing it in the future.

Clear out the workfile and type in the following program:

```
PROGRAM TEST;

VAR
   X : REAL;
   I : INTEGER;

BEGIN
  X := 0;
  FOR I := 1 TO 5 DO
    X := X + 0.2;
  IF X = 1 THEN
    WRITELN ('RIGHT')
  ELSE
    WRITELN ('WRONG')
END.
```

Look over the program. There certainly is nothing complicated or involved here. As you can see, 0.2 is to be summed five times and the result is then tested against 1. But we all know that if you begin with zero, and add 0.2 five times, the result is *always* 1, so what is the big message? If X *is* equal to 1 after the summation, then RIGHT will be printed out; otherwise, WRONG will be printed. **Run the program.** What happened?

Not too surprising, right? Well, let's make a couple of simple changes. **Change the FOR statement to read**

```
FOR I := 1 TO 10 DO
  X := X + 0.1;
```

and run the program. Whoops! What is wrong? Surely, if you begin with zero and add 0.1 ten times, the result is 1. We can check on this by writing the value of X at the same time RIGHT or WRONG is printed out. **Change the IF statement to read**

```
IF X = 1 THEN
     WRITELN ('RIGHT, X = ', X)
ELSE
     WRITELN ('WRONG, X = ', X)
```

The results certainly cry out for explanation. The reported value of X is 1.00000, and still X was not equal to 1 in the IF THEN statement, as shown by the WRONG message.

Let's try one more experiment. **Change the IF statement to read**

```
IF X = 1 THEN
     WRITELN ('RIGHT, X - 1 = ', X - 1)
ELSE
     WRITELN ('WRONG, X - 1 = ', X - 1)
```

and run the program.

Well, now it's clear what is happening. When you wrote out the value of X after the summation, its value *appeared* to be 1. However, when you subtracted 1 from X, the result was *not* 0, but instead was 1.19209E-7. Well then, X must have had the approximate value 1.0000001. This is *close to 1, but it isn't equal to 1 exactly.* If you ask that X be printed out, it will appear as 1.00000 since only six digits are *displayed* by the WRITELN procedure. The test IF X = 1 THEN is testing to see if X is *exactly* equal to 1, and it *isn't*.

You can experiment some more with this program to see where the errors occur. Some tests to try out are these: sum 0.05 twenty times, .02 fifty times, or 0.01 one hundred times.

There are two sources of error that can contribute to the problem. First, the computer represents real numbers internally with only a finite number of significant digits. If you try to express one-third on paper as a real number you would probably write something like .333333. Actually, there should be an infinite number of 3s after the decimal point to represent one third *exactly*. Furthermore, the sum .333333 + .333333 + .333333 is equal to .999999, *not one*. The computer has the same problem that you have in handling fractions with digits that repeat forever, except that the problem comes up in surprising ways. Real numbers, like integers, are represented as sequences of *binary* digits (0 and 1) rather than the *decimal* digits (0 through 9). It just so happens that the decimal number 0.1 looks like this as a binary number:

$$0.000110011001100...$$

It is a *repeating binary fraction*. Since the computer has room for only 23 binary digits of precision, it cannot represent one-tenth exactly.

The moral of this exercise is that whenever you do calculations with real numbers on *any* computer, you should keep in mind the fact that cumulative errors are inevitable and in some cases may be important. The only exact numbers are integers and long integers.

10-9 INTERACTIONS BETWEEN NUMERIC TYPES

You've worked with three different types of numbers now: integer, long integer, and real. As you might suppose, there are times when the computer will convert from one type to another without problem, and other times when the computer will complain if asked to convert. A simple program will let you see which conversions are automatic.

Clear out the workfile and type in the following program:

```
PROGRAM CONFLICT;

VAR
    I1, I2 : INTEGER;
    L1, L2 : INTEGER [12];
    R1, R2 : REAL;

BEGIN
    I1 := 12345;
    L1 := 12345;
    R1 := 12345.0;
    I2 := L1;
    I2 := R1;
    L2 := I1;
    L2 := R1;
    R2 := I1;
    R2 := L1
END.
```

The point of this program is to find out about possible *type conflicts* that may arise in the last six statements. Each of the six statements has a variable on the left side that is of a different type than the value on the right side of the assignment operator.

Run this program. When you get the first compiler error, note carefully which statement the cursor is pointing at. Do not type E. Instead, press the spacebar and go on to the next compiler error. Note down the offending statement. Continue the process until there are no further errors. Then go back to the EDITOR.

This experiment shows that four of your six statements did indeed lead to a *type conflict* error. Note that in the two statements that were legal, there were *integer* values on the right side of the assignments. *Integer values may be assigned to real and long integer variables.*

Change the four statements that caused errors so that they look like this:

```
I2 := TRUNC (L1);
I2 := TRUNC (R1);
L2 := I1;
L2 := TRUNC (R1);
R2 := I1;
R2 := TRUNC (L1)
```

Run the result. This time you should have gotten no compiler errors. As we said earlier, you can use the TRUNC function to *convert* real numbers and long integers to ordinary integers. Thus, the right sides of all six statements are now of type integer, which you can freely assign to *any* numeric variable of whatever type.

Pascal, as you have seen is very forgiving about the use of integer values in places where real or long integer values are expected. Pascal simply *promotes* the integers up to the proper type so as to avoid type conflict errors. This happens not only in assignment statements but also in numeric expressions that mix integers with another numeric type. The following rules sumarize the situation:

> It is *legal* for integers to appear *anywhere* that a real number or long integer is legal.
>
> If integers appear in expressions that contain reals, then integers are automatically *promoted* to reals and the result of the expression is real.
>
> If integers appear in expressions that contain long integers, then integers are automatically *promoted* to long integers and the result of the expression is long integer.
>
> It is *illegal* to mix long integers and reals in the same expression or to use a long integer where a real number or an integer is expected.

Notice the assymetry between the way numbers and strings are handled in Pascal. If it makes sense, integers are *promoted* to reals automatically without any problems. In the same way, characters should be able to be *promoted* to type string. However, you can't concatenate characters to strings, as you saw in Session 9. This is *not* sensible, and is one of the weak points of this implementation of strings in Pascal.

We hope that the different number types and rules for conversion from one type to another have not left you feeling confused. Frankly, the reason that the topic of number types was delayed until relatively late in the book was to avoid the possibility of confusion over minor points that really have very little to do with the language that you are learning. As has already been pointed out, *most* calculations do quite well with integer arithmetic. If you plan to do financial calculations, you will need long integers. Unless you get involved in statistical or scientific calculations, you will rarely need real numbers.

SUMMARY

Now let's summarize what has been covered in this session.

■ **You learned that there are three number types: integer, long integer, and real.**

- The largest integer is **MAXINT** which has the value 32767. The largest negative integer is –32768.

- Long integers can be up to 36 decimal digits long.

- You saw that the largest absolute value of reals is about 3.40282E38. The smallest non-zero absolute value is about 1.17549E–38.

- Pascal scans expressions from left to right, doing the arithmetic in the deepest set of parentheses first.

- When doing arithmetic, multiplication and division (*, /, DIV and MOD) have priority over addition and subtraction (+ and –).

- You used +, –, and * to indicate addition, subtraction, and multiplication respectively, for all numeric types.

- Division of reals is indicated by /. Division of integers is done with either the DIV or MOD operations.

- Both DIV and MOD are permitted with integers, but only DIV is permitted with long integers.

- ABS (X) returns the absolute magnitude of X. X may be integer or real but not long integer.

- SQR (X) returns the square of X. X may be integer or real but not long integer.

- For real X, TRUNC (X) converts the value to type integer and truncates the decimal part of X. For long integer values of X, TRUNC (X) converts the value to type integer so long as the result is within the legal range of integers.

- For real X, ROUND (X) rounds off the number and returns the nearest integer value.

- Arithmetic with real numbers can sometimes produce errors due to conversion from decimal to binary and the fact that reals can only be represented to about seven significant decimal digits.

- Integers are promoted to type long integer in assignment statements and in expressions that contain long integers.

- Integers are promoted to type real in assignment statements and in expressions that contain real numbers.

- Long integers cannot be mixed with reals in the same expression.

Table 10.1 Cumulative Pascal vocabulary. New words introduced in this session are printed in boldface. (Code: a = declared in APPLESTUFF; g = declared in TURTLEGRAPHICS; t = declared in TRANSCEND)

Reserved Words	Built-In Procedures	Built-In Functions	Other Built-Ins
PROGRAM	DELETE	Boolean	Constants
USES	READ	a BUTTON	FALSE
CONST	READLN	a KEYPRESS	TRUE
VAR	WRITE		**MAXINT**
PROCEDURE	WRITELN	Integer	g NONE
FUNCTION	a NOTE	LENGTH	g WHITE
BEGIN	a RANDOMIZE	POS	g BLACK
FOR	g FILLSCREEN	**ROUND**	g GREEN
TO	g GRAFMODE	**TRUNC**	g VIOLET
DOWNTO	g INITTURTLE	a PADDLE	g ORANGE
DO	g MOVE	a RANDOM	g BLUE
REPEAT	g MOVETO		
UNTIL	g PENCOLOR	Real	Types
WHILE	g TEXTMODE	**ABS**	BOOLEAN
IF	g TURN	**PWROFTEN**	CHAR
THEN	g TURNTO	**SQR**	INTEGER
ELSE	g VIEWPORT	t **ATAN**	**REAL**
CASE		t **COS**	STRING
OF		t **EXP**	
END		t **LN**	Units
		t **LOG**	APPLESTUFF
DIV		t **SIN**	**TRANSCEND**
MOD		t **SQRT**	TURTLEGRAPHICS
AND		String	
OR		CONCAT	
NOT		COPY	

QUESTIONS AND PROBLEMS

1. What is the numeric result of each of the following operations?

   a. 25 MOD 10 * 3 + 5 DIV 2

   b. 3 + 4 * 2 MOD 3

   c. ((((2 + 3) * 2) – 2) DIV 7) * 5

   d. ABS (–4.5) / ROUND (2.9) + 0.5

   e. SQR (ABS (TRUNC (2 * 4.2 – 25)))

2. Explain which numeric data types can be used with one another in an arithmetic expression and which cannot. When two different numeric types appear (legally) in an expression, what type does the result of the expression have?

3. For each assignment statement below, tell whether it can be a legal Pascal statement. If so, give all possible types that X can have in order to make the statement legal.

a. X := 0

b. X := 137

c. X := -87524936

d. X := .5632

e. X := 1.7E-4

f. X := 4.3E39

g. X := 32768

h. X := -32768

i. X := '32768'

4. Use the instructions stated in Question 3 for the following statements.

a. X := 5 DIV 2

b. X := 5 DIV 2.0

c. X := 5 / 2

d. X := 5 / 2.0

e. X := 555555 DIV 2

f. X := 555555 / 2

g. X := 5 + 2

h. X := 5 + 2.0

5. Use the instructions stated in Question 3 for the following statements:

a. X := TRUNC (1.3)

b. X := TRUNC (1234567 DIV 1000)

c. X := TRUNC (1234567)

d. X := TRUNC (1)

e. X := TRUNC (SQRT (2))

6. For each value of X given below, state whether TRUNC (X) = ROUND (X), TRUNC (X) > ROUND (X), or TRUNC (X) < ROUND (X).

a. 18.237

b. 18.659

c. −18.13

d. −18.92

(Hint: remember that ">" means "more positive than".)

7. The three statements below are legal Pascal statements.

```
X := 1E10;
Y := X + 1;
IF Y = X THEN
    WRITE ('OOPS!')
ELSE
    WRITE ('OKAY')
```

a. What data type(s) must X and Y be?

b. If the statements are executed in succession, what will be written on the screen? Explain why?

8. Assume that STR1, STR2, NUM1, and NUM2 have the values 'PRICE', 'MARKUP', 6.92, and 1.25 respectively. Explain precisely what screen display will be produced by the following procedure call:

```
WRITELN (STR1 : 10, NUM1 : 10, STR2 : 10, NUM2 : 10)
```

9. What will happen if the following program is run?

```
PROGRAM WHATEVER;

    CONST
        NAME1 = 'BOB';
        NAME2 = 'SUE';

    VAR
        COUNT: INTEGER;

    BEGIN
        FOR COUNT := 3 TO 12 DO
            IF COUNT < 8 THEN
                WRITELN (NAME1 : COUNT)
            ELSE
                WRITELN (NAME2 : COUNT)
    END.
```

10. Write a single program that computes:

   a. The average of all the integers from one to 100,

   b. The average of their squares,

   c. The square root of the number equal to the average of their squares minus the square of their averages.

11. The Pythagorean formula

$$c^2 = a^2 + b^2$$

   relates the lengths of the two perpendicular sides (a and b) of a right triangle to the length of the longest side (c). Write a program that prompts the user to type in the lengths of the two perpendicular sides, separated by a space. The program should then accept the input and write out the length of the longest side.

12. The product of all the integers from one to N is called *N factorial*. Write a program which will compute and write a neatly formatted table giving the exact values for N and N factorial for values of N from one to 30 inclusive. (Caution: you will have to use the "longest" long integers to hold N factorial.)

13. If N is an integer, 1/N is called its *reciprocal*. Write a program that outputs the sum of the reciprocals of N for all integers in the range 1 to NUMBER, where the user types the value of NUMBER when the program is run. Run it several times and describe what happens when NUMBER gets bigger and bigger.

14. Write and run a program, along the lines of the one in question 13, that outputs the sum of reciprocals of the *squares* of N. Describe the result for large NUMBER values.

ELEVEN

SCALAR DATA TYPES AND SETS

In previous sessions you have seen constants, variables, functions, and expressions of a variety of distinct *types*. You have used integers, real numbers, characters, strings, and boolean values in programs. You are probably beginning to wonder how many more distinct data types there are in Pascal. The answer, as you will soon see, is a very large number.

SESSION GOALS

In this session you will explore the *scalar* properties that make integers, characters, and boolean values alike. You will define an entirely new scalar data type of your own choosing, declare variables to be of the new type, and assign new values to these variables. You will use three new built-in functions that work with any scalar values, including ones that you invent. You will see that an entire set of scalar values can be treated as a single piece of data and can be assigned to a variable of a new type called SET. You will find that Pascal contains a facility for finding whether a particular scalar value is a member of a given set, and that it is possible to do arithmetic with pairs of sets.

11-1 WHITE, ORANGE, BLUE: WHAT ARE THEY?

Unless you were unusually alert, we slipped something past you that went unnoticed back in Session 7 while you were learning about graphics. There is a lesson in that, and we will explore it now.

Boot up, set the date, clear the workfile, and enter the following program.

```
PROGRAM LINE;

USES
    TURTLEGRAPHICS;

BEGIN
    INITTURTLE;
    PENCOLOR (WHITE);
    MOVETO (279, 191);
    READLN
END.
```

Run the program. It draws a diagonal line from the middle of the screen (where the turtle starts out) to the upper-right corner and then halts at the READLN call. **Press RETURN to end the program.**

Do you see anything strange about this program? Something that needs further explanation? Look at each word and ask yourself what it is. PROGRAM, for example is a *reserved word.* LINE is a *name* that identifies the program. USES is another reserved word. TURTLEGRAPHICS is the name of a set of programs stored as a *library unit.* BEGIN is another reserved word. INITTURTLE is the name of a procedure declared in the TURTLEGRAPHICS unit. PENCOLOR is the name of another TURTLEGRAPHICS procedure. WHITE is...well it's...it must be a...

What is WHITE anyway? Well, what things could it be? First, we note that WHITE appears in this program as a *parameter* that is being passed to the PENCOLOR procedure. That rules out the possibility of its being a reserved word, such as IF or FOR or WHILE or BEGIN, since reserved words never have *values.*

The things that have values in Pascal are *variables, constants,* and *functions.* Perhaps WHITE is one of these things. If so, it would have to be declared in TURTLEGRAPHICS, and its type and value would have to be established there also. Following that trail a little farther, we naturally ask what the *value* and the *type* of WHITE might be. And the natural answer is to experiment and see. For example, if WHITE is an integer or a real number or a character or a string, then WRITELN (WHITE) will tell us what its value is.

Insert a semicolon after READLN and then the following new line:

```
WRITELN (WHITE)
```

Run the new version.

Well, whatever WHITE is, it does not belong to one of these standard data types. The error message makes that plain. WHITE seems to have a value, but it is not a number, a character, or a string. Very mysterious.

Here's another approach. Does WHITE stand alone, or are there other words that are like WHITE? What else could we substitute for WHITE in the call to PENCOLOR? Well, in Session 7 you used several other words there: BLUE, ORANGE, GREEN, VIOLET, BLACK, and NONE. Whatever these names refer to *they are all of the same type.*

At this point you clearly need some more evidence. **Delete the WRITELN statement. Change program LINE to the following:**

```
PROGRAM LINE;

   USES
      TURTLEGRAPHICS;

   VAR
      COLOR : SCREENCOLOR;

BEGIN
   INITTURTLE;
   COLOR := WHITE;
   PENCOLOR (COLOR);
   MOVETO (279, 191);
   READLN
END.
```

Study the three changes carefully. Run the new version.

This time program LINE works exactly as it did before. Now you have a basis for understanding what is going on. First of all, the added VAR block declares a new variable. Its name is COLOR. Its type seems to be something called SCREENCO-LOR, whatever that may be.

Second, we see that COLOR appears as the *target* of an assignment statement in the BEGIN/END block. That statement,

```
COLOR := WHITE
```

must mean that the variable COLOR is assigned a value equal to the value of WHITE. Ah ha! Since there was no *type conflict* error message, that must mean that WHITE is also of type SCREENCOLOR.

Finally, the successful use of COLOR as the parameter value in the PENCOLOR call confirms our belief that COLOR does indeed have the same value as WHITE, since the program ran as before and drew a white line. WHITE, therefore seems to be a variable or a constant of the new type SCREENCOLOR.

We can tell whether WHITE is a variable or a constant by a simple experiment. **Insert the following assignment line immediately after the one you just added:**

```
WHITE := COLOR;
```

If WHITE is a constant, the compiler will complain about trying to assign a value to it. If it is a variable, on the other hand, then the assignment is legal (though useless in the present case). **Run the program and find out.**

Well, there you have it: WHITE (and the other colors you have used) are *constants of type SCREENCOLOR*. That explains everything, doesn't it. Or does it? If you are like us, you probably feel at this point that a lot of questions have been left dangling. What type *is* SCREENCOLOR, anyway? How did WHITE, BLUE, etc., get to be constants of that type? Do they appear in a CONST block in TURTLEGRA-PHICS? If so, what goes on the right side of the equal sign there?

```
CONST
    WHITE = ???$
    BLUE = ???$
    etc.
```

These are good questions and exactly the ones to keep in mind as you move to the following section.

11-2 SPELLING RULES FOR CONSTANTS

In earlier programs you have written CONST blocks such as

```
CONST
    WIDTH = 280$
    HEIGHT = 192$
    SPACE = ' '$
```

and you have also written assignment statements such as

```
COUNT := 0$
WORD4 := 'COW '
```

WIDTH, HEIGHT, and SPACE are examples of *constants* that were defined by *you*. COUNT and WORD4 are examples of variables. But what are 280, 192, ' ', 0, and 'COW '?

Well, it shouldn't surprise you too much to realize that they too are *conventional names* for the data upon which the computer operates. The three-character sequence 2-8-0 is the way that we humans *spell* a word that stands for the number that represents two hundred eighty things. Pascal, too, allows you to use this *conventional spelling* for the names of numbers. But, *inside the computer*, this same number is represented very differently. At the lowest level of the machine, this number, like all other data, is represented by electric currents flowing or not flowing in discrete circuits.

Just as 280 is a *conventional name* for the *number* it represents, so ' ' is a *conventional name* for the *space character* it represents, and 'COW ' is another *conventional name* for the *string* it represents. Within the computer, 280, ' ', and 'COW ' are all represented by sets of electric current patterns.

The main point here is that 280 is just a *word*, a sequence of characters, and not *really* a number. But it is a word that Pascal knows about and processes correctly according to the rules of arithmetic. In other words, Pascal treats it *like* a number, give or take some of the size and precision limitations you learned about in Session 10.

In the same sense, WHITE, BLUE, BLACK, etc., are words that stand for data of a certain type, called SCREENCOLOR. Just as the words 280 and 372 stand for different INTEGER values, so the words ORANGE and VIOLET stand for two different SCREENCOLOR values. Internal to the computer, as we said, each of these color names is represented by a set of discrete currents, just as integers are.

Likewise, just as the *meaning* of the integers is determined by the way they behave when added, subtracted, multiplied, or divided, so the *meanings* of the colors are determined by the behavior they cause when used in the graphic procedures that expect a parameter of type SCREENCOLOR.

Now we can give answers to some of the questions raised at the beginning of this section. The color names, WHITE, BLUE, etc., did *not* appear on the left side of the equal sign in a CONST block anywhere. In fact, the *only* place they could appear in a CONST block would be on the *right* side of an equal sign. For example, if you think the color produced by PENCOLOR (ORANGE) is really more of a tomato color, then it would be perfectly legal to write

```
CONST
   TOMATO = ORANGE;
```

and then use TOMATO as *your own* constant for that color.

One question remains: how did TURTLEGRAPHICS declare that the standard spelling for these color values would be WHITE, BLUE, etc.? We'll return to that one immediately after the following section.

11-3 SCALAR DATA TYPES

Before defining terms, some experimentation is in order. **Return to the EDITOR. Clear your workfile and type in the following short program;**

```
PROGRAM SCALAR;

  VAR
    X : INTEGER;

BEGIN
  REPEAT
    READLN (X);
    WRITELN (X : 6, PRED (X) : 6, SUCC (X) : 6, ORD (X) : 6)
  UNTIL X = 0
END.
```

It contains three new words: PRED, SUCC, and ORD. What do you think they mean? **Run the program and find out. Type in an integer (other than zero) and press RETURN. Do it again. Try a negative integer. To quit, type a zero and press the RETURN key.**

As the results of this experiment show, PRED (X) means *predecessor* of X, that is, the number that precedes X. Similarly, SUCC (X) means the *successor* of X, the number that succeeds, or follows, X. Finally, ORD (X) seems merely to return the value of X.

PRED, SUCC, and ORD are all functions. You have seen here that each one returns an integer value when X is an integer. These functions are built-in.

Edit your program, replacing INTEGER by CHAR in the VAR block. Also replace UNTIL X = 0 by UNTIL X = '0'. Run again. Type the A key (and press RETURN); the B key; the 1 key; the 2 key; any key. Quit as before using the zero key and RETURN.

The result is different this time and may surprise you. First of all, PRED, SUCC, and ORD can accept a character value as easily as an integer value. Furthermore PRED and SUCC return character values when the parameter has a character value. (In this sense, these functions are as adaptive as the numeric functions SQR and ABS, which are of type integer or real, depending upon the type of the parameter.)

Most significantly, you saw that character values have a predefined *order*. The successor of 'A' is 'B', for example. Furthermore, the ORD function returns a unique integer for each character value. ORD ('A') = 65, ORD ('B') = 66, ORD ('2') = 50, etc. The meaning of ORD is now clearer: it gives the *order number* of the character value that is passed as a parameter to it. (It did the same with integer values, but the order number was equal to the integer value.) The order number of the complete set of Apple Pascal characters varies between 0 and 255, but you can only type a subset of them from the Apple keyboard. (See Appendix F for a complete list of Apple Pascal character values and ORD numbers.)

These two experiments show that character and integer variables have some basic similarities. The set in each case is *finite* and is *ordered* in a definite way, such that each value, except at the extremes, has a successor and a predecessor. Do you think this is also true of strings or of real numbers?

Change CHAR to STRING and run the program. Now change STRING to REAL. Also change UNTIL X = '0' back to UNTIL X = 0. Try again.

The fact that these two programs did not run means that real numbers and strings don't have well-defined successors or predecessors. Think about it. You can always fit some real number between any two other real numbers, and you can always insert another string between two strings so that all three are in dictionary order.

> Integers can be counted. So can characters. Any type of data which has values that can be counted in the same way as integers or characters is said to be a *scalar data type.* INTEGER and CHAR are scalar types, but REAL and STRING are not.

If characters can be counted, then we should be able to use them as limits of a FOR loop, right? **Edit your program as follows and then run it.**

```
PROGRAM SCALAR;

VAR
    X : CHAR;

BEGIN
    FOR X := ' ' TO ']' DO
      WRITELN (X : 6, ORD (X) : 6)
END.
```

This program shows the order numbers of the standard characters that you can type in from your Apple keyboard. The resulting table also shows how two characters will compare: '3' > '2', for example is *true*, since ORD (3) = 51 and ORD (2) = 50. On the other hand '3' > 'A' is *false*, since ORD (A) = 65.

> Scalar types, therefore, can be used to step through FOR loops, while real and string types cannot. For the same reasons, scalar types can be used in CASE statements to enumerate the cases, while reals and strings cannot.

There is a way in Pascal to specify an item of character data by means of its order number. **Change your program as follows.**

```
PROGRAM SCALAR;

    VAR
      X : INTEGER;

    BEGIN
      FOR X := 32 TO 95 DO
        WRITELN (X : 6, CHR (X) : 6)
    END.
```

Run the result and compare its output with that of the previous version.

CHR and ORD are called *inverses* of one another. For example, ORD ('A') = 65 and CHR (65) = 'A'. These two functions allow you to move easily and conveniently between thinking about characters as data of type CHAR and as data of type INTEGER.

There are 256 distinct values of type CHAR. That means that CHR (0) through CHR (255) are all distinct values. CHR (256) is identical to CHR (0), etc. On the other hand, some characters which are distinct from one another will *look* the same when *written* on your screen. That is because your computer uses the same *graphic symbol* for more than one character value. Furthermore, it has no symbols for some values. **Change the first text line of your FOR statement to read**

```
FOR X := 0 TO 255 DO
```

and run again. Use CTRL–S to inspect the sequence of characters.

We haven't said anything about the boolean data type, which has only two values: *true* and *false*. Is boolean a scalar type? **Change your program once more so that it looks like the following:**

```
PROGRAM SCALAR;

    VAR
      X : BOOLEAN;

    BEGIN
      X := 1 > 2;
      WRITELN (ORD (X));
      X := 2 > 1;
      WRITELN (ORD (X))
    END.
```

Note that X is declared to be of type boolean. Then in the BEGIN/END block it is assigned the *truth value* of the expression 1 > 2, which of course is *false*. The next statement writes out the *order number* of this value. The third statement assigns to X the truth value (*true*) of the expression 2 > 1. The last statement writes out its order number. **Run the program.**

Well, that worked; so the boolean type is a particularly simple scalar type, having only two values. The order number of *false* and *true* are 0 and 1 respectively. *True* is the successor of *false*. *False* is the predecessor of *true*.

The above example shows how the boolean value of an *expression* such as 2 > 1 can be assigned to a boolean variable. But what about the boolean *constants* TRUE and FALSE?.

Change your BEGIN/END block to look like this:

```
BEGIN
  X := FALSE;
  WRITELN (ORD (X));
  X := TRUE;
  WRITELN (ORD (X))
END.
```

Run the program.

As you see, this is a legal program and gives the same results as before. TRUE and FALSE, just like WHITE and 280 and 'COW', are *standard spellings* for constants. They are *not* variable names and *cannot* appear on the left side of an assignment statement.

Change your BEGIN/END block once more as follows:

```
BEGIN
  X := FALSE;
  WRITELN (X);
  X := TRUE;
  WRITELN (X)
END.
```

Run it.

The error message here shows that procedure WRITELN (and WRITE) cannot accept a boolean value as a parameter. This is really too bad, since it puts a programming burden on you when you need to write a truth value on the screen. One way of handling that task is shown in the following version of your program:

```
PROGRAM SCALAR;

VAR
   X : BOOLEAN;

PROCEDURE WRITETRUTH (TF : BOOLEAN);
   BEGIN
     CASE TF OF
        TRUE : WRITELN ('TRUE');
        FALSE : WRITELN (' FALSE')
     END (* CASE *)
   END; (* WRITETRUTH *)

BEGIN
   WRITETRUTH (1 > 2);
   WRITETRUTH (2 > 1)
END.
```

The heart of procedure WRITETRUTH is a CASE statement with constant *case labels* of type boolean: TRUE and FALSE. If the parameter value passed to TF is *true* then the string 'TRUE' is written on the screen. Otherwise the string 'FALSE' is written. Since WRITELN can output strings, the program will work. **If you have the time, revise your program as shown and run it.**

So far you have found that the integer, character, and boolean types are each examples of *scalar* types. But what about the screen color type that began this session? Is it also a scalar type? The simplest way to find out is to see whether ORD (WHITE) for example, exists and if so, what it is equal to.

Change your program as follows and run it.

```
PROGRAM SCALAR;

USES
   TURTLEGRAPHICS;

BEGIN
   WRITELN (ORD (WHITE))
END.
```

This experiment proves that the screen colors belong to a scalar type, and that WHITE has an order value of one. **Edit the program, changing WHITE to NONE, ORANGE, BLACK, or VIOLET. Rerun it.**

If you were very patient and systematic you could prove that the full set of TURTLEGRAPHICS color constants and their order numbers are as follows:

NONE	0
WHITE	1
BLACK	2
REVERSE	3
RADAR	4
BLACK1	5
GREEN	6
VIOLET	7
WHITE1	8
BLACK2	9
ORANGE	10
BLUE	11
WHITE2	12

In conclusion, then, you have been introduced to four different types so far in the family of scalar types: INTEGER, CHAR, BOOLEAN, and SCREENCOLOR.

11-4 CREATING NEW SCALAR DATA TYPES

One of the novel features of Pascal is that it permits you to define new scalar data types of your own choosing and to name the constant values of your type to be whatever you want. In this section we return to the question left dangling at the end of Section 11–2: how did TURTLEGRAPHICS declare that the standard spelling for screen color values would be WHITE, BLUE, etc.? More generally, how do you define a new scalar type and the spelling of its legal values?

Let's approach this question from the point of view of a concrete example. In all the earlier sessions dealing with the NOTE procedure, the musical pitch was always specified by a number. You had to remember that a pitch of 20 corresponded to middle C, that 21 was C-sharp, etc. For people who know music it would be much more natural to describe a melody in terms of the conventional names of the notes, rather than the numbers required by procedure NOTE. For example, a procedure to play the C-major scale (the white keys on a piano, beginning with a C-note) would be quite readable if it looked like this:

```
PROCEDURE DOREMI;
  BEGIN
    PLAY (MIDDLEC); PLAY (D);
    PLAY (E); PLAY (F); PLAY (G);
    PLAY (A); PLAY (B); PLAY (HIGHC)
  END; (* DOREMI *)
```

In order to make DOREMI work we would have to do two things: (1) define MIDDLEC, D, etc., to be the proper spellings of *new data values*, and (2) define procedure PLAY such that it accepts a parameter of the new type. We will start with step 1.

Clear out your workfile and enter the following program text:

```
PROGRAM MUSIC;

  TYPE
    MUSICNOTE = (MIDDLEC, CSHARP, D, EFLAT, E, F,
                 FSHARP, G, GSHARP, A, BFLAT, B, HIGHC);

BEGIN
  WRITELN (ORD (MIDDLEC));
  WRITELN (ORD (HIGHC))
END.
```

Run this program.

You have just succeeded in creating a totally new data type. The name of the type is MUSICNOTE. It is declared in a new TYPE block in the declaration section. Legal spellings of its constant values are MIDDLEC, CSHARP, D, etc. When you ran the program you learned that ORD (MIDDLEC) was zero, and ORD (HIGHC) was 12. *For a programmer defined type, the value of ORD is the same as the position of the constant in the list in the TYPE block. The first position is numbered zero.*

Now you can see how the TURTLEGRAPHICS unit specified the spellings of the screen colors. It must contain a TYPE block with the following declaration:

```
TYPE
    SCREENCOLOR = (NONE, WHITE, BLACK, REVERSE,
                   RADAR, BLACK1, GREEN, VIOLET,
                   WHITE1, BLACK2, ORANGE, BLUE,
                   WHITE2);
```

where the order of the names in parentheses established the ORD values of the colors.

Getting back to our task of using MUSICNOTE constants to generate sounds, we need to remember that the built-in procedure NOTE is the only object around that makes a sound, and it requires a pitch parameter of type *integer*. There would be a *type conflict* if you tried to pass MIDDLEC to NOTE, since MIDDLEC is *not* an integer.

The missing link, as you may have guessed, is the ORD function. As you found, ORD (MIDDLEC) is equal to zero. But a pitch value of 20 in the NOTE procedure call results in an audible middle-C pitch. Therefore, we need to use 20 + ORD (MIDDLEC) as the pitch value in the call to NOTE. This basic idea is embodied in the following program:

```
PROGRAM MUSIC#

   USES
     APPLESTUFF#

   CONST
     DURATION = 50#

   TYPE
     MUSICNOTE = (MIDDLEC, CSHARP, D, EFLAT, E, F,
                  FSHARP, G, GSHARP, A, BFLAT, B, HIGHC)#

   PROCEDURE PLAY (ONENOTE : MUSICNOTE)#
     BEGIN
       NOTE (20 + ORD (ONENOTE), DURATION)
     END# (* PLAY *)

   PROCEDURE DOREMI#
     BEGIN
       PLAY (MIDDLEC)# PLAY (D)#
       PLAY (E)# PLAY (F)# PLAY (G)#
       PLAY (A)# PLAY (B)# PLAY (HIGHC)
     END# (* DOREMI *)

BEGIN
   DOREMI
END.
```

Working from the main program level down, we see that the main BEGIN/END block contains only a single call to DOREMI. DOREMI contains eight calls to PLAY, each time passing as a parameter a constant of type MUSICNOTE. PLAY receives that value, computes its ORD (an integer from zero to 12), adds 20 to that, and uses the result as the pitch number in the call to NOTE. (The duration number in the call to NOTE is a global constant declared in the main CONST block. Its name is DURATION and its value is 50.)

Edit your program to look like the text above. Run it. As advertised, this program plays the eight-note C-major scale. It is important to see how it was able to do that and especially to understand the crucial role of procedure PLAY in translating MUSICNOTE values into the correct INTEGER values needed by procedure NOTE. If you have doubts, go back to the program text again and study it closely.

To gain additional familiarity with the concept of defining new scalar data types and using them, let's extend program MUSIC so that it handles the case of scales in different musical *keys*. *Transposing* to different keys, as it is called, is difficult to do on the piano, but easy on the computer. All that is required is to add the same pitch value to each pitch in the calls to NOTE. For example, to raise the C-scale to a C#-scale you have to add one to each pitch in NOTE. But ORD (CSHARP) = 1, so there is an easy way to compute the amount to add. The following program includes this new feature.

```
PROGRAM MUSIC;

  USES
    APPLESTUFF;

  CONST
    DURATION = 50;

  TYPE
    MUSICNOTE = (MIDDLEC, CSHARP, D, EFLAT, E, F,
                 FSHARP, G, GSHARP, A, BFLAT, B, HIGHC);

  VAR
    KEY : MUSICNOTE;

  PROCEDURE PLAY (ONENOTE : MUSICNOTE);
    BEGIN
      NOTE (ORD (KEY) + 20 + ORD (ONENOTE), DURATION)
    END; (* PLAY *)

  PROCEDURE DOREMI;
    BEGIN
      PLAY (MIDDLEC); PLAY (D);
      PLAY (E); PLAY (F); PLAY (G);
      PLAY (A); PLAY (B); PLAY (HIGHC)
    END; (* DOREMI *)

BEGIN
  KEY := MIDDLEC; DOREMI;
  KEY := FSHARP; DOREMI;
  KEY := EFLAT; DOREMI
END.
```

Notice here that the program now has a VAR block where KEY is declared to be a variable of type MUSICNOTE. That means that it will be legal to assign values to KEY, such as BFLAT and CSHARP. Procedure PLAY is also different now: ORD (KEY) has been added to the previous sum of 20 and ORD (ONENOTE). Finally, the main BEGIN/END block now has three calls to DOREMI, each preceded by the assignment to KEY of a value that establishes the starting note of the scale.

Run the program and listen to the three scales.

The first scale you heard was no different from the one before, since the value of KEY was MIDDLEC and ORD (MIDDLEC) is equal to zero; hence, nothing was added to the original pitch values in procedure PLAY. The second scale, however, sounded different. The KEY value was set to FSHARP, and ORD (FSHARP) has the value 6. This number was added to each pitch number in the call to NOTE. A third transposition took place for the third scale.

To convince you further that this new data type is "real", let's use MUSICNOTE values in a FOR loop. **Change your main BEGIN/END block to look like this:**

```
BEGIN
  FOR KEY := MIDDLEC TO HIGHC DO
    DOREMI
END.
```

Run the new version of MUSIC. Notice that the value of KEY steps through the sequence of values MIDDLEC, CSHARP, D, etc., through HIGHC. This makes sense because these values are members of a *scalar* data type and so have a definite, countable order. For the same reason, the boolean expression

```
MIDDLEC < HIGHC
```

is legal and has a value of *true*. You could also use MUSICNOTE constants as case labels in a CASE statement.

11-5 GRAMMAR RULES FOR SCALAR DATA TYPES

The general rule to keep in mind is that data of any scalar type can be used almost anywhere in Pascal that you would have used an integer. Below is a list of legal uses of scalar data.

- **As parameters of ORD, PRED, and SUCC functions.**

- **As the variable, initial value and final value of a FOR statement.**

- **As labels in a CASE statement.**

- **In boolean expressions involving relational operators (>, <, =).**

- **As subscripts of arrays (See Session 12).**

- **As components of arrays (See Session 12).**

- **As components of records (See Session 13)**

- **As subrange delimiters (See Session 12).**

Here are a few places where integers are legal but other scalar types are illegal:

- **In numeric expressions.**

- **As parameters in ABS, SQR and other numeric functions.**

- **As parameters in WRITE and WRITELN procedures.**

- **As parameters in any declared procedure or function that is defined for integer parameters alone.**

All scalar types share two properties with the integers: (1) they have *discrete, countable* values; (2) the values have a definite *order*. Integers have a third property that the others lack: they can represent a *quantity* of something. That is why 8 DIV 2 makes sense, whereas MIDDLEC DIV BFLAT is meaningless. If you keep these similarities and differences in mind, it will always be clear to you when it is a good idea to create a new scalar data type for a particular programming task.

Note that the only built-in functions that will accept as a parameter value *any* scalar type are PRED, SUCC, and ORD. PRED and SUCC take on the same type as the parameter supplied. Thus, SUCC (WHITE) is of type SCREENCOLOR, while SUCC (BFLAT) is of type MUSICNOTE, and SUCC ('A') is of type CHAR. In this sense PRED and SUCC are like ABS and SQR with regard to integer and real number parameters, as stated before.

The ORD function is itself of integer type. ORD (X) returns a number that tells the *position* of the value of X in the *list* of all possible values. In the case of scalar types that you define, the order of the list is the same as the order specified in your *type declaration*. The *first* constant in the list has an order number of *zero*. (Watch out for OBOB!) For integers, ORD (X) = X. For characters, ORD (X) is the same as the so-called *ASCII value* of the character. (This is true of Apple Pascal but may not be true of other versions of Pascal. For a table of these numeric values, see Appendix F.) For boolean data, ORD (X) is zero if X = FALSE and one if X = TRUE.

Not all uses of PRED and SUCC are proper. If X is the first item in the list of data values then PRED (X) is not properly defined. Likewise there is no proper SUCC (X) if X is the last item in the list of legal values of that type. On the other hand, Apple Pascal will give you no error message if you disobey these rules, and you may get incorrect results.

Creating a new scalar type of your own is usually done in a *TYPE block* in the declaration section of the program, a procedure, or a function. As with CONST and VAR blocks, there can be only *one* TYPE block per program (or procedure or function). A type is known *globally* if declared in the main program and is known *locally* if declared in a procedure or function. (This is true of all Pascal names: variables, constants, functions, and procedures.)

The TYPE block must appear after the CONST block (if any) and before the VAR block (if any). The TYPE block begins with the word TYPE and is followed by one or more *type declarations*. Each type declaration is followed by a semicolon. The form of a type declaration is

    name = type

where the *name* is up to you but must conform to the general Pascal rules for names. In program MUSIC the name in the type declaration is MUSICNOTE. On the right side of the equal sign, the word *type* can stand for many different things. In program MUSIC it stands for

    (MIDDLEC, CSHARP, D, EFLAT, E, F,
     FSHARP, G, GSHARP, A, BFLAT, B, HIGHC)

which is just a parenthesized list of the correct spellings of the constant values that are legal for data of type MUSICNOTE. *This form of type declaration is the only way to define a new scalar data type.*

You should realize, however, that the TYPE block can be used for other purposes. If you simply didn't like the word "integer" for example, you could declare

```
TYPE
    WHOLENUMBER = INTEGER;
```

and then declare your variables to be of type WHOLENUMBER. Note that the type declaration here conforms to the above grammar rule: WHOLENUMBER is a *name* and INTEGER is a *type*. In another application that uses many four-character strings it may make sense to declare

```
TYPE
    SHORTSTRING = STRING [4];
```

in your TYPE block and then use the name SHORTSTRING for the type of several string variables declared in your VAR block.

In most situations, you will find that it isn't *necessary* to have a TYPE block at all. In the previous case, for example, it would have been easier to type STRING [4] than SHORTSTRING when declaring the variables. You don't even *need* a TYPE block to define new scalar types. It would have been perfectly legal to write

```
VAR
    KEY : (MIDDLEC, CSHARP, D, EFLAT, E, F,
            FSHARP, G, GSHARP, A, BFLAT, B, HIGHC);
```

which would have both defined the legal values of KEY and identified its type as being distinct from the built-in data types.

So, why have a TYPE block? *The deeper reason for having a separate place for type declarations is so that the program will be easier to read and easier to understand.* If well used, the TYPE block will be the single place to go to find out what the underlying data of the program is like. A close look at the TYPE block and then the VAR block will reveal the *data structures* upon which the *procedures* will operate. By means of these *block structures* in the program text, Pascal forces the attention of both program author and program reader on these two central aspects of any program: data structures and procedures.

11-6 SETS OF SCALAR DATA

It may have crossed your mind earlier in this session that there must be an easier way to write the DOREMI procedure. In the present version of your program it looks like this:

```
PROCEDURE DOREMI;
  BEGIN
    PLAY (MIDDLEC); PLAY (D);
    PLAY (E); PLAY (F); PLAY (G);
    PLAY (A); PLAY (B); PLAY (HIGHC)
  END; (* DOREMI *)
```

Any time that you see a list of very similar statements, one after the other, you should ask yourself whether there is a more *elegant*, less *wordy* way of getting the same result. In your present version of DOREMI you have eight statements in a row, each of which is a call to procedure PLAY. That seems needlessly repetitious.

Repetition suggests doing the same thing again and again, and that should suggest the idea of a *loop structure*. The problem is that the sequence of notes is *not* the complete set of values of type MUSICNOTE; so you cannot simply create a FOR loop exactly like the one in the main BEGIN/END block of the program. You need a mechanism for getting only the notes you want.

That mechanism is the topic of this section. We will change procedure DOREMI so that a FOR statement will loop through *all* the values of type MUSICNOTE. For each note in the loop, DOREMI will *test* it to see whether it is a *member of the set of white-key notes.* That is a new idea. Until now you have not seen a way to test whether a given piece of data is a member of a set. Evidently you will need some new grammatical objects, and Pascal provides them.

```
PROGRAM MUSIC;

  USES
    APPLESTUFF;

  CONST
    DURATION = 50;

  TYPE
    MUSICNOTE = (MIDDLEC, CSHARP, D, EFLAT, E, F,
                 FSHARP, G, GSHARP, A, BFLAT, B, HIGHC);
    NOTESET = SET OF MUSICNOTE;

  VAR
    KEY : MUSICNOTE;
    WHITEKEYS : NOTESET;

  PROCEDURE PLAY (ONENOTE : MUSICNOTE);
    BEGIN
      NOTE (ORD (KEY) + 20 + ORD (ONENOTE), DURATION)
    END; (* PLAY *)

  PROCEDURE DOREMI;
    VAR
      LOOPNOTE : MUSICNOTE;
    BEGIN
      FOR LOOPNOTE := MIDDLEC TO HIGHC DO
        IF LOOPNOTE IN WHITEKEYS THEN
          PLAY (LOOPNOTE)
    END; (* DOREMI *)

BEGIN
  WHITEKEYS := [MIDDLEC, D, E, F, G, A, B, HIGHC];
  FOR KEY := MIDDLEC TO HIGHC DO
    DOREMI
END.
```

Notice that there is a new variable called WHITEKEYS. It is of a new type called NOTESET. NOTESET is defined in the TYPE block to be a SET. This is a reserved word that you have not seen before. Notice further that the FOR-loop in DOREMI now goes through all the notes, but that an IF statement decides whether or not to PLAY each one. **Run the program.**

Program MUSIC sounds exactly the same as before, which is good news. This means that both ways of thinking about this problem work out in practice. Now let's see how this second method actually works. The new idea here is found in the global TYPE block, where NOTESET is declared to be of type SET. This is a new *data structure* and won't be familiar to people who know only Basic or Fortran.

The variable declaration

```
WHITEKEYS : NOTESET;
```

tells two of the three properties of this new variable. Its *name* is WHITEKEYS. Its *type* is NOTESET, which was defined in the TYPE block. As always with variables, its *value* is established by assignment. In your program the statement

```
WHITEKEYS := [MIDDLEC, D, E, F, G, A, B, HIGHC];
```

assigns a value to WHITEKEYS. The value is a set of *names*, each one of which is a constant of type MUSICNOTE. In the assignment statement in your program the set contains eight members, and they correspond to the white-key notes of the diatonic scale. The *value* of WHITEKEYS, therefore, is this *entire* set of eight notes.

Now we turn to the IF statement in procedure DOREMI, since that is where the decision is made whether or not to PLAY a note.

```
IF LOOPNOTE IN WHITEKEYS THEN
    PLAY (LOOPNOTE)
```

If you read this as an English sentence you will see the meaning immediately: if the value of LOOPNOTE is IN the set of WHITEKEYS, THEN PLAY it. That, in fact, is precisely the meaning of the *reserved word* IN in Pascal. It is a *relational operator* like >, <, and =. The phrase

```
LOOPNOTE IN WHITEKEYS
```

is a *boolean expression*, whose value is either *true* or *false*. It is true if the value of the term on the left side of the word IN, namely LOOPNOTE, is *contained* in the set specified by the term on the right side of the word IN, namely WHITEKEYS.

In our example, the FOR statement contained in DOREMI begins by assigning a value of MIDDLEC to the LOOPNOTE variable. But MIDDLEC is indeed a member of the set WHITEKEYS. So LOOPNOTE IN WHITEKEYS is *true*, and the call, PLAY (LOOPNOTE), is carried out: we hear middle C. The second time through the loop, LOOPNOTE is incremented from MIDDLEC to CSHARP. Since CSHARP is *not* in the set WHITEKEYS, the boolean expression is now *false* and the call to PLAY is not carried out: we hear nothing. On the third time through, LOOPNOTE is equal to D, which is in WHITEKEYS; and we hear D played. The process continues until LOOPNOTE reaches HIGHC. Whether each note is played or not depends upon whether it is in the set WHITEKEYS.

Edit your program so that the IF statement looks like this:

```
IF NOT (LOOPNOTE IN WHITEKEYS) THEN
    PLAY (LOOPNOTE)
```

Run the result.

You heard a sequence of scales containing notes *not* in the diatonic scale. The first such scale you heard corresponded to the black keys on the piano. The reserved word NOT simply *negates* the value of the *boolean expression* in parentheses, turning *true* into *false* and *false* into *true*. NOT, as you saw in Session 8, can be used with any boolean expression: NOT (3 > 2) is *false* since 3 > 2 is true, for example. Of course, you would never need to say NOT (A > B), since A < = B means exactly the same thing and is easier to read.

Do you think the *order* of stating the members of a set affects the *value* of the set? **Change your program as follows:**

The global VAR block:

```
VAR
    KEY : MUSICNOTE;
    WHITEKEYS, OTHERKEYS : NOTESET;
```

The main BEGIN/END block:

```
BEGIN
    WHITEKEYS := [MIDDLEC, D, E, F, G, A, B, HIGHC];
    OTHERKEYS := [HIGHC, B, A, G, F, E, D, MIDDLEC];
    IF WHITEKEYS = OTHERKEYS THEN
        WRITELN ('SAME')
    ELSE
        WRITELN ('DIFFERENT')
END.
```

You have added the variable OTHERKEYS, which is of the same type as WHITEKEYS. In the main BEGIN/END block you gave OTHERKEYS a value that *looks* different from the value of WHITEKEYS. The rest of the program will determine whether the two values are the same or different. **Run the program.**

That experiment shows that two sets having the same members are identical in value regardless of the order in which the members are listed. It makes *no* sense to talk about "the fifth member of a set."

It is possible to do arithmetic on sets. The following statements,

```
SET1 := [E, F, G];
SET2 := [D, E];
SET3 := SET1 + SET2;
SET4 := SET1 * SET2;
SET5 := SET1 - SET2
```

will result in values for SET3, SET4, and SET5 as follows:

```
SET3 = [D, E, F, G]
SET4 = [E]
SET5 = [F, G]
```

The plus sign creates the union of the two sets—i.e., a set that contains all the members of both sets. The asterisk creates the intersection of the two sets—i.e., a set that contains only the members that are in both sets. The minus sign creates a set containing all the members of the first set that are not in the second set.

You have also seen earlier that it is possible to compare two sets by means of the relational operators. A = B is true if set A and set B are identical. A <= B is true if A is a subset of B. A >= B is true if B is a subset of A. Note that > and < do not refer to the number of members in the two sets but only to whether one set is contained in the other.

You have already seen that *constants* of type SET are formed by enclosing in brackets a list of values corresponding to the members of the set. (The type of the member is called the *base type* of the set. For example, the base type of NOTESET is MUSICNOTE.) A set with no members is called the *null* set and is represented by the symbol [ ]. Constant sets can also be represented by *subrange* notation. For example ['A'..'Z'] is the set of 26 letters of the alphabet. (Subranges will be discussed more fully in Session 12.)

The following program shows how you can use sets to tell whether a character typed on the keyboard is a letter, a number, or something else.

```
PROGRAM KEYCHECK;

  TYPE
    CHARSET = SET OF CHAR;

  VAR
    LETTERS, NUMBERS : CHARSET;
    CHARACTER : CHAR;

BEGIN
  LETTERS := ['A'..'Z'];
  NUMBERS := ['0'..'9'];
  WRITELN ('TYPE SOMETHING  [Q = QUIT]');
  REPEAT
    READ (CHARACTER);
    IF CHARACTER IN LETTERS THEN
      WRITELN (': IT''S A LETTER')
    ELSE IF CHARACTER IN NUMBERS THEN
      WRITELN (': IT''S A NUMBER')
    ELSE
      WRITELN (': IT''S NOT ALPHANUMERIC')
  UNTIL CHARACTER = 'Q'
END.
```

The variables LETTERS and NUMBERS are of type CHARSET; CHARSET is defined in the TYPE block to be a SET, with base type equal to CHAR. That is, a variable of type CHARSET can have as a value any particular set of characters. The first line of the BEGIN/END block assigns the set of 26 letters to LETTERS, and the second line assigns the set of 10 digits to NUMBERS. The WRITELN call prompts the user. The rest of the program is a REPEAT loop that gets keyboard input of a single character and tests to see whether it is in the set of letters or in the set of numbers or in neither set. The loop writes an appropriate message and continues until you type a Q. (Note that two apostrophes in succession are treated as a single apostrophe in the string constants in the last three WRITELN calls.)

These programs are fairly typical examples of the use of sets as data items in a program. With more experience you will find that sets can often solve some otherwise very tricky programming problems and can help make your intent clearer than if you had taken some other approach.

Here are a few limitations on the use of sets. You cannot have a set of strings, nor a set of real numbers. A set of boolean values, while legal, is useless. A set of arrays (see Session 12) is not allowed (but an array of sets is perfectly fine). A set of records (see Session 13) is illegal also (although a set *can* be contained in a record). You may not define a function to be of type SET (but you can pass a set as a parameter to a function or a procedure). Negative integers and integers greater than 511 may not be included in any set of integers. Finally, sets of more than 512 members are illegal in Apple Pascal.

SUMMARY

■ **In this session you have explored the use of scalar data types and sets of scalar data.**

■ **You found that integers, characters, and boolean data were all examples of scalar data, as were the screencolor values you used in Session 7.**

■ **For each one of these types, the data values were discrete, countable, and ordered.**

■ **You experimented with the PRED, SUCC, and ORD functions and found that they each accepted parameters of any scalar type.**

■ **You used the TYPE declaration block to create your own new scalar type and to declare the legal constant values of that type.**

■ **You followed the TYPE block with a VAR block to define variables of the new type.**

■ **You used the new constant values in assignment statements in the program.**

■ **You found that the WRITE and WRITELN procedures will not accept any scalar values except integers and characters.**

■ **You explored scalar types of your own invention by means of an extended musical example.**

■ **You learned that the TYPE block could be used for other purposes than defining new scalar types.**

■ **You found that an entire set of scalar values could be treated as a single piece of data.**

- You declared variables to be of type SET.

- You found that the members of a set have no order in the set.

- You learned that +, –, and * were legal operations for sets, but with slightly different meanings than for numbers.

- You learned that the relational operators >, <, and =, could be used to compare sets, again with slightly different meanings than for scalar data.

- You found a new relational operator, IN, such that the boolean expression A IN B is true if the value of A is a member of the set B, and false if A is not a member of B.

- You used the NOT operator to negate a boolean expression.

- You found that the value of a set could be specified by a bracketed list of constants or by a bracketed subrange.

Table 11.1 Cumulative Pascal vocabulary. New words introduced in this session are printed in boldface. (Code: a = declared in APPLESTUFF; g = declared in TURTLEGRAPHICS; = declared in TRANSCEND

Reserved Words	Built-In Procedures	Built-In Functions	Other Built-Ins
PROGRAM	DELETE	Boolean	Constants
USES	READ	a BUTTON	FALSE
CONST	READLN	a KEYPRESS	TRUE
TYPE	WRITE		MAXINT
SET	WRITELN	Char	g NONE
VAR	a NOTE	**CHR**	g WHITE
PROCEDURE	a RANDOMIZE		g BLACK
FUNCTION	g FILLSCREEN	Integer	**g REVERSE**
BEGIN	g GRAFMODE	LENGTH	**g RADAR**
FOR	g INITTURTLE	**ORD**	**g BLACK1**
TO	g MOVE	POS	g GREEN
DOWNTO	g MOVETO	ROUND	g VIOLET
DO	g PENCOLOR	TRUNC	**g WHITE1**
REPEAT	g TEXTMODE	a PADDLE	**g BLACK2**
UNTIL	g TURN	a RANDOM	g ORANGE
WHILE	g TURNTO		g BLUE
IF	g VIEWPORT	Real	**g WHITE2**
THEN		ABS	
ELSE		PWROFTEN	
CASE		SQR	Types
OF		t TAN	BOOLEAN
END		t COS	CHAR
		t EXP	INTEGER
DIV		t LN	REAL
MOD		t LOG	STRING
		t SIN	**g SCREENCOLOR**
AND		t SQRT	
OR		String	Units
NOT		CONCAT	APPLESTUFF
IN		COPY	TRANSCEND
		Other	TURTLEGRAPHICS
		PRED	
		SUCC	

QUESTIONS AND PROBLEMS

1. What is the value of each expression given below? (If the expression is illegal, explain why.)

   a. ORD (1)

b. ORD ('1')

c. ORD (1.0)

d. ORD (PRED ('1'))

e. PRED (SUCC ('Z'))

f. SUCC ('ONE')

g. CHR (ORD ('P'))

h. ORD (SUCC (FALSE))

i. ORD (−23)

2. State the type of each of the following built-in functions.

a. ORD

b. CHR

c. ABS

d. SUCC

e. PRED

3. A program contains the following declaration:

```
TYPE
    MONTH = (JAN, FEB, MAR, APR, MAY, JUN,
             JUL, AUG, SEP, OCT, NOV, DEC);
```

What is the value of each expression given below? (If the expression is illegal *or nonstandard* explain why.)

a. ORD (JAN)

b. ORD (DEC)

c. SUCC (SUCC (SUCC (APR)))

d. ORD (SUCC (DEC))

e. PRED (SUCC (SEP))

f. SEP > AUG

4. The program in Question 3 also contains the declaration

```
VAR
   BIRTHMONTH : MONTH;
```

What is the result of executing each of the statements given below? (If the statement is illegal, explain why.)

a. WRITELN (NOV)

b. WRITELN (ORD (NOV))

c. BIRTHMONTH := JUL

d. JUL := BIRTHMONTH

e. BIRTHMONTH := JUL + 2

5. The program in Question 3 contains the following function declaration:

```
FUNCTION MONTHNUM (N: INTEGER) : MONTH;
  VAR
    MO : ??? ;
  BEGIN
    MO := JAN;
    WHILE N > 0 DO
      BEGIN
        MO := SUCC (???);
        N := ???
      ??? ;
    MONTHNUM := ???
  END;
```

Replace each ??? with the proper word such that MONTHNUM (0) returns the value JAN, MONTHNUM (1) returns FEB, etc.

6. If you did Question 5 correctly, function MONTHNUM works properly for parameter values 0 through 11.

a. What does MONTHNUM return for other parameter values?

b. Add an IF statement to MONTHNUM so that an error message is output if the parameter is not in the proper range.

7. A program contains the following assignment statements:

```
SETA := [1..9];
SETB := [2, 4, 6, 8, 10];
SETC := ['1'..'9']
```

Later in the program the following expressions are evaluated. What is the resulting value of each expression? (If the expression is illegal, explain why.)

a. SETA + SETB

b. SETA – SETB

c. SETA * SETB

d. SETB – SETA

e. SETB – SETB

f. SETB – 10

8. Use the information and instructions in Question 7 for the expressions given below.

a. SET A > [3..7]

b. SETA > SETB

c. SETA = SETC

d. 5 IN SETA

e. 10 IN SETA

f. 5 IN SETC

9. A program unit contains the following VAR block.

```
VAR
    COINSET : SET OF (PENNY, NICKEL, DIME)
```

a. How many distinct values can COINSET have? List them all.

b. Explain in English what information a SET variable, such as COINSET, can contain.

10. A program unit contains the VAR block shown in Question 9. For each statement below, say whether it is legal or not. (If it is illegal, explain why.)

a. COINSET := PENNY

b. COINSET := [NICKEL]

c. COINSET := [ ]

d. COINSET := COINSET + [DIME]

e. COINSET := [QUARTER]

f. IF [PENNY] IN COINSET THEN

g. IF NICKEL < DIME THEN

11. Consider the following declaration section of a program unit.

```
TYPE
   MONEY = (PENNY, NICKEL, DIME, QUARTER)$
   MONEYSET = SET OF MONEY$

FUNCTION CENTS (CHANGE : ???) : INTEGER$
   VAR
      COIN : ??? $
      SUM : ??? $
   BEGIN
      SUM := 0$
      FOR COIN := ??? TO ??? DO
         IF COIN IN ??? THEN
            CASE ??? OF
               PENNY : SUM := SUM + 1$
               ??? : ??? := ??? + 5$
               ??? : ??? := ??? + ??? $
               QUARTER : ??? := ??? + ???
            END$ (* CASE *)
      ??? := SUM
   END$ (* CENTS *)
```

Replace each occurrence of ??? by the proper word or number so that the function will return the correct number of cents equal to the total monetary value of the coins represented by the parameter passed to the function. For example, CENTS ([PENNY, DIME]) should return a value of 11.

12. WRITE and WRITELN are unable to accept programmer-defined data types as parameters. Write your own procedure, named WRITEDAY, such that the call WRITEDAY (FRI) causes the string 'FRIDAY' to be written on the screen.

WRITEDAY should work correctly for all data values of type DAYOFWEEK as declared below.

```
TYPE
   DAYOFWEEK = (MON, TUE, WED, THU, FRI, SAT, SUN)
```

(Hint: use a CASE statement.)

13. Given the TYPE declaration in Question 12, you want to be able to declare four variables such that the following assignment statements are all legal.

```
ALL := [MON..SUN];
MWF := [MON, WED, FRI];
TTH := [TUE, THU];
SSU := ALL - MWF - TTH
```

a. Write a VAR block that properly declares the name and type of each of the four variables above. (Note that the last statement will be illegal unless all four types are identical.)

b. What is the value of SSU?

14. NUMSTR is a string whose characters are all numeric digits '0' through '9'. Write a program that prompts the user to type in a positive whole number. The program should then loop through all the characters of NUMSTR and compute the integer value represented by the string. (Hint: ORD (CH) – ORD ('0') is the integer value represented by the character CH if CH is a numeric digit. Looping through NUMSTR from the left works best. Each time you move to the next character, multiply the previous numeric result by 10.)

TWELVE

ARRAYS

In previous sessions you have written many programs that use variables to represent and manipulate data. Sometimes the data were integer or real numbers. Sometimes the data were characters or strings. In Session 11 you learned how to define new types of scalar data. *In all these situations you found that a single variable had a single value.* Towards the end of Session 11 you learned that a variable of type SET contains information about a whole *collection* of values. In this session you will learn another way that a single variable may represent an entire collection of values, such as a list of words or a list of numbers.

Nearly all practical applications of the computer involve the manipulation of lists of data, where each particular element of data is to be handled in the same way as every other data element in the list. It would be tedious to have to give a separate name to each element, and then to have to copy the same program statements again and again for each element. For example, a store owner might keep in the computer a list of the wholesale prices of all items for sale in the store. A useful program might run through the complete list of prices, mark each one up by 40%, add a six percent sales tax, and then print out the net selling price of each item, including tax. It would be painful to have to write

```
NET1 := WHOLESALE1 * 1.4 * 1.06;
NET2 := WHOLESALE2 * 1.4 * 1.06;
NET3 := WHOLESALE3 * 1.4 * 1.06;
    .              .           .        .
    .              .           .        .
    .              .           .        .
NET983 := WHOLESALE983 * 1.4 * 1.06;
```

for the 983 items the store carries. Furthermore, what would happen if the store began to carry 1027 items, or 842 items? The program would have to be rewritten every time the number of items changed.

Life should be easier than this, and it is. The designers of all computer languages have faced up to this basic application need and have provided facilities for dealing with whole lists, and with their individual elements. That is the topic of this session.

SESSION GOALS

You will learn how to declare and how to assign values to a new variable *of type ARRAY*. You will see how to create and use arrays of strings and arrays of integers. You will see how to use *subrange* notation to specify the *dimension* of an array. You will find that only variables, not functions or constants, may be of type array. You will write procedures for *sorting* arrays of data and for *shuffling* arrays of data into random order. You will see examples of *bottom-up* and *top-down* program design. You will use arrays as data structures to represent a list of words and a deck of cards.

12-1 A LIST OF WORDS

Back in Session 9 you wrote a program named SCANNER. It asked you to type in any sentence, and then it broke the sentence up into individual words and wrote each one as a separate line on your screen. The program listing looked like this:

```
PROGRAM SCANNER;

  CONST
    SPACE = ' ';

  VAR
    PHRASE : STRING;
    FIRST : INTEGER;

BEGIN
  WRITELN ('TYPE IN A SENTENCE AND PRESS RETURN');
  READLN (PHRASE);
  WRITELN;
  PHRASE := CONCAT (PHRASE, SPACE);
  WHILE LENGTH (PHRASE)>1 DO
BEGIN
  FIRST := POS (SPACE, PHRASE);
  WRITELN (COPY (PHRASE, 1, FIRST - 1));
  DELETE (PHRASE, 1, FIRST)
END (* WHILE *)
END.
```

Program SCANNER was perfectly adequate for dividing a sentence into words and writing them on the screen. But what if you had wanted, instead, to collect the words in a list in the program and then, at a later time, have another part of the program alphabetize the list, and then have another part write out the alphabetized list. To accomplish this set of tasks you will need some new language elements.

We will introduce the new elements by stages. In the first stage, your program will do nothing more than store each word in a list. We proceed to do that by modifying program SCANNER.

Boot-up Pascal, set the date, clear out the workfile, and enter the EDITOR, as usual. After you have done these steps you will see the FILE? question on your screen. **Press RETURN as usual.**

You saved SCANNER on your PROGRAM: diskette at the end of Session 9, using the Q W exit from the EDITOR described in Section 4–9. In Section 4–10 we showed you a way to move a saved program back into your workfile. Here is a different way that makes use of the Editor's C(OPY command. The new way moves the copy from PROGRAM: directly into the EDITOR's workspace, *not to the APPLE0: workfile*.

At EDIT level type C F. The following message should appear on the screen:

>COPY: FROM WHAT FILE[MARKER,MARKER]?

Remove APPLE0: from the drive and replace it with your PROGRAM: diskette. Type CTRL-Z. Respond to the question by typing PROGRAM:SCANNER and pressing RETURN. After disk activity you should see the text of SCANNER on the screen along with a prompt line warning you to put APPLE0: back in the drive. **Type CTRL-A. Exchange APPLE0: for PROGRAM: and press RETURN. The job is done.** The new workspace copy will be moved out to the APPLE0: workfile the next time you take a Q U exit from the EDITOR. (You can read more about the EDITOR's C(OPY F(ROM FILE command in the Apple Pascal Operating System Reference Manual.)

If you were successful, program SCANNER is now loaded in the workspace, and its text is visible on your screen. (If for some reason SCANNER is *not* saved on your PROGRAM: diskette, then enter INSERT mode and type it in again.)

Now, for the program changes: first, in the *declaration* section, you will add two new variable names, COUNT and WORD, to the VAR block; second, you will *initialize* COUNT to zero just ahead of the WHILE statement; and third, you will delete the WRITELN statement and replace it with two new assignment statements.

Study the program text below and edit program SCANNER so that it is the same as this version. Note that *square brackets* (CTRL-K and SHIFT-M), not parentheses, appear after ARRAY in the VAR block.

```
PROGRAM SCANNER;

  CONST
    SPACE = ' ';

  VAR
    PHRASE : STRING;
    COUNT, FIRST : INTEGER;
    WORD : ARRAY [1..100] OF STRING;

BEGIN
  WRITELN ('TYPE IN A SENTENCE AND PRESS RETURN');
  READLN (PHRASE);
  WRITELN;
  PHRASE := CONCAT (PHRASE, SPACE);
  COUNT := 0;
  WHILE LENGTH (PHRASE) > 1 DO
    BEGIN
      FIRST := POS (SPACE, PHRASE);
      COUNT := COUNT + 1;
      WORD [COUNT] := COPY (PHRASE, 1, FIRST - 1);
      DELETE (PHRASE, 1, FIRST)
    END (* WHILE *)
END.
```

Check the program over carefully and run it. Type in any sentence you want.

There was no output because you deleted the WRITELN statement that previously printed out the sentence; but you should be happy if the program compiled correctly, indicating that the new version is legal Pascal. Now, let's see what the new statements seem to be doing.

As before, the first four lines of the main BEGIN/END block receive *user input* of a line of text, and put a space on the end of the line. The next statement assigns a zero value to the new variable COUNT. After that the WHILE loop is executed (unless the length of PHRASE is 1 or less).

Inside the compound statement of the WHILE loop there are four simple statements. The first one finds the location of the first space character in PHRASE. The next statement gets the current value of COUNT, adds one to it, and assigns the resulting value back to COUNT. The third statement calls the COPY function, which returns as a string value the part of PHRASE from the first character through the character just before the first space. The string returned by COPY, therefore, is the *first word* in PHRASE. In the new version of the program, this string value is assigned to *something new* in Pascal: WORD [COUNT]. More about that later. The final statement in the WHILE loop deletes from PHRASE all characters up to and including the first space.

Then the program execution loops back to the beginning of the WHILE statement. The length of PHRASE is again examined to see whether it contains more words. If so, the steps above are repeated: COUNT is again incremented by one, and the first word of the remaining part of PHRASE is assigned to WORD [COUNT] and also deleted from PHRASE. The loop repeats while the length of PHRASE is greater than one, and quits after that.

Most of the above analysis has been a review of things you learned in Session 9 about strings and the WHILE statement. The new thing here is this business of incrementing COUNT and assigning a value to WORD [COUNT] each time through the loop. What is going on? Try this experiment.

Go to the EDITOR, insert a semicolon after the END that closes the WHILE statement, and add the following WRITELN statements after that. The last few lines of your program should look like this:

```
    END; (* WHILE *)
    WRITELN (WORD [1]);
    WRITELN (WORD [2])
END.
```

Now, run this version and type in a sentence with at least two words in it.

That result looks plausible, doesn't it? You see, on the screen just below the sentence you typed, the first word, and under that, the second word. Recall that your program assigned the first word to WORD [COUNT] when the value of COUNT was equal to one, and it assigned the second word to WORD [COUNT] when COUNT was equal to two. So it isn't terribly surprising that later, when the program wrote WORD [1] and WORD [2] on the screen, you saw the string values that had been assigned to WORD [COUNT] when COUNT was equal to one and two respectively.

Here is another experiment. **Edit your last two WRITELN calls to look like this:**

```
      END; (* WHILE *)
      WRITELN (COUNT);
      WRITELN (WORD [20])
   END.
```

Run the program and type in a sentence with less than 20 words.
You may have gotten nothing, and you may have gotten a screen full of garbage. Why such unpredictable results? Did WORD [20] ever get assigned a value in your program? What was the highest value that COUNT reached in your WHILE loop?

That experiment shows what happens if you try to use the value of an array element before assigning any value to it. It is legal to do so, but the value is not predictable. You saw this problem come up in Session 10.

Go to the EDITOR and change [20] to [200] in the last WRITELN call. Run the result. Press the spacebar to do a warm reboot. Now change [200] to [-2] and run that. Again, press the spacebar and reboot Pascal.

These numbers, –2 and 200, are *outside* the limits, 1..100, appearing after the word ARRAY in the VAR block and they both lead to value range errors at run time. What does this experiment suggest about the meaning of 1..100?

As a final experiment, **delete [-2] so that the final WRITELN call looks like this:**

```
   WRITELN (WORD)
```

Run this version. Did the entire list of words get written on your screen? Normally you can put the name of a variable in the parameter list of a WRITELN call. You declared WORD to be a variable, so what went wrong? Why was there a *type error*?

12-2 GRAMMAR RULES FOR ARRAY VARIABLES

In Pascal, WORD is an example of what is called an *array variable*. WORD [1], WORD [2], etc. are called the *elements* or *components* of the array. The integer (or integer expression) between square brackets is called the *index* or *subscript* of the array. In the present case, WORD is an *array of strings*, since each one of its elements is of type string.

Perhaps a diagram will help clarify things. Let's say that you run program SCANNER and type in the sentence HOW SWEET IT IS. After the WHILE loop finishes execution, the memory of the computer contains the following data in array WORD:

ARRAY WORD

HOW	SWEET	IT	IS	garbage...
WORD[1]	WORD[2]	WORD[3]	WORD[4]	WORD[5]

Each component of WORD contains a single string whose value is one of the words in the sentence you typed in. WORD[5] contains "garbage"—i.e. whatever data happened to be there when you ran the program—since there is no fifth word in the sentence you typed in. Likewise, WORD[6] through WORD[100] contain garbage. Finally, there are no locations in the computer's memory for WORD[0] or less or WORD[101] or greater.

Like all other variables, an array variable has a *name*, a *type*, and a *value*. The *name* and the *type*, as always, must be *declared* before use. This is usually done in the VAR block of the program (or procedure, or function) where the variable is defined. The *value* of an array variable, like all other variables, has to be *assigned* to it, usually by means of assignment statements.

The meaning of the *type* of an array variable needs a closer look than we have given it so far. In the present case you have dealt with an array whose components were all strings. Later in this session, however, you will be using arrays whose separate components are integers. So we need to be careful to distinguish between the type of one array variable and another, even though all array variables are alike in the sense that they represent ordered lists of data items.

The following terminology is often used when talking about array variables. We say that WORD (or any other array variable) is *of type ARRAY*. But since WORD[5] is *of type STRING*, we say that the *component type* of WORD is STRING. Usually all of the above nomenclature is abbreviated. WORD, for example, is described simply as a *string array*.

All array variables have another property that simple variables lack. It is called the *dimension* of the array and tells the legal range of values for the array's subscripts. The dimension, like everything else, except value, must be *declared* prior to use.

With all of this language under our belts, it is easy to explain the declaration line for WORD. It looks like this:

```
WORD : ARRAY [1..100] OF STRING;
```

If you've followed all the above definitions, you'll have no difficulty with this verbal translation: "WORD is an array variable. Its component type is string. Its subscript is an integer that can have any value from one to 100." Note that the two periods (no more, no fewer, and no spaces) between the one and the 100 imply a range of values.

In Pascal this is called *subrange* notation since 1..100 is only part of the complete range of integers. The *legal* range for integers is –32768 to +32767, or –32768..32767 .

Incidentally, you may substitute an *integer subrange* legally anywhere in a Pascal program that the word INTEGER would normally go. For example, the following declaration

```
VAR
     SMALL : -10..10;
```

would mean that SMALL is an integer variable whose legal values will lie between –10 and 10 inclusive. In that case, the statement

```
SMALL := 11
```

would result in a *value range error* message at run time.

Don't think, by the way, that the only word that can go after OF in the ARRAY declaration is STRING. You can have an array of integers, an array of real numbers, an array of characters, or an array of boolean values. You can also have an array of scalar data that you define yourself. More than that, you can have an *array of arrays*. Think of a table of five columns of real numbers, with 40 numbers in each column. Each row is an array of five numbers. And the whole table is an array of 40 *rows*. The following declaration would handle this case:

```
VAR
     TABLE : ARRAY [1..40] OF ARRAY [1..5] OF REAL;
```

which is legally abbreviated as

```
VAR
     TABLE : ARRAY [1..40, 1..5] OF REAL;
```

The assignment statement

```
TABLE [23, 3] := 877.90
```

would store 877.90 in the 23rd row and 3rd column of TABLE. In this case TABLE is said to have *two dimensions*. According to this grammar rule, you can also have arrays of three, four, five, or more dimensions. *Note, however, that each array has exactly one component type.* A table that consists of a column of names and a column of integers *cannot* be represented as a Pascal array. A different type structure, called RECORD, applies to that case. (Session 13 is devoted to records.)

12-3 ALPHABETIZING A LIST OF WORDS

We continue now with our original task of alphabetizing the list of words that program SCANNER has produced. As a first step, we need to be able to see the whole list on the screen. You tried before to do that by the statement

```
WRITELN (WORD)
```

but you found that the built-in WRITELN procedure cannot handle array variables. Evidently you will need to use a FOR loop and write each element of WORD separately.

If you are still at the compile-time error message you got when you tried to write out the array WORD, press E to get back to the EDITOR. Change the last lines of your program to this:

```
    END; (* WHILE *)
    WRITELN;
    WRITELN (COUNT);
    FOR I := 1 TO COUNT DO
      WRITELN (WORD [I])
END.
```

You've probably recognized that the program needs one more change to make it legal. You introduced a new variable, I, but did not declare it. **Add I to the list of integer variables in the VAR block. Then run the program.**

Well, after all these changes the program output is almost exactly back where program SCANNER left it in Session 9. This is another one of those cases where the external behavior of the program stays about the same, but the internal details are quite a bit different. The new version is an improvement over the old one because it contains within it a new *data structure,* namely the array WORD. This means that the data stored in WORD, *whatever that data is,* can be processed further by general procedures that don't know anything about the data contained in WORD, but *do* know how to do various things with *any* array of string values.

The idea of separating a program into *general procedural units* that operate on data, and then establishing communication between the units by passing *data structures* back and forth, is the essence of good computer programming. A language like Pascal gives you a good opportunity to develop this strategy, since Pascal provides both procedural subunits and a large assortment of data structuring techniques.

Towards that goal, let's reorganize program SCANNER to call attention to the three procedural units that make it up. The first thing that SCANNER does is to get *input* from the user. Next it *processes* the input. In the present case, the processing consists of breaking the input sentence into separate words. Finally it performs *output*, in this case, listing the words on the screen. The intent of the main program would be clearer if it looked like this:

```
BEGIN
    GETAPHRASE;
    SCAN;
    SHOWLIST
END.
```

You can get this result simply by first bracketing each group of existing statements with a BEGIN/END, second, preceding each new BEGIN by a PROCEDURE heading, and finally, creating the new procedure call statements.

Use the editor to make your program look like the following. Pay attention to indentation details. Note that the main program BEGIN has been moved below all the procedures. Run the new version and confirm that it works as before.

```
PROGRAM SCANNER;

   CONST
      SPACE = ' ';

   VAR
      PHRASE : STRING;
      I, COUNT, FIRST : INTEGER;
      WORD : ARRAY [1..100] OF STRING;

   PROCEDURE GETAPHRASE;
      BEGIN
         WRITELN ('TYPE IN A SENTENCE AND PRESS RETURN');
         READLN (PHRASE);
         WRITELN
      END; (* GETAPHRASE *)

   PROCEDURE SCAN;
      BEGIN
         PHRASE := CONCAT (PHRASE, SPACE);
         COUNT := 0;
         WHILE LENGTH (PHRASE)>1 DO
            BEGIN
               FIRST := POS (SPACE, PHRASE);
               COUNT := COUNT + 1;
               WORD [COUNT] := COPY (PHRASE, 1, FIRST - 1);
               DELETE (PHRASE, 1, FIRST)
            END (* WHILE *)
      END; (* SCAN *)

   PROCEDURE SHOWLIST;
      BEGIN
         WRITELN;
         WRITELN (COUNT);
         FOR I := 1 TO COUNT DO
            WRITELN (WORD [I])
      END; (* SHOWLIST *)

BEGIN
   GETAPHRASE;
   SCAN;
   SHOWLIST
END.
```

It is a good idea to stop for a minute and compare this listing with the previous version. At first the new version looks more complex, and that may put you off. Functionally, it is identical to the previous one. The main point, however, is that the new version is actually *easier* to understand, since each separate procedural part can be read and analyzed in terms of what it alone does with the data available to it. Program modifications are also easier to make because their effects are easier to localize and identify. If you wanted better looking output, for example, you would know to go to SHOWLIST. If you needed a new variable there, you would simply put a *local* VAR block within SHOWLIST and not worry whether another procedure at the same or a higher level happened to have a variable of the same name. Finally, your procedure units in one program will become the frequently used starting points for solving new programming problems. A good, well-debugged SCAN procedure, for example, can be lifted and copied literally into another program. A good set of procedures are your *software tools* for problem solving.

Now we turn to the task of alphabetizing our list of words. You will need a new procedure (call it SORT) that will start with the WORD array produced by SCAN and will rearrange the words in alphabetical order, returning the alphabetized list in the same WORD array. The new BEGIN/END block of the program will look like this:

```
BEGIN
   GETAPHRASE;
   SCAN;
   SHOWLIST;
   SORT;
   SHOWLIST
END.
```

and will write the list of words both before and after sorting.

How do we sort lists? Books have been written about dozens of different sort procedures, since so many computer applications depend upon having sorted data. (It is a lot easier to find one name in a list of thousands if the list is sorted.) Unfortunately, the fastest sort procedures are not the quickest to write nor the easiest to remember. The sort procedure we will discuss here is fairly easy to remember and will do for lists of up to a hundred or so items.

In your problem, you want the components of WORD to be in alphabetical order. That means that WORD [1] has to be earlier in the dictionary than WORD [2] or WORD [3] or any other word in your array. The list initially produced by SCAN probably will not be in dictionary order. A good way to start checking for correct alphabetization is to compare WORD [1] with all the other words in the array. If WORD [1] is closer to the beginning of the dictionary than any of the other words in the array, there is nothing to do. But what if WORD [2] actually comes ahead of WORD [1] in the dictionary? A simple thing to do would be to interchange the values of WORD [1] and WORD [2]. That is, if WORD [1] was "the" and WORD [2] was "boy", then after the exchange, WORD [1] would be "boy" and WORD [2] would be "the". In effect, "boy" is the new candidate for the first word in the list.

The next step is to compare the value of WORD [1] with WORD [3]. If WORD [3] comes earlier in the dictionary than WORD [1] exchange the two values; otherwise do nothing. Then compare the latest value of WORD [1] with WORD [4]. After going through the whole list, WORD [1] will contain the word that is alphabetically first in the list. Here is the germ of an idea for how to program this initial search for that word.

```
FOR J := 2 TO COUNT DO
   IF WORD [1] > WORD [J] THEN
      exchange the values of WORD [1] and WORD [J]
```

Note that the *greater than sign*, >, compares two strings in *dictionary order*. The expression between IF and THEN is *true* if WORD [1] comes later in the dictionary than WORD [J]. It is *false* if WORD [1] comes earlier than WORD [J] or if the two words are identical.

Now for the exchange operation. Your first impulse is probably to write

```
WORD [1] := WORD [J];
WORD [J] := WORD [1]
```

but that won't work, will it? If at the start WORD [1] contained "the", and WORD [J] contained "boy", then the first statement would cause WORD [1] to contain "boy". The second statement would then assign "boy" to WORD [J], which is what it already contained. The net result is that the word "the" is *lost*.

The way out of this false start is to use a *temporary variable*, which we'll call TEMP. Here is an improved cut at our sorting procedure:

```
FOR J := 2 TO COUNT DO
  IF WORD [1] > WORD [J] THEN
    BEGIN
      TEMP := WORD [1];
      WORD [1] := WORD [J];
      WORD [J] := TEMP
    END (* IF *)
```

This is a good start, even though it only succeeds in getting the alphabetically first word in WORD [1]. That may not seem like much progress, but the rest is really simple when you notice that the same procedure can be applied to WORD [2]. Furthermore, WORD [2] doesn't have to be compared to WORD [1], since we know that WORD [1] is in order. Then, we can repeat the process with WORD [3], again comparing WORD [3] only with WORD [4], WORD [5], etc., since the earlier words are in order by that time.

Since we don't want to have to type the above seven program lines again and again, the answer must be to substitute a *variable name* for the number 1 everywhere it is needed, and then to put the entire FOR loop *inside* another FOR loop. Here is a first cut at that idea.

```
FOR I := 1 TO COUNT DO
  FOR J := I + 1 TO COUNT DO
    IF WORD [I] > WORD [J] THEN
      BEGIN
        TEMP := WORD [I];
        WORD [I] := WORD [J];
        WORD [J] := TEMP
      END (* IF *)
```

Notice that the J-loop always starts at I + 1. (If the J loop started at I, we'd begin by comparing WORD [I] with itself.) Furthermore, there are *three* places where WORD [1] is replaced by WORD [I]. There is still a bug in this procedure, however, and its our friend OBOB—the Off-By-One Bug. What happens when I finally reaches

COUNT in the outer loop? Then J will begin at COUNT + 1. But there is "garbage" stored in WORD [COUNT + 1], since COUNT tells how many words were put in the list by SCAN.

The way out is to use COUNT – 1 for the upper limit of the I-loop. If you think for a minute about the sort method, you'll see that there's no need for I to ever equal COUNT. The list is completely sorted if all but the last word are in order, and the last word is alphabetically greater than any of the sorted words in the list. That, indeed, is the situation.

The final version of this program is given below. Note that in adding PROCEDURE SORT we used a *local variable* I with the same name as a *global variable*. We did not have to worry about that, since the I in SORT is *unknown* elsewhere in the program.

```
PROGRAM DICTIONARY;

  CONST
    SPACE = ' ';

  VAR
    PHRASE : STRING;
    I, COUNT, FIRST : INTEGER;
    WORD : ARRAY [1..100] OF STRING;

  PROCEDURE GETAPHRASE;
    BEGIN
      WRITELN ('TYPE IN A SENTENCE AND PRESS RETURN');
      READLN (PHRASE);
      WRITELN
    END; (* GETAPHRASE *)

  PROCEDURE SCAN;
    BEGIN
      PHRASE := CONCAT (PHRASE, SPACE);
      COUNT := 0;
      WHILE LENGTH (PHRASE)>1 DO
        BEGIN
          FIRST := POS (SPACE, PHRASE);
          COUNT := COUNT + 1;
          WORD [COUNT] := COPY (PHRASE, 1, FIRST - 1);
          DELETE (PHRASE, 1, FIRST)
        END (* WHILE *)
    END; (* SCAN *)

  PROCEDURE SHOWLIST;
    BEGIN
      WRITELN;
      WRITELN (COUNT);
      FOR I := 1 TO COUNT DO
        WRITELN (WORD [I])
    END; (* SHOWLIST *)
```

```
PROCEDURE SORT;
  VAR
    I, J : INTEGER;
    TEMP : STRING;
  BEGIN
    FOR I := 1 TO COUNT - 1 DO
      FOR J := I + 1 TO COUNT DO
        IF WORD [I] > WORD [J] THEN
          BEGIN
            TEMP := WORD [I];
            WORD [I] := WORD [J];
            WORD [J] := TEMP
          END (* IF *)
  END; (* SORT *)
```

```
BEGIN
  GETAPHRASE;
  SCAN;
  SHOWLIST;
  SORT;
  SHOWLIST
END.
```

Note that we have changed the program name to DICTIONARY, since it now does more than just scan a sentence and divide it into words. **Run this program a few times and verify that it works as advertised. Use it to experiment with the meaning of alphabetical order. For example, type the sentence "AA A ADAM AARDVARK". When you are finished, go to the EDITOR and use the Q W option to write the program on your PROGRAM: diskette with the name DICTIONARY. (See Section 4–9 for details.) Then clear out the workfile.**

12–4 TOP-DOWN DESIGN OF A CARD GAME

The following activities deal with elementary data structures and procedures that can be used to represent a card game on the computer. You will quickly see, however, that these data structures have applications that extend far beyond the realm of games.

Earlier in this session you built a program up piece by piece. Then as it took shape and grew in size and complexity, you reorganized it into elementary procedural units. This design approach is sometimes called "bottom-up development", since the detail (bottom-level) work comes first, and the organization into major (top-level) units comes later. In the rest of this session we will reverse the strategy and work in a "top-down" fashion, specifying the main procedural units first and filling in the details later. Experts in problem-solving strategy disagree on the merits of top-down versus bottom-up approaches. Our guess is that people who are good at problem solving tasks move back and forth, starting with a somewhat top-level plan, then working on lower-level details, and using experience there to revise the overall plan. In any event, it is a good idea to learn both approaches.

In any card game simulation one must begin by issuing a fresh deck of cards—exactly 52 in number, all different from one another. An appropriate data representation of the deck is an integer array, which we might name DECK. The value of each card can be represented by 52 distinct integers, perhaps in the *subrange* 1..52. Let's give the name MAKEDECK to the procedure that issues the initial deck, assigning unique values to the DECK array.

We will also need a procedure to shuffle the deck, so as to randomize the sequence of cards. We will call it SHUFFLEDECK, and it must replace the initial sequence of integers stored in the array DECK with a random sequence of the same integers.

It will be important during the development stage to have a procedure to write on the screen the current sequence of cards in the deck, so that we can see whether MAKEDECK and SHUFFLEDECK are working. Let's call it SHOWDECK.

Then we will want to deal a hand of cards to each of the players. For this we will want an appropriate data structure to represent each card in each hand. A two-dimensional array is called for, and a procedure called DEALHANDS will do this task.

In a game like bridge, the play is considerably easier if the cards in each hand are sorted into suit and number order. So a SORTHANDS procedure is appropriate for that task.

Our goal here is *not* to program an entire card game, but rather to see what the first steps toward that goal would be. We will, therefore, stop our top-level planning with the following main program:

```
BEGIN
   MAKEDECK;
   SHOWDECK;
   SHUFFLEDECK;
   SHOWDECK;
   DEALHANDS;
   SORTHANDS
END.
```

In addition to the BEGIN/END block, the main program needs to have CONST, VAR, and PROCEDURE declarations. The number of cards in the deck and the number of hands (players) will be constants for a given game. The list of global variables must include the array representing the card deck and the array representing the cards in each player's hand. Finally, there must be procedure declarations for each one of the procedures named in the BEGIN/END block.

A bare-bones program, therefore would look like this:

```
PROGRAM CARDGAME;

  CONST
    NUMCARDS = 52;
    NUMHANDS = 4;
    SIZEHAND = 13;

  VAR
    DECK : ARRAY [1..NUMCARDS] OF INTEGER;
    HANDS : ARRAY [1..NUMHANDS, 1..SIZEHAND] OF INTEGER;

  PROCEDURE MAKEDECK; BEGIN END; (* MAKEDECK *)

  PROCEDURE SHOWDECK; BEGIN END; (* SHOWDECK *)

  PROCEDURE SHUFFLEDECK; BEGIN END; (* SHUFFLEDECK *)

  PROCEDURE DEALHANDS; BEGIN END; (* DEALHANDS *)

  PROCEDURE SORTHANDS; BEGIN END; (* SORTHANDS *)

BEGIN
  MAKEDECK;
  SHOWDECK;
  SHUFFLEDECK;
  SHOWDECK;
  DEALHANDS;
  SORTHANDS
END.
```

Enter this text into the cleared workfile. See what happens when you run it.
Notice that there were no compiler errors and no run-time errors. CARDGAME
didn't do much, but it ran because it is a legal Pascal program.

12-5 CARDGAME—FILLING IN THE DETAILS

Now we go to work on the details. A minimal program that actually accomplishes
something will need fuller versions of MAKEDECK and SHOWDECK. The job of
MAKEDECK is to issue 52 unique integers to array DECK. A simple FOR loop should
do that.
Edit MAKEDECK to look like this:

```
PROCEDURE MAKEDECK;
  VAR
    I : INTEGER;
  BEGIN
    FOR I := 1 TO NUMCARDS DO
      DECK [I] := I
  END; (* MAKEDECK *)
```

A good starting point for SHOWDECK is found in the general structure of MAKEDECK. **Edit SHOWDECK to look like this:**

```
PROCEDURE SHOWDECK;
    VAR
        I : INTEGER;
    BEGIN
        WRITELN;
        FOR I := 1 TO NUMCARDS DO
            WRITELN (DECK [I])
    END; (* SHOWDECK *)
```

Run the program. Use CTRL-S to stop and start the display when you want to. It may surprise you that the set of cards in the deck is listed twice. That is because the main program calls SHOWDECK twice.

You now have a working program, but the display of information is a bit too raw to be meaningful. What, after all, is card number 20? It would be nice to have SHOWDECK indicate the suit and number of each card. A reasonable convention here would be that the first 13 integers are spades, the next 13 are hearts, the next 13 are diamonds, and the last 13 are clubs. With this definition, then, we can use MOD and DIV to extract face number and suit from the raw integer. For example 20 DIV 13 is one, and 20 MOD 13 is seven. So, 20 corresponds to the seven of hearts. (A suit value of zero is spades.) Here, then, is a first cut at improving SHOWDECK:

```
PROCEDURE SHOWDECK;
    VAR
        I, FACENUMBER, SUITNUMBER : INTEGER;
    BEGIN
        WRITELN;
        FOR I := 1 TO NUMCARDS DO
        BEGIN
            FACENUMBER := DECK [I] MOD 13;
            SUITNUMBER := DECK [I] DIV 13;
            CASE SUITNUMBER OF
                0 : WRITELN (FACENUMBER, 'OF SPADES');
                1 : WRITELN (FACENUMBER, 'OF HEARTS');
                2 : WRITELN (FACENUMBER, 'OF DIAMONDS');
                3 : WRITELN (FACENUMBER, 'OF CLUBS')
            END (* CASE *)
        END (* FOR *)
    END; (* SHOWDECK *)
```

We have used a CASE statement to select which of the four WRITELN calls to make, depending upon the value of SUITNUMBER. FACENUMBER and SUITNUMBER have been added to the local VAR block. Comments have been added to the ENDs to clarify the structure of the program.

Run this version, using CTRL-S from time to time to interrupt the output.

We are getting close; but there is now a new problem, and it looks like our friend OBOB. Right after the "12 OF DIAMONDS" comes the "0 OF CLUBS". We're off by one, again. Evidently FACENUMBER ranges between zero and 12, not one and 13. That is because 13 MOD 13 and 26 MOD 13, etc., are equal to *zero* and *not* 13.

The problem actually goes deeper, since 13 DIV 13 is equal to one, not zero. Therefore the SUITNUMBER of card number 12 is zero (spades), but for card number 13 it is one (hearts). So the suit clicks over one card too soon and the face number at that time goes from 12 to zero. Not only do we have a case of OBOB, we have it in spades.

There are two approaches to solving this problem. One is to diddle around with the MOD and DIV arithmetic, adding and subtracting ones until we get it right. The other way is to recognize that MOD and DIV work best when we do our counting from zero instead of one. Thus, for example, if the first *thirteen* cards were numbered from *zero* to *twelve*, then MOD 13 would work fine and DIV 13 would also, even at the two ends of the range.

Let's choose the second approach and go back to change MAKEDECK as follows:

```
PROCEDURE MAKEDECK;
  VAR
    I : INTEGER;
  BEGIN
    FOR I := 1 TO NUMCARDS DO
      DECK [I] := I - 1
  END; (* MAKEDECK *)
```

Make this change and run the program.

Things are definitely better now, once you accept the idea that the "0 OF CLUBS" is really the ace of clubs, and the "1 OF CLUBS" is really the deuce. Now, at least, we get thirteen cards of each suit. The last remnant of OBOB can be eliminated by adding one to FACENUMBER in SHOWDECK. **Make this change and rerun.**

```
FACENUMBER := DECK [I] MOD 13 + 1;
```

To show you that there is usually more than one way to solve a programming problem, let's look at SHOWDECK from a different perspective. Notice that the CASE statement labels are *consecutive numbers*, not just arbitrary integers. In such a situation you can usually get the effect of different cases by using another *list structure*. Suppose in our example that we had previously defined a string array called SUIT, such that SUIT [0] = 'SPADES', SUIT [1] = 'HEARTS', etc. Then in SHOWDECK we could use SUITNUMBER as the subscript of array SUIT to get the proper word written on the screen. SHOWDECK would look like this:

```
PROCEDURE SHOWDECK#
   VAR
     I, FACENUMBER, SUITNUMBER : INTEGER#
   BEGIN
     WRITELN#
     FOR I := 1 TO NUMCARDS DO
       BEGIN
         FACENUMBER := DECK [I] MOD 13 + 1#
         SUITNUMBER := DECK [I] DIV 13#
         WRITELN (FACENUMBER, ' OF ', SUIT [SUITNUMBER])
       END (* FOR *)
   END# (* SHOWDECK *)
```

To make this method work, of course, we have to *initialize* SUIT to equal 'SPADES', 'HEARTS', etc. The following procedure does that.

```
PROCEDURE INITIALIZE#
  BEGIN
    SUIT [0] := 'SPADES'#
    SUIT [1] := 'HEARTS'#
    SUIT [2] := 'DIAMONDS'#
    SUIT [3] := 'CLUBS'
  END# (* INITIALIZE *)
```

In addition, the SUIT array needs to be declared globally. The main VAR block will have to look like this:

```
VAR
   DECK : ARRAY [1..NUMCARDS] OF INTEGER#
   HANDS : ARRAY [1..NUMHANDS, 1..SIZEHAND] OF INTEGER#
   SUIT : ARRAY [0..3] OF STRING [8]#
```

Finally, the main BEGIN/END block must start with a call to INITIALIZE.

```
BEGIN
  INITIALIZE#
  MAKEDECK#
  SHOWDECK#
  SHUFFLEDECK#
  SHOWDECK#
  DEALHANDS#
  SORTHANDS
END.
```

Make all the above changes. Let INITIALIZE be your first procedure. Run the program.

Which of these two approaches is preferable? Each requires about the same amount of typing. The CASE statement is a little more readable because all of the information needed to understand how it works is located in one place, in SHOWDECK. On the other hand, as this program grows in complexity there will probably be other procedures that will need to use the SUIT array. So, it's a toss-up.

Let's turn next to the problem of specifying the SHUFFLEDECK procedure. One approach would be to simulate physical card shuffling. Another is to focus on the goal, randomizing the deck, and come up with a simple computer procedure for doing that. Since human shuffling is complex and, in fact, doesn't always reach randomness, the second approach looks better.

Here's an easy way to think about randomizing a deck of cards. Start with the whole deck. Pick one of 52 cards at random. Put it aside. Then pick at random one of the 51 remaining cards. Add it to the first one picked. Repeat until there are no more cards.

This process looks easy to implement in a computer program, though there are a few turns in the road. The first random selection process can be accomplished by using a subscript equal to

```
1 + RANDOM MOD 52
```

which gives a random integer in the range one to 52. The second time around, 52 must go down to 51, and then to 50, etc. So we will need a FOR loop that begins to look like this:

```
FOR I := NUMCARDS DOWNTO 1 DO
   BEGIN
      J := 1 + RANDOM MOD I;
      PICK := DECK [J];
```

The first time through the loop J will be an integer between one and 52, the second time, between one and 51, etc. PICK, therefore, will be the card that has been randomly picked from the *remainder* of the deck.

But what do we do with PICK each time through the loop? We could assign it to a different array. But that would take up extra space in the computer's memory. There is a simpler and more elegant solution. Our strategy will be to *exchange* PICK with the last card in the *current* range of cards that we are picking from. The first time through the loop, we will put the 52nd card in the deck at the place where PICK was taken from—*i.e.* at DECK [J]. Then we will put PICK in DECK [52]. The next time through the loop I will equal 51, so J will be a random number between 1 and 51 and PICK will be one of the first *51* cards. Again, we will put the last card in the *current* range, DECK [51] now, into DECK [J] and put PICK into DECK [51]. This process can stop when I reaches 2, by the way. If I were to go all the way down to 1, then J would equal 1 for all values of RANDOM. PICK would equal DECK [1], and then we would exchange DECK [1] with *itself*. Since this step accomplishes nothing, we can safely end the FOR loop at 2 instead of 1. Here is how the whole procedure will look:

```
PROCEDURE SHUFFLEDECK;
  VAR
    I, J, PICK : INTEGER;
  BEGIN
    FOR I := NUMCARDS DOWNTO 2 DO
      BEGIN
        J := 1 + RANDOM MOD I;
        PICK := DECK [J];
        DECK [J] := DECK [I];
        DECK [I] := PICK
      END (* FOR *)
END; (* SHUFFLEDECK *)
```

You will also need a USES block now, since RANDOM is declared in APPLESTUFF.
Fill out PROCEDURE SHUFFLEDECK as above, and add the following USES block:

```
PROGRAM CARDGAME;

  USES
    APPLESTUFF;
```

Run the program and use CTRL-S to examine the shuffled deck.

If you run the program again, you'll see that the sequence of cards produced by SHUFFLEDECK is always the same. That is true, as you probably remember, because RANDOM really is deterministic. The best way way to get a more realistic simulation is by randomizing the seed of the random number generator at the start of the program. You can do that by including a RANDOMIZE call at the beginning of your INITIALIZE procedure.

As you can see, the process of elaborating and extending program CARDGAME can go on for a lot longer; but we will draw it to a halt here. The basic method we have used is one of (1) deciding on a top-level description of the program in terms of procedures and data structures, (2) implementing the procedures, and (3) making successive refinements in the procedures and data structures.

Printed below is a complete listing of CARDGAME in its current state of development. You may want to write it on your PROGRAM: diskette for later use as the starting point for a game that you write.

```
PROGRAM CARDGAME;

  USES
    APPLESTUFF;

  CONST
    NUMCARDS = 52;
    NUMHANDS = 4;
    SIZEHAND = 13;
```

```
VAR
  DECK : ARRAY [1..NUMCARDS] OF INTEGER;
  HANDS : ARRAY [1..NUMHANDS, 1..SIZEHAND] OF INTEGER;
  SUIT : ARRAY [0..3] OF STRING [8];

PROCEDURE INITIALIZE;
  BEGIN
    RANDOMIZE;
    SUIT [0] := 'SPADES';
    SUIT [1] := 'HEARTS';
    SUIT [2] := 'DIAMONDS';
    SUIT [3] := 'CLUBS'
  END; (* INITIALIZE *)

PROCEDURE MAKEDECK;
  VAR
    I : INTEGER;
  BEGIN
    FOR I := 1 TO NUMCARDS DO
      DECK [I] := I - 1
  END; (* MAKEDECK *)

PROCEDURE SHOWDECK;
  VAR
    I, FACENUMBER, SUITNUMBER : INTEGER;
  BEGIN
    WRITELN;
    FOR I := 1 TO NUMCARDS DO
      BEGIN
        FACENUMBER := DECK [I] MOD 13 + 1;
        SUITNUMBER := DECK [I] DIV 13;
        WRITELN (FACENUMBER, ' OF ', SUIT [SUITNUMBER])
      END (* FOR *)
  END; (* SHOWDECK *)

PROCEDURE SHUFFLEDECK;
  VAR
    I, J, PICK : INTEGER;
  BEGIN
    FOR I := NUMCARDS DOWNTO 2 DO
      BEGIN
        J := 1 + RANDOM MOD I;
        PICK := DECK [J];
        DECK [J] := DECK [I];
        DECK [I] := PICK
      END (* FOR *)
  END; (* SHUFFLEDECK *)

PROCEDURE DEALHANDS; BEGIN END; (* DEALHANDS *)

PROCEDURE SORTHANDS; BEGIN END; (* SORTHANDS *)
```

```
BEGIN
    INITIALIZE;
    MAKEDECK;
    SHOWDECK;
    SHUFFLEDECK;
    SHOWDECK;
    DEALHANDS;
    SORTHANDS
END.
```

12-6 ARRAYS AS VARIABLES AND PARAMETERS

In most of your work in this session you have been dealing with the separate *components* of an array. These components are in every sense variables; their type is the same as the *component type* that you declared in the array. For example, DECK [3] is an integer variable in program CARDGAME.

All this attention to the components may have caused you to forget that it is also correct to speak of the whole array DECK as a *single variable* and to use the name that way. For example, if your VAR block contained the declaration

```
DECK, NEWDECK : ARRAY [1..52] OF INTEGER
```

it would be legal (in Apple Pascal, though not all other Pascals) to use these statements in the same program:

```
NEWDECK := DECK;
IF DECK = NEWDECK THEN etc.
```

The first statement would assign all 52 components of DECK to NEWDECK. The boolean expression in the second statement would be *true* if all 52 components of DECK and NEWDECK were equal. The expression would be *false* if any corresponding pair of components were unequal. Note, however, that the above statements would be illegal if NEWDECK and DECK were not of *exactly* the same type. For two arrays to be of the same type, they have to have the same component type *and* the same dimensions.

Not every use of a whole array is legal. You already saw that you could not pass a whole array to the built-in WRITELN procedure. You will also find, if you try to do it, that you cannot define a function to be of type ARRAY. Apple Pascal permits only functions that return *simple data types*: integers, characters, real numbers, boolean values, and user-defined scalar values. Nor does Apple Pascal give you a way to write a constant of type ARRAY. A few extensions of standard Pascal define both array-valued constants and functions.

There is one especially important situation in which you will want to deal with a whole array as a single object. In program CARDGAME your procedure SHOWDECK was designed to display the contents of array DECK on the TV screen. Suppose your program contained another array like DECK, called NEWDECK. How could you use SHOWDECK to display the contents of NEWDECK? That would be hard, because the text of SHOWDECK refers specifically to the array DECK. The only way to get SHOWDECK to work with NEWDECK would be first to assign NEWDECK to DECK and then call SHOWDECK.

There are two things wrong with that approach. First, the previous contents of DECK would be lost. Second, it would require a good deal of computer time to assign all the components of NEWDECK to DECK. The usual way out of this bind is to *parameterize* procedure SHOWDECK so that it will display the contents of *whatever* array is passed to SHOWDECK when it is called. You did this same thing in Session 11, where procedure PLAY was written to play whatever music note was passed to it. The music note was a *simple* variable, whereas DECK is an array; but the idea is the same.

Let's do the obvious thing to SHOWDECK and see whether it works. **Change the heading of SHOWDECK to the following:**

```
PROCEDURE SHOWDECK (CARDS : ARRAY [1..NUMCARDS] OF INTEGER);
```

In the body of SHOWDECK, change DECK to CARDS in the first two assignment statements. Finally, in the main program BEGIN/END block, change the two calls to SHOWDECK to the following:

```
SHOWDECK (DECK);
```

The intent of these changes should be clear to you. You have now written SHOWDECK in terms of a *parameter* whose name is CARDS and whose type is exactly the same as that of DECK. Then your main program calls SHOWDECK and passes the data in DECK to it. **Run the program and see what happens.**

The compiler error message looks ominous. Why does compilation stop right after the word ARRAY, with the message "identifier expected"? It *looks* as though you may not be able to pass an array as a parameter to a procedure, right? Wrong, fortunately. You *can* pass arrays, but the grammar rules of Pascal won't let you do it the way you tried to. A simple set of changes will fix everything. **Go back to the EDITOR and add the following TYPE block after the CONST block in the main declaration part of program CARDGAME:**

```
TYPE
  CARDARRAY = ARRAY [1..NUMCARDS] OF INTEGER;
```

This declaration has simply given a *name* (*i.e.* an "identifier") to the type of array you are using for DECK and CARDS. **Next change the declaration of DECK in the main VAR block to this:**

```
DECK : CARDARRAY;
```

Finally, do the same for CARDS in the heading of SHOWDECK:

```
PROCEDURE SHOWDECK (CARDS : CARDARRAY);
```

In effect, all that you have done by these changes is to substitute the *name* CARDARRAY for the phrase ARRAY [1..NUMCARDS] OF INTEGER. It turns out that this little change is enough to satisfy the grammar rules of Pascal, which does not allow *any* reserved word to appear as a data type in the parameter list of a procedure or function heading. ARRAY is a reserved word.

Run the new version and confirm that the program does exactly what it did in Section 12-4.

Although the new version looks outwardly the same, the inner workings of SHOWDECK are now quite different. SHOWDECK now works on *any* array (of type CARDARRAY) that is passed to it. The main program passes DECK to it. You have succeeded in *parameterizing* SHOWDECK.

12-7 VALUE PARAMETERS AND REFERENCE PARAMETERS

Let's see whether you can also parameterize SHUFFLEDECK in the same way you did SHOWDECK. **Change its heading to**

```
SHUFFLEDECK (CARDS : CARDARRAY);
```

Within the body of SHUFFLEDECK, change DECK to CARDS in all three assignment statements. Finally, in the main program BEGIN/END block, change the SHUFFLEDECK call to this:

```
SHUFFLEDECK (DECK);
```

Run the program.

Whoops! Something is wrong. The program compiled correctly and ran without an error message. But, how come SHUFFLEDECK isn't shuffling the cards any more? The only thing you did was to parameterize it in exactly the same way that you parameterized SHOWDECK. Why did it succeed in one case and not the other?

It turns out that one very, very tiny change will make SHUFFLEDECK work again. **Change the SHUFFLEDECK heading as follows:**

```
SHUFFLEDECK (VAR CARDS : CARDARRAY);
```

Run this version of CARDGAME. As advertised, the addition of the word VAR ahead of the parameter name seems to have fixed everything. But how?

Back in Session 9, when you were learning about the built-in DELETE procedure, we told you there were two different ways to pass parameters to procedures: they could be passed by *value* or by *reference*. These technical terms are not very revealing. A better way to describe value parameters is *one-way* parameters. Reference parameters are *two-way* parameters. A *one-way* or *value* parameter can pass data *into* a procedure or function, but there is no way for the procedure or function to *change* the data passed to it and then *return the new data* via a one-way parameter. For that capability, you need a *two-way* or *reference* parameter.

With those ideas firmly in mind, you can see why SHOWDECK worked, and why SHUFFLEDECK failed at first and then worked later. Notice that procedure SHOWDECK never assigns any *new values* to the components of the array passed as a parameter to it. So a one-way (value) parameter works fine with SHOWDECK. On the other hand, SHUFFLEDECK does change the values of the components of the array passed to it. SHUFFLEDECK *must* have a two-way (reference) parameter to work properly and return the shuffled list back to the caller. You converted the parameter from one-way to two-way by inserting the word VAR ahead of the parameter name. Whenever you do that with parameter name, it means that the parameter can be used by the procedure both to *receive* data from the calling program unit and to *return* data to the caller.

One final question remains: what was SHUFFLEDECK doing with the data passed to it when you declared the parameter to be a one-way (value) parameter? To answer that question you need to understand more about what goes on when you pass a value parameter to a procedure. When that happens, the procedure first makes a *local copy* of all the one-way data sent to it. Then the procedure carries out all its statements, using only the local copy of the data. When the procedure completes its last statement, control goes back to the caller. So SHUFFLEDECK copied all 52 components of DECK into a local array called CARDS. It then shuffled the data in CARDS, *but it did nothing to DECK*. That is why SHUFFLEDECK *seemed* to stop working. In fact, it simply had no way to *communicate* its results back to the main program.

A procedure or function treats a reference parameter quite differently from a value parameter. It does *not* start out by making a local copy of a reference parameter. Instead, the procedure or function *operates directly* on the actual data back in the calling program. Thus, when you finally changed CARDS into a reference parameter, the call SHUFFLEDECK (DECK) caused that procedure to operate on the data actually stored in DECK, not on a local copy of the data, and the shuffling took place properly.

> You *must* use a *reference* parameter if data is to be returned to the calling program unit. You should usually use a *value* parameter when there is only one-way sending of data into the procedure.

There is one exception to the second rule above. Recall that a *local copy* is always made for a value parameter. This takes both computer time and memory space, especially if the parameter is an array. In applications that are time sensitive or lack memory space, it may be necessary to use a reference parameter even when there is to be one-way communication. *However, it then becomes essential to avoid assignment statements that accidentally change the value of the parameter inside the procedure, since the value will also change outside.*

SUMMARY

In this session you have used *array variables* to store and process ordered collections of data. In the first activities you used a *string array* to handle a list of words. Later you used an *integer array* for a list of numbers. In the process of learning the grammar rules for declaring and using array variables, you also developed useful procedures for sorting, shuffling and displaying the data stored in arrays. You also saw examples of top-down and bottom-up programming strategies. The following list reviews particular points of interest.

- Like all other variables, array variables have a name, a type, and a value. A part of the type is the dimension of the array.

- The name, dimension, and component type must all appear in a declaration of the form

  name : **ARRAY** [*dimension*] **OF** *type*

- The usual spelling rules apply to the name. The dimension is in the form of a subrange, such as 1980..1990, or a list of subranges separated by commas. Any Pascal data type, such as INTEGER or STRING, can appear after the reserved word OF. It defines the component type of the array.

- The value of an array variable is the ordered set of elements that are its components. Array variables, like all other variables, receive their values by assignment.

■ Individual components of an array are referred to by their subscript, such as WORD [3] or HAND [4, 10]. The subscript has to be of the same type as the subrange dimension. Attempts to refer to array components with a subscript outside that subrange lead to a value range error at run time.

■ Arrays cannot be passed to the WRITE and WRITELN procedures.

■ Functions and constants may not be of type array.

■ You saw how to write a simple procedure for sorting data.

■ You saw that the relational operator > when used with strings worked on the basis of dictionary order.

■ You learned to use an integer array to represent a deck of cards.

■ You saw how to interpret an integer between zero and 51 in terms of the face value and suit of a playing card.

■ You wrote a procedure to shuffle an array.

■ You passed an array as a parameter to a procedure.

■ You discovered the difference between value and reference parameters.

■ You used the EDITOR's C(opy F(rom file command to move a copy of a file from your PROGRAM: diskette into the workspace.

Table 12.1 Cumulative Pascal vocabulary. New words introduced in this session are printed in bold face. (Codes: a = declared in APPLESTUFF; g = declared in TURTLEGRAPHICS; t = declared in TRANSCEND)

Reserved Words	Built-In Procedures	Built-In Functions	Other Built-Ins
PROGRAM	DELETE	Boolean	Constants
USES	READ	a BUTTON	FALSE
CONST	READLN	a KEYPRESS	TRUE
TYPE	WRITE		MAXINT
ARRAY	WRITELN	Char	g NONE
SET	a NOTE	CHR	g WHITE
VAR	a RANDOMIZE		g BLACK
PROCEDURE	g FILLSCREEN	Integer	g REVERSE
FUNCTION	g GRAFMODE	LENGTH	g RADAR
BEGIN	g INITTURTLE	ORD	g BLACK1
FOR	g MOVE	POS	g GREEN
TO	g MOVETO	ROUND	g VIOLET
DOWNTO	g PENCOLOR	TRUNC	g WHITE1
DO	g TEXTMODE	a PADDLE	g BLACK2
REPEAT	g TURN	a RANDOM	g ORANGE
UNTIL	g TURNTO		g BLUE
WHILE	g VIEWPORT	Real	g WHITE2
IF		ABS	
THEN		PWROFTEN	Types
ELSE		SQR	BOOLEAN
CASE		t TAN	CHAR
OF		t COS	INTEGER
END		t EXP	REAL
		t LN	STRING
DIV		t LOG	g SCREENCOLOR
MOD		t SIN	
		t SQRT	Units
AND			APPLESTUFF
OR		String	TRANSCEND
NOT		CONCAT	TURTLEGRAPHICS
IN		COPY	
		Other	
		PRED	
		SUCC	

QUESTIONS AND PROBLEMS

Questions 1 through 4 refer to the following program:

```
PROGRAM LISTS;

    CONST
        FIRST = 1;
        LAST = 10;

    VAR
        PRICE, COST : ARRAY [FIRST..LAST] OF REAL;

    BEGIN
        PRICE [2] := 1.42;
        PRICE [3] := 1.87;
        <statement3>
    END.
```

1. What are (a) the name, (b) the type, (c) the dimension, and (d) the component type, of the variables declared in the VAR block?

2. For each of the statements below, say what would happen if it were used as statement 3 in program LISTS.

   a. WRITELN (PRICE)

   b. WRITELN (PRICE [3])

   c. WRITELN (PRICE [1])

   d. WRITELN (PRICE [0])

   e. PRICE := 2.79

   f. PRICE [4] := PRICE [3]

   g. PRICE [12] := 3.48

   h. COST := PRICE

3. Explain what would happen in the above program if the first line of the CONST block were changed to each of the following possibilities?

   a. FIRST = -3;

   b. FIRST = 3;

   c. FIRST = 20;

4. What words could be used in place of "REAL" in the VAR block of the above program? (Ignore the statements in the BEGIN/END block.)

5. Write a PROCEDURE block that can be added to program CARDGAME. It should take all the cards currently stored in DECK, reverse their order, and store them back in DECK. The last card is switched to the first position, the next to last to the second, and so on.

6. Examine PROCEDURE SORT in the DICTIONARY program. Explain in detail what would happen if the following changes were made to the text one at a time:

   a. "COUNT – 1" goes to "COUNT".

   b. "I + 1" goes to "I".

   c. Both of the above.

7. Examine PROCEDURE SHOWDECK in the CARDGAME program. What changes would be needed there in order to get the names "ACE", "DEUCE", "THREE", up through "KING" to be written on the screen in place of the numerals one through 13? What other changes would be needed in the program?

8. Write the DEALHANDS procedure for CARDGAME. It should assign the data in DECK to the two-dimensional array HANDS.

9. Write the SORTHANDS procedure for CARDGAME. It should sort each hand separately.

10. Write a SHOWHANDS procedure to display on the screen each hand separately.

11. Consider the following program:

```
PROGRAM WHATISX;

VAR
   X : INTEGER;

PROCEDURE ABC;
   BEGIN
      X := 999
   END;

BEGIN
   X := 0;
   ABC;
   WRITELN (X)
END.
```

a. What will appear on the screen if you run the program? Explain why.

b. Suppose you edit the program, moving the VAR block so that it appears immediately after the procedure heading. Answer the question in part a.

c. Suppose you edit the *original* program so that a *duplicate copy* of the VAR block appears immediately after the procedure heading. Answer the question in part a.

d. Suppose you start with the program as edited in part c and then change both occurrences of X to Y *within procedure ABC.* Answer the question in part a.

12. Consider the following program:

```
PROGRAM GUESSX;

    VAR
      X : INTEGER;

    PROCEDURE ABC (X : INTEGER);
      BEGIN
        X := 999
      END;

    BEGIN
      X := 0;
      ABC (X);
      WRITELN (X)
    END.
```

a. What will appear on the screen if you run the program? Explain why.

b. Suppose you edit the program, moving the VAR block so that it appears immediately after the procedure heading. Answer the question in part a.

c. Suppose you edit the *original* program so that the word VAR appears just before X in the procedure heading. Answer the question in part a.

d. Suppose you start with the program as edited in part c and then change both occurrences of X to Y *within procedure ABC.* Answer the question in part a.

13. Consider the statement

```
A [B] := C
```

a. List all of the data types discussed so far in this book that are legally possible for B.

b. Do the same for C.

14. A program contains the following declarations:

```
TYPE
    DAYOFWEEK = (MON, TUE, WED, THU, FRI, SAT, SUN);
```

Write the *declaration section* and an *initialization procedure* so that the statement

```
WRITE (DAYTIME [TUE])
```

will cause the string 'TUESDAY' to be written on the screen. Similar WRITE statements should work properly for the other days of the week.

15. Consider the following procedure call:

```
STATISTICS (LIST, AVG, STDEV)
```

where LIST is an array of integers defined in the calling program, and AVG and STDEV are real numbers returned by the procedure to the main program.

a. For each variable, state whether it can be a *value* parameter.

b. State whether it can be a *reference* parameter.

16. If LIST in Question 15 contains 1000 numbers, discuss the relative costs and benefits of passing it to STATISTICS as a *value* parameter compared with passing it as a *reference* parameter.

17. The function sketched below is modeled after the POS function for a string. The statement in the calling program

```
LOC := POSITION (PATTERN, MYLIST, 5, 15)
```

causes a search of array MYLIST for the first occurrence of PATTERN, starting at MYLIST [5] and ending with MYLIST [15]. If successful, POSITION returns the value of the subscript. If not, it returns –MAXINT.

```
TYPE
  STRINGARRAY = ARRAY ??? OF ??? ;

FUNCTION POSITION (TARGET : ??? ; LIST : ??? ;
                   START, ??? : ???) : ??? ;
VAR
  I : ??? ;
  FOUND : ??? ;
BEGIN
  POSITION := ??? ;
  ??? := FALSE;
  I := ??? ;
  WHILE I <= FINISH AND ??? ??? DO
    BEGIN
      IF ??? = ??? THEN
        BEGIN
          POSITION := ??? ;
          FOUND := ???
        END; (* IF *)
      I := ???
    END (* WHILE *)
END; (* POSITION *)
```

a. Your job is to replace each occurrence of ??? by the appropriate word, number, or phrase so that the function will work correctly. Assume that TARGET is of type STRING [20]. Assume that the dimension of LIST is from 1 through 50.

b. Could the identical function be used to search an array of integers for a match with a target integer? Explain.

THIRTEEN

RECORDS AND FILES

Session 12 introduced you to the concept of an *array*—an ordered collection of component data items. You dealt there with arrays of integers and arrays of strings. Then, in Session 11 you learned about *sets*—another kind of collection of similar data items. In this session you will explore *records* and *files*—two new data types that, like the above, also represent collections of elementary data components. You will see both how they are similar to and how they differ from the earlier types.

SESSION GOALS

In the first part of this session you will write programs that define and manipulate data of type RECORD. You will see how to deal with whole records and with individual components of a record. The WITH statement will allow you to abbreviate component names. You will study a complex data structure that combines records with arrays and strings.

In the latter part of the session you will write programs that put data into diskette files and get data from them. You will see that files have sequential components and that the components are all of the same Pascal type, which can be any legal type (except FILE itself). You will see how to open and close diskette files and how to input and output components. You will use the EOF function to tell when you reach the end of a file. You will learn about files of characters called TEXT and INTERACTIVE and will use READ, READLN, WRITE, and WRITELN with them.

You will see that these last four procedures, when used without a file name parameter, refer to automatically opened files named INPUT and OUTPUT. You will learn about a similar file named KEYBOARD.

Finally, you will use the R(emove and K(runch commands of the filer.

13-1 DEFINING A VARIABLE OF TYPE RECORD

In Session 12 you used a one-dimensional array of strings to represent a list of words and another one-dimensional array of integers to represent a deck of cards. You also saw how a table of real numbers could be represented by a two-dimensional array of components of type REAL. We called your attention there to the fact that you can use an array only in cases where all components are of the *same* type. Fortunately, there are many situations in which that is true. But there are also situations in which it is not true.

Consider, for example, the data that a company keeps about its employees or that a college keeps about its students. In both cases the fundamental unit of data is a collection of facts about an individual person. For each person, however, there are many separate components of that data, and they are not all of the same type. A partial list of components and their types might look like this:

Component Data	Type
Last name	STRING
First name	STRING
Middle initial	CHAR
ID number	INTEGER
Birth year	INTEGER
Full time	BOOLEAN
Pay rate	LONG INTEGER

As you can see, while it is convenient to think of this entire collection of information as a single set of facts about one person, there is no way to put them all in a single array, because of the component type differences. For that purpose we need a new data type, and Pascal has one.

Let's begin with a slightly simpler example, and then build up from there. Consider the way that dates are often written: 23 FEB 81, for example. We think of the date as containing a useful unit of information; yet it is composed of three elementary components, not all of the same type.

Component Data	Type
Day	INTEGER
Month	STRING
Year	INTEGER

The following program shows how Pascal makes it possible for you to handle these three components separately while, at the same time, allowing you to pull them all together under a single name. **Study the following program carefully.**

```
PROGRAM CALENDAR;

TYPE
   DATE = RECORD
              DAY : 1..31;
              MONTH : STRING [3];
              YEAR : 0..99
          END;

VAR
   TODAY : DATE;

BEGIN
   TODAY.DAY := 23;
   TODAY.MONTH := 'FEB';
   TODAY.YEAR := 81
END.
```

Enter it into your cleared workfile, and run it.

Since there is no output statement in the program, you saw little activity on the screen. The main point, however, is that the program compiled correctly and ran. It's important new feature is found in the TYPE block, where the type DATE is defined to be equal to a structure that begins with the word RECORD and ends with the word END. Between those two reserved words there are three lines containing what looks very much like an ordinary type declaration for a variable. Each line has the form

name : *type*

In the first such line the name is DAY and the type is 1..31, that is, an integer in the subrange 1 to 31. The second name is MONTH and its type is a three-character string. The third name is YEAR and its type is the 0..99 integer subrange.

The VAR block declares that a variable named TODAY is of type DATE. Then in the main BEGIN/END block, we see a series of three assignment statements. The variable names on the left side of each one have a composite form that you have not seen before. The first part of the name is the same as the variable declared in the VAR block. The second part, after a period, comes from the names in the RECORD/END block in the TYPE declaration section. Judging by the types of the constants appearing in the three assignment statements, it seems that this is the place in the program where the three components of the variable TODAY are assigned values.

Carrying the experiment further, let's add another variable of type DATE and use it to generate some output. **Enter the following changes to the latter part of the program.**

```
VAR
    TODAY, TOMORROW : DATE;

BEGIN
    TODAY.DAY := 23;
    TODAY.MONTH := 'FEB';
    TODAY.YEAR := 81;
    TOMORROW := TODAY;
    TOMORROW.DAY := TOMORROW.DAY + 1;
    WRITELN (TOMORROW.DAY);
    WRITELN (TOMORROW.MONTH);
    WRITELN (TOMORROW.YEAR)
END.
```

Run the new version.

Notice here that the new assignment statement

```
TOMORROW := TODAY;
```

has the effect of assigning all three components of TODAY to the corresponding components of TOMORROW. That statement is legal because both variables are of the same type. The next assignment statement

```
TOMORROW.DAY := TOMORROW.DAY + 1;
```

shows that you can do arithmetic with the DAY component. That is true because the DAY component is of type integer (more properly, a *subrange* of integers). In fact the name TOMORROW.DAY could be used *anywhere* in a program that an integer variable name or integer value is legal. Similarly, TOMORROW.MONTH could be used whenever a string variable or value is legal.

> Each component of a variable of type RECORD has its own type and is subject to all the rules that apply to that type.

You probably got tired of typing the record variable names, TODAY and TOMORROW, again and again when you were dealing with the individual components. The full name of a component often gets to be quite long and cumbersome. Pascal gives you a way to get around that problem. **Examine this new version of the program. Make the changes and run the result.**

```
PROGRAM CALENDAR;

TYPE
   DATE = RECORD
            DAY : 1..31;
            MONTH : STRING [3];
            YEAR : 0..99
          END;

VAR
   TODAY, TOMORROW : DATE;

BEGIN
   WITH TODAY DO
     BEGIN
       DAY := 23;
       MONTH := 'FEB';
       YEAR := 81
     END; (* WITH *)
   TOMORROW := TODAY;
   WITH TOMORROW DO
     BEGIN
       DAY := DAY + 1;
       WRITELN (DAY);
       WRITELN (MONTH);
       WRITELN (YEAR)
     END (* WITH *)
END.
```

This version of the program introduces the last Pascal statement type to be covered in this book. The WITH statement is different from all the others in that it can be used only with RECORD variables. The structure of the WITH statement is similar to the WHILE and FOR statements:

WITH *record-name* **DO** *statement*

WITH and DO are reserved words. *Record-name* is the name of a variable of type RECORD. While it is legal for *statement* to mean a *simple statement,* there is little point in using a WITH statement unless you want it to apply to several other statements. So in practice, *statement* almost always means a *compound statement,* bracketed by BEGIN and END.

The effect of the WITH statement is very simple. It attaches the *record-name* to any *component-name* within the body of the (compound) *statement* following the word DO. In effect, the WITH statement allows you to specify the record variable name only once and then to omit it *within the scope of the WITH statement* when referring to each separate component of the record.

In your program you used the first WITH statement to specify TODAY as the record variable name to be attached to DAY, MONTH, and YEAR in the compound statement after the word DO. The second WITH statement specified TOMORROW as the record variable name to be used with those same components. In your first

WITH statement, DAY stands for the TODAY.DAY component; but in the second WITH statement it stands for TOMORROW.DAY.

You should recognize that the WITH statement is mainly a *convenience* feature of Pascal. It does not allow you to do something new or different. It does save typing and may, especially when used with files, improve the efficiency of running the program.

13-2 GRAMMAR RULES FOR THE RECORD DATA TYPE

If you have had some experience using computers before you started to learn Pascal, you probably thought that a *record* had something to do with data kept in a *file* outside the computer. Personnel data, to return to the example that began this session, is usually stored in such files; and people often refer to the information kept about a single individual as making up one record in the file. Later in this session we will discuss the whole question of files and the organization of data within a file.

> The important fact to observe here is that in Pascal, a record is a type of data. There is no built-in link between records and files.

There are two main grammar rules that apply to records. The first tells how to specify the type of a record variable. The second tells how to refer to a whole record or to one of its components.

Recall that a variable gets its type in a VAR block by means of a phrase of this form:

> *variable-name* : *type*

You have already seen that *type* stands for such built-in names as INTEGER, CHAR, STRING, REAL, or BOOLEAN. It also stands for a phrase such as

> **ARRAY** [*dimension*] **OF** *type*

or

> **SET OF** *(constant-name-list)*

or

> **SET OF** *subrange*

To include records as a Pascal data type, all that is necessary is to agree that *type* can also stand for this new phrase:

RECORD *field-specifier(s)* **END**

The phrase begins with the *reserved word* RECORD, which is followed by one or more *field-specifiers* (separated by semicolons) and ends with the *reserved word* END. Each *field-specifier*, furthermore, has the form

field-name : *type*

Going back to program CALENDAR, you can confirm that the segment

```
RECORD
   DAY : 1..31;
   MONTH : STRING [3];
   YEAR : 0..99
END;
```

conforms to this first grammar rule for specifying a record type. That segment could be used anywhere in a program that a *type* is called for. In your program it was used in a TYPE block to define the meaning of the type-name DATE. It would also be legal to omit the TYPE block and instead use the above segment directly in the VAR block:

```
VAR
      TODAY, TOMORROW : RECORD
                        DAY : 1..31;
                        MONTH : STRING [3];
                        YEAR : 0..99
                        END;
```

We don't advise this latter approach. Programs are usually clearer when structured types, such as RECORD and ARRAY and SET, are specified in a TYPE block and given a type name. Furthermore, you will *have* to do that if you intend to define a procedure that will be passed a value of one of these types. There is no other way to declare parameter variables to be of these types, except by giving the type a name.

The second grammar rule for records tells how to refer to a single component of a variable of type RECORD. In such a situation, the form

variable-name.field-name

specifies one single component of the record. *Variable-name* is the name of a variable of type RECORD and *field-name* is one of the names actually used in defining that RECORD type. The type of that component is the same as the type of the *field-name*.

In the previous programming example you found that

```
today.month
```

was the correct name for the MONTH component of the TODAY record, and that its type was STRING [3]. Similarly

```
tomorrow.year
```

referred to the YEAR component of the TOMORROW record. Note that TODAY and TOMORROW by themselves, without a period and a *field-name*, refer to complete records. Note also that the *field-name alone* is used in statements within the scope of a WITH statement. In such a situation the name following the word WITH is used as the *variable name* that identifies the record.

If you've been especially observant you may have noticed that the rule for specifying a record data type allows quite complex data structures. The reason for this is because the definition of a *field-specifier* contains the word *type*. But *type* stands not only for INTEGER, REAL, CHAR, etc., but also for structured types such as ARRAY, SET, and even RECORD itself. Here are a few examples of complex *data structures* that conform to the grammar rules that you have learned. As you will see, they are designed to apply to the problem of dealing with a *data base* containing the names of all classes being taught in a school and the names and grades of all the students in each class.

```
TYPE
   GRADERECORD = RECORD
                    NAME : STRING [20];
                    TESTSCORE : ARRAY [1..10] OF INTEGER
                 END;
   SCORELIST = ARRAY [1..50] OF GRADERECORD;
   CLASSRECORD = RECORD
                    CLASSNAME : STRING [8];
                    PERSON : SCORELIST
                 END;
   CLASSLIST = ARRAY [1..200] OF CLASSRECORD;

VAR
   STUDENT : SCORELIST;
   CLASS : CLASSLIST;
```

With all these declarations it is possible to see that

```
STUDENT
```

is an ARRAY variable containing all the student data for one class, while

        STUDENT [13]

is a RECORD variable containing the data for the 13th student in the class, and that

        STUDENT [13] . NAME

is a STRING variable containing the name of the 13th student, and that

        STUDENT [13] . TESTSCORE

is an ARRAY variable containing all the 13th student's grades, and that

        STUDENT [13] . TESTSCORE [4]

is an INTEGER variable containing the 13th student's grade on the fourth test.

If you have any doubts about these interpretations, this is a good time to stop, reread the preceding paragraph, and review the grammar rules for specifying RECORD and ARRAY types in Pascal. When you are comfortable with the above discussion you will probably be ready for the following conclusions:

First, it should be clear from looking at the VAR block that CLASS is an ARRAY variable. It contains all student names, test scores, and course names for all classes in a school. CLASS is the *whole* data base. You can also tell that

        CLASS [73]

is a RECORD variable containing the course name, student names, and test scores for the 73rd class. Looking more closely,

        CLASS [73] . CLASSNAME

is a STRING variable containing the course name of the 73rd class, while

```
CLASS [73] . PERSON
```

is an ARRAY variable containing the names and grades of all the students in the 73rd class. From here on it's easy, since we are reviewing the previous analysis. As before,

```
CLASS [73] . PERSON [13]
```

is a RECORD variable containing the names and grades of the 13th student in the 73rd class, and

```
CLASS [73] . PERSON [13] . NAME
```

is a STRING variable containing the name of that student, while

```
CLASS [73] . PERSON [13] . TESTSCORE
```

is an integer ARRAY containing the test scores of the 13th student in the 73rd class. Finally, at the lowest level of detail,

```
CLASS [73] . PERSON [13] . TESTSCORE [4]
```

is an INTEGER variable containing the fourth test score of the 13th student in the 73rd class at the school.

The main point to notice here is that Pascal's rules for defining data types allow you to *organize* the data needed for a given computer application and to manipulate the data *at whatever level of detail you want* in various parts of the program.

If you need to pass the whole collection of school data to a procedure, for example, you need only to use the variable CLASS in the parameter list. At the opposite extreme, the statement

```
CLASS [I] . PERSON [J] . TESTSCORE [K] := 93
```

assigns a score of 93 to the Kth grade of the Jth student in the Ith class.

If you are a beginner at Pascal it will be some time before you are writing programs that deal with data of this degree of complexity. Nevertheless, knowing that these features are present in Pascal will help you to evaluate the language and its potential to grow with your needs to handle problems that involve organizing and manipulating large amounts of data. Much of the current enthusiasm for Pascal comes from the rich set of *data structures* that it gives to a programmer by allowing combinations of RECORD, ARRAY, and simple data types. The above example contains arrays of records, records of arrays, and arrays of records of arrays. In fact, the variable CLASS is an array of records of arrays of records of arrays, though saying that doesn't really help you to understand what CLASS is. For that, you need to study the TYPE block and look at examples, just as you have done in this section.

Pascal offers even more flexibility in defining records than you have seen so far. In all of the above examples each record had a fixed format. For example, all variables of type DATE in program CALENDAR contained exactly one string and two integer components. It is possible to define a record data type that allows different variables of that type to have distinct components. Discussion of that particular wrinkle in the Pascal fabric would take us far afield. Since this is a beginners book, we will leave that to the more advanced texts listed at the end of this book.

13-3 DEFINING A VARIABLE OF TYPE FILE

In the remainder of this session you will be experimenting with a very special data type called FILE. Among all Pascal data types, FILE is unique. The value of a variable of type FILE is determined by data that is located *outside* the main memory of the computer. The value of every other type of variable is determined by data in the main memory. This fact imposes many restrictions on what one can do with the FILE variables. For example, although it is legal to put the name of any other type of variable on either side of an assignment statement, this is illegal for FILE variables. You cannot *assign* a FILE value to a FILE variable. (Before long you will see how FILE variables get their values.) Nor can a FILE be a component type of an ARRAY or RECORD type.

Despite these restrictions, you will soon discover that the FILE variable is Pascal's principal way of moving data into the main memory from the keyboard, out from the main memory to the screen, and in both directions to and from diskettes. Our main focus now will be on data storage on diskettes and data retrieval from diskettes, but you should keep in mind the fact that Pascal receives data from your keyboard and sends data to your TV screen in exactly the same way that it deals with data on diskettes. More about that later.

Let's see how to write a program that does nothing more than put the numbers from 1 to 100 into the disk file APPLE0:NUMBER.DATA

Clear out your workfile. Type the following program into your workspace.

```
PROGRAM FILEIT;

  VAR
     COMPONENT : INTEGER;

BEGIN
  FOR COMPONENT := 1 TO 100 DO
     WRITELN (COMPONENT)
END.
```

Run the above program. There should be no surprises here as you see the numbers appear on your screen. The following program shows all the changes needed to convert the previous version to one that sends its output to the diskette instead of the screen.

```
PROGRAM FILEIT;

  VAR
     COMPONENT : INTEGER;
     DATAFILE : FILE OF INTEGER;

BEGIN
  REWRITE (DATAFILE, 'APPLE0:NUMBER.DATA');
  FOR COMPONENT := 1 TO 100 DO
    BEGIN
      DATAFILE^ := COMPONENT;
      PUT (DATAFILE)
    END; (* FOR *)
  CLOSE (DATAFILE, LOCK)
END.
```

Enter all of the changes. Use SHIFT-N to type the circumflex sign (∧) in the assignment statement. Run the program.

If you saw no compile-time or run-time errors, the program seemed to have worked. (If you got errors, follow instructions to get back to the EDITOR and fix them.) You won't be sure that all is well until you try to get the data back from the diskette, of course, but you can, at least, check the directory of APPLE0:. **Enter the FILER, type L, the diskette name, and press RETURN.** Towards the bottom of the list you should find a new file name, NUMBER.DATA, with a length of one block. That looks good.

Before trying to get the data back, let's have a closer look at the changes you made in your program. **Re-enter the EDITOR.**

The first change was in the VAR block, where you added the new line

```
   DATAFILE : FILE OF INTEGER;
```

You know from the grammar rules for the VAR block that the word on the left side of the colon must be the name of a *variable* and that the phrase on the right side must be a *data type*. This line, therefore, defines DATAFILE to be a variable *of type FILE*, a data type that you have not worked with before. Notice also that the complete phrase, FILE OF INTEGER, suggests that DATAFILE has many *components* and that each one is of *component type* INTEGER. The name DATAFILE refers to the whole collection of data. We have not yet described how to refer to a single component of DATAFILE.

Like a variable of any other type, a variable of type FILE represents data. What can be done with that data will depend upon the *operations* and the *procedures* that are available for that data type. For INTEGER data, arithmetic operations are available as well as functions such as SQR and ABS. For STRING data there are procedures for concatenation and deletion. For SCREENCOLOR data there are procedures for drawing lines in several different colors. The question, then, is this: what operations and procedures are available for data of type FILE?

For answers, look at the text of program FILEIT. You will see three places where variables of type DATAFILE appear in parameter lists of procedure calls. You will also see the name DATAFILE∧ used in an assignment operation. When you understand what is happening in each of these four statements, you will understand most of what there is to know about FILE data.

The first procedure call in the program is

```
   REWRITE (DATAFILE, 'APPLE0:NUMBER.DATA');
```

and its effect is to *open a file that will receive output*. REWRITE takes care of one or two bookkeeping matters and finally concludes by identifying the program variable named DATAFILE with the specific disk file called APPLE0:NUMBER.DATA. You should *not* get the idea that any data in the computer is moved to the diskette at this time. The data isn't even defined yet. Furthermore, in most applications there would not be enough room in the computer's main memory to hold all the data at once. That, in fact, is one of the chief reasons for using disk files.

Within the body of the FOR statement this assignment statement appears:

```
   DATAFILE^ := COMPONENT;
```

Whatever DATAFILE∧ is, it has to be a variable name (since it is the target of an assignment statement) and it has to be of type INTEGER (since a type-mismatch error would have occurred otherwise). Looking back at the VAR block, you would probably guess the right answer: DATAFILE∧ is the name of one *component* of DATAFILE. The spelling rule for components of an ARRAY variable requires square brackets after the variable name. The spelling rule for components of a RECORD variable requires a period and field name after the variable name. In the same fashion, the spelling rule for a component of a FILE variable requires a circumflex (SHIFT–N) after the variable name.

The assignment statement in your program, therefore, is assigning the current value of COMPONENT to one component of DATAFILE. "Which component?", you might ask. The spelling rule for FILE components, unlike that for RECORD and ARRAY components, doesn't allow you to distinguish one component from another. The reason for this comes out of a fundamental fact about a variable of type FILE.

> At any one time, only one component of a FILE variable is available for direct manipulation by a Pascal program. The name of that component is the name of the FILE variable, followed immediately by a circumflex (SHIFT–N).

The next statement in your program

```
PUT (DATAFILE)
```

is a procedure call in which the name of your FILE variable is passed as a parameter to PUT. Its effect is very simple. It puts a *copy* of the data currently in DATAFILE ∧ into the disk file APPLE0:NUMBER.DATA. The data goes on the diskette in a *sequential* fashion, starting at the beginning location established originally by the REWRITE procedure, which opened the disk file. Each successive PUT operation puts a *copy* of the current value of DATAFILE ∧ into the *next sequential location* on the diskette. (Note that PUT does not *change* the value of DATAFILE∧.)

Once you have opened a file, therefore, all that you have to do to put sequential data into it is, first, to assign the value of the data to the file variable *component*, and, second, to carry out the PUT operation on that file variable. Your program FILEIT, therefore, writes the numbers from 1 to 100 as successive integer values in the open disk file APPLE0:NUMBER.DATA.

The final statement in the program,

```
CLOSE (DATAFILE, LOCK)
```

does exactly what it says. After execution, the variable called DATAFILE is no longer associated with your diskette file or any other file. DATAFILE is *closed*. An attempt to execute a PUT statement on a closed file is illegal. Failure to close a file before a program finishes can leave the file in an indeterminate state. *Always close any open files before the program comes to an end.*

The word LOCK in the CLOSE parameter list is an instruction to make the new file permanent in the directory of APPLE0: with the name NUMBER.DATA. It also puts an *end-of-file mark* just after the last file component that was put on the disk. If you had used the word NORMAL instead of LOCK, or had not put any word after DATAFILE, the CLOSE procedure would have deleted the new file from the directory. (Such a temporary file, often called a *scratch file*, can be used for intermediate storage of amounts of data too big to fit in the main memory.''

Before attempting to get the data back, let's create another data file of a different type. **Change your program as follows.**

```
PROGRAM FILEIT;

VAR
    COMPONENT : CHAR;
    DATAFILE : FILE OF CHAR;

BEGIN
    REWRITE (DATAFILE, 'APPLE0:LETTER.DATA');
    FOR COMPONENT := 'A' TO 'Z' DO
        BEGIN
            DATAFILE^ := COMPONENT;
            PUT (DATAFILE)
        END; (* FOR *)
    CLOSE (DATAFILE, LOCK)
END.
```

Note that CHAR has replaced INTEGER in two places in the VAR block. DATAFILE is now a *file of characters*. Note also that the disk file name is now LETTER.DATA. Finally, the FOR statement now goes from 'A' to 'Z'. Note, on the other hand, that the *internal* name, DATAFILE, is the same as before, and that the two statements that define a component of DATAFILE and put it on the diskette are also unchanged. The strategy for outputting file components of type CHAR is exactly the same as for file components of type INTEGER *or any other component type, however complex.*

Run the new version. Then go to the FILER and check the APPLE0: directory again. You should find that LETTER.DATA has joined NUMBER.DATA there.

13-4 GETTING DATA OUT OF DISK FILES

Now that you have put data items into files, let's see how to get them back out. We'll start with LETTER.DATA. The changes to your program are fairly simple. **Return to the EDITOR. Change the program so that it looks like this:**

```
PROGRAM FILEIT;

  VAR
    I : INTEGER;
    COMPONENT : CHAR;
    DATAFILE : FILE OF CHAR;

  BEGIN
    RESET (DATAFILE, 'APPLE0:LETTER.DATA');
    FOR I := 1 TO 26 DO
      BEGIN
        COMPONENT := DATAFILE^;
        GET (DATAFILE);
        WRITELN (COMPONENT)
      END; (* FOR *)
    CLOSE (DATAFILE)
  END.
```

Run the changed version. Then return to the EDITOR.
  Your new program has the following changes.

1. A call to RESET replaces the call to REWRITE.

2. The FOR loop counts from 1 to 26, indexed by the new integer variable I.

3. The assignment statement

```
COMPONENT := DATAFILE^
```

reverses the original order of the variable names.

4. GET has replaced PUT.

5. We have added a WRITELN call, to see the current value of COMPONENT on the TV screen.

  RESET, as you may have guessed, opens the APPLE0: diskette file LETTER.DA-TA and identifies it with your Pascal variable DATAFILE. The main difference between RESET and REWRITE is that RESET can only be used with *existing* disk files. RESET, therefore, is the appropriate one to use when opening a file from which you want to get *input*, while REWRITE is the only choice for creating a new disk file and opening it for *output*. (REWRITE is usually preferable as well when you want to send new data to an existing disk file.)
  After opening LETTER.DATA for input, the program repeats 26 times the following set of statements:

```
COMPONENT := DATAFILE^;
GET (DATAFILE);
WRITELN (COMPONENT)
```

The GET procedure is the inverse of the PUT procedure: PUT *sends a copy* of DATAFILE∧ to the *current location* on the diskette; GET *receives a copy* of the data at the *current location* on the diskette and assigns it to DATAFILE∧. GET and PUT are the elementary file input and output (I/O) procedures in Pascal.

While studying this new version of your program, you should note carefully the *order* of statements in the FOR loop. *Your assignment statement precedes your GET call.* This may seem strange: how did DATAFILE∧ get its value the first time around the loop? The answer points up another difference between RESET and REWRITE. RESET normally does an automatic GET after it opens the file. (There is one exception to this rule, and we'll come to it in Section 13-9.) REWRITE does not do a GET. In your current program, therefore, the RESET procedure moves a *copy* of the first component ('A') of the file into the computer, where it can be manipulated via the name DATAFILE∧. That is why the assignment statement works the first time around the loop. (If you're wondering why RESET does an automatic GET, you'll soon see.)

Finally, note that the parameter list for CLOSE contains only the name of the file variable. The word LOCK could have been included, but it has no effect on a file that has been opened by means of the RESET procedure.

It would be a simple matter to edit your program to input all the numbers in NUMBER.DATA, but we'll leave that as a problem for you to do at the end of this session.

13-5 FILE INPUT USING THE EOF FUNCTION

You have seen that the RESET call does an automatic GET. Then your program's FOR loop did 26 more GETs, for a total of 27. But there were only 26 letters in the disk file. What happened on the 27th time that

```
GET (DATAFILE)
```

was carried out? What was the value of DATAFILE∧ after that?

The following program variation will introduce you to a new *boolean function* that will reveal more of what is going on.

```
PROGRAM FILEIT;

  VAR
    COMPONENT : CHAR;
    DATAFILE : FILE OF CHAR;

BEGIN
  RESET (DATAFILE, 'APPLEO:LETTER.DATA');
  WHILE NOT EOF (DATAFILE) DO
    BEGIN
      COMPONENT := DATAFILE^;
      GET (DATAFILE);
      WRITELN (COMPONENT)
    END; (* WHILE *)
  CLOSE (DATAFILE)
END.
```

The main change is the replacement of the FOR loop with a similar WHILE loop. The body of the two loops remains the same. In addition, I has been removed from the VAR block. **Make the changes and run the program.**

The new version works, but how? Recalling the rules for the WHILE statement, you will remember that the body of the loop is executed as long as the expression after WHILE remains *true*. For NOT EOF (DATAFILE) to be true, EOF (DATAFILE) must be *false*. EOF stands for "end of file". As you have seen by running the program successfully, EOF was false at first and remained false until the last file component was input.

The EOF function normally returns a value of *false*. If any GET attempts to input data past the end-of-file marker (put there when the file was created), then EOF returns a *true* value, and the value of DATAFILE∧ becomes *undefined*. Your new input program makes use of this behavior of the EOF function in the WHILE statement to decide when to stop input. This method of using WHILE NOT EOF when getting input from a file is usually better than using a counting loop, since you do not need to know in advance how many components are in the file.

This application is a good opportunity to show why Pascal has both a WHILE statement and a REPEAT statement. You might have been tempted to write your file input loop like this:

```
REPEAT
  COMPONENT := DATAFILE^;
  GET (DATAFILE);
  WRITELN (COMPONENT)
UNTIL EOF (DATAFILE)
```

In fact, this approach would have worked *in the present case*. But if you had used it in a *general* file input program, sooner or later it would have gotten you in trouble.

Recall that the body of a REPEAT loop is *always* done once. What would have happened if the data file had been completely empty? Then the first thing in the file would be the end-of-file marker. As soon as the RESET procedure was carried out along with its automatic GET, EOF would have become true. But the REPEAT statement would not examine EOF until the loop was done once. In the meantime, the program would be treating DATAFILE∧ as though it had meaningful data, which would not be true. Use of the WHILE statement avoids this problem altogether. You should note also that neither a REPEAT loop nor a WHILE loop would work properly if RESET *failed* to do a GET initially. That is why RESET works the way it does.

13-6 GRAMMAR RULES FOR THE FILE DATA TYPE

In previous parts of this book you have seen that the word *type* in Pascal stood for words, such as INTEGER, CHAR, REAL, BOOLEAN, and STRING, and also for phrases, such as SET OF 'A'..'Z' and ARRAY [1..10] OF REAL. In the early part of this session, you saw that 'type' also stands for very complex RECORD structures. Now you see that 'type' must also include a new FILE phrase of the following form

FILE OF *type*

FILE and OF are both reserved words. As before *type* means everything you have seen it stand for before. The one thing it may *not* stand for is another FILE type: you may not have a file of files. The following, however, are all legal:

```
FILE OF CHAR
FILE OF REAL
FILE OF [0..15]
FILE OF SET OF CHAR
FILE OF ARRAY [1..3, 1..10] OF INTEGER
FILE OF RECORD
          I, J, K : INTEGER;
          ST : ARRAY [0..3] OF CHAR
       END
```

The *component type* or *base type* of a FILE type is defined by the word or phrase after the phrase FILE OF in the definition of the FILE type. For example, a FILE variable defined by the next to last example above would have a component whose type was ARRAY [1..3, 1..10] OF INTEGER. If the name of the variable was LISTFILE, then LISTFILE∧ would refer to one entire two-dimensional array in the "file of arrays". Likewise, LISTFILE ∧ [2, 5] would refer to one of the integers in that array. Bear in mind that however complicated the component type may be, *one entire component* is always available to your program after it has opened the file. If the component is a *structured type* such as an ARRAY or a RECORD, all its sub-components are available.

13-7 TEXT FILES, READ, AND WRITE

Return to the EDITOR. Change the declaration of DATAFILE to read:

```
DATAFILE : TEXT
```

Run the program. The fact that the program runs and produces the same result as before tells you that TEXT is a legal file type, and that it is a synonym for FILE OF CHAR.

Now edit your program again as follows:

```
PROGRAM FILEIT;

  VAR
    COMPONENT : CHAR;
    DATAFILE : TEXT;

BEGIN
  RESET (DATAFILE, 'APPLEO:LETTER.DATA');
  WHILE NOT EOF (DATAFILE) DO
    BEGIN
      READ (DATAFILE, COMPONENT);
      WRITELN (COMPONENT)
    END; (* WHILE *)
  CLOSE (DATAFILE)
END.
```

Run it. Identical results this time suggest that the READ procedure is synonymous with the pair of statements

```
COMPONENT := DATAFILE^;
GET (DATAFILE);
```

This idea turns out to be true whenever DATAFILE is of type TEXT (or FILE OF CHAR) and COMPONENT is of type CHAR.

Let's explore TEXT files a bit further. **Go to the FILER and type E, for E(xtended List Directory.** Reading down the rightmost column, notice that one of the files in the directory, SYSTEM.WRK.TEXT, is identified by the word TEXT. Perhaps you could use your present program to get input from that file and write its contents on the screen. **Return to the EDITOR and change the RESET call as follows:**

```
RESET (DATAFILE, 'APPLEO:SYSTEM.WRK.TEXT');
```

Run the program.

Indeed, you can use your program to read this or any other TEXT file, one character at a time. Actually, you can do a lot better than that. **Change your program again so that it looks like this:**

```
PROGRAM FILEIT;

  VAR
    COMPONENT : STRING;
    DATAFILE : TEXT;

  BEGIN
    RESET (DATAFILE, 'APPLEO:SYSTEM.WRK.TEXT');
    WHILE NOT EOF (DATAFILE) DO
      BEGIN
        READLN (DATAFILE, COMPONENT);
        WRITELN (COMPONENT)
      END; (* WHILE *)
    CLOSE (DATAFILE)
  END.
```

You changed the type of COMPONENT from CHAR to STRING, and you changed READ to READLN. **Run the program.**

No, you're not back in the EDITOR. The final version of your program has told you two very important facts about TEXT files and the READLN procedure. It is clear that READLN is reading one "line" at a time out of SYSTEM.WRK.TEXT and storing the characters in COMPONENT, now a string variable. That must mean that this particular TEXT file contains *end-of-line* markers as well as an *end-of-file* marker. Such is the case. In fact, Pascal has an EOLN function that behaves similarly to EOF. It is unlikely that you will have much need for it, however, since the READLN procedure automatically reads everything until the end-of-line marker.

Now let's apply this final version of the program to your LETTER.DATA file. **Return to the EDITOR. Change the RESET parameter list back to this:**

```
RESET (DATAFILE, 'APPLEO:LETTER.DATA');
```

Run the program.

Since you did *not* put any end-of-line markers in LETTER.DATA when you created it, READLN treats *the whole file* as a single line, using the end-of-file marker as equivalent to end-of-line. (This would only work for a short file, since the maximum string length allowed in Apple Pascal is 255 characters.

The thing to note here is that the READLN procedure, with a file name and a string variable as parameters, gives you a completely general way to get input from a TEXT file that is divided into separate lines. The final version of your program is a prototype for this situation.

As the final experiment in this section, let's see how to put those end-of-line markers into a TEXT file. We'll do this by modifying your program to make a second disk copy of SYSTEM.WRK.TEXT. To do that, you have to open a new file for output. Then you have to send each line of output to that file. Finally, you have to close the file and LOCK it. **Edit your program as follows:**

```
PROGRAM FILEIT;

  VAR
    COMPONENT : STRING;
    DATAFILE : TEXT;
    OUTFILE : TEXT;

BEGIN
  RESET (DATAFILE, 'APPLE0:SYSTEM.WRK.TEXT');
  REWRITE (OUTFILE, 'APPLE0:COPY');
  WHILE NOT EOF (DATAFILE) DO
    BEGIN
      READLN (DATAFILE, COMPONENT);
      WRITELN (OUTFILE, COMPONENT)
    END; (* WHILE *)
  CLOSE (DATAFILE);
  CLOSE (OUTFILE, LOCK)
END.
```

Note that the only necessary change in the WRITELN call was the addition of the file variable, OUTFILE, to the parameter list. **Run the program.**

The lack of output on the screen suggests that WRITELN sent its output to OUTFILE, which was opened in the REWRITE call as APPLE0:COPY. **Go to the FILER and do an E(xtended List Directory.** Note, indeed, that you now have a new APPLE0: file named COPY.DATA. It contains, line for line, all of the text that was in SYSTEM.WRK.TEXT, *including* end-of-line markers created by the WRITELN calls. (The suffix ".DATA" is added to all disk file names created by the REWRITE procedure, unless you have already included the suffix.)

To understand WRITELN in detail, it is easier to start with the WRITE procedure. If OUTFILE is a file variable of type TEXT and CH is a variable of type CHAR, then

```
WRITE (OUTFILE, CH)
```

is *exactly equivalent* to this sequence:

```
OUTFILE^ := CH;
PUT (OUTFILE)
```

Similarly, if ST is a variable of type STRING, then

```
WRITE (OUTFILE, ST)
```

is *exactly* equivalent to this loop:

```
FOR I := 1 TO LENGTH (ST) DO
   BEGIN
      OUTFILE^ := ST [I];
      PUT (OUTFILE)
   END
```

WRITELN is just like WRITE in the above examples, except that it puts an end-of-line marker into the file after the last character output.

WRITE, WRITELN, READ, and READLN, when called with a file variable as the first parameter in the parameter list, are straightforward generalizations of the same procedures you have been using all along to send output to the screen and get input from the keyboard. The parameter list in all situations may contain several variables, and their types may be CHAR, STRING, INTEGER or REAL. WRITE and WRITELN *convert* the data, whatever its initial type, into a sequence of characters, suitable to be PUT into a TEXT file. Similarly, READ and READLN will GET a sequence of characters out of a TEXT file and will *attempt to convert* them into data of types that match the variables in the parameter list. Conversion won't succeed if the characters don't correspond to the data type: letters where digits are expected, for example.

> Input data conversion *always* succeeds for character or string variables, however, and they provide the only *safe* way for a program to use the READ or READLN procedures with unknown data.

You should note carefully that these four procedures—READ, READLN, WRITE, and WRITELN—can be used *only* with a file variable whose component type is CHAR. If X is an integer or a real number, WRITE (X) is perfectly legal, since it first converts X to a sequence of characters and then sends them to the TV screen. If

OUTFILE is of type TEXT or FILE OF CHAR, then WRITE (OUTFILE, X) is also legal, and for the same reason. But if OUTFILE is of type FILE OF INTEGER or FILE OF REAL, then it is *illegal* in Apple Pascal to use the statement WRITE (OUTFILE, X). (Some other versions of Pascal allow this use of WRITE.)

> The final version of program FILEIT is a good starting point for any future program that gets input from a TEXT file and puts output into another TEXT file. Study it carefully and remind yourself what each statement does.

There is one last point worth noting about TEXT files. You may have noticed in the Extended Directory Listing two strange things about file COPY. Though it is supposed to contain all the text in SYSTEM.WRK.TEXT, which is four blocks long, COPY is only one block long. Furthermore, SYSTEM.WRK.TEXT is identified in the rightmost column by the word TEXT, while COPY is identified by the word DATA. What is going on?

In fact, SYSTEM.WRK.TEXT (or any other file with a .TEXT as a suffix) has more data in it than just text. The first two blocks, for example, contain information that must be available to the EDITOR if you are to succeed in bringing the file into the workspace. When a Pascal program opens such a file, however, these blocks are skipped over and the first READ, READLN, or GET begins with the first *text* character in the file. What is contained in COPY, therefore, is just the text part of SYSTEM.WRK.TEXT.

Now is a good time to learn about another feature of the FILER. Notice that when you used the FILER's Extended Directory Listing command you saw at the bottom of the screen a phrase similar to this:

```
13/13 FILES, 23 UNUSED, 17 IN LARGEST
```

This means that the largest piece of *consecutive* free storage space on the diskette is 17 blocks long, out of a total free storage space of 23 blocks. One or more UNUSED areas account for the other six blocks.

Many file activities require the use of consecutive storage locations. For example, if you are editing a large workfile, you will not be able to quit and update (Q U) unless there is enough consecutive storage to hold the new version of SYSTEM.WRK.TEXT. The message "ERROR WHILE WRITING FILE" results when there is not enough consecutive storage space.

Furthermore, many small activities, such as creating new files or removing old ones, can result in *fragmentation* of unused storage space. Obviously, it would be nice to retain consecutive space on the diskette. **From the FILER, type K. To the question "CRUNCH ?", answer with the diskette name APPLE0: and a RETURN.** As a safety measure, the FILER asks

```
FROM END OF DISK, BLOCK 280? (Y/N)
```

Type Y. Messages appear telling you that various files are being "moved forward" and that the diskette is now "crunched". **Do another E(xtended Directory.** Notice now that all of the UNUSED space is consecutive.

> It is a good practice from time to time to K(runch your diskette to get maximum consecutive storage.

13-8 INTERACTIVE FILES, INPUT, OUTPUT, AND KEYBOARD

You saw in the last section that the TEXT data type means exactly the same thing as FILE OF CHAR. Apple Pascal offers still another file data type, called INTERACTIVE, which is similar to, but not exactly the same as, TEXT. That is the topic of this section.

To see the difference clearly, let's start out with an earlier version of program FILEIT. **Remove the five lines you just added to FILEIT, and make the changes shown below.**

```
PROGRAM FILEIT;

  VAR
    COMPONENT : CHAR;
    DATAFILE : TEXT;

  BEGIN
    RESET (DATAFILE, 'APPLE0:LETTER.DATA');
    WHILE NOT EOF (DATAFILE) DO
      BEGIN
        READ (DATAFILE, COMPONENT);
        WRITELN (COMPONENT)
      END; (* WHILE *)
    CLOSE (DATAFILE)
  END.
```

Note that each READ will input one character now, and that the disk file name is LETTER.DATA. **Run the program.** If you made the changes correctly, you saw the 26 letters of the alphabet appear in a column on the TV screen.

Change the word TEXT in your VAR block to INTERACTIVE, and run again. The results should be *nearly* the same, but not exactly. For some reason your program wrote an extra Z at the bottom of the list of letters. When you understand why that happened you will know the basic difference between the TEXT and INTERACTIVE data types.

Recall that for the TEXT data type the statement

```
READ (DATAFILE, COMPONENT)
```

was exactly equivalent to this pair:

```
COMPONENT := DATAFILE^;
GET (DATAFILE)
```

That is, the character variable called COMPONENT was first assigned the value of the *current* component of DATAFILE. After that, the GET procedure input a new value for DATAFILE^. Recall also that to make this sequence work for the first character in the file, it is necessary to do a GET as soon as the file is opened, and RESET does that automatically.

Now for the differences. If a file variable is declared to be of type INTERACTIVE, then the RESET procedure does *not* do an automatic GET. Furthermore, the statement

```
READ (DATAFILE, COMPONENT)
```

is exactly the same as *this* pair:

```
GET (DATAFILE);
COMPONENT := DATAFILE^
```

That is, the order of the GET and the assignment statements is reversed. These two differences work together in such a way that the first READ after a RESET correctly picks up the first character in the file, and each successive READ gets the next character. That much is true whether the file is TEXT or INTERACTIVE.

The difference shows up at the end of the file. Suppose that LETTER.DATA contained just the single character A, followed by the end-of-file marker. If the data type were declared as TEXT, then the RESET statement would do a GET. That would make DATAFILE∧ = 'A'. The first READ statement would assign 'A' to COMPONENT and then would do another GET. That GET would set EOF to *true,* and the WHILE loop would exit.

Now let's see what happens if the data type were declared to be INTERACTIVE. The RESET would *not* do a GET. The READ would do a GET, making DATAFILE∧= 'A', and then would assign 'A' to COMPONENT. Since the READ does not do a second GET, EOF remains *false:* there has been no attempt to input data *beyond* the end-of-file marker. Therefore, the WHILE loop is *not exited*, and a second READ is done. This time the GET causes EOF to become *true,* but it leave DATAFILE∧in an *undefined* state. "Undefined" means that different versions of Pascal will handle the situation differently. Apple Pascal leaves DATAFILE∧ equal to its previous value, which is the previous character read. Finally, the READ assigns this incorrect value to COMPONENT. The WHILE loop then exits, since EOF has become *true.*

Now you can see why the present version of your program wrote two Zs on the TV screen before quitting. To avoid this problem, you would have to change the program logic in the BEGIN/END block as follows:

```
BEGIN
  RESET (DATAFILE, 'APPLEO:LETTER.DATA');
  REPEAT
    READ (DATAFILE, COMPONENT);
    IF NOT EOF (DATAFILE) THEN
      WRITELN (COMPONENT)
  UNTIL EOF (DATAFILE);
  CLOSE (DATAFILE)
END.
```

> This is a rather ugly and inefficient control structure. You should avoid it by declaring your file variable to be of type TEXT when dealing with disk text files.

Why have the INTERACTIVE type if it presents so many problems? Well, there is one situation in which the TEXT approach fails miserably, and that is when a program tries to do a READ *from the keyboard.* When any Pascal program first starts running, the keyboard is automatically opened as a file with the name INPUT. If INPUT were of type TEXT, then an automatic GET would be done from the keyboard and your program would halt, waiting for you to type something. If you typed a Q, for example, then the value would be given to INPUT∧, and the first READ statement would assign 'Q' to the variable in the READ statement. Then it would do another

GET, which would halt the program again and wait for more input. That is obviously bad.

Apple Pascal avoids this problem by declaring INPUT as being of type INTERACTIVE. There is no GET from the keyboard when INPUT is first opened. Furthermore, each READ *starts* with a GET, which causes a halt at the right time. Then when a character is typed in, its value is given to INPUT∧ which is assigned to the variable in the READ statement.

So you can see that you have been using an INTERACTIVE type of file all along, whenever you used a READ or READLN statement, such as

```
READLN (A, B, C)
```

You could also have written that statement like this:

```
READLN (INPUT, A, B, C)
```

If the first parameter in the list is not the name of a file, then INPUT is assumed for READ and READLN procedure calls. Another file, named OUTPUT, is similarly opened for all programs and is assumed for the WRITE and WRITELN procedures when the first parameter is not a file name. OUTPUT is also of type INTERACTIVE, although the difference between TEXT and INTERACTIVE is insignificant for output: the WRITE procedure works the same way for both.

Apple Pascal opens one last file automatically for every running program. It is called KEYBOARD and is of type INTERACTIVE. It is legal to do a GET or READ or READLN from KEYBOARD. The result is exactly the same as if you had used those procedures with the INPUT file, except that the characters you type in response are *not* automatically written on the screen. Suppose, for example, that you wanted the user of your program to respond to a question by typing one letter out of the set (A, B, C, D, E). The following statements would have the *apparent* effect of *disabling* all the keys on the keyboard except the five you want. Then, when one of those five was typed, it would be written on the screen.

```
REPEAT
   READ (KEYBOARD, CH)
UNTIL CH IN ['A'..'E'];
WRITE (CH)
```

This program segment is typical of the use of the KEYBOARD file. It gives you a very nice tool for building a friendly input validation procedure as part of a program that converses with the user.

13-9 REMOVING FILES FROM A DISKETTE

Now that you know how to create data files on your diskette, you will face an information pollution problem if you do not discard useless files. **After you have completed this session, including the problems, come back to this point and tidy up your diskette.**

Let's suppose you are ready to remove the LETTER.DATA file. **Go to the FILER and type R.** The prompt line at the top of the screen says

```
REMOVE ?
```

Type APPLE0:LETTER.DATA and press RETURN. If all went well, you are now looking at the confirmation prompt,

```
UPDATE DIRECTORY ?
```

which gives you a way out if you discover to your horror that you asked to remove some precious file. For example, if you had typed SYSTEM.EDITOR instead of LETTER.DATA above, then you could now type N and all would be forgiven.

Type Y to confirm. That pops you back to the FILER level. **Type E and APPLE0: and RETURN.** Note that the name LETTER.DATA is not in your directory. In its place is the word < UNUSED >, followed by a one. This means that one block of storage has been returned. **Repeat all the above steps for each file you want to get rid of.**

After you remove any files, you should K(runch the diskette again to regain as much consecutive space as possible. **Type K and respond to the questions as before.**

SUMMARY

In Session 12 you learned about the ARRAY data types for dealing with collections of data components, all of the same type. In this session you saw that the RECORD data type permits you to handle a collection of components of distinct types. You also saw how the FILE data type allows you to move data of any other type into and out of the main memory of the computer.

- **RECORD components were referred to by their field names, separated from the record name by a period.**

- **There was no presumed order among the components of a record.**

- **The value of one record could be assigned as a whole to another record variable of the same type.**

- The WITH statement allowed you to omit the record variable name from component names.

- You wrote programs to create a disk file of integer components and one of character components.

- You used the FILE OF phrase to declare a variable of type FILE.

- You used a file variable name in procedure calls affecting the data associated with that file.

- You used the REWRITE call to open a new disk file for receiving output.

- You used the circumflex accent mark as a suffix on the file name to refer to the current component of the file.

- You used the PUT procedure to output a single component to the open file.

- You used the CLOSE procedure with a LOCK parameter to close the open file and make a permanent entry in the diskette directory.

- RESET opened an existing disk file for input.

- You used GET to input the next component of a file.

- You found that RESET does an automatic GET (except for file variables of type INTERACTIVE).

- EOF was used to detect input past the end-of-file marker.

- TEXT was an abbreviation for FILE OF CHAR.

- READ and READLN could be used with TEXT files. If CH is a CHAR variable, then

```
READ (INFILE, CH)
```

was exactly equivalent to

```
CH := INFILE^;
GET (INFILE)
```

if INFILE was declared to be of type TEXT.

- If INFILE was declared to be of type INTERACTIVE, however, the above READ call was equivalent to

```
GET (INFILE)
CH := INFILE^
```

- **WRITE and WRITELN could also be used with TEXT or INTERACTIVE files. In both cases,**

```
WRITE (OUTFILE, CH)
```

was equivalent to

```
OUTFILE^ := CH
PUT (OUTFILE)
```

- **READ, READLN, WRITE, and WRITELN, when used without any file name, referred to INPUT and OUTPUT, which were opened automatically.**

- **These four procedures could handle CHAR, STRING, INTEGER, and REAL parameters, converting each value to (or from) a sequence of characters for output to (or input from) a file of characters.**

- **Three file variables, INPUT, OUTPUT, and KEYBOARD, were declared by the system to be of type INTERACTIVE and were opened automatically when the program execution began.**

- **Input from KEYBOARD was like that from INPUT, except that the characters typed did not appear on the screen.**

- **You used the FILER's E(xtended List Directory, K(runch, and R(emove commands.**

Table 13.1 Cumulative Pascal vocabulary. New words introduced in this session
are printed in bold face. (Code: a = declared in APPLESTUFF; g =
declared in TURTLEGRAPHICS; t = declared in TRANSCEND)

Reserved Words	Built-In Procedures	Built-In Functions	Other Built-Ins
PROGRAM	**CLOSE**	Boolean	Constants
USES	DELETE	**EOF**	FALSE
CONST	**GET**	**EOLN**	TRUE
TYPE	**PUT**	a BUTTON	MAXINT
ARRAY	READ	a KEYPRESS	g NONE
RECORD	READLN		g WHITE
SET	**RESET**	Char	g BLACK
FILE	**REWRITE**	CHR	g REVERSE
VAR	WRITE		g RADAR
PROCEDURE	WRITELN	Integer	g BLACK1
FUNCTION	a NOTE	LENGTH	g GREEN
BEGIN	a RANDOMIZE	ORD	g VIOLET
FOR	g FILLSCREEN	POS	g WHITE1
TO	g GRAFMODE	ROUND	g BLACK2
DOWNTO	g INITTURTLE	TRUNC	g ORANGE
DO	g MOVE	a PADDLE	g BLUE
REPEAT	g MOVETO	a RANDOM	g WHITE2
UNTIL	g PENCOLOR		
WHILE	g TEXTMODE	Real	Types
IF	g TURN	ABS	BOOLEAN
THEN	g TURNTO	PWROFTEN	CHAR
ELSE	g VIEWPORT	SQR	INTEGER
CASE		t ATAN	**INTERACTIVE**
OF		t COS	REAL
WITH		t EXP	STRING
END		t LN	**TEXT**
		t LOG	g SCREENCOLOR
DIV		t SIN	
MOD		t SQRT	Variables
			INPUT
AND		String	**KEYBOARD**
OR		CONCAT	**OUTPUT**
NOT		COPY	
IN			Units
		Other	APPLESTUFF
		PRED	TRANSCEND
		SUCC	TURTLEGRAPHICS

QUESTIONS AND PROBLEMS

1. You need to manipulate a list of employee's names and social security numbers. Define a data type for a single variable that will contain all the data for all the employees. How would you refer to the social security number of the 87th employee?

2. If Pascal had no RECORD type, how would you approach the above problem?

3. Set up the TYPE declaration for the following situation. You want STUDENT.ID to be an integer ID number and you want STUDENT.NAME to be the entire name of a student. But you also want STUDENT.NAME.FIRST to be just the first name and STUDENT.NAME.LAST to be the last name. (Hint: use a record of records.)

4. What VAR declaration would you use to define a file variable such that each file component was one student record as defined in Question 3? If the file variable name is STUFILE, what is the type of STUFILE^? What data would be contained in STUFILE^?

5. How do you open STUFILE in Question 4 for output? For input? How do you close it in each case?

6. STUFILE in Question 4 has just been opened for input. Is STUFILE^ defined at that point? If so what is its value?

7. STUFILE in Question 4 has just been opened with a REWRITE call. Is STUFILE^ defined at that point? If so, what is its value?

8. Use the type declaration of Question 3 to write the steps necessary to output an ID number of 27862, last name of SMITH, and first name of ALFRED, to the next component of the diskette file opened as STUFILE.

9. OUTFILE is a FILE of INTEGER. What do these three statements do?

```
OUTFILE^ := 23;
PUT (OUTFILE);
PUT (OUTFILE)
```

10. Consider the version of program FILEIT on page 320. Explain what would happen if LETTER.DATA were empty.

11. Suppose that in the version of FILEIT on page 320, DATAFILE had been declared to be INTERACTIVE instead of FILE OF CHAR. Explain why the program would give unpredictable results? Would the first character on the screen represent the first character in the file? What about the last character? What about the ones between?

12. Write a program to input the numbers in the file APPLE0:NUMBER.DATA.

13. Someone gives you a diskette that contains a file of characters divided by end-of-line markers that are never more than 80 characters apart. Write a program to input the file and display the contents on the screen. Would the program have to be changed if you didn't know there were any end-of-line markers?

14. Explain the difference between the way READ works for TEXT and for INTERACTIVE file openings.

RECURSION

Most people have seen recursion in pictures. A recent magazine cover, for example, contained a picture of a TV set that was turned on and showed a picture of the same TV set, which was turned on and showed a picture of the same TV set, which was turned on, etc. Such a picture is called *recursive* because one of the objects in the picture *is* the picture itself. It would be impossible to describe the contents of the picture without referring to the picture itself. The picture *recurs* in its own definition. Many programming problems are easier to express by means of definitions that contain the name of the thing being defined. Pascal permits you to do that sort of thing, and you will experiment with examples in this session.

SESSION GOALS

Your main goal in this final session is to see how to analyze a problem in terms of functions and procedures that call themselves. You will write such a recursive function to compute the sum of a series of integers. You will see how complex pictures can be described in terms of recursive procedures. You will learn that every recursive procedure must have a way to prevent infinite recursion. You will investigate an extended example of a mutually recursive program that simulates a Mondrian painting.

14-1 RECURSIVE ARITHMETIC

Suppose you are given the task of summing all the integers from one to 100. How would you do it?

Certainly the most straightforward way would be to start with a variable (call it SUM) equal to zero and then add each number from one to 100 to it. Let's write such a program in two parts: a *function* that returns the sum of the first NUM integers, and a call to that function with a parameter value of 100. Here is such a program:

```
PROGRAM ADDEM;

  FUNCTION SUM (NUM : INTEGER) : INTEGER;
    VAR
      I, TOTAL : INTEGER;
    BEGIN
      TOTAL := 0;
      FOR I := 1 TO NUM DO
        TOTAL := TOTAL + I;
      SUM := TOTAL
    END; (* SUM *)

BEGIN
  WRITELN (SUM (100))
END.
```

Enter this program in a new workfile and run it. You should see the answer, 5050, appear on your TV screen just below the "RUNNING..." message.

That method was quite clear-cut and may at first seem to be the only way to handle this kind of problem. In fact, there are several other ways. The following approach involves *recursion*.

You want SUM (100). Suppose you knew the value of SUM (99). Then you could get what you want by the simple formula

$$SUM (100) = SUM (99) + 100$$

which says that the sum of the first 100 integers is equal to the sum of the first 99 integers, plus 100. That certainly is true, but you *don't* know the value of SUM (99), do you? Perhaps not, but by the same argument it must be true that

$$SUM (99) = SUM (98) + 99$$

and in general,

$$SUM (NUM) = SUM (NUM - 1) + NUM$$

Of course, there is a problem with the above approach: it keeps defining unknown things in terms of other things that are also unknown. *Sooner or later we must know some value of SUM.* And indeed, you *do* know a particularly easy case:

$$SUM (1) = 1$$

In a strictly logical sense, therefore, it is correct to define SUM (NUM) by these two equations:

$$SUM\ (1) = 1$$

$$SUM\ (NUM) = SUM\ (NUM - 1) + NUM$$

where NUM is assumed to be any positive integer. This is called a recursive definition because the name SUM *recurs* in the definition of SUM.

A remarkable feature of Pascal is that it allows you to define functions and procedures in this same recursive fashion. Study the following version of function SUM carefully and try to understand how it works. **Edit your program to look like this version:**

```
PROGRAM ADDEM;

    FUNCTION SUM (NUM : INTEGER) : INTEGER;
    BEGIN
        IF NUM = 1 THEN
            SUM := 1
        ELSE
            SUM := SUM (NUM - 1) + NUM
    END; (* SUM *)

BEGIN
    WRITELN (SUM (100))
END.
```

Note that the entire BEGIN/END block of function SUM consists of a single IF statement with a THEN block and an ELSE block. If the parameter value in a call to SUM had been set equal to 1, then the function returns a 1. That much is easy to see. Now let's see what happens with the call to SUM (2). In this case the parameter value is *not* equal to 1, so the ELSE block is executed. It assigns to SUM the value of SUM (1) + 2. Since the parameter value equals 1, this *second* call returns a value of 1, as we have already seen. Since SUM (1) = 1, it follows that SUM (1) + 2 = 3; and that is the value that gets assigned to SUM and so gets returned as the value of SUM (2).

A SUM (3) call would work in the same sort of way. The ELSE block would be carried out, assigning to SUM the value of SUM (2) + 3. But SUM (2) is a new call to SUM. Once again, the ELSE BLOCK *in that second edition of the function* would be carried out, assigning to the *second edition* of SUM the value of SUM (1) + 2. But SUM (1) is *still another* call to SUM. Finally, the THEN block *in the third edition of the function* gets carried out, assigning to the *third edition* of SUM the value one. Since there are no more calls, the *third* edition of SUM returns with that value, one. That result is then added to 2 and assigned to the *second* edition of SUM, which returns a value of 3. Finally, that result is added to 3 and assigned to the *first* edition of SUM which returns a value of 6 for SUM (3), which is the final result.

Now run the recursive version of the program and confirm that it works as advertised.

Perhaps the easiest way to think about recursion in Pascal is to imagine that each internal call to SUM creates a totally new copy of the function with its own independent set of names and values that are known *locally* within that copy but are not known to the earlier copy that called the new one into being. Think of the call, SUM (100), as creating 100 independent copies of the SUM function, *each of which* has a statement of the form SUM := ... Nevertheless, the name SUM in the 100th copy is independent of the name SUM in the 37th copy and all other copies. Each copy is like a *sibling* of the other copies, and Pascal's general rule about the scope of variable names (and other names) applies also to successive copies of a recursive function or procedure.

Some implementations of recursion actually do create a separate copy for every call; so this way of thinking about recursion is not just conceptual. Apple Pascal, however, does not create copies of the actual program statements. Instead, it stacks up copies of just the local variables. However it is done, handling recursion takes both processor time and memory space. Despite that price, a recursive definition is often the clearest way to define a process.

We shall soon return to other examples of recursion, but before we do, let's look one last time at the problem of summing consecutive integers. It turns out that neither the direct FOR loop approach nor the recursive approach would pass muster as good programming. There is a far simpler way, and folklore has it that the great mathematician, Karl Friedrich Gauss, figured it out in 1785 when he was a small child at school. His teacher, annoyed at some misbehavior, required as punishment that he add all the numbers from one to 100. The child thought about it for a few seconds and reported the correct result: 5050. His method was to notice that

$$
\begin{array}{rcrcl}
1 & + & 100 & = & 101 \\
2 & + & 99 & = & 101 \\
3 & + & 98 & = & 101 \\
  & . & . & & . \\
  & . & . & & . \\
  & . & . & & . \\
49 & + & 52 & = & 101 \\
50 & + & 51 & = & 101 \\
\end{array}
$$

Thus there were 50 occurrences of 101. The answer had to be 50 times 101, or 5050. This way of doing things is summed up by the formula

SUM = NUM * (NUM + 1) DIV 2

for the sum of the first NUM positive integers.

Edit your program as follows. Then run it and check the time needed.

```
PROGRAM ADDEM;

   FUNCTION SUM (NUM : INTEGER) : INTEGER;
      BEGIN
         SUM := NUM * (NUM + 1) DIV 2
      END; (* SUM *)

   BEGIN
      WRITELN (SUM (100))
   END.
```

14-2 RECURSIVE PICTURES

The example of recursion that began this session was a pictorial one. In this section you will see how to define recursive pictures of your own. **Clear out your workfile and enter the following nonrecursive program.**

```
PROGRAM SQUARES;

   USES
      TURTLEGRAPHICS;

   PROCEDURE SQUARE (SIZE : INTEGER);
      VAR
         I : INTEGER;
      BEGIN
         FOR I := 1 TO 4 DO
            BEGIN
               MOVE (SIZE);
               TURN (90)
            END
      END; (* SQUARE *)

BEGIN
   INITTURTLE;
   MOVETO (44, 0);
   PENCOLOR (WHITE);
   SQUARE (191);
   READLN
END.
```

The main program first initializes the Apple window so that it is looking at the graphic page and sets the pen color to NONE. The next statement moves the "turtle" to the bottom of the screen near the left edge. The next line sets pen color to WHITE. The fourth line calls SQUARE with a size value of 191. The last line creates a program halt so that you can examine the picture. Your procedure SQUARE is very simple. It merely does a move in its initial direction (to the right, as set by INITTURTLE) a distance equal to the value of the SIZE parameter. Then it turns 90 degrees counterclockwise. These two steps are repeated four times. At the end, the turtle is back where it started and is pointed to the right again.

Run the program. When you have finished looking at the square, press RETURN and then go back to the EDITOR.

As it stands, your program now draws a picture of a square. Suppose instead that you wanted a picture of a square that contained within it a picture of a slightly smaller square that contained within it a picture of a still smaller square, that contained...etc. The following modification of SQUARE should do the trick:

```
PROCEDURE SQUARE (SIZE : INTEGER);
   VAR
   I : INTEGER;
   BEGIN
     IF SIZE > 1 THEN
       BEGIN
         FOR I := 1 TO 4 DO
           BEGIN
             MOVE (SIZE);
             TURN (90)
           END;
         SQUARE (TRUNC (SIZE * 0.9))
       END (* IF *)
   END; (* SQUARE *)
```

Make the above changes. Note that recursion occurs in the THEN block, which first *draws* a square, just as before, and then *calls* SQUARE with a size 90% that of the size it was called with. (Note that the expression SIZE * 0.9 is of type REAL. The TRUNC function turns the result back to INTEGER, as required for the parameter type in the definition of SQUARE.)

The entire procedure is now a single IF statement, which is what prevents infinite recursion. Sooner or later the shrinking size parameter will equal one. When that happens, SQUARE does nothing, and that stops the recursive sequence of calls.

Run the program. Press RETURN when you're through looking at the display. As promised, you have produced a picture of a square containing a picture of a square containing... A slight variation of this program is even more interesting. **Go to the EDITOR. Change the THEN block as follows:**

```
FOR I := 1 TO 4 DO
   BEGIN
     MOVE (SIZE);
     TURN (90)
   END;
MOVE (1 + TRUNC (SIZE * 0.1));
TURN (5);
SQUARE (TRUNC (SIZE * 0.9))
```

Run this version. Then return to the EDITOR and study the two statements you added and their effects. Each square now contains a picture of a rotated square, containing a picture of a rotated square, containing...

Now let's make another small change in the definition of SQUARE. **Delete the two statements you just added. Move the call to SQUARE inside the FOR statement. Change 0.9 to 0.45.** The new version of the THEN block should look like this:

```
BEGIN
  FOR I := 1 TO 4 DO
    BEGIN
      MOVE (SIZE);
      TURN (90);
      SQUARE (TRUNC (SIZE * 0.45))
    END;
END (* IF *)
```

With this new version, SQUARE will draw one side of a square, turn 90 degrees, and then call for a picture of a smaller square to be drawn at that corner before continuing with the next side of the original square. What do you think will result? **Run the program and find out.**

14-3 ANOTHER RECURSIVE PICTURE

Probably the best way to get a feeling for recursive programming is by means of examples. This section is devoted to another simple graphic example of a recursive procedure. It draws members of a family known as *dragon curves*. **Clear out your workfile and enter the following program.**

```
PROGRAM DRAGONCURVE;

   USES
      TURTLEGRAPHICS;

   VAR
      LEV : INTEGER;

   PROCEDURE DRAGON (SIZE, LEVEL : INTEGER);
      VAR
         NEWSIZE : INTEGER;
      BEGIN
         IF LEVEL <= 0 THEN
            MOVE (SIZE)
         ELSE
            BEGIN
               NEWSIZE := ROUND (SIZE * 0.707);
               TURN (45);
               DRAGON (NEWSIZE, LEVEL - 1);
               TURN (-90);
               DRAGON (NEWSIZE, LEVEL - 1);
               TURN (45)
            END (* IF *)
      END; (* DRAGON *)

BEGIN
   INITTURTLE;
   FOR LEV := 0 TO 10 DO
      BEGIN
         PENCOLOR (NONE); MOVETO (70, 50);
         PENCOLOR (WHITE); DRAGON (140, LEV);
         READLN
      END (* FOR *)
END.
```

To understand this program, start with the main BEGIN/END block. A FOR loop first puts the turtle at the starting point (70, 50); second, the main BEGIN/END block calls DRAGON with a size parameter of 140 screen units and a "level" parameter equal to the loop variable; finally the program halts, awaiting a RETURN from the keyboard. Each time through the loop the process is repeated, but the level parameter goes up by one.

Now, study the definition of DRAGON.

As with any other recursive procedure, you will have the essential idea when you see what happens in the two special cases: the non-recursive case and the simplest recursive case.

The nonrecursive case for DRAGON occurs when the level parameter equals zero. In that case DRAGON simply draws a line of length equal to SIZE in the current direction of the turtle. The simplest recursive case occurs when the level parameter is equal to one. In that case, the following sequence of events takes place:

1. The turtle is turned 45 degrees counterclockwise.

2. DRAGON is called with a smaller size and a level value of zero. So a shorter line is drawn in a direction 45 degrees above the horizontal.

3. The turtle is turned 90 degrees clockwise.

4. DRAGON is called again with the same smaller size and zero level value. Again a shorter line is drawn, this time in a direction *below* the horizontal. The beginning of the second line is connected to the end of the first line.

5. The turtle is turned 45 degrees counterclockwise. Its heading is now the same as it was originally.

Note that the magic number 0.707 is chosen here so that the turtle will end up in the same location where the nonrecursive case would have left it after the horizontal straight-line move.

Run the program. The first picture is the nonrecursive case. **Now press RETURN and examine the simplest recursive case. Was that what you expected? Before pressing RETURN, try to figure out what the level = 2 picture will look like. Press RETURN and see. Continue examining curves of higher and higher degree of recursion.**

You probably noticed that at a level of 5 the curve began to cross itself. This can be avoided by the simple tactic of *alternating* the 45 degree turns so that the first is counterclockwise, the second is clockwise, etc. To do that you need a SIGN parameter in the parameter list of DRAGON. Here is the changed version:

```
PROCEDURE DRAGON (SIZE, LEVEL, SIGN : INTEGER);
  VAR
    NEWSIZE : INTEGER;
  BEGIN
    IF LEVEL <= 0 THEN
      MOVE (SIZE)
    ELSE
      BEGIN
        NEWSIZE := ROUND (SIZE * 0.707);
        TURN (45 * SIGN);
        DRAGON (NEWSIZE, LEVEL - 1, 1);
        TURN (-90 * SIGN);
        DRAGON (NEWSIZE, LEVEL - 1, -1);
        TURN (45 * SIGN)
      END (* IF *)
  END; (* DRAGON *)
```

Make this change. Then change the FOR loop of the main BEGIN/END block as follows:

```
FOR LEV := 0 TO 10 DO
   BEGIN
      FILLSCREEN (BLACK);
      PENCOLOR (NONE); MOVETO (70, 50);
      PENCOLOR (WHITE); DRAGON (140, LEV, 1);
      READLN
   END (* FOR *)
```

This time each pass through the loop begins with a screen erase. Also, the main program calls DRAGON with a third parameter of value equal to one. This means that SIGN will equal one at the outer level of the call to DRAGON. Therefore the first turn will be in the +45 degree direction, which is counterclockwise, as before.

Run the program and examine carefully the picture produced at levels zero, one and two of recursion. You should find that levels zero and one are exactly the same as before. Level two produces the first difference. Instead of looking like this,

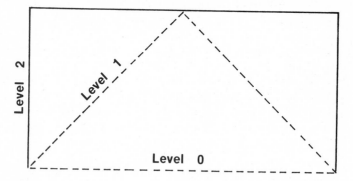

it looks like this:

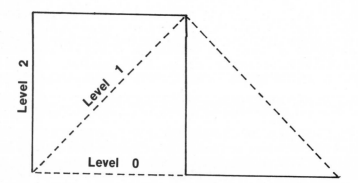

That result is the effect of alternating the SIGN values between +1 and –1. **Try to predict what the dragon curve will look like for LEV = 3. Press RETURN and see. Check the rest of the levels.**

14-4 MUTUAL RECURSION

So far you have seen several examples of recursive functions and procedures. In each case the BEGIN/END block had a logical path that was nonrecursive and another logical path in which the function or procedure called itself. Such a situation is called *simple recursion*. It is also possible to have more complex types of recursion. Procedure A could call procedure B. Procedure B could call procedure C. At this point you might conclude that procedures A and B are nonrecursive. But what would you say if a reading of procedure C showed that it could call procedure A? Is C the recursive one? Or is it A? Or B?

This situation is called *mutual recursion*. The set of procedures A, B, and C would be called mutually recursive, since a call to any one of them could cause recursion to occur. This section will consider a graphic example of mutual recursion.

Piet Mondrian, the Dutch painter who lived from 1872-1944, created a series of canvases that had a strong similarity to one another. Each one had a solid white background with solid black horizontal and vertical bars distributed in a somewhat random fashion over the surface. The bars were of a fairly uniform thickness. A few of the enclosed rectangles were painted in brilliant primary colors.

Our goal in this section is to define a program that reproduces some of the attributes of a Mondrian painting of that type. Here is our basic strategy: we define two similar procedures whose task is to receive a given rectangle and slice it at random into two smaller rectangles. Procedure VERTICAL, for example, receives a rectangle defined by the four parameters LEFT, RIGHT, BOTTOM, and TOP. It picks a number at random between LEFT and RIGHT. Call it MID. Then it draws a vertical bar at MID, from BOTTOM to TOP. Now it has produced two new rectangles. One is specified by LEFT, MID, BOTTOM, TOP; the other by MID, RIGHT, BOTTOM, TOP. Then procedure VERTICAL calls its twin brother, HORIZONTAL, twice. The first time it passes the lefthand rectangle and the second time, the righthand rectangle. HORIZONTAL's job is to divide the received rectangle into smaller rectangles, to draw a horizontal bar between them, and then to call VERTICAL twice, passing each of the two new rectangles.

You can see from the above description that HORIZONTAL and VERTICAL are going to be mutually recursive procedures. Let's start with a *non*recursive program that contains the first steps in this direction. **Study the listing below, expecially procedure VERTICAL and the main BEGIN/END block.**

```
PROGRAM MONDRIAN;

  USES
    APPLESTUFF, TURTLEGRAPHICS;

  VAR
    CH : CHAR;

  PROCEDURE VERTICAL (LEFT, RIGHT, BOTTOM, TOP : INTEGER);
    VAR
      MID, SPAN : INTEGER;
    BEGIN
      SPAN := RIGHT - LEFT + 1;
      MID := LEFT + RANDOM MOD SPAN;
      PENCOLOR (NONE); MOVETO (MID, BOTTOM);
      PENCOLOR (BLACK) ; MOVETO (MID, TOP)
    END; (* VERTICAL *)

BEGIN
  RANDOMIZE;
  INITTURTLE;
  REPEAT
    FILLSCREEN (WHITE);
    VERTICAL (0, 279, 0, 191);
    READ (CH)
  UNTIL CH = 'Q'
END.
```

Note in procedure VERTICAL that SPAN is assigned a value equal to the entire width of the rectangle. Then SPAN is used in the expression RANDOM MOD SPAN to compute a pseudorandom integer between zero and SPAN − 1. That number is added to LEFT and assigned to MID. MID, therefore, is a random number in the subrange LEFT..RIGHT. The next two lines of VERTICAL draw a vertical line at the point where the distance from the left edge *of the screen* is MID. So far, that is all that VERTICAL can do.

Now let's look at the main BEGIN/END block. The first statement calls RANDOMIZE, to vary the seed of the random number generator. INITTURTLE does the usual graphics mode initializations. The rest of the main block is a single REPEAT statement. It begins by filling the screen with the color WHITE. Next, it calls VERTICAL, passing parameters for the left, right, bottom, and top of the full graphic screen. Finally, it halts with the READ call, waiting for the user to touch any key. If the input character is a Q, the program stops. Otherwise the REPEAT loop continues.

Clear out your workfile. Enter the above program and run it. Press the spacebar a few times to experiment with the program. Then type Q to quit. Well, that won't win any art contests, but it's a start. As you saw, VERTICAL did what we told it to do, drawing randomly placed vertical lines on the screen.

Before turning to the definition of its twin, HORIZONTAL, let's do a bit of stepwise refinement on VERTICAL. First, those thin vertical lines were poor representations of Mondrian's bold black stripes. We need an area-filling procedure that will replace the line-drawing steps in VERTICAL. Here is a simple one:

```
PROCEDURE FILL (L, R, B, T : INTEGER;
                     COLOR : SCREENCOLOR);
   BEGIN
      VIEWPORT (L, R, B, T);
      FILLSCREEN (COLOR)
   END; (* FILL *)
```

FILL has a 5-item parameter list. The first four are integers that define the left, right, bottom, and top of the rectangle to be filled with color. The fifth parameter tells what color to use. Since it is declared to be of type SCREENCOLOR, the *value* of that parameter can be BLACK, WHITE, BLUE, etc. Notice that we have decided to enter the parameter list on two lines of text, since it is a long one. That is legal in Pascal, since a RETURN can be used whenever a space is legal. FILL does two things: it defines a viewport equal to the rectangle passed to FILL; then it fills the rectangle with the color value passed as the fifth parameter to FILL.

Now let's see how to use FILL to draw the solid black bars that we want in our picture. Suppose we define a constant, called HALF, that represents about half the desired width of a bar. Then the call

```
FILL (MID - HALF, MID + HALF, BOTTOM, TOP, BLACK)
```

would draw a vertical black bar centered at MID and having a total thickness equal to 2 * HALF + 1. Here, then is a revision of the first version of MONDRIAN:

```
PROGRAM MONDRIAN;

  USES
    APPLESTUFF, TURTLEGRAPHICS;

  CONST
    HALF = 4;

  VAR
    CH : CHAR;

  PROCEDURE FILL (L, R, B, T : INTEGER;
                         COLOR : SCREENCOLOR);
    BEGIN
      VIEWPORT (L, R, B, T);
      FILLSCREEN (COLOR)
    END; (* FILL *)

  PROCEDURE VERTICAL (LEFT, RIGHT, BOTTOM, TOP : INTEGER);
    VAR
      MID, SPAN : INTEGER;
    BEGIN
      SPAN := RIGHT - LEFT + 1;
      MID := LEFT + RANDOM MOD SPAN;
      FILL (MID - HALF, MID + HALF, BOTTOM, TOP, BLACK)
    END; (* VERTICAL *)

BEGIN
  RANDOMIZE;
  INITTURTLE;
  REPEAT
    FILLSCREEN (WHITE);
    VERTICAL (0, 279, 0, 191);
    READ (CH)
  UNTIL CH = 'Q'
END.
```

Enter the changes and run the new version.

So far, so good. Now let's write a HORIZONTAL procedure modeled after VERTICAL. Here is a simple and direct translation:

```
PROCEDURE HORIZONTAL (LEFT, RIGHT, BOTTOM, TOP : INTEGER);
  VAR
    MID, SPAN : INTEGER;
  BEGIN
    SPAN := TOP - BOTTOM + 1;
    MID := BOTTOM + RANDOM MOD SPAN;
    FILL (LEFT, RIGHT, MID - HALF, MID + HALF, BLACK)
  END; (* HORIZONTAL *)
```

Enter this new text into your program immediately after procedure FILL and before procedure VERTICAL.

The next step is to modify procedure VERTICAL so that after it draws its vertical bar it will call HORIZONTAL, passing the rectangle on the left side of the bar, and then will again call HORIZONTAL, this time passing the rectangle on the right side of the bar. Here is how VERTICAL should look:

```
PROCEDURE VERTICAL (LEFT, RIGHT, BOTTOM, TOP : INTEGER);
  VAR
    MID, SPAN : INTEGER;
  BEGIN
    SPAN := RIGHT - LEFT + 1;
    MID := LEFT + RANDOM MOD SPAN;
    FILL (MID - HALF, MID + HALF, BOTTOM, TOP, BLACK);
    HORIZONTAL (LEFT, MID - HALF -1, BOTTOM, TOP);
    HORIZONTAL (MID + HALF + 1, RIGHT, BOTTOM, TOP)
  END; (* VERTICAL *)
```

Enter the two new lines into VERTICAL. Then run the program. Press the spacebar a few times. Then type Q to quit.

Except for an obvious "bug", things are looking up. VERTICAL drew its black bar; it called HORIZONTAL, which drew a horizontal bar in the lefthand rectangle; then VERTICAL called HORIZONTAL again, resulting in a horizontal bar in the righthand rectangle. The bug shows up when you press the spacebar, expecting the screen to erase. It doesn't. The problem comes from an interaction between the FILLSCREEN call in the main BEGIN/END block and the VIEWPORT call in procedure FILL. Each call to FILL resets the viewport to a narrow bar *and leaves it that way*. FILLSCREEN always fills in the *current* viewport. It works fine the first time, since the initial viewport is the full screen. It fails after that.

You can fix the bug by replacing the FILLSCREEN (WHITE) call (in the main BEGIN/END block) by a call to FILL, as follows:

```
FILL (0, 279, 0, 191, WHITE);
```

Make this change and run again. This time you should start with a new white screen each time you press the spacebar.

Now that VERTICAL is drawing its bar and then calling HORIZONTAL, and HORIZONTAL is drawing its horizontal bars, all that remains is to have HORIZONTAL call VERTICAL twice, first passing the lower rectangle and then the upper one. VERTICAL would then do its number and then call HORIZONTAL, etc.

Let's see how to handle this case of mutual recursion. The first step is fairly obvious. As before, we must make HORIZONTAL into a twin of VERTICAL. That is, we need to add two new call statements back to the calling procedure. **Change HORIZONTAL as follows.**

```
PROCEDURE HORIZONTAL (LEFT, RIGHT, BOTTOM, TOP : INTEGER);
   VAR
      MID, SPAN : INTEGER;
   BEGIN
      SPAN := TOP - BOTTOM + 1;
      MID := BOTTOM + RANDOM MOD SPAN;
      FILL (LEFT, RIGHT, MID - HALF, MID + HALF, BLACK);
      VERTICAL (LEFT, RIGHT, BOTTOM, MID - HALF -1);
      VERTICAL (LEFT, RIGHT, MID + HALF + 1, TOP)
   END; (* HORIZONTAL *)
```

Now each procedure will compute a division into two smaller rectangles, draw a bar between them, and call its twin twice, first with one of the new rectangles and then with the other. Let's see if that works. **Try to run the program as it stands.**

If you didn't make any typing errors, compiling should have halted immediately after appearance of the word VERTICAL in procedure HORIZONTAL. **Type E to go back to the EDITOR.** Note that the compiler's complaint is that VERTICAL is an "undeclared identifier". Of course, you *have* defined VERTICAL, but the definition occurs *later in the text* of the program. *Pascal insists firmly that all words be defined before first use.*

The standard solution to this problem is to move the text of the definition ahead of the place where it is first used. But if you move the text of procedure VERTICAL ahead of the text of HORIZONTAL, you will still be in hot water. Note that the text of VERTICAL uses the word HORIZONTAL, so the compiler would complain that HORIZONTAL was an "undeclared identifier."

Suddenly it looks as though mutual recursion is ruled out on a technicality. Pascal, however, offers a way out of the woods. As things stand with your program now, the compiler is complaining because it doesn't know anything about the word VERTICAL. In fact, all that the compiler needs to know about VERTICAL *at this point* is the information contained in the heading:

```
PROCEDURE VERTICAL (LEFT, RIGHT, BOTTOM, TOP : INTEGER)
```

If that much of procedure VERTICAL could be placed ahead of procedure HORIZONTAL in the text of your program, the compiler would be quite happy when it saw the word VERTICAL later.

Pascal has a special way of allowing you to do exactly that. Here are the steps.

1. Put the *complete* heading of the procedure (or function), including the parameter list, ahead of the first procedure (or function) that refers to it.

2. Follow the heading immediately by the reserved word FORWARD and a semicolon.

3. Put the rest of the declaration of the procedure (or function) later in the text of your program, duplicating the heading *but omitting any parameter list this time.*

Here is how these changes would look in your program:

```
PROCEDURE VERTICAL (LEFT, RIGHT, BOTTOM, TOP : INTEGER);
   FORWARD;

PROCEDURE HORIZONTAL (LEFT, RIGHT, BOTTOM, TOP : INTEGER);
   VAR
      MID, SPAN : INTEGER;
   BEGIN
      SPAN := TOP - BOTTOM + 1;
      MID := BOTTOM + RANDOM MOD SPAN;
      FILL (LEFT, RIGHT, MID - HALF, MID + HALF, BLACK);
      VERTICAL (LEFT, RIGHT, BOTTOM, MID - HALF -1);
      VERTICAL (LEFT, RIGHT, MID + HALF + 1, TOP)
   END; (* HORIZONTAL *)

PROCEDURE VERTICAL;
   VAR
      MID, SPAN : INTEGER;
   BEGIN
      SPAN := RIGHT - LEFT + 1;
      MID := LEFT + RANDOM MOD SPAN;
      FILL (MID - HALF, MID + HALF, BOTTOM, TOP, BLACK);
      HORIZONTAL (LEFT, MID - HALF -1, BOTTOM, TOP);
      HORIZONTAL (MID + HALF + 1, RIGHT, BOTTOM, TOP)
   END; (* VERTICAL *)
```

Make the above changes. Run the new version. This time there should be no compile-time errors. As required by Pascal, all words are declared in the text prior to first use.

Everything is fine, except that the program doesn't work the way we intended. The first vertical bar is drawn correctly. The lefthand horizontal bar is drawn. Then a vertical bar goes into the lower lefthand rectangle, etc. The problem is that each division leaves unfinished business that *never* gets attended to. This is a case of *infinite recursion*.

In fact, it looks as though the computer has stopped working. After about 45 seconds, however, the graphic screen disappears and you should see the message

```
STACK OVERFLOW
S# 1, P# 2, I# 7
PRESS RESET
```

Don't press RESET! Disaster has struck. Infinite recursion has used up all the computer's memory. You will have to do a cold reboot. **Remove APPLE0:, replace it with APPLE3:, and press RESET. When prompted, exchange APPLE0: for APPLE3:, and again press RESET. When the COMMAND prompt appears, type E.** You're back in business.

You should not have been surprised at the outcome, since we broke one of the cardinal rules of recursive programming.

> Every recursive procedure definition must contain a nonrecursive path.

In our program, VERTICAL *always* calls HORIZONTAL, and HORIZONTAL *always* calls VERTICAL. The only path through either procedure is a recursive one.

To avoid infinite recursion, you need to specify some criterion for deciding when to cut off the chain of recursive calls. In Section 14–3 you saw how to use a "level" parameter for that purpose, and you could easily do the same thing here. For variety, however, we'll use a somewhat more naturalistic graphic criterion.

You recall that the black bars are nine screen units wide. Sooner or later the division process will make the size of the rectangles passed to HORIZONTAL or VERTICAL so small that further division is pointless. Note that the variable named SPAN has a value equal to the distance to be divided by the bar. If you were to define a global constant named MINSPAN, then testing SPAN against MINSPAN would give you a criterion for whether or not to divide the rectangle and continue the recursion. For example, procedure HORIZONTAL would look like this:

```
PROCEDURE HORIZONTAL (LEFT, RIGHT, BOTTOM, TOP : INTEGER);
   VAR
      MID, SPAN : INTEGER;
   BEGIN
      SPAN := TOP - BOTTOM + 1;
      IF SPAN >= MINSPAN THEN
         BEGIN
            MID := BOTTOM + RANDOM MOD SPAN;
            FILL (LEFT, RIGHT, MID - HALF, MID + HALF, BLACK);
            VERTICAL (LEFT, RIGHT, BOTTOM, MID - HALF -1);
            VERTICAL (LEFT, RIGHT, MID + HALF + 1, TOP)
         END
   END; (* HORIZONTAL *)
```

With this change, HORIZONTAL stops calling VERTICAL as soon as the width of the passed rectangle is less than MINSPAN. **Make this change to HORIZONTAL. Make an identical change to VERTICAL. Change your CONST block as follows:**

```
CONST
   HALF = 4;
   MINSPAN = 40;
```

Run the new version. Press the spacebar five or six times to see the variety of pictures. Type Q to quit.

Now let's add some color. Note that in the new version of HORIZONTAL and VERTICAL, *nothing* happens when recursion finally comes to an end. That is true because the IF statement in each procedure does not contain an ELSE block. All that we need to do is add an ELSE block which colors in the rectangle that did *not* get divided further. Here is how the complete IF statement would look for procedure HORIZONTAL.

```
IF SPAN >= MINSPAN THEN
   BEGIN
      MID := BOTTOM + RANDOM MOD SPAN;
      FILL (LEFT, RIGHT, MID - HALF, MID + HALF, BLACK);
      VERTICAL (LEFT, RIGHT, BOTTOM, MID - HALF -1);
      VERTICAL (LEFT, RIGHT, MID + HALF + 1, TOP)
   END
ELSE
   ADDCOLOR (LEFT, RIGHT, BOTTOM, TOP)
```

Make the changes above in both HORIZONTAL and VERTICAL.

The next task is to define procedure ADDCOLOR. The following steps will use a probabilistic approach, rather like rolling a die to decide what color to use:

```
PROCEDURE ADDCOLOR (L, R, B, T : INTEGER);
   BEGIN
      CASE RANDOM MOD 10 OF
         0 : FILL (L, R, B, T, ORANGE);
         1 : FILL (L, R, B, T, BLUE)
      END (* CASE *)
   END;
```

RANDOM MOD 10 produces random integers in the range 0..9. If the result is zero, the rectangle is filled with orange. If the result is one, it is filled with blue. If the result is greater than one, it is left white. **Enter the above procedure into the text of your program immediately after the end of procedure FILL. (Why there?) Run the result.**

We'll leave the Mondrian problem at this point of development. It is still a far cry from being an automatic generator of masterpieces, but the program does exhibit a few of the characteristics of Mondrian's paintings. More to the point here, it shows how to employ simple recursive methods and random events to produce structures of apparent complexity. For future reference, the following is a listing of the final version of your program.

```
PROGRAM MONDRIAN;

  USES
    APPLESTUFF, TURTLEGRAPHICS;

  CONST
    HALF = 4;
    MINSPAN = 40;

  VAR
    CH : CHAR;

  PROCEDURE FILL (L, R, B, T : INTEGER;
                          COLOR : SCREENCOLOR);
    BEGIN
      VIEWPORT (L, R, B, T);
      FILLSCREEN (COLOR)
    END; (* FILL *)

  PROCEDURE ADDCOLOR (L, R, B, T : INTEGER);
    BEGIN
      CASE RANDOM MOD 10 OF
        0 : FILL (L, R, B, T, ORANGE);
        1 : FILL (L, R, B, T, BLUE)
      END (* CASE *)
    END;

PROCEDURE VERTICAL (LEFT, RIGHT, BOTTOM, TOP : INTEGER);
  FORWARD;

PROCEDURE HORIZONTAL (LEFT, RIGHT, BOTTOM, TOP : INTEGER);
  VAR
    MID, SPAN : INTEGER;
  BEGIN
    SPAN := TOP - BOTTOM + 1;
    IF SPAN >= MINSPAN THEN
      BEGIN
        MID := BOTTOM + RANDOM MOD SPAN;
        FILL (LEFT, RIGHT, MID - HALF, MID + HALF, BLACK);
        VERTICAL (LEFT, RIGHT, BOTTOM, MID - HALF -1);
        VERTICAL (LEFT, RIGHT, MID + HALF + 1, TOP)
      END
    ELSE
      ADDCOLOR (LEFT, RIGHT, BOTTOM, TOP)
  END; (* HORIZONTAL *)
```

```
PROCEDURE VERTICAL;
  VAR
    MID, SPAN : INTEGER;
  BEGIN
    SPAN := RIGHT - LEFT + 1;
    IF SPAN >= MINSPAN THEN
      BEGIN
        MID := LEFT + RANDOM MOD SPAN;
        FILL (MID - HALF, MID + HALF, BOTTOM, TOP, BLACK);
        HORIZONTAL (LEFT, MID - HALF -1, BOTTOM, TOP);
        HORIZONTAL (MID + HALF + 1, RIGHT, BOTTOM, TOP)
      END
    ELSE
      ADDCOLOR (LEFT, RIGHT, BOTTOM, TOP)
  END; (* VERTICAL *)

BEGIN
  RANDOMIZE;
  INITTURTLE;
  REPEAT
    FILL (0, 279, 0, 191, WHITE);
    VERTICAL (0, 279, 0, 191);
    READ (CH)
  UNTIL CH = 'Q'
END.
```

SUMMARY

You have seen in this session that is is legal in Pascal for a function or a procedure to call itself recursively. You have also investigated four different examples of recursion.

- You saw that when a function or procedure calls itself, it is exactly as though it had called another function or procedure that happened to be an exact copy of itself.

- You saw that each such copy has its own set of local variables not known to the caller.

- You found that infinite recursion occurs and causes a fatal "stack overflow" error if the function or procedure lacks a nonrecursive path.

- You saw how to use a "level" parameter to decide when to stop recursion.

- You wrote mutually recursive procedures that call one another.

- You used the reserved word FORWARD to allow placement of a procedure heading before its first use in the text of a program.

- You used an abbreviated heading later in the text at the start of the main body of the procedure whose full heading included the FORWARD declaration.

Table 14.1 Cumulative Pascal vocabulary. New words introduced in this session are printed in bold face. (Code: a = declared in APPLESTUFF; g = declared in TURTLEGRAPHICS; t = declared in TRANSCEND)

Reserved Words	Built-In Procedures	Built-In Functions	Other Built-Ins
PROGRAM	CLOSE	Boolean	Constants
USES	DELETE	EOF	FALSE
CONST	GET	EOLN	TRUE
TYPE	PUT	a BUTTON	MAXINT
ARRAY	READ	a KEYPRESS	g NONE
RECORD	READLN		g WHITE
SET	RESET	Char	g BLACK
FILE	REWRITE	CHR	g REVERSE
VAR	WRITE		g RADAR
PROCEDURE	WRITELN	Integer	g BLACK1
FORWARD	a NOTE	LENGTH	g GREEN
FUNCTION	a RANDOMIZE	ORD	g VIOLET
BEGIN	g FILLSCREEN	POS	g WHITE1
FOR	g GRAFMODE	ROUND	g BLACK2
TO	g INITTURTLE	TRUNC	g ORANGE
DOWNTO	g MOVE	a PADDLE	g BLUE
DO	g MOVETO	a RANDOM	g WHITE2
REPEAT	g PENCOLOR		
UNTIL	g TEXTMODE	Real	Types
WHILE	g TURN	ABS	BOOLEAN
IF	g TURNTO	PWROFTEN	CHAR
THEN	g VIEWPORT	SQR	INTEGER
ELSE		t ATAN	INTERACTIVE
CASE		t COS	REAL
OF		t EXP	STRING
WITH		t LN	TEXT
END		t LOG	SCREENCOLOR
		t SIN	
DIV		t SQRT	Variables
MOD			INPUT
		String	KEYBOARD
AND		CONCAT	OUTPUT
OR		COPY	
NOT			Units
IN		Other	APPLESTUFF
		PRED	TRANSCEND
		SUCC	TURTLEGRAPHICS

For a complete list of all the words for the Pascal vocabulary, see Appendix C.

QUESTIONS AND PROBLEMS

1. Write a recursive function that returns the value of the sum

    1 + 1/2 + 1/3 + .. + 1/N

    for any positive value of N. Be sure to make the function REAL.

2. Write a recursive function that returns the value of the sum

    1 − 1/2 + 1/3 − 1/4 + .. ± 1/N

    for any positive N. (Hint: the built-in function ODD (N) has the boolean value *true* if N is an odd integer and *false* if N is even. Use ODD to decide whether to add or subtract 1/N.)

3. Pictured below are the first three levels of a recursive picture. Write a procedure to draw the picture for any non-negative level.

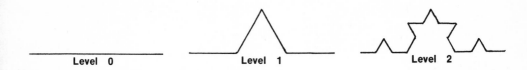

Level 0   Level 1   Level 2

4. Write a recursive procedure to draw pictures in a family, the first two members of which are

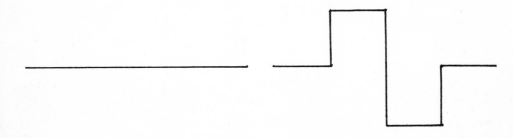

5. Write a recursive procedure to draw pictures in the family whose fourth member is this:

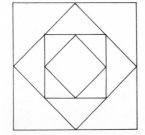

6. Write a recursive procedure to draw pictures in the family whose third member is this:

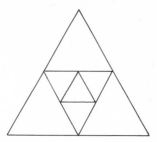

7. Write two mutually recursive procedures named SQUARE and TRIANGLE that draw the family whose fifth member is this:

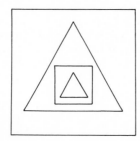

(Hint: after each figure is drawn, you will have to set pen color to NONE, do some MOVEs and TURNs, and then set pen color back to WHITE, in order to move the next figure inside the current one.)

8. Write two mutually recursive functions named SUM and PRODUCT that return the value of the expression

(...(((1 + 2) * 3 + 4) * 5 + 6) * 7 + ... + (N − 1) * N)

for any N greater than zero. How will the main program decide whether to call SUM or PRODUCT to get the right answer for a given N?

WHERE DO YOU GO FROM HERE?

We said in the Introduction that our intention as writers was not to have the last word on the subject of Pascal but instead to get you off to a good start. In fact, if you have done most of the activities set out in these 14 sessions, you will have come a long way towards a fairly deep working knowledge of the language. You know all the statement types except one (the GOTO statement), all the built-in data types except one (pointers), and nearly all the reserved words. You have used the majority of the built-in functions, procedures and constants available in Apple Pascal. And you have used all of the important system commands for entering, editing, running, and saving programs.

Nevertheless, our book is not the last Pascal book you will ever read. Nor should it be, since it cannot satisfy all of your future needs. For one thing, this book is a dismal failure as a reference manual, either for the language or for the operating system commands. For reference purposes you want a complete, concisely written, sequentially organized, precise set of definitions, rules and explanations of each topic—something like a dictionary or a grammar book in the case of a human language.

We have deliberately avoided the reference manual format in this book because reference manuals are hard to learn from unless you already have a working knowledge of the subject. You didn't learn your native language from a dictionary or a grammar book. You learned it through a sequence of situations in which you were trying to communicate with other people already "programmed" to communicate in that language. You said things, tried out expressions, and saw what worked and what didn't. As years went by, somehow you ended up "knowing" your language. Nevertheless, you probably continue to forget grammar rules, correct spellings, and precise meanings. It would be painfully difficult to have to go back through all your original learning situations starting with "mama", "dada", and "doggie", in order to check up on a grammar rule or a correct pronunciation.

Our book has been an attempt to give you a sequence of revealing "learning situations" in which you have tried to communicate with a computer already programmed to understand Pascal. You wrote things, tried out expressions, and saw what worked and what didn't. As the weeks went by, somehow (we hope) you ended up "knowing" Pascal. Even so, there will be times when you forget a grammar rule, a correct spelling, or a precise meaning in Pascal. While we have worked carefully to provide a thorough index for this book, you will generally do better to turn to other sources both for reference purposes and to learn new things about Pascal.

You may have already begun to do that. (One reader of the manuscript of this book reported with great satisfaction that after the first six or seven sessions he was able for the first time to read and understand the Apple Pascal Language and Operating System Reference Manuals as well as other Pascal textbooks.) You may also have found, as your knowledge of Pascal grew, that it became more efficient for you to learn by reading about the outcomes of the experiments we proposed for you than by actually carrying out the experiments. These are signs that it is time to read other books and manuals, such as the ones below.

SUGGGESTED PASCAL REFERENCE BOOKS

The books listed here are ones that we believe will be worth your time and attention either for reference or further study.

Apple Pascal Operating System Reference Manual (Apple Computer, Inc, Cupertino, CA, 1979).

This book, plus a 14-page addendum, is your complete guide to the EDITOR, the FILER, and the inner workings of the operating system. It also shows you how to write and assemble programs written in the assembly language for the 6502 microprocessor in your Apple. You will find this book quite easy to read and follow.

Beginners Guide to the UCSD Pascal System, Ken Bowles (Byte Books, Peterborough, NH, 1979)

Apple Pascal is based on UCSD Pascal, which was written by Ken Bowles and his colleagues at the University of California, San Diego. **Beginners Guide** supplements the information in the first book in this list and gives more details about the way things work. It seems to be aimed mainly at people who would like to implement UCSD Pascal on new computers. There are small differences between Apple Pascal and UCSD Pascal, but **Beginners Guide** is the only other book about the operating system commands and is probably worth having.

Apple Pascal Language Reference Manual, (Apple Computer, Inc., Cupertino, CA, 1979).

Despite the name, this book does not describe the Pascal Language. It and its 16-page addendum document the differences between Apple Pascal and "Standard Pascal" as described in the Jensen and Wirth book below. It also contains a careful description of all built-in procedures and functions available in Apple Pascal. The book and addendum describe a variety of "compiler options" and explain how to create special "units", such as APPLESTUFF, and add them to the system library.

Pascal User Manual and Report, Kathleen Jensen and Niklaus Wirth (Springer Verlag, NY, 1978).

> This is the Bible of Pascal, presented by the Creator. To some people, Pascal is nothing more nor less than the language formally defined in this book. And it is a very formal document, used mainly as a reference book when issues of grammar and meaning come up. This book, when combined with the one immediately above, gives you a complete, precise definition of the version of Pascal used by the Apple II computer system.

Programming in Pascal, 2nd Edition, Peter Grogono (Addison Wesley, Reading, MA, 1980).

> This university-level textbook is quite clearly written and well organized for reference purposes. The large sample programs that tie the book together are nice examples of serious use of the data structures possible in Pascal. This is a good place to learn about the pointer data type and its application. The version of Pascal used here is CDC 6000 PASCAL, which is the "official" version written under the guidance of Niklaus Wirth.

A Practical Introduction to Pascal, I.R. Wilson and A.M. Addyman (Springer-Verlag, New York, 1979).

> Brevity and clarity are the chief merits of this outstanding book. It follows the traditional textbook format, but a quick reading of its 150 or so pages will help you to summarize all of the things you know, fill in the vacancies, and tie down a few loose ends.

THE ART AND CRAFT OF PROGRAMMING

You now know the main features of a major programming language. You have seen dozens of examples of short programs. But there is still much to learn about the practice of programming. Your situation is not unlike that of a person who has learned to speak a human language, knows a fairly large vocabulary, and has learned most of the grammar rules. It takes more than that to know how to write well. First of all, you need to have ideas. Then you need to know how to express them clearly, logically, concisely and in a well organized fashion.

These same needs occur in computer programming. The ideas in programming are called *algorithms*. You know some algorithms already. For example, you know how to sort a list of strings or numbers, how to shuffle a list, how to play a musical scale, how to draw graphic objects, and quite a few other useful things. There are many practical programming problems that you are already equipped to solve. There are a good many more that you probably cannot handle yet because you aren't familiar with the necessary algorithms. So one important direction to move will be toward the acquisition of knowledge about fundamental algorithms—the "software tools" that you can apply to many different problems.

The other equally important need is the development of a clear, logical, concise well-organized *style* of writing computer programs. If you succeed in this, your programs will be easy to read, easy to follow, easy to change, and easy to model new programs upon. Learning good programming style is like learning good writing style. It takes practice, practice, and more practice. You must see good models of clear programming style, and you must write and revise, revise, and revise.

The books listed in this section are suggestions for further readings that may help you to learn some new programming ideas and to write them clearly and stylishly.

Pascal with Style—Programming Proverbs, H. Ledgard, et al, (Hayden, Rochelle Park, NJ, 1979).

"Things is 'round to help learn programmers, especially them who don't want to pick up no more bad habits, to program good, easy, the first time right, and so somebody else can figger out what they done and why." That sentence introduces a gem of a book that is easy to read and full of wisdom and practical guidance. A must.

Algorithms + Data Structures = Programs, Niklaus Wirth (Prentice-Hall, Englewood Cliffs, NJ, 1976).

Jef Raskin, in the preliminary Apple Pascal reference manual, sums up this book nicely: "St. Nick's classic, must reading after you've gotten familiar with Pascal. May well expand your programming horizons."

Systematic Programming: An Introduction, Niklaus Wirth, (Prentice-Hall, 1973).

This book is of, by, and for computer scientists and students of computer science. Required reading if you're thinking of entering this field or simply want to know what it looks like from the viewpoint of a leading practitioner.

A Discipline of Programming, E. Dijkstra, (Prentice-Hall, 1976).

The same comments apply to this as to Wirth's **Systematic Programming.** Dijkstra is the person who in 1968 blew the whistle on the GOTO statement and triggered the birth of "structured programming", an idea fully incorporated into Pascal.

LAST WORDS

We hope that you will follow our advice and read what other people have to say about Pascal and about programming. At the same time, we also hope that your work in carrying out the activities in this book has taught you the value of experimentation in learning (and putting to the test what authorities say) about computers and their programs.

> As we said at the outset, the computer, like the physical world around us, *is* what it *does* and not necessarily what someone *says* about it. When in doubt, experiment and see for yourself.

GETTING STARTED WITH A SINGLE DISK DRIVE

First of all, be patient; you have about an hour of very mechanical tasks ahead of you. At the end of that time you will have (1) gone through a checklist of your computer system, (2) learned the "boot-up" procedure for Pascal, (3) learned how to format blank diskettes before use, and (4) learned how to copy one diskette on to a formatted blank diskette. This appendix is subdivided into these four parts.

A-1 SINGLE DRIVE CHECKLIST

1. **Do you have at least two blank diskettes?** If not, stop here until you get them.

2. **Is your Language System already installed in your computer?** If not, stay here and install it according to the Apple Language System Installation and Operating Manual (Catalog # A2L0024 (030–0059–00)).

3. **Do you have a single disk drive connected to your computer?** If you have more than one drive, stop here and go to Appendix B.

4. **Make sure the power is turned off and the Apple is plugged into a grounded outlet before touching any circuit cards.**

5. **Is your disk drive plugged into the DRIVE 1 connector on the disk controller card?** Take off the top of your Apple and see if the ribbon cable is properly connected. If not, disconnect carefully and reconnect to the DRIVE 1 connector. (To remove the top of your Apple, snap the rear corners up vertically. Then slide the loose top to the rear.)

6. **Is your disk controller card plugged into your Apple in slot 6?** Slot 6 is the next to last slot at the right end of the row of eight slots inside your Apple (viewed from the front). If the card is in another slot, carefully rock it back and forth to remove it, and replace it in Slot 6.

7. **Is your computer connected to a TV receiver or monitor?** If not, connect it directly to a monitor or through an RF modulator and game connector switch to a TV receiver.

At this point you should be able to answer "yes" to all of the above questions in the checklist. If so, you are ready to "boot-up" Pascal on your Apple.

A-2 SINGLE-DRIVE BOOT-UP PROCEDURE

Your goal here is to get your computer turned on and properly loaded with the information it needs in order to run the Pascal language and operating system properly. Your system diskettes contain that information.

1. **Turn on the TV power switch.** Turn the volume down. If you have a game connector, switch it to the setting that says GAME or TV SCOREBOARD, or the like; then turn the TV receiver to the proper channel.

2. **If the power to your Apple is on, turn it off.** The power switch is on the back and is easily reached with the left hand. When it is off the POWER light at the lower-left corner of the keybard is also off.

3. **Insert the APPLE3: diskette into the disk drive.** Lift the drive door fully open. Hold the diskette in your right hand, palm up, with your thumb on the printed label. Insert the diskette carefully into the drive and lower the door until it snaps shut.

4. **Turn on the computer power switch.** The POWER light will come on, the red "IN USE" light on the disk drive will come on, and you will hear the drive spinning and clicking. On your TV screen you will immediately see the phrase "APPLE][". In a few seconds the screen lights up with at-signs. A second later the disk drive stops whirring, its red light goes out, and the screen clears except for a white rectangle at the upper left. Immediately after that, the following text appears:

```
INSERT BOOT DISK WITH SYSTEM.PASCAL
ON IT, THEN PRESS RESET
```

(Note: if no such text appears, it means that you are using Apple Pascal Version 1.0 diskettes. See Appendix H for further information.)

5. **Remove the APPLE 3: diskette and insert the APPLE0: diskette into the disk drive.** Handle the diskettes carefully, palm up with the thumb on the label. Close the door.

6. **Press the keyboard key marked "RESET".** If nothing happens, hold the CTRL key down and press the RESET key. The RESET key is in the upper-right corner of the Apple keyboard; the CTRL key is at the extreme left. After about 15 seconds of more red lights, at-signs, and whirring disk sounds, the following message appears on your TV:

```
WELCOME APPLE0, TO APPLE II PASCAL 1.1

BASED ON UCSD PASCAL II.1

CURRENT DATE IS 30-JAN-81



(C) APPLE COMPUTER INC. 1979, 1980
(C) U.C. REGENTS 1979
```

About a second later all activity stops and the following line appears at the very top of your screen:

```
COMMAND: E(DIT, R(UN, F(ILE, C(OMP, L(IN
```

The appearance of this line tells you that you have successfully booted up Pascal and your computer is ready for your command. (The current date may be different.)

A-3 SINGLE-DRIVE FORMATTING PROCEDURE

The following steps show you how to convert new blank diskettes into properly formatted blanks for use with your Pascal System. (The same method is used for recycling old non-Pascal diskettes containing useless information.) It is a good idea at this time to format as many blank diskettes as you have.

"Formatting" means writing information on the magnetically sensitive surface of the diskette. The information is put on the diskette in a regular pattern that marks off the whole surface into a set of concentric circular *tracks* and subdivides each one of these into a small number of arcs or *sectors*. Your computer uses these markers to put data on the diskette in well defined places so that it can be retrieved correctly later.

If the COMMAND line is not at the top of your TV screen, go back to part A-2 above and boot up Pascal on your Apple.

1. **With the COMMAND: line at the top of your screen, type an X on your keyboard.** The computer will ask "EXECUTE WHAT FILE?"

2. **Remove APPLE0: from the drive and replace it with APPLE3:.** Handle the diskettes with care. Close the door fully.

3. **Type APPLE3:FORMATTER and press the RETURN KEY.** If you find a typing error before pressing RETURN, use the left-arrow key to backspace over to the error. Then retype from there on. If all goes well, the red light on the drive will come on and the disk will whirr. Then the screen will say

```
APPLE DISK FORMATTER PROGRAM

FORMAT WHICH DISK (4, 5, 9..12) ?
```

If it doesn't say this, start over again at step 1. (Apple Pascal refers to the disk drive that is plugged into drive 1, slot 6, as Volume #4.)

4. **Remove APPLE3: from the drive and replace it with a blank diskette.** Be sure not to let a diskette with valuable information on it get into the drive by mistake. Set safely aside all your prerecorded diskettes during the next several steps.

5. **Type a 4 on your keyboard and then press the RETURN key.** If the diskette was blank, you will hear it going through the formatting process for half a minute. The screen will say "NOW FORMATTING DISKETTE IN DRIVE 4." (If the diskette had been previously formatted, you'll be asked if you really want to destroy its contents. Just type N at that point unless you really do want to destroy the contents, in which case type Y.) When the formatting is complete, the screen will ask, once more, "FORMAT WHICH DISK (4, 5, 9..12) ?"

6. **Remove the formatted diskette from the drive.** Use a felt-tip pen (not a ball point pen or pencil!) and write "Pascal" on its label in small letters, to indicate that it has been formatted.

7. **Place another blank diskette in the drive and repeat steps 5 and 6.** It is a good idea to format several diskettes at this time.

8. **With the last diskette you have formatted removed from the drive, press the RETURN key.** The computer will say

```
PUT SYSTEM DISK IN #4 AND PRESS RETURN
```

9. **Put APPLE0: in the drive, close the door and press RETURN.**

At the bottom of the screen, you'll see "THAT'S ALL FOLKS...", and the COMMAND: line will quickly appear at the top of your TV screen. The formatting cycle is over.

A–4 SINGLE-DRIVE COPY PROCEDURE

Now, at last, you are ready to make a back-up copy of the important information on each of your system diskettes. You will copy one diskette at a time, transferring the information to one of the blank diskettes you just formatted in Section A–3. Since you have only a single disk drive, and since one diskette holds far more information than can fit in the memory of your computer, the transfer has to be done in many small steps. Each step consists of (1) moving a portion of the original diskette's data into the computer's main memory, (2) exchanging the original diskette and the blank in the disk drive, (3) writing the data on the blank, (4) reading the data back to verify that it was correctly written, and (5) exchanging the diskettes again.

This is the place where you will wish you had either two disk drives or four hands. However, with patience and perseverence you will be able to make the necessary back-up copies of your valuable APPLE0: and APPLE3: diskettes, and any other Pascal diskettes you want to duplicate, including your BASICS diskettes.

If you do not see the COMMAND: line at the top of your TV screen, better go back to Section A-2 and boot up Pascal properly. Then return to this section.

You must have at least two properly formatted blank diskettes. If not, go back to Section A-3.

Make certain that the APPLE0: diskette is in your disk drive. (It will be there if you started this section immediately after finishing either Sections A-2 or A-3.)

1. **With the COMMAND: line on the TV screen, type the F key.** The COMMAND: line goes away and is replaced by the FILER: line.

2. **With the FILER: line on the TV screen, type the T Key.** The screen responds by saying "TRANSFER ?"

3. **Remove APPLE0: from the disk drive and replace it with the first diskette you want to copy.** For the rest of these directions, we assume you will be copying "APPLE3:", but the next time around, remember to substitute "APPLE0:" or whatever other diskette you are copying for "APPLE3:" in steps 4 - 11 below.

4. **Type the name of the diskette you are copying, followed by the RETURN key.** (APPLE3: the first time around.) *Be sure to type the colon as part of the diskette name.* The screen will respond by asking "TO WHERE ?" (If you accidentally leave out the colon or make another typing error, the screen will say "NO SUCH VOL ON-LINE <SOURCE>". You must then start over at step 2.)

5. **Answer by typing BLANK: (including the colon) on your keyboard and pressing RETURN.** "BLANK:" is the name the formatter automatically gives to newly formatted diskettes. The screen responds by asking "TRANSFER 280 BLOCKS ? (Y/N)". If you get any other message, follow the instructions and when the FILER line appears, go back to step 2.

6. **Type Y on your keyboard.** (The N answer would be used to prevent the copy operation in case you decided not to go ahead.) After a while the screen says

```
PUT IN BLANK:
TYPE <SPACE> TO CONTINUE
```

(If instead, you get any other message, it means that you made a typing error back in step 5. To correct it you have to reboot as shown in Section A-2 and start over at step 1.)

7. **Remove the original diskette (APPLE3:) and replace it with the blank diskette. Then press the spacebar.** The screen asks "DESTROY BLANK: ?" giving you a last chance to prevent the operation. For example, if by mistake you forgot to take APPLE3: out before pressing the spacebar, the screen would ask "DESTROY APPLE3: ?", and you would be glad to type N and start over at step 2.

8. **Type Y on your keyboard.** The actual copying now begins. Your Apple cannot hold all of the original diskette contents in memory, so it only copies a small part at a time on the duplicate. In a short time, the screen will say

```
PUT APPLE3: IN UNIT #4
TYPE <SPACE> TO CONTINUE
```

9. **Remove BLANK:, replace with APPLE3: and press the space bar.** In a few moments the screen will say

```
PUT BLANK: IN UNIT #4
TYPE <SPACE> TO CONTINUE
```

10. **Remove APPLE3:, replace with BLANK: and press the spacebar. (It's a good idea to keep one diskette in one hand, and the other diskette in the other hand.) Repeat steps 9 and 10 about 20 times.** Finally the screen announces

```
APPLE3:                         --> BLANK:
```

11. **Remove BLANK: from the drive and write APPLE3: on the label with a felt-tip pen.**

12. **Press RETURN to clear the screen, go back to step 2, and repeat all steps with APPLE0: in place of APPLE3:.** You should always have at least one back-up copy of each of these two diskettes.

13. **Put your original, write-protected diskettes on a shelf away from your computer. Never use them except to make copies.**

If you came to this appendix from Session 1 of this book, you are now ready to return there, at last, and resume learning Pascal. Before doing that, however, you may be ready for a break, and now is a good time to take one. **Turn off the power on your computer.** Whenever you're ready, turn back to Section 1–1

GETTING STARTED WITH A DUAL DISK DRIVE

First, consider yourself lucky. Getting started with a dual-disk drive system takes about a third as many steps as with a single drive. You should be through in about 20 minutes. On the other hand, the steps are very mechanical and uninforming, so accuracy and patience are called for.

After you have completed this appendix you will (1) have gone through a checklist of your computer system, (2) learned the "boot-up" procedure for a dual-disk system, (3) learned how to format blank diskettes before use, (4) learned how to use the two drives to copy one diskette on to a formatted blank diskette, and (5) learned how to disconnect your second drive so as to convert back to the single-drive system upon which the main body of this book is based.

Readers who have only one disk drive should take comfort from item 5 above. Once past the initial start-up business of making back-up copies of APPLE0: through APPLE3:, everyone will be on the same basis. In fact, there is no particular advantage to having two drives while you are learning to write and run Pascal programs.

B-1 DUAL-DRIVE CHECKLIST

1. **Do you have at least two blank diskettes?** If not, stop here until you get them. (Four blanks are better.)

2. **Is your Language System already installed in your computer?** If not, stop here and install it according to the Apple Language System Installation and Operating Manual (Catalog # A2L0024 (030–0059–00)).

3. **Do you have two disk drives connected to your computer?** If you have only one, you're in the wrong appendix; go back to Appendix A.

4. **Make sure the power is turned off and the Apple is plugged into a grounded outlet before touching any circuit cards.**

5. **Are both drives connected into the same disk controller card?** Take off the top of your Apple and see whether the ribbon cables are properly connected. (To remove the top, snap the rear corners vertically up. Then slide the loose top to the rear.) If the cables are connected to different cards, carefully disconnect one cable and reconnect it to the other card. **Note carefully which cable is connected to "Drive 1" and which goes to "Drive 2". Mark the disk units accordingly.**

6. **Is your disk controller card plugged into your Apple in Slot 6?** Slot 6 is the next to last slot at the right end of the row of eight slots inside your Apple (viewed from the front). If the card is in another slot, carefully rock it back and forth to remove it, and replace it in Slot 6.

7. **Is your computer connected to a TV receiver or monitor?** If not, connect it directly to a monitor or through an RF modulator and game connector switch to a TV receiver.

At this point you should be able to answer "yes" to all of the above questions in the checklist. If so, you are ready to "boot-up" Pascal on your Apple.

B-2 DUAL-DRIVE BOOT-UP PROCEDURE

Your goal here is to get your computer turned on and properly loaded with the information it needs in order to run the Pascal language and operating system properly. Your system diskettes contain that information.

1. **Turn on the TV power switch.** Turn the volume down. If you have a game connector, switch it to GAME, TV SCOREBOARD, or the like. Turn the TV receiver to the proper channel.

2. **If the power to your Apple is on, turn it off.** The power switch is on the back and is easily reached with the left hand. When it is off the POWER light at the lower-left corner of the keyboard is also off.

3. **Insert the diskette marked "APPLE1:" in drive 1.** Lift the drive door fully open. Hold the diskette in your right hand, palm up, with your thumb on the printed label. Insert the diskette carefully into the drive and lower the door until it snaps shut.

4. **Insert the diskette marked "APPLE2:" into drive 2.** Close the door fully.

5. **Turn on the computer power switch.** Everything is automatic from here on, but here is what you should see. The keyboard POWER light will come on, the red "IN USE" light on drive 1 will come on and you will hear the drive spinning and

clicking. On your TV screen you will see the phrase "APPLE]][". In a few seconds the screen lights up with at-signs. A second later the screen clears, disk drive 1 stops whirring, its red light goes out, and disk drive 2 and its red light turn on briefly. Then drive 1 comes back on and after a few more seconds, the following message appears on your TV screen:

```
WELCOME APPLE1, TO APPLE II PASCAL 1.1

BASED ON UCSD PASCAL II.1

CURRENT DATE IS 31-JAN-81




(C) APPLE COMPUTER INC. 1979, 1980
(C) U.C. REGENTS 1979
```

About a second later, all activity stops as the following line appears at the very top of your screen:

```
COMMAND: E(DIT, R(UN, F(ILE, C(OMP, L(IN
```

It signals to you that you have successfully booted up Pascal on your computer, which is now awaiting your command. (The date may be different.)

B-3 DUAL-DRIVE FORMATTING PROCEDURE

The following steps show you how to convert new blank diskettes into properly formatted blanks for use with your Pascal System. (The same method is used for recycling old Pascal diskettes containing useless information.) It is a good idea at this time to format as many blank diskettes as you have.

"Formatting" means writing information on the magnetically sensitive surface of the diskette. The information is put on the diskette in a regular pattern that marks off the whole surface into a set of concentric circular *tracks* and subdivides each one of these into a small number of arcs or *sectors*. Your computer uses these markers to put data on the diskette in well defined places so that it can be retrieved correctly later.

If the COMMAND: line is not at the top of your TV screen, go back to part B-2 above and boot up Pascal on your Apple.

1. **With the COMMAND: line at the top of your screen, type an X on your keyboard.** The computer will ask "EXECUTE WHAT FILE?"

2. **Remove APPLE2: from drive 2 and replace it with APPLE3:.** Handle diskettes and drive doors with care. Close the door fully. (Leave drive 1 as is throughout the formatting process.)

3. **Type APPLE3:FORMATTER and press the RETURN key.** If you find a typing error before pressing RETURN, use the left-arrow key to backspace over to the error. Then retype from there on. If all goes well, the red light on drive 2 will come on and the disk will whirr. Then the screen will say

```
APPLE DISK FORMATTER PROGRAM

FORMAT WHICH DISK (4, 5, 9..12) ?
```

If it doesn't say this, start over again at step 1. (Apple Pascal refers to the disk drive that is plugged into drive 1, slot 6, as Volume #4. It refers to drive 2, slot 6, as Volume #5. Now is a good time to label your drives accordingly.)

4. **Remove APPLE3: from drive 2 and replace it with a blank diskette.** Be sure not to let a diskette with valuable information on it get into drive 2 by mistake. Set safely aside all your prerecorded diskettes during the next several steps.

5. **Type a 5 on your keyboard and then press the RETURN key.** If the diskette was blank, you will hear it going through the formatting process for half a minute. The screen will say "NOW FORMATTING DISKETTE IN DRIVE 5." (If the diskette had not been previously formatted, you'll be asked if you really want to destroy its contents. Just type N at this point unless you really do want to destroy the contents, in which case type Y.) When the formatting is complete, the screen will ask, once more, "FORMAT WHICH DISK (4, 5, 9..12) ?"

6. **Remove the formatted diskette from drive 2.** Use a felt-tip pen (not a ball-point pen or pencil!) and write "Pascal" on its label in small letters, to indicate that it has been formatted.

7. **Place another blank diskette in drive 2 and repeat steps 5 and 6.** It is a good idea to format several diskettes at this time.

8. **With the last diskette you have formatted removed from drive 2, press the RETURN key.** At the bottom of the screen, you'll see "THAT'S ALL FOLKS...", and the COMMAND: line will quickly appear at the top of your TV screen. Formatting is over.

B-4 DUAL-DRIVE COPY PROCEDURE

Now, at last, you are ready to make a back-up copy of the important information on each one of your system diskettes. You will copy one diskette at a time, transferring the information to one of the blank diskettes you just formatted in

Section B–3. The original system diskette will go into drive 1 and the blank into drive 2. Since a diskette holds far more information than can fit in the memory of your computer, the transfer has to be done in small steps; but the process is automatic once you begin it. Each step consists of (1) moving a portion of the original diskette's data into the computer's main memory, (2) writing it on the blank diskette, and (3) reading the data back to verify that it was correctly written.

If you do not see the COMMAND: line at the top of your TV screen, better go back to Section B-2 and boot up Pascal properly. Then return to this section.

If you do not have at least two blank formatted diskettes, go back to Section B-3. Make certain that the APPLE1: diskette is in drive 1. (It will be there if you started this section immediately after finishing either Sections B–2 or B–3.)

1. **With the COMMAND: line on the TV screen, type the F key.** The COMMAND: line goes away and is replaced by the FILER: line.

2. **With the FILER: line on the TV screen, type the T key.** The screen responds by saying TRANSFER ?

3. **Remove APPLE1: from disk drive 1 and replace it with the first diskette you want to copy.** For the rest of these directions, we assume you will be copying APPLE3: but the next time around, remember to substitute APPLE0: or whatever diskette you are copying for APPLE3: in steps 4 – 9 below.

4. **Type the name of the diskette you are copying followed by the RETURN key.** (APPLE3: the first time around.) *Be sure to type the colon as part of the diskette name.* The screen will respond by asking TO WHERE ? (If you accidentally leave out the colon or make another typing error, the screen will say NO SUCH VOL ON-LINE <SOURCE>. You must then start over at step 2.

5. **Remove whatever diskette is in drive 2 and replace with a formatted blank diskette.** This a critical step! Your computer thinks that you intend whatever diskette is in drive 2 to be treated as a blank. You wouldn't want to let a valuable diskette remain in drive 2 at this point.

6. **Answer the TO WHERE ? question by typing BLANK: on your keyboard and then pressing RETURN. Be sure to include the colon after BLANK.** BLANK: is the name the formatter automatically gives to newly formatted diskettes. The screen responds by asking TRANSFER 280 BLOCKS ? (Y/N). If you get any other message, go back to step 2.

7. **Type the Y key on your keyboard.** (The N key would be used if you decided to prevent the copy operation for any reason.) Your Y answer means that you want to copy the whole diskette. The computer checks to make sure the diskettes you named are both on-line and in the correct drives. The computer gives you one last chance to confirm that you really know what you are doing. It asks DESTROY BLANK: ? to remind you that the copy operation will destroy the contents of whatever was on the destination diskette. Since that is exactly what you want to do, go to step 8. If you got any other message, it means you either made a typing error or put the wrong diskette in drive 2. Either way, leave the diskettes alone, press the spacebar, and start over at step 2.

8. **Type Y on your keyboard.** Your computer spends the next 30 seconds or so copying the contents of the diskette in drive 1 on the blank diskette in drive 2. Finally the screen announces

9. **Remove BLANK: from drive 2 and write APPLE3: on the label with a felt-tip pen.**

10. **Repeat the whole process, by pressing RETURN and going to step 2, for the other system diskettes.** Be sure to remember to substitute their names for APPLE3: in all the above steps. A copy of APPLE0: is essential.

11. **Put your original, write-protected diskettes on a shelf away from your computer. Never use them except to make copies.**

12. **Turn off the power on your computer.**

B–5 CHANGING BACK TO A SINGLE-DRIVE SYSTEM

Except for making duplicate copies of diskettes, this book is written for use with a single-drive system. While it is possible to leave both drives connected and pretend that you have a single-drive system, sooner or later you will put a diskette in the wrong drive and get very confusing results. Our strong advice is that you follow the steps below for disconnecting and putting away one of your disk units temporarily.

1. **If the POWER light is on, turn off the power switch on the rear of your computer but leave it plugged into a grounded outlet.** The keyboard POWER light will go out.

2. **Remove the lid of your computer.**

3. **Carefully remove the ribbon cable from the card connector labelled DRIVE 2.** (You may have to remove the card to do this. If so, be sure to put it back in slot 6.)

4. **Replace the lid.**

5. **Put the unused disk drive away on a shelf.**

If disconnecting drive 2 turns out to be very inconvenient, perhaps because someone else needs to use the same comptuer with two drives, then you can treat drive 1 as if it were the only drive. We advise you to turn drive 2 around and place it as far away as the cable will allow, so that you don't accidentally put a diskette into it. Then make sure there is no diskette in it when you boot up Pascal. Use the boot-up procedure in Section 1–1, with the APPLE0: and APPLE3: diskettes. In either situation, you will have no further need for the APPLE1: and APPLE2: diskettes while you are learning Pascal with this book. Set these diskettes aside for the time you resume using drive 2 as explained in Appendix G.

NAMES, RESERVED WORDS, AND BUILT-IN NAMES

A *name* in Pascal is any sequence of characters that begins with a letter of the alphabet and is followed by zero or more characters which are either letters or decimal digits. Listed below are examples of legal and illegal names.

Legal Names	Illegal Names
WRITE	HOT-SHOT
X	HOT SHOT
A23	23A
AVERYLONGNAME	A$
PIC392A	PIC.39

In Apple Pascal, only the first eight characters of long names are significant. For example, the Apple Pascal compiler would treat the names NUMBEROFEMPLOY-EES and NUMBEROFHOLIDAYS as equivalent to one another and to the name NUMBEROF. The usual result is a compile-time error message that complains about an "identifier declared twice".

Pascal names fall into one of three categories: reserved words, built-in words, and programmer-defined names. Reserved words, as the name implies, have a use and a meaning that is an invariant part of the Pascal language. You may not use a reserved word as the name of a variable, constant, procedure, or the like. Built-in words have a predefined meaning within Apple Pascal, but is it legal to change their meanings by taking them over as names of your own variables, etc. If you do so, they lose their former meaning.

The following table contains a complete list of all Pascal resrved words and built-in words. The words shown in **bold face** are the ones that you have used in this book. (For information about the other words, see the "Apple Pascal Language Reference Manual", especially Chapters 3, 5, and 7.) For specific page references to the use of the bold-face words in the present book, see the Index headings, "Built-in words", and "Reserved words".

Reserved Words	Built-In Procedures	Built-In Functions	Other Built-Ins
PROGRAM	**CLOSE**	Boolean	Constants
UNIT	**DELETE**	**EOF**	**FALSE**
INTERFACE	EXIT	**EOLN**	**TRUE**
IMPLEMEN- TATION	FILLCHAR	ODD	**MAXINT**
	GET	UNITBUSY	NIL
USES	GOTOXY	a **BUTTON**	g **NONE**
LABEL	HALT	a **KEYPRESS**	g **WHITE**
CONST	INSERT	g SCREENBIT	g **BLACK**
TYPE	MARK		g **REVERSE**
PACKED	MOVELEFT	Char	g **RADAR**
ARRAY	MOVERIGHT	**CHR**	g **BLACK1**
RECORD	NEW		g **GREEN**
SET	PAGE	Integer	g **VIOLET**
FILE	**PUT**	BLOCKREAD	g **WHITE1**
VAR	**READ**	BLOCKWRITE	g **BLACK2**
PROCEDURE	**READLN**	IORESULT	g **ORANGE**
EXTERNAL	RELEASE	**LENGTH**	g **BLUE**
FORWARD	**RESET**	MEMAVAIL	g **WHITE2**
SEGMENT	**REWRITE**	**ORD**	
FUNCTION	SEEK	**POS**	Types
BEGIN	UNITCLEAR	**ROUND**	**BOOLEAN**
FOR	UNITREAD	SCAN	**CHAR**
TO	UNITWAIT	SIZEOF	**INTEGER**
DOWNTO	UNITWRITE	TREESEARCH	**INTERACTIVE**
DO	**WRITE**	**TRUNC**	**REAL**
REPEAT	**WRITELN**	a **PADDLE**	**STRING**
UNTIL	a **NOTE**	a **RANDOM**	**TEXT**
WHILE	a **RANDOMIZE**	g TURTLEANG	g **SCREENCOLOR**
IF	a TTLOUT	g TURTLEX	
THEN	g CHARTYPE	g TURTLEY	Variables
ELSE	g DRAWBLOCK		**INPUT**
CASE	g **FILLSCREEN**	Real	**KEYBOARD**
OF	g **GRAFMODE**	**ABS**	**OUTPUT**
WITH	g **INITTURTLE**	**PWROFTEN**	
GOTO	g **MOVE**	**SQR**	Units
END	g **MOVETO**	t **ATAN**	**APPLESTUFF**
	g **PENCOLOR**	t **COS**	CHAINSTUFF
DIV	g **TEXTMODE**	t **EXP**	**TRANSCEND**
MOD	g **TURN**	t **LN**	**TURTLEGRAPHICS**
	g **TURNTO**	t **LOG**	
AND	g **VIEWPORT**	t **SIN**	
OR	g WCHAR	t **SQRT**	
NOT	g WSTRING		
IN		String	
		CONCAT	
		COPY	
		STR	
		Other	
		PRED	
		SUCC	

COMMAND STRUCTURE OF APPLE PASCAL

Each command of the Apple Pascal Operating System consists of a single character, usually generated by a single key-press on the Apple keyboard. The meaning of a given character depends on the context or "level" of the system that you are currently at. The set of levels and commands are organized in a tree-structured fashion, the main trunk of which is the COMMAND level. From COMMAND level you can climb out some branch to reach any other level or command.

The two main branches connected to the COMMAND trunk are the EDIT and FILER levels, each of which contains many other branches or commands. Most of the operating system commands you have learned in this book are EDITOR and FILER commands. The two tables which follow provide a complete list of all the levels and commands of the Apple Pascal Operating System. Table D-1 shows the EDITOR command structure, and Table D-2 shows the FILER and all other command levels that can be reached from the main trunk, including commands that can be used at any level.

Commands shown in **bold face** are ones that you have used in this book. (For information about the other commands, see the "Apple Pascal Operating System Reference Manual". For specific page references to the use of the bold-face commands in the present book, see the Index—especially the "E(dit level" and "F(iler" headings.

Table D-1 Complete table of the EDITOR levels of Apple Pascal. Those features studied in this book are shown in bold face type.

	Exit to escape from accidental entry			Exit to escape from accidental entry
E(ditor	**ESC RETURN or QE**	Text Changing Commands		
Q(uit editor and	**R**	**I(nsert text**		**ESC**
U(pdate workfile		**CTRL-C (Normal exit)**		
E(xit with no update		**D(elete text**		**ESC**
R(eturn to editor	**Q**	**CTRL-C (Normal exit)**		
W(rite to named file	**RETURN**	**C(opy text from**		**ESC**
E(xit from EDITOR		**B(uffer**		
R(eturn to EDITOR		**F(ile**		
S(ave with same name		**X(change characters**		**ESC**
		CTRL-C (Normal exit)		
Cursor Moving Commands		R(eplace text in mode of		ESC
Right-arrow (Move cursor right)		L(iteral replacement		ESC
Left-arrow (Move cursor left)		T(oken replacement		ESC
CTRL-L (Move cursor down)		V(erify replacement		
CTRL-O (Move cursor up)		S(ame-string option		
RETURN (Move cursor to beginning		Z(ap deletion		
of next line)				
Spacebar (Move cursor to next		Formatting Commands		
character)		**A(djust indentation**		
J(ump to	**ESC**	L(eft		
E(nd of text		C(enter		
B(eginning of text		R(ight		
M(arker in file		**Cursor control keys**		
P(age move		**CTRL-C (Normal exit)**		
=(start of I, F, R block		M(argin set		
F(ind text pattern as:				
L(iteral characters		Miscellaneous Editing Commands		
T(oken		S(et		ESC
S(ame-string option		M(arker		RETURN
		E(nvironment		Spacebar
		A(utomatic indentation		
		F(illing		
		L(eft margin set		
		R(ight margin set		
		P(aragraph margin set		
		T(oken default		
		C(ommand character		
		V(erify editor status		

Table D-2 Complete table of other command levels of Apple Pascal. Those features studied in this book are shown in bold face type.

Exit to escape from accidental entry

F(iler
Q(uit the filer	**F**
G(et a file from diskette	RETURN
S(ave the workfile	RETURN
N(ew workfile	**RETURN**
W(hat is the workfile?	
V(olumes on line?	
L(ist the directory	**RETURN**
E(xtended directory list	**RETURN**
C(hange name	**RETURN**
R(emove file from diskette	**RETURN**
T(ransfer a file	**RETURN**
D(ate setter	**RETURN**
P(refix for volume name	RETURN
B(ad blocks on diskette	RETURN
X(amine bad blocks?	RETURN
K(runch files together	**RETURN**
M(ake directory entry	RETURN
Z(ero diskette and reformat	RETURN
? Show additional commands	**RETURN**

C(ompile workfile
R(un program in workfile
X(ecute compiled program
I(nitialize the system
A(ssemble 6502 program
L(ink program segments
U(ser restart
H(alt and cold reboot
M(ake exec file
S(wap option

Commands Available at Any Level
RESET Attempts cold reboot of Pascal
CTRL-A Toggle to other half of CTRL-A
    Pascal page
CTRL-S Stop and restart program CTRL-S
    having screen output
CTRL-Z Set horizontal scroll CTRL-A
CTRL-@ Warm reboot
CTRL-F Flushes output buffer
CTRL-E Enables reverse-video mode
    and toggles keyboard between
    upper and lower case
CTRL-W Enables reverse video and
    sets keyboard to upper case
    for next character only

Commands Available at Any Level Except EDIT
CTRL-R Enables video reverse
CTRL-T Disables video reverse and
    sets keyboard to upper case

SIZE AND QUANTITY LIMITS IN APPLE PASCAL

DATA LIMITS

Range of CHAR values: CHR (0)..CHR (255)

Range of INTEGER values: –32768..32767

Range of long integers: as many decimal digits as declared, up to a maximum of 36, not including the sign.

Range of REAL values: –3.40282E38..3.40282E38

Smallest positive REAL value: 1.17549E–38

Precision of REAL values: approximately 7 decimal digits.

Maximum STRING length: 255 characters.

Largest SET: 512 members. Sets of integers must be in the range 0..511

BUILT-IN FUNCTION AND PROCEDURE RANGES

Range of RANDOM numbers: 0..32767

Range of PADDLE numbers: 0..255

Range of NOTE pitch values: 0..255

Range of musical pitch values: 1..50

Range of NOTE duration values: 0..255

Range of PWROFTEN parameter: 0..37

TEXT PAGE DIMENSIONS

Horizontal range: 0..79

Vertical range: 0..23

Upper left corner: (0, 0)

Apple window looks at only 40 characters of the full text page.

GRAPHIC PAGE DIMENSIONS

Horizontal range: 0..279

Vertical range: 0..191

Lower left corner: (0, 0)

MEMORY LIMITS AND SIZES

All memory units are given in *words*. One word is equal to two bytes.

Data type	Words used
Boolean	1
CHAR	1
INTEGER	1
REAL	2
STRING	41
STRING [N]	1 + N DIV 2
INTEGER [N]	2 + (N – 1) DIV 4
ARRAY [1..100] OF INTEGER	100
ARRAY [1..100] OF 0..255	100
ARRAY [1..100] OF 0..15	100
ARRAY [1..100] OF CHAR	100
PACKED ARRAY [1..100] OF 0..255	50
PACKED ARRAY [1..100] OF 0..15	25
PACKED ARRAY [1..100] OF CHAR	50
FILE	310

Maximum space for user program and variables: 18,850 words without swapping and 19,950 with swapping.

Opening and closing a file does not change the amount of available memory.

Setting a string variable equal to the null string (") does not regain any available memory.

OTHER LIMITS

Largest editable file: 34 blocks without swapping and 40 blocks with swapping.

Maximum number of procedures or functions in a single compilation: 149

Maximum size of a compiled procedure or function: 600 words plus any local variables.

ORD AND CHR VALUES OF ASCII CHARACTER SET

Within a running Pascal program, all character values from CHR (0) through CHR (255) are legal and are distinct from one another. However, not all of them may be input from the keyboard nor written on the screen. This table lists the 128 characters of the American Standard Code for Information Interchange (ASCII) character set and, for each one, shows the ORD value, the Apple key that generates the character, whether that key can be read by a Pascal program, and what happens when a Pascal program writes the character on the Apple screen.

Character values CHR (128) through CHR (255) have no standard ASCII names or graphic symbols and may not be typed on the Apple keyboard. If such a character is written on the Apple screen by a WRITE (CH) call in a Pascal program, the result is the same as for the character whose ORD value is 128 less.

ORD value	ASCII name	Apple key	Notes
0	NUL	CTRL-@	1,2,A
1	SOH	CTRL-A	1,3,A
2	STX	CTRL-B	A
3	ETX	CTRL-C	1,4,A
4	EOT	CTRL-D	A
5	ENQ	CTRL-E	1,5,A
6	ACK	CTRL-F	1,6,A
7	BEL	CTRL-G	B
8	BS	CTRL-H left-arrow	
9	HT	CTRL-I	A
10	LF	CTRL-J	D
11	VT		1,A
12	FF	CTRL-L	E
13	CR	CTRL-M RETURN	1,8,F
14	SO	CTRL-N	A
15	SI	CTRL-O	A

For explanation of notes, see pages 388-389.

ORD value	ASCII name	Apple key	Notes
16	DLE	CTRL-P	G
17	DC1	CTRL-Q	A
18	DC2	CTRL-R	H
19	DC3	CTRL-S	1,9,A
20	DC4	CTRL-T	I
21	NAK	CTRL-U	A
		right-arrow	
22	SYN	CTRL-V	A
23	ETB	CTRL-W	1,10,A
24	CAN	CTRL-X	11,A
25	EM	CTRL-Y	J
26	SUB	CTRL-Z	1,12,A
27	ESC	ESC	A
28	FS		1,K
29	GS	CTRL-SHIFT-M	A
30	RS	CTRL-SHIFT-N	L
31	US		1,M
32	SP	space-bar	
33	!	!	
34	"	"	
35	#	#	
36	$	$	
37	%	%	
38	&	&	
39	'	'	
40	(	(	
41	)	)	
42	*	*	
43	+	+	
44	,	,	
45	-	-	
46	.	.	
47	/	/	
48	0	0	
49	1	1	
50	2	2	
51	3	3	
52	4	4	
53	5	5	
54	6	6	
55	7	7	
56	8	8	

INPUT NOTES

The following notes refer to the effect of attempting to type a particular Apple keyboard character in response to the statement READ (KEYBOARD, CH), where CH is of type CHAR. In the accompanying table, the *absence* of a note number in the last column means that input succeeds and that CH is equal to the corresponding ASCII character. Presence of a note number means that you should read the numbered note below.

1. Character cannot be input from Apple keyboard.
2. Causes a warm reboot.
3. Togles Apple window left or right; clears horizontal scroll mode.
4. Sets EOF and EOLN to TRUE.
5. Toggles alphabetic keys between upper and lower case; enables reverse-video display of upper case letters subsequently written on Apple screen.
6. Toggles keyboard between locked and unlocked state.
7. Okay for single character READ, but in string READLN, deletes previous character.
8. Sets EOLN to TRUE; CH = SP.
9. Toggles screen between locked and unlocked state. In locked state, keyboard input goes into a buffer and is used as soon as screen is unlocked.
10. Enables upper case for next character only.
11. Okay for single character READ, but for string READLN, deletes all characters to the start of the string.
12. Sets horizontal scroll mode.
13. Keyboard must be in lower case mode. See note 5.

ORD value	ASCII name	Apple key	Notes
57	9	9	
58	:	:	
59	;	;	
60	<	<	
61	=	=	
62	>	>	
63	?	?	
64	@	@	
65	A	A	
66	B	B	
67	C	C	
68	D	D	
69	E	E	
70	F	F	
71	G	G	
72	H	H	
73	I	I	
74	J	J	
75	K	K	
76	L	L	
77	M	M	
78	N	N	
79	O	O	
80	P	P	
81	Q	Q	
82	R	R	
83	S	S	
84	T	T	
85	U	U	
86	V	V	
87	W	W	
88	X	X	
89	Y	Y	
90	Z	Z	
91	[	CTRL-K	
92	\		1,P
93	]	SHIFT-M	
94	∧	∧	
95	—	—	1,Q
96	'		1,N
97	a	A	13,N
98	b	B	13,N
99	c	C	13,N
100	d	D	13,N
101	e	E	13,N
102	f	F	13,N

OUTPUT NOTES

The following notes refer to the effect of attempting to WRITE a particular character on the Apple screen by means of a WRITE (CH) statement, where the value of CH is a character. In the accompanying table, the *absence* of a note letter in the last column means that output succeeds and that the corresponding ASCII symbol is displayed on the screen at the current cursor position, and the cursor is moved one position to the right. Presence of a note letter means that you should read the corresponding note below.

A. Output causes no effect on the Apple screen.
B. The "bell" is beeped.
C. Cursor moves left one character. (backspace)
D. Cursor moves down one line. (linefeed)
E. Cursor moves "home" (top, left corner); screen is erased. (formfeed)
F. Cursor moves to extreme left and down one line. (newline)
G. Character following CH is lost. Instead, its ORD value minus 32 is used to indent the following characters that number of spaces.
H. Sets reverse-video display mode for upper case letters.
I. Sets regular video display mode.
J. Cursor moves to "home".
K. Cursor moves right one character.
L. Deletes following characters to end of line; cursor moves to "home".
M. Cursor moves up one line.
N. Upper case character is displayed.
P. Reverse-slash character is displayed.
Q. Underscore character is displayed.

ORD value	ASCII name	Apple key	Notes
103	g	G	13,N
104	h	H	13,N
105	i	I	13,N
106	j	J	13,N
107	k	K	13,N
108	l	L	13,N
109	m	M	13,N
110	n	N	13,N
111	o	O	13,N
112	p	P	13,N
113	q	Q	13,N
114	r	R	13,N
115	s	S	13,N
116	t	T	13,N
117	u	U	13,N
118	v	V	13,N
119	w	W	13,N
120	x	X	13,N
121	y	Y	13,N
122	z	Z	13,N
123	{		1,N
124	|		1,N
125	}		1,N
126	~		1,N
127	DEL		1,N

For explanation of notes,
see pages 388-389.

USING TWO DISK DRIVES

You only need one disk drive throughout this book while you are learning Pascal on the Apple computer. Although a single drive is no handicap in the learning stages, you will soon discover its limitations as you begin to develop longer and more numerous programs. These limitations are due to the fact that the APPLE0: diskette has very little room left over for your programs. The system programs take 248 blocks of the total of 280 blocks of diskette storage, leaving you only 32 blocks. Since each text file uses a minimum of 4 blocks and each code file, a minimum of 2 blocks, you cannot store many programs or data files on APPLE0:. That is the reaon why we show you how to save programs on a second diskette. (See Section 4–9.)

You can increase your storage capacity on APPLE0: by about 50% if you are willing to do without the compiler error messages. Simply remove (Type R under the FILER) SYSTEM.SYNTAX from APPLE0: and then K(runch the diskette. When you get compiler errors, you will continue to be told the error number, but you will have to turn to the back of this book to read the text of the message.

Since none of the other system files can be removed without making your use of a single-drive system either inconvenient or impossible, your only recourse will be to invest in a second drive, and we recommend that you do so if you intend to write many Pascal programs in the future. The rest of this Appendix explains differences between using single-drive and dual drive systems.

The dual-drive boot-up process, explained in detail in Section B–2 of Appendix B, is quite similar to the single-drive boot-up. The only difference is that diskette APPLE1: goes into drive 1 and APPLE2: goes into drive 2 before turning on the power switch. When you power up, the entire boot-up process is automatic and you do not need to touch the diskettes again.

If you press the RESET key at any time, it causes a complete "cold boot", just as though you had turned off the power switch and turned it back on. With a single-drive system and APPLE0: in the drive, you get into trouble; a cold boot requires that you have APPLE3: in your drive. But with a dual-drive system you normally have both APPLE1: and APPLE2: in the drives, and so the cold reboot succeeds. (You still lose what is in your workspace, or course.)

In order to establish a correspondence between what we say in the main part of this book and what you will do with a dual-drive system, you need only substitute "APPLE1:" for "APPLE0:" in almost every place in the book. In a single-drive system, APPLE0: is what is called your "boot disk". In a dual-drive sytem, APPLE1:, which *must* be placed in drive 1, is your boot disk. Listed below are the system files supplied on these two diskettes:

APPLE0:

APPLE 1:

SYSTEM.APPLE
SYSTEM.PASCAL
SYSTEM.MISCINFO
SYSTEM.COMPILER
SYSTEM.EDITOR
SYSTEM.FILER
SYSTEM.LIBRARY
SYSTEM.CHARSET
SYSTEM.SYNTAX
SYSTEM.WRK.TEXT
SYSTEM.WRK.CODE

SYSTEM.APPLE
SYSTEM.PASCAL
SYSTEM.MISCINFO

SYSTEM.EDITOR
SYSTEM.FILER
SYSTEM.LIBRARY
SYSTEM.CHARSET
SYSTEM.SYNTAX
SYSTEM.WRK.TEXT
SYSTEM.WRK.CODE

The major differences are that APPLE1: contains SYSTEM.APPLE, but it lacks SYSTEM.COMPILER. The file SYSTEM.APPLE (which is also on APPLE3:) is *necessary* for the first stage of the cold boot-up. Furthermore, it has to be located on the diskette in drive 1 if this stage of boot-up is to succeed. So you can use either APPLE3: or APPLE1: (or any other diskette you create that contains SYSTEM.APPLE) placed in drive 1 to initiate the boot-up.

To complete the boot-up, drive 1 must hold a diskette containing the files SYSTEM.PASCAL and SYSTEM.MISCINFO. If they are *missing*, then the computer will halt and ask you to "insert the boot disk" into drive 1, which the Pascal system refers to as "volume 4"; drive 2 is "volume 5". Thus, if you start the boot-up with APPLE3: then you need to put APPLE0: into the drive to complete the boot-up. But if you start with APPLE1:, then there is no need to switch diskettes in drive 1. APPLE1: contains all the necessary files for a complete bootup.

The long file SYSTEM.COMPILER, which is missing from APPLE1:, is contained on APPLE2: (along with several additional files not contained on any of the other system diskettes). The result is that APPLE1: contains 75 blocks of free space for your programs and data, and APPLE2: contains 112 blocks more. The additional free space on APPLE1: allows you to write and edit quite long workfiles, while the space on APPLE2: is best used to save programs and data files.

The method of saving programs described in Section 4–9 works about the same way with a dual-drive system. The two differences are that the diskette for program storage is normally APPLE2: rather than PROGRAM:, and that there is no need to remove any diskette from the drives. These same two changes apply to the method given in Sections 4–10 and 12–1 for recalling saved programs from a second diskette. There are other methods of saving and recalling diskette text files (see the G(et and S(ave commands in the FILER) with a dual-drive system. You can read about them in the "Apple Pascal Operating System Reference Manual."

With this understanding, you are ready to install drive 2 in your Apple computer. To so so, simply turn off the power switch and reverse all the steps given at the end of Appendix B.

DIFFERENCES BETWEEN VERSIONS 1.0 AND 1.1 OF APPLE PASCAL

Apple Pascal diskettes sold with Apple Language Systems prior to November, 1980, contained Version 1.0. Although that edition of the software contains a number of known bugs, as well as other differences from Version 1.1, you may still use this book with Version 1.0 diskettes. Before starting each session, however, you should check this appendix for any differences that will show up in that session.

SESSION 1

Page 11.

At the end of Step 4 of the boot-up process, no message appears on the screen. Proceed with Step 5.

Page 12.

At the end of Step 6 of the boot-up process the "WELCOME" message is slightly different.

Page 13, top.

The "version identifier" in square brackets is II.1 instead of 1.1.

Page 13, bottom.

The "version identifier" for the FILER is C.2.

Page 16, top.

The right half of the Pascal page contains only the two letters LT. The S(WAP and M(AKE EXEC commands are not available in Version 1.0.

SESSION 2

Page 21, bottom.

The "version identifier" for the EDITOR is E.6F.

Page 23, bottom.

The RESET key is somewhat less of a disaster in Version 1.0. You still lose any text that was in your workspace, but you don't have to turn off the power switch and do the complete "cold reboot" process. The RESET key in Version 1.0 does an automatic "warm reboot", at the end of which you are at the COMMAND level. The RESET key spells trouble in either version, of course.

Page 25, top.

The Q(UIT level of the EDITOR does not have a S(AVE option in Version 1.0. This book does not use the S option, so you will not miss it.

Page 25, middle.

The question "THROW AWAY CHANGES SINCE LAST UPDATE?" does *not* appear. There is no warning that you are about to lose the changes. In other words, typing Q E in Version 1.0 is the same as typing Q E Y in Version 1.1.

Page 31, question 7.

The question is okay, but the answer for Version 1.0 is different than for Version 1.1.

SESSION 3

Page 36, bottom.

The "version identifier" for the compiler is B2B.

Page 37, top.

The number of "WORDS" left available is 2124. Programs compiled under Version 1.0 do not take up as much space in the computer as those compiled under Version 1.1.

Sessions 4, 5, and 6

No differences.

SESSION 7

WARNING: All graphic programs shown in this session and future sessions must be modified to run correctly under Version 1.0. If they are not modified, they will leave your computer in "graphic mode" and you will not be able to see anything you type or anything the computer writes on the Pascal text page. (If this happens, press the RESET key for a warm reboot.) The needed modification is the addition of a

TEXTMODE procedure call as the last statement executed by any graphic program, as shown below.

Page 130, PROGRAM SKETCH.

The last statement of the program must be a TEXTMODE call. The final lines should look like this:

```
    END; (* FOR *)
  TEXTMODE
END.
```

Page 132, program text at bottom of page.

Change final lines as follows:

```
    UNTIL BUTON (0);
  TEXTMODE
END.
```

Page 135, program text at top and bottom.

Change final lines as on p. 132.

Page 136, program text.

Change final lines to:

```
  UNTIL BUTTON (1);
  TEXTMODE
END.
```

Page 138; program text.

Change final lines to:

```
K                UNTIL BUTTON (1);
L     4            TEXTMODE
M               END.
```

Page 139, paragraph 1, lines 1 and 5.

Change "three" to "four."

Page 139, paragraph 2, last 3 lines.

Change to "but line K, which ends statement 3, *does* need a semicolon to separate it from statement 4."

Page 141, program text at top.

Change final lines to agree with the change on page 136.

Page 147, program text.

Ditto.

SESSION 8

Page 168, screen messages at top and middle.

No message appears or halt occurs after CTRL-SHIFT-P is pressed, but system reinitialization does take place as described.

Page 168, screen message at bottom.

The numbers are different from the ones shown.

Page 171, program text.

Change final lines so that the last statement is followed by a semicolon and a call to TEXTMODE.

SESSION 9

No differences.

SESSION 10

Page 210, 211.

Wherever the book says that –32768 will appear on the screen, instead you will see ––2768. This is a bug in Version 1.0.

Page 213, bottom insert.

The last two lines of the screen message will be

```
S# 0, P# 255, I# 10812
TYPE <SPACE> TO CONTINUE
```

Page 214, paragraph 3 and bottom line.

Ignore warning. Follow screen directions and press spacebar for a warm reboot.

SESSION 11

Page 237, 239, program LINE.

Insert a semicolon and the word TEXTMODE after the READLN call.

Page 242, last bold face paragraph.

Due to a bug in Version 1.0, the compiler will *fail* to detect an error when you change X to type REAL, but the program will also fail when it is run. You will probably have to turn off power and reboot.

SESSION 12

Page 269, top.

You may *not* use the C(opy F(rom file method with version 1.0. Instead, use the F(ile T(ransfer method given in Section 4.10.

SESSION 13

No differences.

SESSION 14

Pages 339, 342, 346, 348, 355.

In the main BEGIN/END block of each program, the final statement must be followed by a semicolon and a call to TEXTMODE.

Page 351

Instead of the STACK OVERFLOW message at the bottom of the page, infinite recursion will cause a catastrophic failure. Your only recovery method is to turn off the power and reboot.

APPENDIX A

Page 366

At the end of step 4 of the boot-up process, no message appears on the screen. Proceed with step 5.

Page 367, top.

The "WELCOME" message is slightly different.

APPENDIX B

Page 373

The "WELCOME" message is slightly different.

APPENDICES C, D, E

No significant differences.

APPENDIX F

Notes 5, 10, H, and I don't apply. There is no lower case or reverse video mode.

SOLUTIONS TO PROBLEMS

SESSION 1

1. COMMAND level. FILER. L, V, D.

3. The screen clears and the COMMAND prompt reappears.

5. F V. FILER. Type Q.

7. Type Q.

9. The FILER program is loaded into the main memory. Without APPLE0: there would be no place to get the FILER program, and an error message would appear.

SESSION 2

1. E RETURN I CTRL-C P A S C A L Q U

3. When there is no workfile on APPLE0:, you get the message. When there is a workfile, no message appears, and a copy of the workfile appears on the screen.

5. Type ESC.

7. Yes. Answer the question by typing N; then Q U.

SESSION 3

1. F N Y

3. Q E F L A P P L E 0 : RETURN

5. A copy of the buffer goes into the workspace, and the EDIT prompt line appears.

7. Move the cursor to the start of line 2; type D RETURN RETURN CTRL-C.

9. Starting on the line below the prompt line, there will appear these two lines:

```
IT WAS THE BEST OF TIMES,
IT WAS THE WORST OF TIMES.
```

SESSION 4

1. Q E F N Y Q E

3. A type conflict occurs whenever a value of one data type appears in a statement that expects a value of a different, conflicting type.

5.
```
PROGRAM NUMBERS;

VAR
   I : INTEGER;

BEGIN
  FOR I := 1 TO 15 DO
    WRITELN (I)
END.
```

7. Enter the FILER. Type C. Put diskette BLANK: into drive. Type "BLANK:" and press RETURN. Type "TAXES:" and press RETURN. Put APPLE0: in drive. Type Q.

9. Enter the EDITOR. Type Q W. Insert diskette ABC: into drive. Type ABC:SONIC.TEXT and press RETURN. Insert APPLE0: into drive. Type E or R.

11. If the line is a Pascal statement and it is to be inserted after another statement, put the cursor at the end of the latter statement. Type I, a semicolon, and press RETURN. Type the new line, but do not press RETURN. Type CTRL–C.

13. It is illegal to use a reserved word as a variable name or any other programmer-defined name. It is legal to use built-in words for variable names, but the words lose their standard meanings.

15. Any single Pascal statement is a simple statement. A compound statement is a sequence of two or more simple statements, separated by semicolons, and bracketed by BEGIN and END. A null statement is a statement containing no characters.

SESSION 5

1. Assignment, procedure call, and FOR.

3. The same number will appear on two successive lines at the left margin each time. The numbers are 0, 3, 4, 5. There are three statements.

5. If the program contains more than one statement that calls the procedure, then the body of the procedure would have to be duplicated in each place.

7. a. 1

   b. 2–14

   c. 16–18

9. TOP is your parent. BOTTOM is your child.

11. HENRY := 5 is okay anywhere. GWEN := 10 is okay for statement 1 or statement 2. LUKE := 2 is okay for statement 1. HENRY is a global variable.

13. Name and type are declared in the parameter list in the procedure heading. Value is passed to it by the call statement parameter.

15.
```
      PROCEDURE DIATONIC (KEY : INTEGER);
         BEGIN
            NOTE (20 + KEY, PADDLE (1));
            NOTE (22 + KEY, PADDLE (1));
            NOTE (24 + KEY, PADDLE (1));
            NOTE (25 + KEY, PADDLE (1));
            NOTE (27 + KEY, PADDLE (1));
            NOTE (29 + KEY, PADDLE (1));
            NOTE (31 + KEY, PADDLE (1));
            NOTE (32 + KEY, PADDLE (1));
         END; (* DIATONIC *)
```

SESSION 6

1. a. 2

   b. 3

   c. 0

   d. 5

   e. 0

   f. 0

   g. error

   h. error

3. Compute (237 – 37) MOD 7. If it is zero, the 237th day is Monday. If it is 1, the day is Tuesday, etc.

5. Seed = 1, Factor = 37

Next-number	Next-number x factor
1	37
3	111
11	407
40	1480
48	1776

7. Seed = 43, Factor = 10

Next-number	Next-number x factor
43	430
43	430
43	430

Yes. There are "bad factors".

9. No. Yes. Yes.

11. An assignment statement.

13.
```
FUNCTION FIFTHPWR (N : INTEGER) : INTEGER;
   BEGIN
      FIFTHPWR := N * N * N * N * N
   END; (* FIFTHPWR *)
```

15. Spacebar, RETURN, P, F.

17. Numeric prefix causes an equal number of repetitions. Slash causes repetition until further moves are impossible.

19. a. J B F / B E G I N /

b. J B 2 F / B E G I N /

c. J B / F / B E G I N /

SESSION 7

1. Boolean variables may only have two values—*true* and *false*. They can be used with boolean operators, such as OR. Integer variables may have many different values and can be used with arithmetic operators, such as + and DIV.

3. It will halt the program by repeatedly calling the BUTTON function until it returns the value *true*.

5. Yes.

7.
```
PROGRAM RND100;
  USES
    APPLESTUFF;
  BEGIN
    REPEAT
      WRITELN (RANDOM MOD 101)
    UNTIL BUTTON (0)
  END.
```

9.
```
PROGRAM RNDRECT;

  USES
    APPLESTUFF, TURTLEGRAPHICS;

  CONST
    WIDTH = 280; HEIGHT = 192;

  VAR
    X1, X2, Y1, Y2 : INTEGER;

  BEGIN
    INITTURTLE; FILLSCREEN (WHITE);
    REPEAT
      X1 := RANDOM MOD WIDTH;
      X2 := RANDOM MOD WIDTH;
      Y1 := RANDOM MOD HEIGHT;
      Y1 := RANDOM MOD HEIGHT;
      PENCOLOR (NONE); MOVETO (X1, Y1);
      PENCOLOR (BLACK); MOVETO (X2, Y1);
      MOVETO (X2, Y2); MOVETO (X1, Y2);
      MOVETO (X1, Y1);
      REPEAT UNTIL BUTTON (0) OR BUTTON (1)
    UNTIL BUTTON (1)
  END.
```

11.
```
PROGRAM SKETCH;

  USES
    APPLESTUFF, TURTLEGRAPHICS;

  CONST
    WIDTH = 280; HEIGHT = 192;

  VAR
    X, Y, HALFWID, HALFHT : INTEGER;

BEGIN
  INITTURTLE;
  PENCOLOR (BLACK);
  HALFWID := WIDTH DIV 2;
  HALFHT := HEIGHT DIV 2;
  VIEWPORT (0, HALFWID, 0, HALFHT);
  REPEAT
    FILLSCREEN (WHITE);
    REPEAT
    X := RANDOM MOD HALFWID;
    Y := RANDOM MOD HALFHT;
    MOVETO (X, Y)
    UNTIL BUTTON (0) OR BUTTON (1)
  UNTIL BUTTON (1)
END.
```

13.
```
PROGRAM GRID;

  USES
    APPLESTUFF, TURTLEGRAPHICS;

  CONST
    WIDTH = 280; HEIGHT = 192; STEP = 20;

  VAR
    X, Y : INTEGER;

BEGIN
  INITTURTLE; FILLSCREEN (WHITE); X := 0;
  REPEAT
    PENCOLOR (NONE); MOVETO (X, 0);
    PENCOLOR (BLACK); MOVETO (X, HEIGHT);
    X := X + STEP
  UNTIL X >= WIDTH;
  Y := 0;
  REPEAT
    PENCOLOR (NONE); MOVETO (0, Y);
    PENCOLOR (BLACK); MOVETO (WIDTH, Y);
    Y := Y + STEP
  UNTIL Y >= HEIGHT;
  REPEAT UNTIL BUTTON (1)
END.
```

SESSION 8

1. Improperly typed numbers cause run-time errors that halt the program.

3. A prior touching of any readable key on the Apple keyboard sets the value of KEYPRESS to TRUE. Executing a READ or READLN call sets it back to FALSE.

5. TURN (D) turns D degrees counterclockwise from the current heading; TURNTO (D) sets the current heading to be D degrees counterclockwise from the zero-degree direction, which is to the right.

7. Yes. The expression after CASE has boolean values TRUE and FALSE, as do the case labels.

9.
```
IF X > 5 THEN
    WRITELN ('GREATER')
ELSE
    WRITELN ('LESS THAN OR EQUAL')
```

11 a.
```
IF A > 0 THEN
    IF B > 0 THEN
        WRITE ('X')
    ELSE
ELSE
    WRITE ('Y')
```

11 b. i) X

ii) nothing

iii) Y

iv) Y

13.
```
PROGRAM TOLLBRIDGE;

    VAR
       TRUCK, RUSHHOUR, CARPOOL : BOOLEAN;

    FUNCTION YES (QUESTION : STRING) : BOOLEAN;
       VAR
         ANSWER : CHAR;
       BEGIN
         WRITE (QUESTION); READ (ANSWER); WRITELN;
         IF ANSWER = 'Y' THEN
           YES := TRUE
         ELSE
           YES := FALSE
       END;  (* YES *)

    BEGIN
      TRUCK := YES ('IS IT A TRUCK? ');
      CARPOOL := YES ('3 OR MORE PEOPLE? ');
      RUSHHOUR := YES ('IS IT RUSH HOUR? ');
      IF TRUCK THEN
        WRITELN ('TOLL = $1.00')
      ELSE IF NOT RUSHHOUR THEN
        WRITELN ('TOLL = 25 CENTS')
      ELSE IF CARPOOL THEN
        WRITELN ('NO CHARGE')
      ELSE
        WRITELN ('TOLL = 50 CENTS')
    END.
```

15.
```
PROGRAM ARBITRARY;

    VAR
       X : INTEGER;

    BEGIN
      WRITELN ('ENTER ANY INTEGER');
      WRITELN ('AND PRESS RETURN');
      READLN (X);
      IF (X >= 1) AND (X <=20) THEN
        BEGIN
          IF X = 1 THEN
            WRITELN (X, 'ST')
          ELSE IF X = 2 THEN
            WRITELN (X, 'ND')
          ELSE IF X = 3 THEN
            WRITELN (X, 'RD')
          ELSE
            WRITELN (X, 'TH')
        END (* IF *)
    END.
```

17.

```
         PROGRAM TEST;

           VAR
             N1, N2, N3 : INTEGER;

         BEGIN
           WRITELN ('TYPE IN THREE INTEGERS');
           WRITELN ('SEPARATED BY SPACES.');
           WRITELN ('THEN PRESS RETURN');
           READLN (N1, N2, N3);
           IF N1 > N2 THEN
             IF N2 > N3 THEN
               WRITELN (N3, ' ', N2, ' ', N1)
             ELSE IF N1 > N3 THEN
               WRITELN (N2, ' ', N3, ' ', N1)
             ELSE
               WRITELN (N2, ' ', N1, ' ', N3)
           ELSE
             IF N3 > N2 THEN
               WRITELN (N1, ' ', N2, ' ', N3)
             ELSE IF N1 > N3 THEN
               WRITELN (N3, ' ', N1, ' ', N2)
             ELSE
               WRITELN (N1, ' ', N3, ' ', N2)
         END.
```

19.

```
          PROGRAM PIANO;

            USES
              APPLESTUFF;

            CONST
              DURATION = 30;


            VAR
              KEY : CHAR;
              PITCH : INTEGER;

          BEGIN
            REPEAT
              READ (KEY);
              CASE KEY OF
                'A': PITCH := 20;
                'W': PITCH := 21;
                'S': PITCH := 22;
                'E': PITCH := 23;
                'D': PITCH := 24;
                'F': PITCH := 25;
                'T': PITCH := 26;
                'G': PITCH := 27;
                'Y': PITCH := 28;
                'H': PITCH := 29;
                'U': PITCH := 30;
                'J': PITCH := 31;
                'K': PITCH := 32;
                'Q', 'R', 'I', 'O', 'P',
                'Z', 'X', 'C', 'V', 'B',
                'N', 'M', ',', '.': PITCH := 0
              END; (* CASE *)
              NOTE (PITCH, DURATION)
            UNTIL BUTTON (0)
          END.
```

SESSION 9

1. String.

3. String.

5. a. 19

   b. 'IS WORTH TWO IN THE BUSH A BIRD IN THE HAND '

   c. 11

   d. 40

   e. 0

   f. 21

   g. 1

7. a. 'BIRD IN THE HAND '

   b. 'ISTH TWO IN THE BUSH '

   c. 'A BIN THE HAND '

9.
```
    BEGIN
      FIRST := POS (SPACE, PHRASE);
      IF FIRST > 1 THEN
         WRITELN (COPY (PHRASE, 1, FIRST - 1);
      DELETE (PHRASE, 1, FIRST)
    END (* WHILE *)
```

11.

```
PROGRAM COUNTMATCHES;

VAR
    TARGET, SOURCE : STRING;
    LTARG, P, COUNT : INTEGER;

BEGIN
    WRITE ('TARGET PATTERN = '); READLN (TARGET);
    WRITE ('SOURCE STRING = '); READLN (SOURCE);
    LTARG := LENGTH (TARGET) - 1;
    P := POS (TARGET, SOURCE);
    COUNT := 0;
    WHILE P > 0 DO
      BEGIN
        COUNT := COUNT + 1;
        DELETE (SOURCE, 1, P + LTARG);
        P := POS (TARGET, SOURCE)
      END; (* WHILE *)
    WRITELN (COUNT, ' OCCURRENCE(S)')
END.
```

13. Legal statements are: a, c, e, and f.

15. Input string is 'ABCDEF'. Output is

```
A
 B
  C
   D
    E
     F
```

with a leading space in front of the A, 2 spaces in front of the B, etc.

SESSION 10

1. a. 17

   b. 5

   c. 5

   d. 2.00000

   e. 256

3. (I = integer, L = long integer, R = real, S = string)

    a. ILR

    b. ILR

    c. L

    d. bad format

    e. R

    f. too big

    g. LR

    h. ILR

    i. S

5. a. ILR

    b. ILR

    c. too big to convert to integer

    d. ILR

    e. ILR

7. a. real

    b. 'OOPS!'; X is an 11-digit number, but only the leading 7 digits are kept for any real number. Adding 1 to X will not affect those 7 digits, so 1E10 and 1E10 + 1 have exactly the same representation in Apple Pascal.

9.
```
          BOB
           BOB
            BOB
             BOB
              BOB
              SUE
               SUE
                SUE
                 SUE
                  SUE
```

11.
```
PROGRAM PHTHAGOREAN;

  USES
    TRANSCEND;

  VAR
    A, B, C : REAL;

BEGIN
  WRITELN ('TYPE IN THE LENGTHS OF');
  WRITELN ('THE TWO PERPENDICULAR SIDES');
  WRITELN ('SEPARATED BY A SPACE. THEN');
  WRITELN ('PRESS RETURN.');
  WRITELN;
  READLN (A, B);
  WRITELN;
  C := SQRT (A * A + B * B);
  WRITELN ('LONGEST SIDE HAS LENGTH ', C);
END.
```

13.
```
PROGRAM RECIPROCAL;

  VAR
    N, NUMBER : INTEGER;
    SUM : REAL;

BEGIN
  WRITELN ('ENTER A POSITIVE INTEGER');
  WRITELN ('AND PRESS RETURN');
  READLN (NUMBER);
  SUM := 0;
  FOR N := 1 TO NUMBER DO
    SUM := SUM + (1 / N);
  WRITELN ('SUM OF RECIPROCALS IS ', SUM);
END.
```

SESSION 11

1. a. 1

   b. 49 (see Appendix F)

   c. illegal, since real numbers cannot be counted.

   d. 48

e. 'Z'

f. illegal, since a string doesn't have a unique successor.

g. 'P'

h. 1

i. −23

3. a. 0

b. 11

c. JUL

d. 12, which is legal in Apple Pascal but nonstandard.

e. SEP

f. TRUE

5.
```
        FUNCTION MONTHNUM (N : INTEGER) : MONTH;
        VAR
          MO : MONTH;
        BEGIN
          MO := JAN;
          WHILE N > 0 DO
            BEGIN
              MO := SUCC (MO);
              N := N - 1
            END;
          MONTHNUM := MO
        END;
```

7. a [1..10]

b. [1,3,5,7,9]

c. [2, 4, 6, 8]

d. [10]

e. []

f. illegal, since 10 is not a set.

9. a. There are 8 possible sets.

b. The value of COINSET tells whether or not each *possible* member of the set is an *actual* member of COINSET.

11.
```
        TYPE
           MONEY = (PENNY, NICKEL, DIME, QUARTER);
           MONEYSET = SET OF MONEY;

        FUNCTION CENTS (CHANGE : MONEYSET) : INTEGER;
           VAR
              COIN : MONEY;
              SUM : INTEGER;
           BEGIN
              SUM := 0;
              FOR COIN := PENNY TO QUARTER DO
                 IF COIN IN CHANGE THEN
                    CASE COIN OF
                       PENNY : SUM := SUM + 1;
                       NICKEL : SUM := SUM + 5;
                       DIME : SUM := SUM + 10;
                       QUARTER : SUM := SUM + 25
                    END; (* CASE *)
              CENTS := SUM
           END; (* CENTS *)
```

13.
```
        VAR
           ALL, MWF, TTH, SSU : SET OF DAYOFWEEK;
```

SESSION 12

1. a. PRICE and COST

   b. ARRAY

   c. FIRST..LAST

   d. REAL

3. a. Nothing

   b. A "value range error" would be reported at run time when the first assignment statement was executed.

   c. A compile-time error would occur, since the dimensions must be declared in *ascending* order.

5.
```
PROCEDURE REVERSEDECK;
  VAR
    I, J, TEMP : INTEGER;
  BEGIN
    FOR I := 1 TO NUMCARDS DIV 2 DO
      BEGIN
        J := NUMCARDS - I + 1;
        TEMP := DECK [I];
        DECK [I] := DECK [J];
        DECK [J] := TEMP
      END (* FOR *)
  END; (* REVERSEDECK *)
```

7. The WRITELN statement in SHOWDECK would have to be changed to

```
WRITELN (FACE [FACENUMBER], ' OF ', SUIT [SUITNUMBER])
```

In addition, INITIALIZE would need 13 new assigment statements to give proper string values to array FACE. Finally, the VAR block would need the following new declaration:

```
FACE : ARRAY [1..13] OF STRING [5];
```

9.
```
PROCEDURE SORTHANDS;
  VAR
    H, I, J, TEMP : INTEGER;
  BEGIN
    FOR H := 1 TO NUMHANDS DO
      FOR I := 1 TO SIZEHAND - 1 DO
        FOR J := I + 1 TO SIZEHAND DO
          IF HANDS [H, I] > HANDS [H, J] THEN
            BEGIN
              TEMP := HANDS [H, I];
              HANDS [H, I] := HANDS [H, J];
              HANDS [H, J] := TEMP
            END (* IF *)
  END; (* SORTHANDS *)
```

11. a. 999, since X is a *global* variable and ABC changed its value.

b. A compile-time error message appears, complaining that the X in the main BEGIN/END block is "undeclared". This happens because the only VAR block is the *local* one inside ABC.

c. 0 appears now, because the two X's are different. ABC affects only its own, *local* X, while the main program affects only the *gobal* X.

13. a. INTEGER, CHAR, BOOLEAN, any programmer defined scalar data type.

b. Any data type discussed so far, including ARRAY. For example, if C were a one-dimensional array and A were two-dimensional, then the statement would assign all components of C to one "row" of A.

15. a. LIST may be a value parameter, but AVG and STDEV may not.

b. All three may be defined as reference parameters.

17. a.

```
TYPE
    STRINGARRAY [1..50] OF STRING [20];

FUNCTION POSITION (TARGET : STRING [20]; LIST : STRINGARRAY;
                   START, FINISH : INTEGER) : INTEGER;
    VAR
      I : INTEGER;
      FOUND : BOOLEAN;
    BEGIN
      POSITION := -MAXINT;
      FOUND := FALSE;
      I := START;
      WHILE I <= FINISH AND NOT FOUND DO
        BEGIN
          IF TARGET = LIST [I] THEN
            BEGIN
              POSITION := I;
              FOUND := TRUE;
            END; (* IF *)
          I := I+1
        END (* WHILE *)
    END; (* POSITION *)
```

b. No. It would be necessary to declare en entire new function with parameters of type INTEGER and ARRAY of INTEGER.

SESSION 13

1.
```
      TYPE
        WORKERLIST = ARRAY [1..NUMWORKERS] OF
                        RECORD
                          NAME : STRING;
                          SSNUM : INTEGER [10]
                        END;
```

If EMPLOYEE is of type WORKERLIST, then EMPLPOYEE [87] SSNUM is the social security number of the 87th employee.

3.
```
      TYPE
        STUREC = RECORD
                   ID : INTEGER;
                   NAME : RECORD
                            FIRST : STRING [20];
                            LAST : STRING [20]
                          END  (* INNER RECORD *)
                 END; (* OUTER RECORD *)
```

5. For output:

> REWRITE (STUFILE, 'disk file name')
> CLOSE (STUFILE, LOCK)

For input:

> RESET (STUFILE, 'disk file name')
> CLOSE (STUFILE)

7. No, it is undefined.

9. The first statement assigns the value 23 to the current component of OUTFILE. The second statement sends that value to the output file opened as OUTFILE. The third statement sends that same value (23) to the output file. The result is that the output file will have the value 23 in two successive locations.

11. For INTERACTIVE files, RESET does not do an automatic GET, so DATAFILE^ is undefined at the start. If the file is empty, EOF (DATAFILE) remains false until after the first GET. Therefore, the first character on the screen would be spurious. The rest (if any) would be correct.

.3.

```
PROGRAM READIT;

  VAR
    COMPONENT : STRING;
    INFILE : TEXT;

BEGIN
  RESET (INFILE, 'disk file name');
  WHILE NOT EOF (INFILE) DO
    BEGIN
      READLN (INFILE, COMPONENT);
      WRITELN (COMPONENT)
    END; (* WHILE *)
  CLOSE (INFILE)
END.
```

SESSION 14

1.

```
FUNCTION SERIES (NUM : INTEGER) : REAL;
  BEGIN
    IF NUM = 1 THEN
      SERIES := 1
    ELSE
      SERIES := SERIES (NUM - 1) + 1 / NUM
  END; (* SERIES *)
```

3.

```
PROCEDURE SNOWFLAKE (SIZE, LEVEL : INTEGER);
VAR
  NEWSIZE : INTEGER;
BEGIN
  IF LEVEL = 0 THEN
    MOVE (SIZE)
  ELSE
    BEGIN
      NEWSIZE := ROUND (SIZE / 3);
      SNOWFLAKE (NEWSIZE, LEVEL - 1);
      TURN (60);
      SNOWFLAKE (NEWSIZE, LEVEL - 1);
      TURN (-120);
      SNOWFLAKE (NEWSIZE, LEVEL - 1);
      TURN (60);
      SNOWFLAKE (NEWSIZE, LEVEL - 1)
    END (* IF *)
END; (* SNOWFLAKE *)
```

5.
```
           PROCEDURE DIAMOND (SIZE : INTEGER);
             VAR
               I : INTEGER;
             BEGIN
               IF SIZE > 1 THEN
                 BEGIN
                   FOR I := 1 TO 4 DO
                     BEGIN
                       MOVE (SIZE);
                       TURN (90)
                     END; (* FOR *)
                   MOVE (SIZE DIV 2);
                   TURN (45);
                   DIAMOND (TRUNC (SIZE * 0.707))
                 END (* IF *)
             END; (* DIAMOND *)
```

7.
```
           PROCEDURE TRIANGLE (SIZE : INTEGER);
             FORWARD;

           PROCEDURE SQUARE (SIZE : INTEGER);
             VAR
               I : INTEGER;
             BEGIN
               IF SIZE > 1 THEN
                 BEGIN
                   FOR I := 1 TO 4 DO
                     BEGIN
                       MOVE (SIZE);
                       TURN (90)
                     END; (* FOR *)
                   PENCOLOR (NONE); MOVE (SIZE DIV 10);
                   TURN (90); MOVE (SIZE DIV 10); TURN (-90);
                   PENCOLOR (WHITE);
                   TRIANGLE (SIZE * 8 DIV 10)
                 END (* IF *)
             END; (* SQUARE *)

           PROCEDURE TRIANGLE;
             VAR
               I : INTEGER;
             BEGIN
               IF SIZE > 1 THEN
                 BEGIN
                   FOR I := 1 TO 3 DO
                     BEGIN
                       MOVE (SIZE);
                       TURN (120)
                     END; (* FOR *)
                   PENCOLOR (NONE); MOVE (SIZE DIV 3);
                   TURN (90); MOVE (SIZE DIV 10); TURN (-90);
                   PENCOLOR (WHITE);
                   SQUARE (SIZE DIV 3)
                 END (* IF *)
             END; (* SQUARE *)
```

COMPILER ERROR MESSAGES

1: Error in simple type
2: Identifier expected
3: 'PROGRAM' expected
4: ')' expected
5: ': ' expected
6: Illegal symbol (possibly missing ';' on line above)
7: Error in parameter list
8: 'OF' expected
9: '(' expected
10: Error in type
11: ' ' expected
12: ' ' expected
13: 'END' expected
14: ';' expected (possibly on line above)
15: Integer expected
16: '=' expected
17: 'BEGIN' expected
18: Error in declaration part
19: Error in <field-list>
20: '.' expected
21: '*' expected
22: 'Interface' expected
23: 'Implementation' expected
24: 'Unit' expected
50: Error in constant
51: ': =' expected
52: 'THEN' expected
53: 'UNTIL' expected
54: 'DO' expected
55: 'TO' or 'DOWNTO' expected in for statement
56: 'IF' expected
57: 'FILE' expected
58: Error in <factor> (bad expression)
59: Error in variable
101: Identifier declared twice
102: Low bound exceeds high bound
103: Identifier is not of the appropriate class
104: Undeclared identifier
105: Sign not allowed
106: Number expected
107: Incompatible subrange types
108: File not allowed here
109: Type must not be real
110: <tagfield> type must be scalar or subrange
111: Incompatible with <tagfield> part
112: Index type must not be real
113: Index type must be a scalar or a subrange
114: Base type must not be real
115: Base type must be a scalar or a subrange
116: Error in type of standard procedure parameter

117: Unsatisfied forward reference
118: Forward reference type identifier in variable declaration
119: Re-specified params not OK for a forward declared procedure
120: Function result type must be scalar, subrange or pointer
121: File value parameter not allowed
122: A forward declared function's result type can't be re-specified
123: Missing result type in function declaration
124: F-format for reals only
125: Error in type of standard procedure parameter
126: Number of parameters does not agree with declaration
127: Illegal parameter substitution
128: Result type does not agree with declaration
129: Type conflict of operands
130: Expression is not of set type
131: Tests on equality allowed only
132: Strict inclusion not allowed
133: File comparison not allowed
134: Illegal type of operand(s)
135: Type of operand must be boolean
136: Set element type must be scalar or subrange
137: Set element types must be compatible
138: Type of variable is not array
139: Index type is not compatible with the declaration
140: Type of variable is not record
141: Type of variable must be file or pointer
142: Illegal parameter solution
143: Illegal type of loop control variable
144: Illegal type of expression
145: Type conflict
146: Assignment of files not allowed
147: Label type incompatible with selecting expression
148: Subrange bounds must be scalar
149: Index type must be integer
150: Assignment to standard function is not allowed
151: Assignment to formal function is not allowed
152: No such field in this record
153: Type error in read
154: Actual parameter must be a variable
155: Control variable cannot be formal or non-local
156: Multidefined case label
157: Too many cases in case statement